THE FOOD REVOLUTION

Also by Dr Tom Sanders

The Vegetarian's Healthy Diet Book

Also by Peter Bazalgette

BBC Food Check

THE
FOOD
REVOLUTION

Dr Tom Sanders
and Peter Bazalgette

BANTAM PRESS

LONDON · NEW YORK · TORONTO · SYDNEY · AUCKLAND

TRANSWORLD PUBLISHERS LTD
61–63 Uxbridge Road, London W5 5SA

TRANSWORLD PUBLISHERS (AUSTRALIA) PTY LTD
15–23 Helles Avenue, Moorebank, NSW 2170

TRANSWORLD PUBLISHERS (NZ) LTD
Cnr Moselle and Waipareira Aves,
Henderson, Auckland

Published 1991 by Bantam Press
a division of Transworld Publishers Ltd
Copyright © Dr Tom Sanders & Peter Bazalgette 1991

A catalogue record for this book is available from the British Library

ISBN 0–593–02182–7 Csd
ISBN 0–593–02315–3 Pbk

Typeset in Palatino by
Chippendale Type Ltd., Otley, West Yorkshire

Printed in Great Britain by
Mackays of Chatham PLC, Chatham, Kent

DEDICATION

To the nutrionist John Rivers who always put things
in perspective.

ACKNOWLEDGEMENTS

The authors would particularly like to thank Tim Hincks who researched Sections II and V and Lorna Todd, MA (Oxon), MSc (London), who compiled and tested *The Food Revolution* Questionnaire. In addition we are grateful to the following for their help:

Alcohol Concern; Professor Bruce Ames; Anheuser-Bush Europe Ltd; Margaret Ashwell; Professor Arnold Bender; Sir David Benton; British Heart Foundation; British Library; The British Medical Association; British Nutrition Foundation; British Psychological Society; Janet Cade, Southampton University; Capital Radio; Caterer and Hotelkeeper; Compass Catering; Helen Conn, Forum Chemicals; Coronary Prevention Group; Richard Cottrell; Dunn Nutrition Unit; David Edwards, The Food Hygiene Bureau; The European Commisson; The Family Heart Association; Food From Britain; *The Food Magazine*; Friends of the Earth; Gardiner Merchant; Geoff Harrington, Meat & Livestock Commission; Harrods; Health Education Council; Heinz; Institute of Food Research; International Food Information Service; James Rhodes Associates; Susan King; Kings College, London; *The Lancet*; McCain; Market Research Company of America; Ministry of Agriculture, Fisheries and Food; Liz Moore; Professor Donald Naismith; National Consumer Council; Mike Nelson; *New England Journal of Medicine*; Office of Population Census and Surveys; Tony Painter, Law Labs Ltd; Public Health Laboratory Service; Sheela Reddy; Rowett Research Institute; Royal Society of Medicine; Royal Society for the Prevention of Accidents; Willy Russell; Sainsbury's; Linda Saunders; Sea Fish Industry Authority; Soil Association; St Ivel; Stirling University Marine Laboratory; Tea Council; Tesco; UIP/Paramount; US Food and Drug Administration; Vandenburghs; Vegetarian Society; Which?; Which? Way To Health; Theresa Wickham; Richard Woolfe; Ruth Yahal; Professor John Yudkin.

Finally we would like to express our gratitude to Mark Lucas and Ursula Mackenzie.

CONTENTS

SECTION V – THE CONSUMERS' GUIDE   221

SECTION VI – A–Z DIRECTORY   325

PREFACE

HOW TO GET THE BEST OUT OF
THE FOOD REVOLUTION

The Food Revolution enables you to understand how your body uses food and how to discover the small changes to your diet that will revolutionize your health and change your life. It is partly a manual of self-analysis, partly a family handbook and partly a convenient work of reference.

Complete *The Food Revolution* Questionnaire in Section II and discover how well or badly you eat and drink – small changes in your diet can yield massive benefits. In the same section, the Liberation List details the foods you need to eat regularly to stay healthy and live longer.

Section III – Getting Away With It – explains the *real* risks associated with food and what you can get away with.

In Section IV – the Seven Ages of Man – look up your own age group to discover your special dietary needs – everyone from babies to vegetarian teenagers, anything from middle-age spread to elderly loss of appetite. Then there is the Liberation Diet which shows you how to put the Liberation List into practice. And whether you need to lose weight, reduce your cholesterol or lower your blood pressure there is a special diet here for you.

Section V – the Consumers' Guide – contains all you need to know about handling food, from shopping to cooking. It includes valuable advice on how to avoid food poisoning and the best-ever guide to food labelling – if you crack the code you can reap the benefits.

Section VI – an A–Z Directory – answers all your questions about nutrition and food safety. Keep it on the shelf and consult it as a handy reference. It is written in a practical and unemotional way so you can employ it as an antidote to food scares as they arise!

Finally, our Index enables you to find your way around *The Food Revolution* effortlessly. Whenever you hear or read a food term that perplexes you – in a magazine or newspaper, on radio or television, from your doctor or on a food label – use the index to run it to earth. *The Food Revolution* will cut through the jargon and provide you with the facts.

SECTION I
INTRODUCTION

If you are after fad diets, six week 'instant cures' or the body of a film star, then you are reading the wrong book. If on the other hand you would like to harness the power of food to revolutionize your health then . . . welcome to *The Food Revolution*.

What do we mean by The Food Revolution? We could be referring to the new technology which allows us to micro-wave instant meals in seconds. Or we might be alluding to the modern distribution that delivers strawberries to us in winter and sprouts in summer or to the genetic engineers who are breeding tomatoes with built-in pesticides. All these things are indeed happening but they are incidental to our Food Revolution. Our revolution has yet to happen, but when it does it will transform the way we eat – in the 1990s and beyond.

So much disease is diet-related, so much of it can be avoided. By making small changes to the food we eat we can revolutionize our health. But first we need to understand how food interacts with our bodies. You might suppose that this is something we already know about. Having just emerged from the 1980s – the much vaunted decade of healthy eating – can *The Food Revolution* really offer anything new? That depends on how much we have actually learnt about food as we move into the 1990s.

Here are a couple of questions for you:

- Should you reduce your calories?
- Should you increase your intake of energy foods?

When these two questions were asked in a national poll in 1984 half the respondents said 'Yes' to both. In fact, calories and energy are the same thing and so if it is right to reduce calories it must be wrong to increase our intake of energy foods. What this proved was that half of us did not under-stand what calories are. Had we learnt more by 1989? In that year MORI put the following statements to 2,000 adults. See which you think are true and which false.

- Pregnant women who have a normal well-balanced diet still need to take extra vitamins and minerals.

72 per cent answered wrongly and 10 per cent couldn't answer at all.

- Margarine high in polyunsaturates contains less fat than ordinary margarine or butter.

61 per cent answered wrongly and 17 per cent couldn't answer at all.

- In a normal person's diet most of the energy or calories should come from protein.

53 per cent answered wrongly and 19 per cent couldn't answer at all.

- Growing children who have a normal well-balanced diet still need to take extra vitamins and minerals.

34 per cent answered wrongly and 5 per cent couldn't answer at all.

How do you think you did? We are not going to give you the answers straight away, but they can all be found in *The Food Revolution*. However, what the above poll illustrates is just how vague we are about a subject that should matter to us more than anything – our food and health. Many of us clearly know little and understand less about the food we eat and how it affects our bodies. Imagine a survey in which we were asked 'Are you a virgin?' to which 60 per cent of us responded 'Don't know'. We display just that level of ignorance about food, which is certainly as important as sex and (arguably) as enjoyable.

Living as we do in an age of food scares – pesticides, additives, salmonella, listeria, BSE – it is essential we fight known dangers rather than illusory or unproven ones. For example, take the list in the previous sentence. None of the terrible hazards mentioned there compare with the threat of heart disease, cancer or alcohol-related disease.

Why do we understand so little about food and nutrition? Basically because we are fed a constant diet of half-truths, misinformation and scares by the media, by food producers, well-meaning but misguided activists and others with an axe of one sort or another to grind. Let us give you examples, starting with some newspaper articles.

I cut my risk of a heart attack in half. My trial proves oat bran is a lifesaver.

Jeers of disbelief greeted last week's claim that eating oat bran cereal helps prevent heart attacks. But I tried it – and it works. For three weeks I included 4oz a day of oat bran in my diet. At the end of the trial my cholesterol level was down by 25 per cent – slashing my chances of a heart attack in half!

In fact the jeers of disbelief may not have been entirely misplaced. This trial proves nothing. The crucial question is whether the journalist's fat consumption was the same both before and during the test. Forcing all that bran into his stomach – the equivalent of four servings of bran every day! – it would be surprising if much room was left for anything else, let alone fat. But he made no record of whether the rest of his diet remained constant or not. His uncontrolled experiment shows a far, far greater reduction in cholesterol than has been noted in the properly regulated studies. For that reason alone the article is highly dubious (*see* Section VI, p353).

Scientists do an about turn over polyunsaturates.

A team at Cambridge University's department of clinical pharmacology has concluded that people who eat large amounts of polyunsaturates, hoping for protection from heart disease, could be putting themselves at increased risk. The scientists have shown that when polyunsaturated fats are processed by the body a surge of 'free radicals' – oxygen in a highly reactive form – can sometimes result. These alter the chemical structure of cholesterol – rich substances circulating in the blood. Those substances play a vital role in body maintenance, but when transformed by free radicals they can enter blood vessel walls where they begin the disease process that causes blockages.

This article caused an enormous stir. We have all been told to cut down on saturated animal fats and consume more polyunsaturated fats. Were we wrong if we heeded the dulcet voice-overs of Terry Wogan and rushed out to buy polyunsaturated Flora? Well, the article seemed very technical and persuasive. Unfortunately it quoted a Professor Morris Brown who, though he spoke on the issue, had not done the research into polyunsaturates. He subsequently wrote a letter disowning the story. While Dr Mitchison, the scientist who had actually done the research in question, was quite clear on the subject: 'The paper got it all wrong.' (*See* Section III, p89 and Section VI, p392).

Cancer link to ketchup.

Tomato ketchup and brown bread contain alarming amounts of a cancer-linked chemical, it was claimed yesterday. Other foods including apples, carrots, pears and potatoes are also contaminated with ethylene thiourea (ETU), which is used in fungicide crop sprays. It has been linked with lung, liver and thyroid cancer, as well as birth defects. The health alert was issued by Friends of the Earth and Parents for Safe Food, who commissioned tests on products sold by many high street stores.

Should we and our children all have stopped eating tomato ketchup and bread immediately? There was one crucial fact missing from this article which emerged later. When the Ministry of Agriculture, Fisheries and Food carried out their own tests on exactly the same food they found residues of the fungicide to be much lower. A measure of the Ministry's accuracy was their correct discovery that the two pressure groups had deliberately spiked one of the samples by adding ETU to it. It is true that experts in the US had concluded that ETUs ingested in relatively large quantities over a long period of time could cause cancer. So the Americans had banned the relevant chemical from use as a fungicide. But what was the real level of risk? The newspaper never asked that question. Is ketchup more of a risk to us than the highly saturated fat in the sausage we pour it on to? Assessment of genuine risk is vital but sadly neglected (*see* Section III, p153).

Now yoghurt is linked with cancer in women.

Women who eat lots of yoghurt and cottage cheese could be sentencing themselves to death, a shock report revealed last night. For chilling new statistics have shown that eating large amounts of dairy produce – especially yoghurt – increases the chances of developing cancer of the ovaries. An American specialist has warned women to cut down drastically on these foods, and milk as well, if they want to stay healthy.

Was it true that women had been sentencing themselves to death? In fact only women with a low level of a particular enzyme are at risk because of their difficulty in processing one element of lactose into glucose. That element is called galactose. It allegedly increases the chances of ovarian cancer. But there was no quoted evidence as to how many women suffer from this and so once again no indication of the level of risk.

In fact, because yoghurt is fermented milk you would not expect much lactose to be left in yoghurt. The process of fermentation would have already broken down most of the lactose. Following the argument of the 'American specialist' (actually a team at Harvard University) milk would represent much more of a danger. It not only contains more lactose but we also consume much more of it. Indeed, a different American study – twenty years in the making but not meriting a mention in this newspaper article – came to a very different conclusion about milk. The researchers concluded that milk and cheese consumption are unrelated to ovarian cancer mortality.

You could also consider evidence from Bulgaria. Certain groups of people in Bulgaria live to an exceptionally old age. Whatever else is proved by this it should be noted that the Bulgarians eat very large quantities of yoghurt in their diet! With any question of diet and health you can expect to find conflicting studies. To come to even a rudimentary view of where the truth lies you need to consider *all* the studies. Quoting just one without reference to the others serves little purpose. Meanwhile, dairy cows can sleep more easily in their stalls in the knowledge that what they produce is not entirely poisonous. (For the truth about diet and cancer, *see* Section III, p119.)

Baby brain damage peril of micro milk.

> Milk reheated in microwaves could damage babies' brains, scientists have discovered. They say rapid reheating turns harmless proteins in the milk into poisonous chemicals . . . The Austrian scientists have found that microwaves can turn milk proteins into a variation of naturally occurring amino acids which the bodies of young babies cannot absorb. The acids can build up in key organs like the liver or brain and damage them.

A crucial revelation, you may well think. After all, around one home in two now has a microwave and many parents use them to warm milk. There was just one small problem with this story, one that the Austrians' paper had not revealed and the author of the newspaper article had not included. When the milk was heated for one minute (the normal time needed to warm milk) *no observable change* occurred to the milk proteins. The amino acids only showed up after prolonged heating in a closed test tube for ten minutes, which actually caramelized the milk. However, another newspaper went one better when pulling this and other microwave scares together.

100,000 a year may end up dead.

> The news that microwave ovens may turn the ingredients in normally safe foods into potentially toxic substances has to be taken very seriously. With 10 million microwaves in use today, in a few years they could be killing more people than cigarettes. That's currently 100,000 a year.

This prediction, based on the earlier misapprehensions, was later described by an experienced statistician as extremely irresponsible. As for the Austrian scientist who wrote the original paper, he had this to say about the threat to babies' brains: 'There is no link. I am horrified, completely horrified, about this distortion.'

Coffee can stop you having babies.

Women yearning to become mothers may be wrecking their dreams by drinking too much coffee. Two cups a day can halve the chances of becoming pregnant, say scientists. For addicts who make regular trips to the coffee machine the chances of conceiving may only be 25 per cent. The revelation emerged from a study by American doctors who found the intake of the coffee drug caffeine affected fertility.

It is a pity to let the facts spoil a good story or, as one writer put it, 'to drag facts in like so many unwanted dogs'. But here are a couple the journalist may not have been aware of. Dr Wilcox from Harvard University who carried out the research says that all the women involved did become pregnant, but some not as quickly as the others. Wilcox argues that coffee never 'stopped' pregnancy but merely delayed it, while a similar study carried out at about the same time, which involved twenty-eight times as many women, found no evidence whatsoever for this adverse effect from coffee (*see* Section VI, p355).

Woozy pilots in diet drinks probe.

Pilots are to undergo tests amid fears that low-calorie drinks make them a danger in the air. The drinks, based on artificial sweeteners, may trigger dizziness and blurred vision at the controls. The scare follows a report that a pilot had a seizure soon after landing and is being tested for reaction to low-calorie drinks.

This warning could be as crucial to drivers as the advice not to drink and drive. There had, in fact, been an article in the US General Aviation Safety Leaflet reporting pilots' fears that artificial sweeteners had this effect. It was, however, merely anecdotal. A test in October 1989 on 108 subjects who consumed low-calorie drinks found no persistent changes to their wakefulness. Subsequently, the *Flight Safety Bulletin* of the Civil Aviation Authority in Britain has advised anyone who suffers from symptoms of light-headedness or dizziness to seek the advice of a physician. To attribute such symptoms to an artificial sweetener 'could be a serious error', they say. Nevertheless, this scare was reported in both magazines and

and newspapers in 1990 without any mention of the October test or the British CAA's advice. In this way suspicion becomes fact and possible myths are perpetuated. (*See* Section VI, p334).

These journalistic scoops – each worthy of a Pulitzer – will come as no surprise to those familiar with the excesses of Fleet Street. So we should not express too much surprise that many of these stories are difficult to substantiate and all of them were capable of scaring – not to say panicking – large numbers of people. However, what they underline is the absence of reasoned and reasonable information about food. And this is a problem often compounded by food producers. Consider the following cases.

MILK AND OSTEOPOROSIS

Some post-menopausal women suffer calcium loss which can lead to brittle bones and painful fractures. Doctors accept that the menopause and physical inactivity are the chief causes of this condition. Exercise can actually decrease the rate of bone loss. And hormone replacement or drug therapy are the only known medical treatments. The amount of calcium in a woman's diet is obviously not irrelevant, but on its own is neither the primary cause of, nor cure for osteoporosis.

Enter the milk producers. In the mid-1980s, medical experts were becoming much more aware of osteoporosis as the main cause of hip and leg fractures in the elderly. Milk is an important source of calcium. So here was a selling opportunity taken up faster than you can say Drinka-Pinta-Milka-Day. Unigate launched a calcium-enriched milk called Calcia. Express Dairies – not to be outdone – came up with Vital. With Calcia was a leaflet which read:

> As women move through their adult years the danger of developing brittle bones (osteoporosis) increases. This danger can be reduced by ensuring your diet contains the correct amount of calcium.

In August 1987, the Advertising Standards Authority upheld

a complaint against this leaflet stating that 'the leaflet included claims that the dangers of osteoporosis would be reduced by ensuring the correct amount of calcium in the diet.' The leaflet was withdrawn. Express Dairies had to withdraw similar claims admitting the difficulties of finding a scientific basis for them. But the story did not end there. In April 1989 posters appeared on advertising hoardings showing a chummy milkman with a ready smile leaning against his float. 'Worried about osteoporosis? Consult a specialist' ran the legend beside him. The National Dairy Council now admit that they would not use this advertisement again. But the ending of such misleading campaigns does not correct the erroneous impression they leave behind.

VITAMINS AND INTELLIGENCE

In January 1988 QED, the BBC's respected documentary science series, broadcast a sensational edition. It reported on a study in which a group of schoolchildren at Darland High School in North Wales had been given multi-vitamin pills over a period of eight months. These had shown a significant increase in non-verbal intelligence while other children who had been given nothing or merely placebos showed no increase at all. Gwilym Roberts, a science master, had called in Dr David Benton from the University of Swansea to carry out the experiment because he suspected the poor diet of some of his pupils was behind their apparent lack of ability at school.

The results appeared to be a resounding confirmation of his theory and the newspapers needed little encouragement. All that week vitamins were proclaimed to be the answer to low IQs. Armies of parents set out like locusts to chemists and health shops and within two days the shelves were cleared.

Neither Dr Benton nor Mr Roberts are qualified nutritionists. It was not long before experts in the field began to scrutinize the results closely and they did not like what they found. Subsequent investigations culminated in a letter to *The Lancet* signed by, amongst others, one of the authors of this book. Their complaints were that:

21

- no bona fide nutritionist took part in the experiment;
- no accurate method of recording the food intake was used and no appropriate food database had been employed to determine the adequacy or otherwise of the children's existing diets;
- the pills contained compounds which are not vitamins for humans at all; they have no nutritional value;
- the level of iron was only one-tenth of the UK's Recommended Daily Amount (RDA);
- the statistical analysis was seriously flawed.

In fact, a 1986 report from the Department of Health had found that in general the diets of British schoolchildren were not deficient in vitamins and minerals – the only exceptions being iron and vitamin D. Dr Benton's study flew in the face of the 1986 report and, indeed, of several subsequent studies. One was published in the *British Journal of Nutrition* in 1990 by Dr Nelson and Professor Naismith. It involved a much larger group of schoolchildren and all the food they ate was carefully weighed and recorded. *No significant correlation was found between school performance and consumption of vitamin supplements.* The report also found that the children's general intake of vitamins was, in the majority of cases, well above the RDA's. The only notable exception was, once again, iron.

Another study by Dr Geraldine MacNeill – which was also published in *The Lancet* – attempted to repeat Dr Benton's study, but with improvements to the method. Her conclusion? 'Vitamin and mineral supplementation does not improve the performance of schoolchildren in tests of reasoning.' Dr MacNeill added that you can correct deficiencies in most aspects of health by changing diet rather than by adding supplements to tackle everything that arises. In other words, eat food not pills.

Dr Benton subsequently was not able to replicate his initial findings. He now says, 'There has been a silly amount of publicity. It is all far from proven . . . we have no answers as yet.' And we could leave it at that were it not for a worrying development.

Emboldened by the instant sales of their pills, various vitamin manufacturers came out with new products which exploited the unproven but widely disseminated idea that vitamin supplements can increase a child's intelligence. Two managed to embody 'IQ' into their name and a third is simply called 'Top Marks'. But in October 1990 one of the companies deleted 'IQ' from their product range. And with good reason – diet and its relationship to performance at school will be researched and debated for a long time yet, but at the moment there is no proof that children are either deficient in vitamins or that vitamins will boost their IQ. (*See* Section VI, p410.)

MINERAL WATER AND BACTERIA

In 1988 a certain Water Authority came to resent the healthy image bottled mineral water had achieved at the expense of tap water (less so now, perhaps). So the authority did a simple analysis of both, knowing full well what they would find. Their tap water had far fewer bacteria in it than the bottled mineral water. They released the results to a couple of MPs who duly mounted an offensive on bottled waters in the House of Commons. This then received the publicity the authority had intended.

What was the truth of the matter? Of course bottled mineral waters have bacteria in them – they are meant to be a natural, unprocessed product, straight from an environment teeming with harmless bacteria (much as our own bodies are). Of course tap water contains fewer bacteria. Tap water has had chemicals pumped into it to kill as many organisms as possible. What the Water Authority had done, in their small way, was add to the sum of misinformation about food bacteria.

CHEESE AND LISTERIA

In 1989 the Department of Health revealed that it had discovered some soft, rinded cheeses like Brie and Camembert had relatively high concentrations of the notorious bacterium, listeria monocytogenes. The Department concluded (as other experts had before) that this presented a particular threat to pregnant women, capable of causing miscarriages and still births.

Dairy Crest is the massive cheese-making arm of the Milk Marketing Board. They make some soft, rinded cheeses – Lymeswold for one. They were immediately quoted in a newspaper to the effect that the government's warning only related to cheeses made from unpasteurized milk. (Subsequently, two government ministers also gave the impression that unpasteurized cheeses were a particular problem.) It was not true. In fact, the worst known outbreak of listeria poisoning (in which thirty-seven people died) was caused by a Swiss cheese made from *pasteurized* milk. But the damage was done and in the confusion that ensued small cheese-makers – producing cheese the traditional way, from unpasteurized milk – suffered a drop in sales. As for the rest of us, we understood even less about food poisoning than we had before.

Such firm pronouncements help no one if in reality little is known about the problem, even by the experts. It still is not known how widespread cases of listeria poisoning are or what level of listeria poses a threat and to whom. The 1990 Richmond Report revealed a fascinating fact which no one noticed when it was initially published because it was tucked away in an appendix. It stated that Department of Health research had shown listeria was present in 1.5 per cent of *pasteurized* milk. This meant that the milk was being unhygienically processed to the tune of two or three million pints a week. How much of a threat these contaminated bottles really represent is not known. No doubt the Milk Marketing Board would have been upset had anyone exploited the lack of scientific knowledge about listeria to launch a scare about the safety of milk. But what is sauce for the goose . . .

PEAS AND PRESERVATIVES

In the mid-1980s there was much public concern about additives in food, much of which persists today. (How much of a danger they really are we consider a little later.) 'Negative labelling' became the vogue for food manufacturers. No can or packet was complete without a tag saying 'no preservatives' or 'no artificial colours'.

24

Like many others, Batchelors Peas jumped on the bandwagon by placing a prominent triangle on their tinned peas saying 'no preservatives'. Very helpful. In fact canned food has never needed preservatives because it is itself a method of food preservation (*see* the Consumers' Guide, p232). Far from helping us understand how our food is prepared, this negative labelling hinders us from achieving that knowledge. If Batchelors had placed television advertisements at the same time explaining how the canning process works that would be a different matter. The irony is that their processed peas *do* contain tartrazine, a food colouring, to which there is strong public resistance. But they make less of a song and dance about that – it is only in the small print.

Perhaps Batchelors and the rest of the processed food industry should contemplate a new version of negative labelling – a panel that simply says, 'No kidding'.

When it comes to food scares – whether food poisoning, additives, pesticides and cancer, vitamins and intelligence – one of the biggest problems we have is that the risk attached to eating one food or avoiding another is never assessed for us. The media want a good story and the manufacturers want to promote their product in the best possible light. But the proper assessment of risk is something we should all be learning to look at closely. Fed on a diet of half-truths and scares about a whole range of foods, how else are we to know what to take seriously and what to dismiss? To illustrate this point, a television company asked a representative sample of viewers what worried them most about food in the autumn of 1989. Here is what they said:

	%
Additives	20
Food poisoning	18
Residues of pesticides/fungicides	18
Food's nutritional value	12

So even late in a year in which so many food-poisoning scares had occurred in Britain – salmonella, listeria and botulism – additives still worried people the most. And while effectively giving equal importance to food additives, food poisoning and pesticides, we put nutrition and healthy eating a poor fourth. Is this a balanced and informed view of risk, firmly founded on the laws of probability? Not according to Sir Herman Bondi, former chief scientist to the government: 'If I had one wish it would be that the general public understood probability.' Professor Richard Southwood, the man asked to investigate the risk represented by Bovine Spongiform Encephalopathy ('mad cow disease' or BSE), says that we need only to isolate and then tackle the *main* avenues of risk.

In May 1990, thousands of schools took beef off their lunch menus. BSE had been around for five years but the education chiefs picked this moment to panic about the dangers of catching the disease by eating beef. Since another disease, scrapie, had been in sheep for two hundred years and BSE had developed from scrapie, the logic of their action was that we should never have been eating lamb at all. But lamb stayed on the menu and beef came off. Professor Southwood himself had reported in 1989 that there was only a 'remote' risk of BSE spreading to humans. Many people thought that if there was any risk at all it was quite right to give up beef. But is that the criterion we apply, for example, to driving cars? There is a real risk of a fatal accident but the benefit of driving far outweighs that risk. So most of us own cars.

You can find out more about BSE in Section VI. But the episode does exemplify a more general lesson. Professor Southwood points to a human emotion, especially powerful when it comes to food, which dictates risk management. It is dread. We are all capable of fear and of believing that small risks will affect us personally. This can lead us to alter our eating patterns irrationally. Will Waites, Professor of Microbiology at Nottingham University, favours setting up an independent risk centre which could assess health risks and keep the public properly informed. According to him:

The risk from microbiology contamination is a thousandfold greater than that due to environmental contamination. While the risk due to pesticide residues and food additives is about a hundred times smaller again.

Perhaps all newspaper editors should have this statement pinned to their walls. The column inches devoted to food additives alone demonstrate that journalists have a rather different set of priorities. So many scare stories about additives had appeared by the mid-1980s that consumers took the E-numbers they saw on packets to be a warning. In fact, under an EC system of classification, additives are given E-numbers as a guarantee of their safety. By the end of the decade, food manufacturers had reverted to listing additives under their full chemical name so as not to alarm their customers and in the process negated the purpose of the E-number system.

The root of the problem is that we have been led to believe we are quite likely to suffer allergic or intolerant reactions to food additives. Books like *E for Additives* have, quite legitimately, listed some of the reactions that have been observed. However, what they do *not* list is how *likely* we are to be afflicted in this way. Doctors Ian Pollock and John Warner, senior paediatricians at St George's Hospital, decided to test how many children really suffer hyperactivity caused by food additives. Their results were published in 1990.

Pollock and Warner studied thirty-nine children, aged between two and fifteen, whose parents thought they were hyperactive. The children were given opaque capsules daily for seven weeks. For five weeks the capsules were placebos containing entirely neutral material. For the other two weeks a mixture of azo dyes was introduced. Azo dyes are the food colourings which are considered most suspect, such as tartrazine, sunset yellow, amaranth and carmoisine. These were given to the children in doses massively higher than they would consume in their normal diet. Only two sets of parents correctly identified the weeks when their children were given the colourings and even they could have reached their conclusions by chance.

It seems quite clear that far fewer children are hyperactive as a result of food additives than parents believe and that any direct physical link is difficult to prove. This was also the conclusion of two other studies in High Wycombe and Manchester. None of them deny that a tiny, tiny minority of children may suffer genuine additive-induced hyperactivity. But all these experts agree that it is ridiculous for us to have become so obsessed by the subject. As Dr Pollock puts it, 'it is unfair to children to put them on a restrictive diet when it is unproven that colourings cause hyperactivity.' Indeed, in cases where children have been proved to be food-sensitive it has been to a wide variety of natural foods – for example, oranges, wheat and soya – not unnatural additives.

Compare the song and dance about additives to the subject of naturally occurring toxins, which receive little or no publicity. A 1987 Ministry of Agriculture study found that eleven out of fifty-nine samples of crunchy peanut butter from health food shops contained more than ten times the permitted level of aflatoxins (a potentially carcinogenic mould toxin). Now there *is* something to be worried about, given the wide range of naturally occurring toxins.

More recently, public concern about pesticide and fungicide residues in food has been growing. This was well illustrated by the controversy over daminozide, an apple spray, more commonly known by its trade name Alar. This chemical can help delay maturity when apples are growing so that they end up bigger and more vividly coloured. Thus, in the US it was used on red apples such as Red Delicious, but not on green apples like Granny Smiths. In Britain Alar was mainly used to increase the yield on trees and stop the apples falling off too early. Some tests on rats found no link between Alar and cancer. Further tests found that, in massive quantities, it could cause cancer in mice but not hamsters and dogs. A television documentary in the US caused pandemonium when it said that Alar should be banned, arguing that government safety levels (aimed at reducing risk of cancer to one in a million) ignored the fact that children eat more fruit than adults and were therefore in greater danger. In particular, the programme argued that the active carcinogen mainly occurred after Alar is heated, whether in making juice, sauce or pies.

Casting doubt on the safety of apple-pie in the US is like telling Italians that pasta kills you. The result was mass hysteria. One parent even called out the police to stop the school bus her daughter was travelling on and reclaim the apple from her lunch-box. This inspiring example of mother love misunderstood the debate on a number of levels:

- Alar was only used on a minority of apples.
- Alar was probably only carcinogenic, if at all, when heated.

28

- The scientific evidence was conflicting.
- Rats and mice may be good pointers towards carcinogenity, but they hardly provide total proof.
- No one had worked out how often people were exposed to Alar in their daily diet.

In short, no one had published a reliable assessment of the real risk involved. However, another mother, rather better known than the one who called out the police, reacted just as strongly. Meryl Streep was before long appearing in nation-wide commercials calling for Alar's withdrawal in the US. Her campaign succeeded. So outraged was the American Council of Science and Health that it published its own advertisements in major newspapers saying: 'Our food supply is safe. There is no scientific merit to charges that pesticide residues in our produce cause cancer in human beings.'

In Britain, the comic actress, Pamela Stephenson, founded a similar campaign to get Alar banned. It is called Parents for Safe Food. She was successful to the extent that Alar has now been withdrawn worldwide. Her campaign, launched for the best of motives, was an object lesson in dealing with multi-national companies and government inaction. But the Ministry of Agriculture still maintains that Alar is safe. Where does the truth lie in this episode? The work of an American professor could provide the key. He has spent the best part of five years attempting to inject sense where there is hysteria and guidance where there is panic.

Bruce Ames is Director of the National Institute of Environmental Sciences Centre at the University of Berkeley in California. He argues that while animal cancer tests alone cannot be used to predict absolute cancer risks in humans, the results of such experiments can help us work out the relative risk between chemicals *if we include how often we come into contact with them*. Professor Ames has developed a measurement of cancer risk called a Herp – human exposure divided by rodent potency. In other words, how much we eat of something is set against how easily it kills a rat. It is very refreshing to find an American casting a sceptical eye on 'the dead rat syndrome'. Hardly a day goes by without a scientific journal or newspaper reporting that a US laboratory some-where has detected cancer in rats force fed on some staple element of our diet. Coupled with this has been the development of an incredibly sensitive machine – the mass spectrometer – which has made it possible to trace pesticide residues to a tiny and almost meaningless level. So when the dead rat syndrome is linked to the merest trace of the same pesticide present in human food everyone hits the panic button. But Professor Ames has now decided on a new approach. He is linking the tests on animals to both the frequency and level of our exposure to a given pesticide and he argues that, in any case, we consume vast quantities of naturally occurring pesticides in fruit and vegetables every day. He has come to some very interesting conclusions:

A can of diet cola has a Herp of 0.006 per cent. The average daily intake of a food preservative AF2 has a Herp 300 times smaller at 0.0002 per cent.

Naturally occurring toxins (nature's pesticides) in 5g of brown mustard have a Herp of 0.07 per cent. The Herp for a daily average intake of the man-made pesticide PCB is 0.0002 per cent – massively lower in risk. And as for the 100g of cooked bacon we might consume with the mustard – cooking generates mutagens, toxins and carcinogens giving it a Herp of 0.003 per cent. That's more than ten times riskier than the PCB residue!

A final point of contrast – one mushroom (which contains a cocktail of natural toxins) has a Herp of 0.1 per cent and a glass of beer a Herp as high as 2.8 per cent. (Are Meryl Streep and Pamela Stephenson now going to start a campaign to ban mushrooms and beer?)

Using his method of risk assessment, Professor Ames says that the possible cancer hazard from Alar in a daily glass of apple juice is eighteen times smaller than that from the aflatoxins in a daily peanut butter sandwich and 1,000 times smaller than that from a daily glass of beer. This he illustrates in the table opposite.

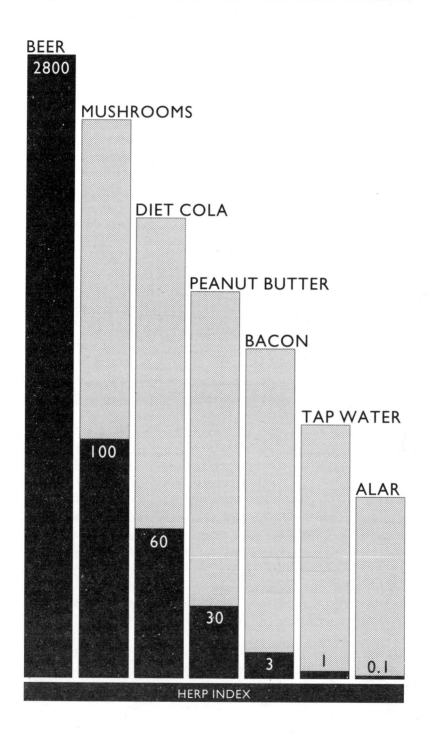

RELATIVE CANCER RISK

BEER
2800

MUSHROOMS
100

DIET COLA
60

PEANUT BUTTER
30

BACON
3

TAP WATER
1

ALAR
0.1

HERP INDEX

Contrast this with the claims made by the Natural Resources Defence Council (NRDC) in the US – the pressure group which set Meryl Streep off in the first place. It predicted that *1 in 4,000 children exposed to Alar before the age of six would then get cancer later in life*. But the Environmental Protection Agency (EPA), a US government body, later insisted that the NRDC figures could not serve as a basis for banning Alar because of 'flaws in test methodology and documentation'. NRDC had gauged Alar's cancer potency using data that had been emphatically rejected four years before as inappropriate and unreliable by the independent US Scientific Advisory Panel. NRDC had also estimated average intake of Alar in too small a survey. The EPA came up with a very different risk estimate – *that only 4.5 people in every 100,000 would contract cancer if exposed to Alar over a lifetime*. That, by the way, is an infinitesimal risk. Most people would probably not be exposed to Alar consistently over a lifetime. While some other cause of death (disease or accident) would in all likelihood do for those who were so exposed long before cancer intervened. Nevertheless, the EPA did ban Alar because they finally concluded it exceeded their risk threshold of one in every million. But they added:

It is important to understand that risk estimates based on animal testing are fairly rough and do not accurately predict human disease. For example, EPA risk estimates mean that there is a 95 per cent certainty that the risk is no higher than estimated by the agency. It may be lower and may even be zero.

The truth is that naturally occurring toxins in the foods we eat every day pose a far greater threat to us than negligible quantities of man-made pesticides and food additives. On average, Professor Ames estimates that we ingest 10,000 times more by weight of natural pesticides than of man-made pesticide residues. In all we take in between 5,000 and 10,000 different natural pesticides – eating cabbage alone involves consuming forty-nine natural pesticides. Ames concludes that there are more carcinogens in a single cup of coffee than in all the man-made pesticides we eat in a year *and it is well-established that coffee intake is not linked with cancer*.

Professor Ames says that when you test naturally occurring

pesticides on animals more than half of them are carcinogenic. However, this does not mean we are at risk, merely that humans, who live in a world of natural toxins, are well protected by their bodies' own defences:

We have tried in our scientific work to put into perspective the tiny exposures to pesticide residues by comparing them to the enormous background of natural substances ... If we spend all our efforts on minimal, rather than important, hazards we hurt public health. Most risk comes from food-borne bacteria and poor diet.

By 'poor diet' Professor Ames is referring to the heart disease and cancer that arise from eating an unbalanced diet. Along with the less fatal problem of bacteriological food poisoning, it is heart disease and cancer that pose by far the greatest threat to us. Both can be diet-related. It is this very real threat that *The Food Revolution* seeks to tackle. To persist in directing all our nervous energy towards additives and pesticides is like the airline pilot who is worried that he has spilt coffee on his trousers when his aeroplane has gone into a nosedive. There are many pressing reasons why we should be concerned about the use of pesticides and fungicides by farmers. In particular, the delicate balance of our eco-system is clearly under threat. But the specific danger of residues in food has been blown out of all proportion. Likewise, it is important to scrutinize food additives closely, particularly the ones that allow manufacturers to disguise cheap, unhealthy food. But the problems of hyper-activity have been exaggerated. No one can doubt that the pursuit of pesticide manufacturers and food manufacturers by pressure groups has been a good thing. Many companies have rightly had to change their policies as a result. But when it comes to the specific safety of the food on our plate we have lost sight of the wood because of the profusion of trees.

Food poisoning, as Professor Ames would agree, is defi-nitely known to pose something of a threat to us. But here, as elsewhere, there is still much work to be done to work out the size of the risk. Official government statistics tell us that in 1989 there were around 54,000 cases of confirmed food poisoning in England and Wales. The key question is how many cases went unreported. Many of us who suffer what we take to be food poisoning merely sit it out. If we do go to the

33

doctor he or she may prescribe something to help us but the majority of GPs won't take samples for analysis. Only if samples were sent to the Public Health Laboratory would it be possible for the existence of a bug to be confirmed. To estimate the real number of cases of food poisoning in Britain, health officials tend to multiply the number of confirmed cases by ten. Others in the US use a multiple of 100. So all we can say with confidence is that in 1989 there were between 540,000 and 5.4 million cases of food poisoning.

Assessing the risk from listeria is, if anything, even more difficult. We have already related how in 1989 the Department of Health advised pregnant women not to eat soft cheese. Their own uncertainty becomes apparent when you consider that they were acting on a survey of soft cheese they had carried out *three* years before. It took them that long to decide that there was a risk. Some bacteriologists believe that listeria (which, if it has any effect at all, normally results in mild, flu-like symptoms) causes many of the thousands of miscarriages which women suffer every year. But the official statistics merely number the annual cases at about twenty. One of the problems here is that the listeria bacterium is endemic in our environment and indeed is carried in many of our bodies. It has been found in many pre-cooked chilled meals and prepared salads, as well as the soft cheeses and milk we mentioned earlier. This said, it has never been ascertained what level of listeria constitutes a danger and to whom, nor whether avoiding certain foods would expose us to a health and nutrition risk greater than the risk of listeriosis. But the level of risk would be different for children, adults, the sick, the elderly and pregnant women.

Earlier we quoted Professor Waites' contention that the risk from microbiological contamination is much greater than environmental contamination and massively greater than the risk represented by pesticide residues or food additives. But to put food poisoning itself into context he also wrote:

Given that there are about 50,000 food-borne illnesses reported each year in England and Wales, taking the worst case scenario and assuming this represents one per cent of actual cases, this would represent 5 million meals a year which produced illness. However, such a figure would be only 0.01 per cent of the total number of meals eaten.

Salmonella, listeria and other food poisoning bacteria will always be with us. In order to reduce the risk considerably below Professor Waites' 0.01 per cent of meals there are some basic rules of food handling we can follow. These are set out in Section V – the Consumers' Guide.

Since we constantly stress the vital connection between diet and health you might imagine that family doctors would be a fund of good advice. Not so.

In 1988, Dr Jan Francis monitored how 128 doctors and nurses dealt with patients at risk from heart disease because of high levels of blood cholesterol.

- Thirty-seven of these health professionals did not understand that polyunsaturated fats should be increased as a proportion of total fat intake.
- Twenty-five told patients to lose weight when they were not overweight.
- Thirty-seven gave advice on what to avoid but offered no suggestions about eating more healthy food such as fruit, vegetables and various carbohydrates.

None of this is at all surprising when you learn that there is no individual examination paper for nutrition in any medical degree course. A 1983 report from the British Nutrition Foundation found that nutrition was poorly served. A follow-up in 1987 revealed that only three of Britain's twenty-nine medical schools had even discussed the report and that nutrition was still not given great prominence in their medical exams. Four medical schools set no nutrition questions at all and four others were not even interested enough to respond to the follow-up.

Not surprisingly, Britain has few professors of nutrition at its medical schools. One of the few, Professor John Garrow of St Bartholomew's, says that for years the situation has been awful and is only slowly improving. But Professor Garrow accepts that any improvements made now (and various bodies are looking at how to achieve this) will not help doctors already qualified:

> Often their understanding is astonishingly poor and gleaned from the media. It is therefore often untrue and often contradictory . . . A lot of people go to their GPs for dietary advice but most find that they do not have enough fundamental knowledge to deal with questions sufficiently.

If good diet is fundamental to good health then this is a lamentable state of affairs. And if doctors know little what hope is there for the rest of us?

Food and nutrition as a subject is treated with equally scant regard in our schools. Provisional figures for children taking GCSE in 1988 show that whereas around 600,000 took English and Mathematics only 175,000 studied Home Economics. For the small minority who did study Home Economics to examination level, food accounted for only a minority of the syllabus. Since then Home Economics has become part of a 'core curriculum' subject called Technology. All eleven- and twelve-year-olds have to study Technology, but the emphasis given to food and nutrition depends very much on the importance individual schools attach to it. There is some coverage of nutrition and food bacteria in science subjects but it is hardly given priority.

How are the eleven-year-olds who get to study food and nutrition taught? Often very well by teachers who have become the poor relations of the new 'core curriculum'. They are short of funds and thus short of attractive course material. They have to fall back on a vast array of booklets, posters and videos thoughtfully provided free by food manufacturers. Let us give you some examples:

The Biscuit, Cake, Chocolate and Confectionery Alliance has published a series of leaflets amongst which is *Biscuits, Cakes, Chocolate and Confectionery: Everyday Foods for Everyone.* It states, quite correctly, that such products '. . . now provide a significant and enjoyable part of our diet.' Of course there is nothing wrong, as such, with any of these foods in moderation. But as the Alliance admits, they have become a significant part of our diet. So much so that they account for a part of the saturated fat that causes the appalling level of heart disease in Britain. The leaflet then goes on to inform its junior audience that biscuits and the rest 'have established themselves as part of a healthy balanced diet.' What about a healthy balanced education? It is true that in a further leaflet the nutritional breakdown of biscuits and confectionery is explored, including saturated fats. But saturated fat is certainly not given as much importance as health experts give it.

The British Soft Drinks Association publish *Soft Drinks Today* – a leaflet produced under the heading 'New Generation Home Economics' and labelled as 'suitable for GCSE'. Essentially, the leaflet describes how soft drinks are made and what goes into them. But it does touch on health: 'Soft drinks provide a means of obtaining the fluid which is essential to a healthy body. They are also fun to drink.' Strangely, though, the dangers of tooth decay are not covered. The 1989 COMA report on sugar from the Department of Health (*Dietary Sugars and Human Diseases*) said that the sucrose we add to our diet is a significant cause of tooth decay and should be reduced. Carbonated drinks are a significant source of sucrose in our diet. Is it not time the British Soft Drinks Association told the whole story?

The British Sugar Bureau, funded by the sugar producers, has produced large quantities of educational material over the years. A 1986 video which claimed that sucrose was not the main cause of tooth decay was withdrawn after complaints from dentists. More recently a leaflet, produced by the Dental Health Foundation (an organization partly funded by the Bureau), was also withdrawn after complaints that sucrose was omitted from a list of foods which cause tooth decay.

The National Dairy Council is the beneficent body which has bestowed *Michael the Milkbottle* upon infant schools. Michael lives in Milkland where 'all the people are healthy, kind and live for ever . . . we have plenty of milk, butter, cream and cheese and lots of other foods and our people are very healthy.' Now while it is a mistake to put small children on low fat diets (they need considerable quantities of fat from their mothers' milk onwards) this is a question of education for the future. Does the preceding paragraph give small children the right idea about diet?

The Butter Information Council publish 'A Project for Infant Schools' (Key Stage I of the National Curriculum) called *Changes*. Children are given a sheet to fill in answering the question 'Which do you like with your toast?' The choice they are given is cheese, strawberry jam, a poached egg, baked beans, spaghetti and butter. Not margarine or some other spread, you notice, but butter.

Mazola produce a leaflet called *Understanding Cholesterol*. On one page it explains where the fat in our diet can be found. Foods that are high in polyunsaturated fats are 'some fish, Mazola corn oil, Mazola sunflower oil'. A curiously short list strangely dominated by one oil manufacturer.

The Shredded Wheat Fibre Information Centre has produced a leaflet on healthy eating. On the cover is a beautiful photograph of all the wonderful foods nature has to offer mankind – fruit, vegetables, grain, pulses, meat and fish. In addition, there are some everyday foods which man has processed for himself – pasta, dried fruit, bread and cheese. And there, nestling in the forefront, is a piece of shredded wheat. Almost God-given, you might say.

What about the education we receive as adults? We have already looked at the quality of nutritional information in popular newspapers. Books are also a common source. In fact, hardly a week goes by when there are not four, and quite often rather more, food paperbacks in the top ten bestsellers. The majority of them are so-called diet books – that is, weight loss programmes, but losing weight is only a small part of the story. *The Food Revolution* is not a diet book in the usual sense of the phrase. It does not offer an eight-week regime designed to render the body beautiful. Instead, it proves how narrow a diet most of us eat and shows how only a few minor changes can revolutionize our health . . . for the rest of our lives. Heart attacks, cancer, obesity, diabetes and bowel disease – known as 'diseases of affluence' – are the major health problem facing western countries today and so often they are diet-related. We need to know how to eat in order to avoid them.

We have shown how we worry about things that are not

important and ignore those that are crucial. We have looked at the appalling amount of misinformation about food which abounds. And we have demonstrated that we do not know nearly enough about nutrition as a result.

Here, at last, is the anti-scare food book. Everything you wanted to know about eating but no one would tell you. How our dietary needs vary at different ages – how to lose weight sensibly and permanently – a consumers' guide to help with shopping and the best cooking methods – the basics of family nutrition – the latest research on foods which help prevent diseases like cancer – and a comprehensive directory which you can keep on the shelf to use as a handy reference. In short, this book is a food bible designed to help you enjoy eating and live longer. The message of the 1980s always seemed to be *don't*. The message for the 1990s has to be a positive one: *do* eat these foods and enjoy the benefit.

All of us can take part in *The Food Revolution*. What we need to know is not only contained in this book, it is now being printed on food products. Being a food revolutionary is easy when you know how. Perhaps you would like to start by analysing your own diet. You will be surprised at the results.

SECTION II

THE FOOD REVOLUTION

THE QUESTIONNAIRE

You are about to begin an in-depth exploration of your own diet. Relax. This is strictly between you and this book. Just find yourself a quiet corner where you won't be disturbed for twenty minutes or so, and put your feet up. The aim is not to increase your angst. All you have to do is take a deep breath, pick up a pencil, and tell the truth. No one else need ever know.

Let's try something simple for starters. What does the word 'meal' mean to you? Did 'food eaten as part of a structured social occasion with time, place and sequence rules' flit through your mind? No? Oh well, let's just say that a meal is one of those more or less regular occasions when you sit down at table and eat, usually with a knife, fork or spoon. It can be a light meal – like a bowl of cereal for breakfast – or a main meal, like meat-and-two-veg. What about the word 'snack'? You needn't feel compelled to think of it as wicked. Try substituting: 'any small amount of food that's eaten quickly between, or in place of, structured meals'. It's perfectly normal to include snacks somewhere in your diet.

In *The Food Revolution* Questionnaire that follows, just circle the answer of your choice – whether it's A, B or C – then add up your scores to see how you have done in the Analysis section which follows each set of questions.

Fine, now before we start probing for the candid details of your diet, why don't we take an overall look at your dietary patterns.

In other words . . .

41

NEVER MIND THE QUALITY, CHECK THE BREADTH

RECORD YOUR ANSWER ON RIGHT

Q1 How many meals do you eat in a normal day?
A. Three – one main meal and two lighter meals
B. Two – one main meal and one light meal
C. One

Q2 Here's an example of the main meals your next-door neighbour might eat in a fortnight, excluding any puddings:

Mon (1) sausages, mashed potato, baked beans
Tue (1) cottage pie, peas
Wed (1) lasagne, salad
Thu (1) steak, boiled potatoes, French beans
Fri (1) fried fish, chips, peas
Sat (1) pizza, garlic bread, salad
Sun (1) roast beef, Yorkshire pudding, roast potatoes, sprouts
Mon (2) spaghetti bolognaise
Tue (2) steak, chips, peas
Wed (2) sausages, chips, baked beans
Thu (2) baked potato, chilli con carne filling
Fri (2) fish fingers, boiled potatoes, peas
Sat (2) chicken curry
Sun (2) roast beef, Yorkshire pudding, roast potatoes, sprouts

Let's look at the number of different types of main meals your neighbour had.

Well, the two Sunday meals were identical, and there's not much difference between meals Mon (1) and Wed (2) (sausages, potatoes, baked beans), Thur (1) and Tues (2) (steak, potatoes, green veg), or between meals Fri (1) and Fri (2) (fish, potatoes, green veg), is there? So you could say that their diet revolved around $(14 - 4) = 10$ basic meals.

Now try to jot down the **main meals** you've eaten over the last two weeks:

WEEK 1	**WEEK 2**
MON:	MON:
TUES:	TUES:
WED:	WED:
THURS:	THURS:
FRI:	FRI:
SAT:	SAT:
SUN:	SUN:

How many different types of main meals did *you* have?

A. More than 12
B. 8 to 12
C. Less than 8

Q3 Breakfast means different things to different people. It could be toast with jam or marmalade; bacon-and-eggs; some sort of breakfast cereal; coffee, cigarette and morning paper . . .

Whatever it is, is it true to say that you *usually* have the same thing for breakfast every day?

A. Yes, I tend to have the same kind of thing most days
B. No, I eat a different type of breakfast each morning

Q4 Now, what about those eating events between meals . . . Which statement best describes the number of snacks you have in an average day?

A. I nibble at food throughout the day
B. I usually have two or three snacks a day
C. I tend to have one snack a day
D. I never eat between meals

Q5 What's in a snack? Well, we've decided, in theory, that snacks can be made up of *any* small amount of food eaten between, or instead of, meals. In practice, it doesn't seem to work out that way.

One snacker described her typical snack-pattern as:

morning break-time – packet of crisps
mid-afternoon – tea and biscuits
mid-evening – fruit, usually an apple

Do *you* tend to choose the same foods for your snacks each day?

A. Yes, I might try a different brand, but I usually eat the same type of snacks in the course of a day
B. No, I make a point of eating a completely different type of snack-food each day

ANALYSIS

Now add up your scores
1. If you answered A score 2, for B score 1, for C 0.
2. A 2, B 1, C 0
3. A 0, B 2
4. A 2, B 1, C 1, D 0
5. A 0, B 2

So, your variety score is [   ]

SCORE 7–10

You're a natural gourmand, aren't you? Variety is the spice of life to you and you enjoy experiencing the taste and texture of a wide range of foods. This sensation-seeking tendency will ensure your dietary repertoire is never dull, but beware that your consuming passion for palatable pleasures doesn't lead you to become a little too *fleshy* yourself – especially if you chose answer A to question 4.

SCORE 4–6

Well, there's nothing *unusual* about your repertoire – pretty run of the mill, really. But don't you feel you're missing out sometimes? Extend your range a little and add a touch of colour to your palate. It just might brighten things up a bit.

SCORE 0–3 No one could accuse you of being promiscuous in your tastes where food is concerned. In fact, you bind yourself to a very monotonous diet indeed. Could it be that you are *afraid* of experimenting with different dishes? Why not give yourself permission to try out some new dietary combinations. Who knows, you might even discover things you really like.

INTERPRETATION

You might be surprised that most people have a limited repertoire of foods. There is nothing wrong with that. We asked you these questions to make you think about what you consume. You probably had some difficulty remembering what you had to eat. Most people do and this is one reason why we don't mind eating the same foods again and again. If you have to shop and cook for other people regularly the thought must have gone through your mind, 'Oh, what are we going to eat tomorrow?'. The fact is we all have our favourite dishes and a limited repertoire of perhaps as few as eight to twelve basic meals. This means that you can easily modify those meals to make them more healthy. We are going to show you how small changes can help you keep fit and stay well.

Now we need to take a closer look at the *quality* of your diet. After all, two food repertoires might include the same number of items, but be as different as chalk and cheese.

We'll begin with a frank question.

DO YOU KNOW THE FATS OF LIFE?

Q1 What do you usually spread on your bread?

A. Butter – there's no substitute for taste, is there?
B. Margarine – any brand will do, as long as it's cheap!
C. Only a margarine or low-fat spread that's high in polyunsaturates

Q2 What do you tend to use for cooking?

A. Lard, dripping or butter – it makes food taste like home-cooking
B. Vegetable oil, these days, maybe olive or sunflower oil

Q3 Do you eat deep-fried foods – for example, fried chicken and chips or fish and chips or doughnuts?

A. Yes, regularly – I love 'em!
B. Occasionally – now and again I'll treat myself to chips or something
C. Never – I loathe greasy foods

Q4

Look at each of the following statements and decide whether it applies to you:

		Yes	No
A.	I always choose lean meat	[ ]	[ ]
B.	I trim off any fat I can see on the meat before I cook it	[ ]	[ ]
C.	I rarely eat lamb	[ ]	[ ]
D.	I rarely eat poultry or fish	[ ]	[ ]
E.	I mostly leave the fatty bits of the meat on my plate	[ ]	[ ]
F.	I can't resist those crunchy bits of bacon rind, or a crispy roast chicken skin, and as for pork crackling . . . !	[ ]	[ ]

Q5

Hamburgers, sausages, sausage rolls, bought meat pies, pâté, Cornish pasties and the like are all categorized as 'meat products'. How often do you eat meat products as part of a meal or as a snack in a typical week?

A. Most days
B. About four or five times a week
C. Up to twice a week on average
D. Never

Q6

Which statement best describes the amount of cheese you eat in a day on average?

A. Up to 30g (1oz) – that's about a small matchbox sized piece of cheese
B. 30 to 100g (1 to 3.5oz)
C. Over 100g (3.5oz) – I'm coming back as a mouse in my next life!

Q7

What type of milk do you use?

A. Gold top milk – nothing but the best
B. Ordinary milk – who needs 'chalky water'!
C. Semi-skimmed milk
D. Skimmed milk – now I've got used to it, anything else tastes awful

ANALYSIS

Now add up your scores
1. A 0, B 0, C 2
2. A 0, B 2
3. A 0, B 1, C 2
4. A Yes – 1, No – 0 B Yes – 1, No – 0
   C Yes – 1, No – 0 D Yes – 0, No – 1
   E Yes – 1, No – 0 F Yes – 0, No – 1
5. A 0, B 0, C 1, D 2
6. A 2, B 0, C 0, D 0
7. A 0, B 0, C 2, D 4

So, your fats of life score is [   ]

SCORE 0–8 Sorry to have to say this, but it looks like there's a thing or two your mother didn't tell you. Maybe you regard yourself as a chip off the old block ('fried food was good enough for Dad . . . '), but this isn't a very healthy attitude, especially if you scored zero for questions 4F, 5A, or 6C.

SCORE 8–13 Not bad but you could do better.

SCORE 14–20 Where the fats of life are concerned, you've little to worry about. But check the interpretation section before moving on . . .

INTERPRETATION

Avoiding heart disease and possibly some types of cancer means eating less fatty food and using oils instead of hard fats. Most of the wrong type of fat we get comes from butter, cheese, full-cream milk and meat fats. The fattiest meats are the meat products and remember meat pies are the worst because of the pastry. Fish, poultry, and lean meat are fine – there is no need to avoid red meat. Low-fat spreads or margarines high in polyunsaturates are healthier alternatives to butter. But if you are a butter addict then just don't eat too much. Most people consume about 35g a day – that's about 1¼oz – so the choice is yours: either eat less than half an ounce of butter a day or change to a low-fat spread or margarine high in polyunsaturates.

GREENGROCER PHOBIA

Some people confess to being bananas about salads, fruit and veg. Whereas other people regard it as rabbit food.

Q1

Look at the following list:
apples, apricots, nectarines, oranges, peaches, pears, tangerines.

What's your *honest* reaction to the thought of eating these items raw?
A. Ugh – I wouldn't touch one with a barge-pole, let alone eat it – unless it was in a pie or flan maybe
B. OK, I suppose. I eat one of those about three times a week
C. Fine – I usually have a piece of fresh fruit every day
D. Delicious! I regularly chomp my way through several pieces of fruit each day

Q2

Which statement best sums up your *everyday* attitude to leafy green vegetables and carrots?

A. No thanks, I'll stick to meat and potatoes
B. Yes – a dinner would be a bit dull without them
C. Great! I either have cooked veg or a salad with both lunch and dinner

Q3

How do you usually cook your vegetables?

A. Microwave
B. Steam
C. Sweat them in a small volume of water with a knob of butter
D. Boil in a saucepan full of water with salt
E. Boil in a saucepan full of water without salt

ANALYSIS

Now add up your scores
1. A 0, B 0, C 2, D 1
2. A 0, B 1, C 2
3. A 2, B 2, C 1, D 0, E 1

SCORE
4–6

Good you're a true green. A word of warning, though, if you chose answer (D) for question 1 – too much fruit can actually dull your smile by promoting dental caries.

SCORE
0–4

If you chose answer (A) to questions 1 and 2, then you've revealed yourself to be a hardened case of 'greengrocer-phobia'. Your attitude to fruit and vegetables needs examining in more detail. See below to find out why.

INTERPRETATION

A regular intake of fruit and green, yellow and orange vegetables, besides being a good source of vitamins A and C, may also prevent heart disease and cancer. But if you eat fruit too frequently between meals, the sugar naturally present in the fruit can cause tooth decay. When you cook vegetables it's best to microwave or steam them without adding salt. If you boil them in a large amount of water you will be losing most of the vitamins in the cooking water. If you add butter to vegetables be careful not to overdo it. Just add a very small knob.

You've already come quite some way in separating the wheat from the chaff in your diet. Now we'll examine whether you take the rough with the smooth.

TESTING YOUR FIBRE

Q1 **Your Daily Bread**
How many slices of *wholemeal* bread do you have each day?

A. Eight
B. Six
C. Four
D. Two
E. One
F. None

How many slices of *white* bread do you have each day?

G. Eight
H. Six
I. Four
J. Two
K. One
L. None

Q2 **Breakfast Cereals**
Which breakfast cereal do you tend to eat in the morning? (Choose the most similar type if your usual brand is not shown.)

A. All-Bran
B. Muesli
C. Shredded Wheat, Weetabix
D. Cornflakes, porridge, Sugar Puffs
E. Special K, Rice Krispies, Frosties, Cocopops
F. I don't eat cereal regularly for breakfast

Q3 Spuds
If you eat potatoes, how often do you tend to have them?

A. Twice a day
B. Daily
C. Three to four times a week
D. Two to three times a week
E. I don't usually eat potatoes

Q4 Pasta
If you eat pasta, how often do you tend to have it?

A. Twice a day
B. Daily
C. Three to four times a week
D. Two to three times a week
E. I don't usually eat pasta

Q5 Rice
If you eat rice, how often do you tend to have it?

A. Twice a day
B. Daily
C. Three to four times a week
D. Two to three times a week
E. I don't usually eat rice

Check Your Pulse Rating
Which of the following would you
have in a typical day?

A. Peas
B. Green beans
C. Baked beans
D. Lentils
E. None of these in a typical day

ANALYSIS

Add up the numbers you have scored
1. A 20, B 15, C 10, D 6, E 2.5, F 0,
   G 8, H 6, I 4, J 2.5, K 1.5, L 0
2. A 15, B 6, C 4, D 1.5, E 0, F 0
3. A 4, B 2, C 1, D 0.5, E 0
4. A 8, B 4, C 2, D 1, E 0
5. A 6, B 3, C 1.5, D 0.5, E 0
6. A 4, B 2.5, C 10, D 4, E 0

Your fibre score is [   ]

SCORE 25+
You're a person who ensures you've
got plenty of fibre – definitely not a
type to sit around waiting for things to
happen. Check below for why you
should maintain this positive
approach.

SCORE 15–25
You're already going through the
motions where fibre is concerned, but
there's some room for improvement.
Find out how simple it is to enhance
your performance . . .

SCORE
0–15

This refusal of yours to take the rough with the smooth explains why you're probably finding things a bit of a strain. You're placing an unnecessary burden on your well-being and it's time you learnt how to loosen up a bit. Do yourself a favour and read the interpretation section *straightaway*.

INTERPRETATION

Fibre prevents constipation. The British still spend a lot of money on laxatives. If you scored less than 15 and are the constipated type then eating more fibre-rich food could save you pounds per anum per annum. A high intake of fibre-rich food may also help prevent diverticular disease (inflammation of the large bowel).

FOR TRUE GREENS

Q1

This question is for vegetarians only – that is, people who do not eat meat, fish or poultry.

Which of the following is true?
A. I drink at least half a pint of milk a day
B. I eat at least 30g (1oz) of cheese a day
C. I eat eggs at least three times a week
D. I don't eat milk, cheese or eggs

ANALYSIS

Add up the numbers you have scored
for estimate of your vitamin B_{12} intake.

A. 1
B. 0.5
C. 1
D. 0

So, your vitamin B_{12} score is [   ]

INTERPRETATION

If you scored less than 2 you could be at risk from vitamin B_{12}
deficiency. If you are a vegan then you must supplement
your diet with vitamin B_{12} or use foods fortified with the
vitamin. Many foods acceptable to vegetarians and vegans
are supplemented with the vitamin.

THE MEANING OF FOOD – HOW DO YOU RELATE TO YOUR PLATE?

If you stop to think about it, food isn't just something you
stick in your face when you feel hungry. Food *means* things to
us all. Different foods have different meanings. Food can
function as a status symbol – like serving caviare at a party. Or
as sign of friendship – like giving a box of chocolates to your
neighbour. People will eat the caviare or the chocolates not
necessarily because they're peckish, but because they've learnt
that doing so is part of the rules applying to a particular social
situation. Imagine how you'd feel if your neighbour refused
to take the chocolates because she didn't feel like sweets!

Food doesn't only have meanings we share with others, it
also has private meanings for ourselves. For many people,
sweet food represents comfort and security. Think how often
people eat sweets not because they're hungry, but because
sweets taste nice and make them feel better. Certain foods
can acquire negative or threatening meanings – for example,

57

some people associate highly-palatable foods with gaining weight, which, in turn, is linked to fears about losing their attractiveness. Eating these foods will prompt an anxiety response in such consumers.

Whether or not you are consciously aware of it, you too have your own menu of food meanings and responses and this influences the kind of diet you eat. Answering the following questions *honestly* will help you confront this aspect of your appetite. Ready? Time to spill the beans.

Q1 **Just supposing . . .**

A. There's something tasty in the fridge. Would you go and finish it off? (Well, it's a shame to let it go to waste . . . ')
Frequently [ ]
Occasionally [ ]
Never [ ]

B. You're on an aeroplane and the stewardess is handing out those little plastic trays with the little plastic titbits. Would you polish off the lot even if you weren't hungry? ('What the hell, it's free, isn't it . . . ?')
Frequently [ ]
Occasionally [ ]
Never [ ]

C. You're preparing a meal. Would you nibble as you went along? ('One for the pot and one for me and one for the pot and . . . ')
Frequently [ ]
Occasionally [ ]
Never [ ]

D. You've had a row with your partner or boss. Would you take it out on the biscuit tin?
Frequently [ ]
Occasionally [ ]
Never [ ]

E. It's late at night and you're alone with the telly. Would you nibble away at something to console yourself?
Frequently [ ]
Occasionally [ ]
Never [ ]

Q2 Decline or fall?

A. Do you try to eat less at meal-times than you'd really like to?
Frequently [ ]
Occasionally [ ]
Never [ ]

B. When offered food or drink, do you turn it down because you're worried about your weight?
Frequently [ ]
Occasionally [ ]
Never [ ]

C. Do you make a point of choosing low calorie meals and/or counting calories?
Frequently [ ]
Occasionally [ ]
Never [ ]

ANALYSIS

1. Count up the number of times you chose 'frequently', 'occasionally', or 'never' for **question 1**. Which response did you choose *most often*?

Frequently
Deep down inside you know you're something of a food junky – just the sight of food turns you on and when things go wrong you crave your food-fix. You're not necessarily overweight, but if you don't wean yourself off this habit of comfort-eating you might end up that way – which isn't very healthy.

Occasionally

You're human and you can get tempted to eat when you're not hungry – but if your other answers were 'nevers' then, by and large, you've got your appetite under control. No real harm in indulging your whims once in a while, unless you're inclined to put on weight. But remember the temptation is there and try not to get hooked.

Never

You rarely yield to food unless you're hungry and you don't use it as an emotional prop. On the face of it, this is a healthy attitude. But before you congratulate yourself prematurely, check your rating for the next question . . .

2.   Count up the number of times you chose 'frequently', 'occasionally', or 'never' for **question 2**. Which response did you choose *most often*?

Before we analyse your answers to this question, there's one more thing we need to know. 'Would a doctor say you were overweight?'

If you are *not* overweight

and you mostly answered . . .

Frequently

You treat life like a permanent slimming diet, don't you? It's wise not to go overboard at the smorgasbord, but there's no need to keep quite such a tight hold on your intake. Letting go doesn't mean you'll be sunk by the fatty you fear within. Regain a more balanced attitude to food by following a balanced diet, and you'll find the scales will steady themselves.

Occasionally or never
As long as you continue to eat from
need and not greed, you'll stay on the
right lines.

If you are overweight

and you mostly answered . . .

Frequently
Well done – you're taking positive
action to fight the flab! Make sure
you're eating sensibly, though, and not
starving yourself in your desire to lose
weight too quickly.

Occasionally or never
Hmm. If you're only slightly chubby
and comfortable that way, you'll
probably get away with it. If you're fat,
you may be storing up problems for
yourself. Read on *then* decide if it's
worth the risk.

Q3 Playing the numbers game . . .

How many of the following
statements are true of you? [   ]

- I never buy processed food
- I feel guilty if I've eaten something
  with an E-number in it
- I avoid all foods which contain
  added sugar
- I only eat organic produce

Q4 Healthy, wealthy and . . . ?

If you had to choose, which of the
following would you say are the *five*
most important items to spend your
money on for healthy eating?

A. Organic food
B. High-fibre foods (wholemeal bread, breakfast cereals, pulses)
C. Additive-free foods
D. Foods with no added sugar
E. Lean meat and fish
F. Biscuits and snackfoods
G. Green, orange and red vegetables
H. Low-fat products (skimmed/ semi-skimmed milk, low-fat spreads)
I. Diet drinks
J. Mineral water
K. Fresh fruit and fruit juice

3. If *any* of these statements applied to you, then you must learn to relax about food! Whatever the food terrorists tell you, you can actually do none of these things and still live a happy and wholesome life. Armed with that, food-shopping need never be so stressful for you again.

4. Answers B, E, G, H, K score 1 point each, the rest score zero. Add up the number of points that you have scored.

So your healthy eating score is [   ]

INTERPRETATION

SCORE OF 5 You sound as if you've got a well-adjusted attitude to food purchase. If you put your money where your mouth is, you've got the recipe for a healthy diet!

SCORE 3–4 You still need a little guidance with your priorities – but one or two changes is all it takes to get full marks for your shopping basket.

SCORE 0–2 When it comes to shopping, you're a bit mixed up, aren't you? But don't despair, a few simple guidelines will straighten out your shopping list in no time at all – and save you hours of agonizing at the check-out.

RISKY TENDENCIES

Ask most people what kind of person they'd call a risk-taker and they'll probably come up with a daredevil stuntman, wheeler-dealer whizz-kid or someone else equally dynamic and glamorous. Actually risk-takers come in all shapes and sizes, especially when it's a question of gambling with one's health. You might not think you have a fate-tempting lifestyle, but you may be wrong. In this last phase of the analysis you're going to have to be a little tough-minded with yourself as we put this to the test and see how well your diet stands up to the risks you're taking. And remember, if you're going to dine with the devil you'd better sup with a long spoon . . .

Q1 Sitting it out?
Which of the following statements best describes you?

A. Most of my days are spent sitting or standing and I don't really exercise on any regular basis
B. I exercise so that I'm moderately breathless for at least twenty minutes three times a week
C. I'm a serious athlete in training/ my job involves heavy manual work

Q2

The Wicked Weed
Are you a cigarette-smoker?

A.   No, certainly not!
B.   'Fraid so, up to ten a day
C.   Gasp . . . It's – er – over ten a day!

Q3

Tubby or not tubby . . .
Look at the following weight-for-height chart:

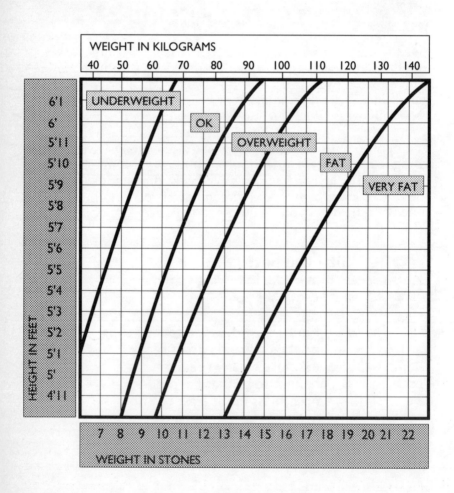

Do you fall into the fat or very fat bands?

A. Yes
B. No

If you do, are you . . .

C. Pear-shaped (your hips are bigger than your waist)
D. Apple-shaped (your waist is bigger than your hips)

 Relative Danger
Has a parent, brother or sister of yours suffered from heart disease under the age of fifty-five?

A. Yes
B. No

ANALYSIS

Add up all the numbers that you scored for questions 1 to 4 to find your coronary heart disease (CHD) risk score:

1. A 2, B 0, C 0
2. A 0, B 1, C 4
3. A 2, B 0, C 0, D 2
4. A 10, B 0

So, your CHD risk score is [   ]

INTERPRETATION

Heart disease tends to run in families. If your CHD score is 20 and you got a low score on the Fats of Life section (p47) you are a prime candidate for a heart attack. It's time to take some action. If you scored 10 on question 4 you need to be particularly careful about your diet, especially if you got a low score on the Fats of Life. Your risk of heart disease increases with age and women usually get heart disease ten years later than men. Diet is believed to be the underlying cause of heart disease. Regular exercise may help protect from heart disease and is certainly good for people who have already had one heart attack. If you are apple-shaped rather than pear-shaped then you are more likely to die from heart disease. If you are overweight, losing weight will cut your risks. Even if you scored zero you could reduce your risks by changing your fat intake. If you are a smoker then what you eat and drink matters even more both for avoiding heart disease and cancer – you need to make sure that you eat plenty of fruit and leafy vegetables.

Falling under the influence

There's one unit of alcohol in:

- one small glass of sherry
- one average glass of wine
- half a pint of beer, lager or cider
- one measure of spirits

Would you say you drink on average:

If you're a man:
A. At least 7 units a day
B. 3 to 7 units a day
C. Up to 3 units a day
D. Never touch a drop

If you're a woman:
A. At least 5 units a day
B. 2 to 5 units a day
C. Up to 2 units a day
D. Never touch a drop

ANALYSIS

5.   A excess, B high, C low, D zero

So, your alcohol intake rating is [   ]

INTERPRETATION

If you are in the low or zero grades, that's fine. If you are
pregnant you shouldn't be drinking at all. If you smoke as
well as drink you are at high risk from mouth and throat
cancer. If you are in the high grade B, then you should try to
cut down. If you are in the excess grade A, then you are
already damaging your health.

Q6 Grin and bear it?
Which of the following do you admit
to:

		Yes	No
A.	I brush my teeth *every* day	[ ]	[ ]
B.	I floss my teeth *every* day	[ ]	[ ]
C.	I frequently eat bread/cakes/biscuits/sweets/fruit between meals	[ ]	[ ]
D.	I frequently drink sugar-sweetened drinks between meals	[ ]	[ ]

ANALYSIS

6. Add up the numbers that you scored for question 6 to find your dental disease risk score:

A. Yes–0, No–1
B. Yes–0, No–2
C. Yes–3, No–0
D. Yes–1, No–0

So, your dental disease risk score is [   ]

INTERPRETATION

If you've scored zero you're doing well. Tooth decay is caused by bacteria growing on residual food particles left in the mouth after eating. Bacteria grow very well on starchy and sugary foods to produce acid which erodes the enamel and causes bad breath. Preventing tooth decay and gum disease is simple:

- avoid eating sugary foods frequently between meals;
- brush your teeth regularly with a fluoride toothpaste;
- remove any residual food particles between your teeth with dental floss.

ANALYSING YOUR DIET

Wait till he finds out he's gettin' chips an' egg for his tea tonight. Well, it's Thursday, isn't it? And on Thursday it has to be steak. It's the eleventh commandment, isn't it? Moses declared it. 'Thou shalt give thy fella steak every Thursday and if thou doesn't thy fella will have one big gob on him all night long.

Shirley Valentine

Now that you have analysed your own diet with the help of our questionnaire, we hope you will have discovered a lot about your eating habits – the way you approach fat, fruit and vegetables, fibre, alcohol and, of course, how broad or narrow your diet is. Shirley Valentine's husband – and he is not alone – expected the same seven evening meals every week. The monotony of this and other aspects of their marriage drove Shirley into the arms of a Greek lover. But it is possible to vary our diets without embarking on extra-marital affairs. Indeed, it can provide an added spice to life as well as yield enormous health benefits. For we eat not just to sustain ourselves but also for the immense pleasure of it. Eating is a sensual act. Like many sensual acts it brings with it pleasure and guilt in equal quantities. The purpose of *The Food Revolution* is to capitalize on that pleasure principle and encourage you to extend your repertoire a bit. But the guilt we will leave to the puritans who seem to believe that eating, like one or two other of life's pleasures, is no more than a necessary evil. So at the end of this section there is not a list of foods we *ought not* to eat. (There is no such thing as a bad food, there are only bad diets where we get the balance wrong.) Instead, we list the foods we positively *ought* to eat, every day and every week. This chapter is about variety and good health. One leads to the other and both help us enjoy our food to the utmost.

However you emerged from our diet analysis we can assure you that there are millions of others like you. But in case you need persuading as to the nature of everyone's eating habits we have assembled the incontrovertible evidence from a wide variety of sources. We have carefully built up a picture of how the British nation eats and the results are very revealing.

The market research company, Taylor Nelson, have been

monitoring the way we eat since 1974. They have persuaded 5,500 people – accounting for 2,100 households – to fill in regular food diaries which describe what they eat. Giles Quick masterminds this operation:

> People's foods are still very monotonous. The average meal-time looks much the same as it did ten years ago. Some products have gone through changes – like yoghurt – but basically people are still eating meat, potatoes and bread with a few vegetables. Our diets are dominated by a handful of products. It's still fish on Friday and a roast on Sunday.

In February 1990 this is what Taylor Nelson discovered about what we eat, meal by meal (each table shows the percentage of meals which featured the listed foods):

Breakfast	% of appearances
Bread and rolls	68
Cereals	66
Yellow fats:	
(butter, marg, etc)	51
Marmalade	32
Eggs	13
Fruit	10
Bacon	9
Jam	8
Sweet/savoury spreads	5
Salad/veg	3
Sausages	2
Diet bread	2
Dried fruit	2
Cheese	2
Yoghurts	1
Root veg	1
Tinned fruit	1
Sweet biscuits	1
Fresh soft fruit	1
Baked beans	1

Although the traditional fried breakfast is in steady decline (8 per cent) it is interesting to note that it is still a good deal more popular than, say, yoghurt (1 per cent). And clearly the majority of breakfasts merely feature cereal or bread and marmalade. Breakfast, by the way, is our most popular meal-time. It is the one we are least likely to skip. Now let's take a look at our lunch-time preferences:

Lunch	% of appearances
Bread	55
Yellow fats	35
Fresh potatoes	29
Salad veg	22
Fruit	21
Cheese	20
Fresh root veg	16
Cakes	14
Prepared veg	14
Sauces	13
Gravy	12
Prepared savoury dishes	12
Fresh leaf veg	11
Cold meats	10
Eggs	9
Beef	8
Poultry	7
Yoghurt	6
Fresh fruit	6
Canned soup	6
Baked beans	6
Frozen and canned fish	3
Fresh and smoked fish	2

As more women work, lunch has declined, although it is still the second most important eating occasion. Convenience of preparation is highly valued – 82 per cent of lunches are cold. Bread is commonest because of the popularity of sandwiches. There is quite a variety of foods in this table but salad vegetables only occur at about one lunch in five and fresh leaf vegetables at only one lunch in ten. Fish fares even worse.

We will have something to say about all this at the end of this chapter. Next we move on to tea-time:

Tea-time	% of appearances
Bread	51
Yellow fats	42
Cakes/tarts	34
Fresh potatoes	24
Salad veg	23
Prepared veg	15
Cheese	14
Fresh root veg	12
Sauces/dressings	11
Fresh fruit	10
Eggs	10
Prepared savoury dishes	10
Cold meats	9
Jam	8
Baked beans	7
Ice-cream	7
Beef	7
Poultry	6
Sweet biscuits	6
Fresh leaf veg	5
Frozen fish	5
Canned fish	4
Fresh and smoked fish	3

Tea-time is a much less important eating occasion than it used to be. The vast majority of homes only eat it intermittently. It is children and the elderly who eat tea more regularly. Finally, let's see how the evening meal features in the day's diet:

Evening meal	% of appearances
Fresh potatoes	49
Bread	32
Frozen veg	28
Fresh root veg	27
Salad veg	24
Yellow fats	24
Sauces	18
Cakes	17
Fresh fruit	16
Gravy products	16
Prepared savoury dishes	16
Beef	14
Fresh leaf veg	14
Ice-cream	12
Poultry	12
Cheese	12
Eggs	9
Fresh soft fruit	7
Baked beans	7
Sauces	7
Prepared potatoes	7
Frozen fish	7
Yoghurts	7
Sausages	7
Cream	6
Pork	6
Lamb	6
Fresh seed veg (eg, peas, beans, sweetcorn)	6
Hot pies	6
Cold meats	6
Fresh and smoked fish	5
Pasta	3

Our evening meal is steadily becoming more important to us and will shortly overtake lunch to become the second most frequent meal. The major changes recently have been a decline in desserts and a growth in the popularity of poultry, fresh leaf vegetables and pasta. Sales of fresh fish have also been increasing. All this sounds very virtuous but we must temper our sense of self-congratulation. These important and delicious foods still only feature in a minority of meals.

So, what can we conclude from this analysis of our eating habits? Two simple points, really:

- That we rely on a very narrow range of foods for the majority of our meals.
- That only a few small changes could greatly change our diet (say, eating more green vegetables and fish).

Does this conclusion – drawn from Taylor Nelson's research – match the facts as known? Let's examine five commonly expressed opinions about food.

I. WE'RE EATING A GREATER VARIETY OF FOODS

When you walk into the average supermarket the range and choice is so overwhelming it is difficult to believe how narrowly we still eat. Indeed, the plentifully stocked shelves of British food shops have recently reduced several visitors from Eastern Europe to tears. Their reaction underlines the wealth of choice we have and how lucky we are to have it. Do we exploit it properly? Not on the evidence we have looked at so far. But are things beginning to change? Tesco – who sell us one seventh of all we eat and drink in this country – say that our tastes are broadening and becoming more cosmopolitan. These are their three most popular ready-cooked recipe meals:

- Chilli Con Carne
- Lasagne
- Chicken Tikka Masala

And Tesco admit they have the greatest difficulty persuading us to buy a traditional British dish, beef stew and dumplings.

But what proportion of our meals feature these chilled convenience dishes? Although a rapidly growing market, it is still very small (and fears about listeria do not help it – *see* p377 in the Consumers' Guide). In fact, only one in a thousand meals eaten at home feature such dishes. As yet, like the yoghurt we mentioned earlier, convenience meals have a very small influence on the way we eat.

Southampton University's Janet Cade recently led a team which analysed the diets of 2,400 men and women aged between thirty-five and fifty-four. They were drawn from Ipswich, Stoke and Wakefield. She found that only twenty-nine people in this large group had a diet that matched the major dietary guidelines for healthy eating established since 1980. Janet Cade then set out to answer a very interesting question. How did the diets of these twenty-nine 'model eaters' differ from the average eating habits of the whole 2,400 people? To find out, her team selected another twenty-nine of their subjects at random and compared their diets to those of the 'model eaters'. They took a range of foods and worked out the average number of grams per person per day eaten by the respective groups.

FOODS	MODEL EATERS	RANDOM SELECTION
	grams per person per day	
Total bread	126	140
– wholemeal	62	16
– brown	27	18
– white	37	106
Other cereals (such as pasta, rice, breakfast cereals, crispbreads)	80	25
Butter	0.5	8
Margarine	2	9
Polyunsaturated margarine	10	1
Whole milk	122	250
Skimmed milks	146	0
High fat cheese	4	15
Fruit	140	37
Vegetables (not potatoes)	180	96
Potatoes	198	140
Lean meat and poultry	77	52
Fatty meat	14	36
Fish	35	32
Cakes, puddings, biscuits and ice-cream	36	147
Sweets and chocolate	7	0.3
Added sugar (eg, to tea or coffee)	16	16

So what were the key differences between the two groups? The model eaters consumed:

MORE   wholemeal bread, other cereals, skimmed milks, polyunsaturated margarine, fruit and vegetables, poultry, lean meat.

LESS   white bread, butter, full fat margarine, whole milk, high fat cheese, fatty meat.

Perhaps we could have predicted such differences. However, what is much more surprising is that the model eaters consumed about the same amount of cakes, puddings, biscuits and ice-cream and actually ate *more* sweets and chocolate! As we suggested in the Introduction, you do not need to wear a hair shirt to eat sensibly.

We have already shown we are not really eating a greater variety of foods. But the twenty-nine model eaters in this survey (a tiny minority) certainly did. When compared to the random group the model eaters ate a greater range of breads, cereals, milks and fruit. But we have news for the model eaters. They may get top marks when judged against the dietary guidelines of the 1980s but in the 1990s we all ought to eat more fish. That goes for the model eaters too. Only five of them ate white fish and only four of them ate fatty fish. Could do better!

However, everyone in Janet Cade's survey of three English towns, comes out better than the Scots do in a study carried out in the mid-1980s. The Scots have just about the highest rate of heart disease in the world. There are many factors which can contribute to this including smoking, lack of exercise, alcohol consumption and too much saturated fat in the diet. But there is another factor. Look at the extraordinarily high number of people in middle age who ate *no* fresh fruit or *no* green vegetables whatsoever.

Age group	% who ate no fresh fruit		% who ate no green veg	
	Men	Women	Men	Women
40–59	20	10	12	7

Approximately 1 in 4 men and 1 in 10 women ate *no fresh fruit at all*. Approximately 1 in 9 men and 1 in 7 women ate *no green vegetables whatsoever*. And areas with the highest proportion of people eating no fresh fruit or vegetables suffered correspondingly high rates of death from heart disease.

We will explain in detail why fruit and green vegetables are so good for us in the next section of the book. But for the moment let the figures from Scotland serve as further evidence – if such evidence is needed – of how appallingly narrow some of our diets are. Now let's consider the popular idea that our diets are getting healthier.

2. MEALS SUCH AS BACON AND EGGS AND COOKED PUDDINGS HAVE GONE INTO SHARP DECLINE

Absolutely true. Our consumption of bacon and sausages at breakfast has fallen by as much as 25 per cent since 1985, while hot puddings have declined by 20 per cent in the same period. So what has taken the place of these heavy, fatty foods? Although we have been eating much more yoghurt it still only appears at 1 per cent of breakfasts, 6 per cent of lunches and 7 per cent of evening meals. To find the answer you have to look beyond meal-times themselves. We have become very fond of snacks.

According to the analysis, 40 per cent of our eating at home is accounted for by informal snacks rather than formal meal-times. This indicates that getting on for half of our energy intake is from snacks rather than meals. And one in four of these snack occasions features sweet biscuits. According to the Biscuit, Cake, Chocolate and Confectionery Alliance we eat eighteen such biscuits a week topped up with the equivalent of three chocolate bars. Of course, there is nothing necessarily wrong with biscuits and chocolate, it depends how often we eat them and whether such snacks are taking the place of meals. But if they *do* supplant a proper meal then we have a real problem.

In any event, while our taste for such products increases at such a pace we can hardly pat ourselves on the back for eating fewer hot puddings or bacon and egg breakfasts. This was borne out dramatically by the Department of Health's *The Dietary & Nutritional Survey of British Adults* (1990) which analysed the food eaten by 2,000 people aged between sixteen and sixty-four. In each case, the Department of Health took a period of a week, carrying out the research between 1986 and 1987. They found that:

- In 1980 8 per cent of women and 6 per cent of men were obese.
- In 1986/7 12 per cent of women and 8 per cent of men were obese.

So for all the lip service paid to healthy eating, obesity appears to be a growing problem, albeit for a minority.

3. WE ARE EATING LESS WHOLE MILK, BUTTER AND RED MEAT AND FAR MORE LOW-FAT MILKS AND SPREADS

Absolutely true again. The Ministry of Agriculture's *National Food Survey* shows that during the 1980s we have:

- reduced our weekly consumption of butter from 4.05oz to 1.75oz – a dramatic decline;
- reduced our weekly consumption of carcase meats from 28oz to 24oz – (ie, a fall of around 15 per cent);
- increased our weekly consumption of low-fat milks from nothing to 1oz a week – they now account for more than 33 per cent of milk sales;
- increased our weekly consumption of low-fat spreads from nothing to 1.6oz – ie, approximately the same as the amount of butter that we eat.

But before we once more congratulate ourselves on our collective good sense it is worth remembering this:

- In 1984 a government report on heart disease recommended that, as a nation, we should only derive 35 per cent of the energy in our diet from fat.
- In 1980 the figure was in fact 42.6 per cent.
- By early 1990 it had only fallen to 41.4 per cent.

And during that time the amount of saturated, animal fat we were eating hardly declined at all.

We get our energy from four sources – fat, carbohydrates, protein and alcohol. The two major sources are fat and carbohydrate (starch and sugars). According to the Department of Health's Dietary Survey, these are the actual foods from which we get our energy:

79

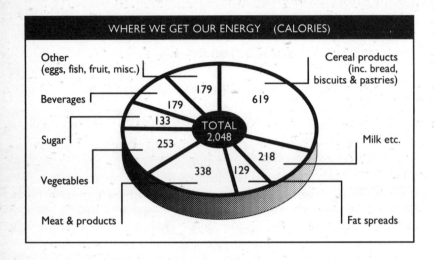

WHERE WE GET OUR ENERGY (CALORIES)

Other (eggs, fish, fruit, misc.) — 179
Beverages — 179
Sugar — 133
Vegetables — 253
Meat & products — 338
TOTAL 2,048
129
218
619 — Cereal products (inc. bread, biscuits & pastries)
Milk etc.
Fat spreads

Looking at the foods, we can see why almost 40 per cent of our energy intake is fat. It comes from meat and meat products, fat spreads, milk and a range of biscuits and pastries. Breaking it down still further, here are the foods from which we derive the fat in our diet:

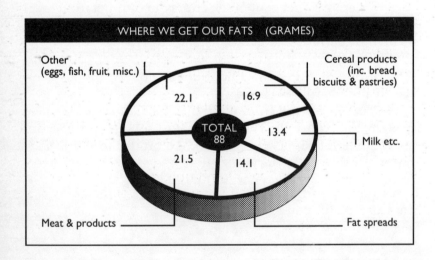

WHERE WE GET OUR FATS (GRAMES)

Other (eggs, fish, fruit, misc.) — 22.1
Meat & products — 21.5
TOTAL 88
14.1
13.4 — Milk etc.
16.9 — Cereal products (inc. bread, biscuits & pastries)
Fat spreads

It is the saturated animal fats in our diet that make the level of cholesterol in our blood high. And a high level of cholesterol puts us at risk of heart disease. The Department of Health's survey painted a bleak picture on this front:

- Almost 67 per cent of those surveyed had an undesirably high level of cholesterol.
- More than 80 per cent were eating more fat and saturated fat than is recommended (particularly in Scotland and the South-East).

One other point is crucial. The Department of Health's survey covered all food consumed. The figures we were quoting earlier from the *National Food Survey* only cover food eaten at home. As a result, the survey shows a decline in our consumption of red meat, while in fact nationally there has been no such decline. The answer to this puzzle is that more and more of us eat out. Fast-food hamburger chains now dominate our high streets and, as a consequence, we are eating almost as much fatty, red meat as ever. In the US the problem is even more pronounced, with hamburgers contributing more fat to the overall diet than any other food – 7.2 per cent of total fat. Hot dogs and ham come a close second.

In Britain between the mid-1970s and the mid-1980s, we increased the money we spent on eating out by more than 200 per cent. By 1985, takeaways alone accounted for 25 per cent of all meal occasions. And by 1989 we were eating almost 4 million takeaway meals a year. It has been shown that men now get at least a third of their calories from eating out and women at least a quarter.

Sandwiches are the most popular takeaway food followed by fish and chips. But hamburgers are also massively popular, accounting for about one in five takeaways. Food eaten outside the home is more likely to have a high-proportion of fat than home-cooked food. Hamburgers are a case in point. At the time of writing, a Big Mac and chips yielded 43g of fat. Since our daily requirement is 75g to 80g, McDonalds were generously providing more than half of what we need in a day. The food processing and catering industries rely more on fat than we do at home.

Our overall appetite for fatty foods when eating out was

demonstrated very neatly in the course of an investigation carried out by the Institute of Food Research in Norwich. They asked seventy people between the ages of fifteen and sixty-four to keep a record of the food they ate for three days. The vast majority ate something away from home during that time. It showed that *eating out contributed more than half the fat in their diets*. But the high levels of fat are no surprise when you consider that we often treat ourselves when eating out. The food groups contributing most significantly to the Norwich seventy's intake when eating out were:

- Meats
- Sugars
- Alcohol
- Fish and chips

There is nothing wrong with a treat if we can get the overall balance right. That is the crucial question.

So the true picture as to our eating habits is not as clear cut as some of our more careless assumptions would lead us to believe. But then neither is our approach to cooking all that it might seem when we are eating at home.

4. WE'RE USING MORE HEALTHY COOKING METHODS THESE DAYS

Once again, on the face of it this statement is true. Here is an analysis of how we cooked our evening meals in 1989:

	% of appearances
Boiled	52
Roast/baked	33
Fried	23
Grilled	23

The most important development has been a recent increase in grilling and a fairly dramatic decline in frying (for some surprising advice on the best cooking methods, *see* the Consumer's Guide – p369). On average, we eat three fewer fried meals per fortnight than we did in 1985.

But how significant are these statistics when compared to the enormous growth in snacks such as biscuits? As we have already noted, 40 per cent of our eating at home is in the form of snacks. This is borne out by the decline in home cooking:

- Between 1980 and 1987, there was a 33 per cent decline in home cooking.
- Those over the age of sixty-five still include at least one item of home-cooked food in 75 per cent of their meals.
- Those aged between seventeen and twenty-four consume an item of home-cooked food in just 17 per cent of their meals.

In other words, the younger we are the less likely we are to cook and the more likely we are to eat convenience foods or eat out. So once again, although the statistics seem encouraging, the real story is rather different.

5. NOWADAYS EVERYONE KNOWS ABOUT HEALTHY EATING

Only hermits and astronauts can have missed the plethora of articles and television programmes about healthy eating which have cropped up over the last decade. But to what extent do we pay lip service to such ideals and to what extent do we act on them?

Capital Gold is a commercial radio station in London playing the hits of the fifites, sixties and seventies to ageing hippies. Each Friday morning disc jockey 'Diddy' David Hamilton asks listeners to send in the supermarket bill for their weekly family shop. He picks one out of the hat and pays it. One week we followed up seventeen of the families who had sent in their bills and analysed the food they had bought. All but one said they believed in healthy eating. Let's see whether they put that belief into action when deciding how to spend their housekeeping.

On average, the Capital Gold listeners spent:

- 11% on cakes, puddings, biscuits, confectionery
- 11% on meat products (burgers, pies, pâtés, etc)
- 8% on carcase meats
- 8% on fresh vegetables (excluding potatoes)
- 6% on processed vegetables (excluding potatoes)
- 6% on cereals (including bread)
- 3% on fresh fruit
- 2.5% on fish
- 2% on potatoes
- 1% on poultry

We should bear in mind that meat is the most expensive of foodstuffs and potatoes the cheapest. But compare their expenditure on cakes, puddings, biscuits and confectionery (11 per cent) with that on fresh fruit (3 per cent). Compare what they spent on meat and meat products (19 per cent) with poultry and fish (3.5 per cent). While it is true that they did spend a good deal on vegetables, it is also clear that much of their energy comes from meat and fatty, sugary foods rather than starch-rich ones (eg bread and potatoes).

One of the shoppers we spoke to said she believed in a healthy diet with plenty of fresh vegetables and fish and very little fatty red meat. In fact, she spent 15 per cent on meat and meat products, 17 per cent on biscuits, cakes and confectionery and bought no fish at all!

Another shopper claimed that she and her family had a high fibre, low-fat diet with lots of fresh food. In fact, she spent 34 per cent on meat and meat products, 11 per cent on biscuits, cakes and confectionery, 7 per cent on soft drinks *but only 3 per cent on fresh vegetables and 1 per cent on bread.*

A third woman said she ate lots of vegetables, few fatty foods and few biscuits and cakes. In fact she bought no poultry or fish and no fresh fruit either. She even told us that in the cause of healthy eating she had cut down on potatoes and bread (valuable carbohydrates) and was trying to persuade her husband to do the same!

What can one conclude from this random sample of shoppers?

- Most of us pay lip service to healthy eating, few of us put it into practice.
- Many of us are thoroughly confused as to what constitutes a good diet.

So now we have looked at five commonly held views:

- that we are eating a greater variety of foods;
- that unhealthy meals such as bacon and eggs and cooked puddings are in decline;
- that we are eating less fatty foods and more low-fat ones;
- that we are using healthier cooking methods;
- that everyone knows about healthy eating.

We have demonstrated that while each proposition appears to be true on the surface, the reality is rather different. There are changes – small changes – we can make to our diet which could dramatically improve our health. In the next section but one we look at these in detail for each age group. For the moment it is worth repeating that the purpose of this book is to help you enjoy eating and live longer. Nowhere do we recommend draconian regimes. We have seen that in Janet Cade's study of three English towns the 'model eaters' ate just as many cakes, biscuits, puddings and ice-creams as the others, and more chocolate. But they had adjusted their diets in other ways. Similarly, Dr Michael Nelson led a study in Cambridge in 1985 which compared 'healthy' eaters to 'unhealthy' eaters. Nelson concluded that the latter group only needed to make small changes to improve their diets dramatically. He also noted that the 'healthy' men consumed more white bread and milk than the others, and the 'healthy' women ate more meat, chips and cakes.

So there is no such thing as a bad food. Yet so often we read of foods we should eat less of or avoid altogether. Food and drink seem to have become inextricably linked with the twin spirits of prohibition and guilt. Since we spend one-tenth of our lives eating we intend to help correct this gloomy state of affairs. To that end, we have compiled a list of foods that we *ought* to eat. We hope you will look upon it as a liberating influence.

THE LIBERATION LIST

Lean meat, cheese or beans/pulses/nuts	once a day
Fish (favouring the more oily species)	twice a week
Wholemeal bread, potatoes, rice or pasta	with each main meal
Green leaf veg or green salad veg	every day
Carrots	twice a week
Fruit (favouring citrus)	every day
Milk (⅓ pt or more if skimmed)	every day

The only problem with the Liberation List is one of perception. Many of us believe that we do not like, say, oily fish or green leaf vegetables. But there are so many different types of each on offer in the shops and so many more ways of cooking them that the choice is effectively infinite. Here are a few examples to whet your appetite:

OILY FISH (above 5 per cent fat)

Amberjack, **Anchovy**, Arctic Char, Bonito, Buffalo, Butterfish, **Carp**, Cisco, **Eel**, **Herring**, Inconnu, Lake Sturgeon, **Mackerel**, **Pilchards**, Pompano, Sablefish, **Salmon**, **Sardine**, Shad, **Shark**, Spiny Dogfish, Spot, **Sprat**, Swordfish, **Trout**, **Tuna**, **Whitebait** (baby herring or sprat).

The more commonly available fish are indicated in heavy type.

GREEN LEAF AND SALAD VEGETABLES

Artichoke, Asparagus, Beansprouts, Broccoli, Brussel Sprouts, Cabbage (many varieties), Cauliflower, Celery, Chicory, Chinese Leaves, Chives, Fennel, Kale, Lettuce (many varieties), Mangetout, Parsley, Salad Cress, Salsify, Seaweed, Spinach, Spring Onions, Watercress.

FRUIT

Apple, Apricot, Asian Avocado, Pear, Babaco, Banana, Bilberries/Blueberries, Blackberries, Blackcurrant, Carambola, Cherry, **Clementine**, Cranberry, Damson, Dates, Figs, Gooseberry, Greengage, Grape, **Grapefruit**, Guava, Kiwifruit, **Kumquat**, **Lemon**, **Lime**, Loganberry, Lychee, Mango, Mangosteen, Melon, Minnela, Nectarine, **Orange**, Passion Fruit, Paw Paw, Peach, Pear, Physalis, Pineapple, Plum, Pomegranates, **Pomela**, Raspberry, Redcurrant, Rhubarb, **Satsuma**, Sharon Fruit, Strawberry, Sweetie, Tamarillo, **Tangerine**, Tangor, Topaz, Ugli, Water Melon.

Widely available citrus are indicated in heavy type.

BEANS AND PULSES

Adzuki, Black Peas, Black-eyed Beans, Black Kidney Beans, Black Beans, Borlotti Beans, British Field Beans, Broad Beans, Brown Lentils, Butter Beans, Cannellini/Alubia Beans, Chick Peas, Flageolet Beans, Full Medames Beans, Green/Laird Lentils, Green Split Beans, Maple/Carlin Peas, Marrow Fat Peas, Mung Beans, Pinto Beans, Red Kidney Beans, Red Split Lentils, Rose Cocoa Beans, Soya Beans, Yellow Split Peas.

NUTS

Almonds, Brazils, Cashews, Chestnuts, Coconut, Hazelnuts, Macadamias, Peanuts, Pecans, Pine Kernels, Pistachios, Walnuts.

In this second section of *The Food Revolution* you have analysed your own diet for its shortcomings and discovered the truth about the British diet. The value of analysing your own diet is that each person's nutritional needs are different. The two most critical factors are age and sex. In the Seven Ages of Man – Section IV – we examine how our nutritional needs change as we get older. For specific advice you can turn to the age-group to which you belong. But before that Section III outlines the diseases we can all avoid if we eat well – what we call 'Getting Away With It'.

SECTION III

GETTING AWAY WITH IT

INTRODUCTION

Since virtually everything you can think of has been linked with some disease or disorder, you might well wonder whether any food is safe to eat. But although eating may involve risk, not eating results in certain death. Eating is like any other pleasurable activity – *you need to know what you can get away with.*

Food is a complex mixture of chemicals. Now, if the term 'chemical' evokes a hostile response in you, perhaps we should explain that chemicals are not just the products of the chemical industry such as pesticides, petrol, food additives. In fact, *everything is made up of chemicals, including our bodies.* The chemicals supplied by food include the nutrients needed for health as well as other substances, both harmful and beneficial. In this section we identify the main risks to health from food and suggest how you can best avoid them.

Everything we do involves risk. For example, travelling involves considerable risk – yet this does not stop us riding bicycles or driving cars. The problem is that our perspective on risk is often distorted by catastrophes. Most people can remember the horror of the explosion of a PanAm flight over Lockerbie in Scotland. As a result we have a fear of flying, yet flying is far safer than driving a car or bike.

Air crashes get banner headlines but the hundreds of people who die suddenly from a heart attack every day aren't news unless they are famous. Mass death shocks us, as does the idea that the risk is beyond our control. A study in America asked people to guess how many people died every year from heart disease. Most people guessed it was around 40,000 – *but the true number is nearer one million.* When they were asked to guess how many people died from botulism every year they said about 1,000, whereas the true number was one.

How we react to a risk is as distorted as the way we

perceive it. Imagine how you would react if a jumbo jet crashed because of pilot error every week – you would be horrified. But in Britain the equivalent of a jumbo jet full of middle-aged men die every week from heart disease. Even though we know how to prevent these deaths, as a nation we are doing little about it. We will avoid foods if they are associated with an immediately harmful effect (as with food poisoning) but are reluctant to change our eating habits when the harmful effects are not so obvious, as with heart disease. If you have a toothache you will tend to avoid hot, sweet or cold foods because the pain is excruciating. Yet if you *don't* have toothache you won't necessarily stop gorging yourself on sweets – even if you are warned that they will rot your teeth. Doctors have the same problem persuading people to give up smoking. Many smokers say they will give up smoking when 'they have to'. But by the time they think they have to it will be too late. The damage will already have been done. *Preventing disease means changing factors that increase risk.* The difficulty is convincing people that such changes will genuinely improve their lives.

We use the phrase 'Getting away with it' not in a slipshod or dishonest way but to identify what really matters and those key changes required to minimize risk. For example, if you have a child playing in a room with an open fire the fire poses an obvious hazard to the child. There are various ways of tackling the problem. You can remove the child from the room where it enjoys playing, you can rip the fire out and lose the benefit of heating or you can install a safety guard in front of the fire. Most people would opt for the last approach because they know that the fireguard is quite adequate protection. Such an approach exemplifies the art of getting away with it.

'Getting away with it' also implies a degree of uncertainty. You can minimize risk but you can also be unlucky. However, this doesn't mean you don't have to be careful! Let's take another example. Bicycle accidents are a major cause of child fatalities. Most parents know that riding a bicycle is a hazard for children, but don't stop them doing it because they know it gives them great pleasure. The trick is to reduce the risks by making sure that children receive instruction in road safety, wear protective head gear and don't ride on busy roads. We are suggesting that you adopt the same approach towards food and act rationally. This involves identifying the main hazards and ranking them in order of importance. Once you have identified what the major risks are then at least you know what you are up against.

To help you distinguish the risks that really matter from the ones that do not, we have prepared a table – 'the Risk Business' (*see* over). It ranks the food risks according to the evidence associated with each and in an order that is generally accepted by the experts concerned with food safety. You can compare the hazards to our health posed by different foods. Start at the bottom and see how the size of the risk spirals as you move up the page.

You can see that pesticides and food additives rank lowest (a testament to the important laws and stringent tests that apply to them). While up there at the top is the danger of diet-related diseases such as heart attacks and cancer caused by nutritional imbalance. It is so much more important than the other risks, yet shockingly neglected.

So what steps can we take to decrease the real health risks posed by food? Well, fortunately a number of dietary guidelines have been developed over the years to help us. These guidelines fall into two main categories. The first category is concerned with 'getting enough', in other words, meeting the body's requirements for nutrients. Experts tend to agree on the nature of these requirements. The second category is preventing diet-related disorders such as heart disease. Here opinions differ markedly when it comes to the treatment and prevention of diet-related disease. Even so, there is still a reasonable degree of consensus on the role of diet in preventing obesity, coronary heart disease, cancer and tooth decay. In this and the following section we look at both categories in the most practical way possible. In the pages that follow it is crucial to remember that we have all sorts of reasons for eating and drinking – minimizing the risk to health from eating is only one of the factors influencing our food choice. What we eat also depends upon what we can afford and how we are brought up. Food plays an important social function from an early age. Imagine a child's birthday party without a cake or a wedding reception without drink. Food is used to

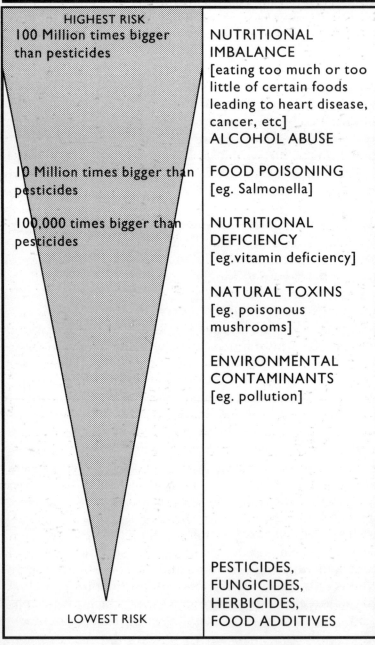

THE RISK BUSINESS

HIGHEST RISK
100 Million times bigger than pesticides

NUTRITIONAL IMBALANCE
[eating too much or too little of certain foods leading to heart disease, cancer, etc]
ALCOHOL ABUSE

10 Million times bigger than pesticides

FOOD POISONING
[eg. Salmonella]

100,000 times bigger than pesticides

NUTRITIONAL DEFICIENCY
[eg. vitamin deficiency]

NATURAL TOXINS
[eg. poisonous mushrooms]

ENVIRONMENTAL CONTAMINANTS
[eg. pollution]

PESTICIDES, FUNGICIDES, HERBICIDES, FOOD ADDITIVES

LOWEST RISK

reward as well as to celebrate – typically a woman is given chocolates, a man a bottle and a child sweets.

As we have seen, food means different things to people. For some it is just fuel for survival, others just live to eat. It can provide comfort and reassurance as the old Elstree Studio films depicted – 'You better sit down and have a nice cup of tea, love.' Each society has its own set of beliefs about food and eating patterns are strongly interwoven with religious belief. Certain foods are taboo in some cultures – pork is forbidden to Muslims and Jews, beef to Hindus. In parts of Africa, children are forbidden to eat eggs because it is believed that if they do they will turn into thieves. In Indonesia, it is taboo to give young women big bananas! Newspapers have scandalized us by suggesting that in 1992 New Forest ponies may land up on the French dinner plates. Most Britons would also be horrified if they were given dog to eat, yet it is commonly eaten in China.

An attack on our food is often seen as an attack on our culture. John Gummer, the Minister of Agriculture, attacked vegetarianism in the wake of the BSE scare saying it was an attack on Christian values. Perhaps more vegetarians were offended by the sight of John Gummer and his daughter on television eating beefburgers than by his attempt to reassure the British public that beef was safe. So what you choose to eat may be a political statement. For example, if you buy organic food it may be because you are concerned about the environment. You may buy free-range eggs because you think that battery farming is barbaric. You may not have bought fruit from South Africa because you were an opponent of apartheid.

Even from an early age we learn to choose foods because we like them, not because of their nutritional value. The newborn baby has an innate preference for sweet foods and a dislike for those which taste bitter. As we grow up, we acquire tastes for foods that we innately reject. We add condiments like mustard, pepper and chilli to food even though they set our mouths on fire. We're not solely concerned with satisfying our hunger.

While growing up, we acquire a lot of emotional luggage associated with food that can be a burden in later life. Food likes and dislikes are common but unhealthy. Anorexia nervosa and Bulimia nervosa are now well-recognized eating disorders in adolescent girls and young women. There is an incredible amount of pressure placed on women to look as skinny as a rake. This causes many women to be obsessed with the pursuit of slenderness and leads to a rejection of their normal body image. Excessive slimming also unsexes women. It suppresses the production of the sex hormone oestrogen so that secondary sexual characteristics are not expressed. Eating, like sex, is often a focus for neurotic disorders.

Allergies to certain common foods – for example, wheat, eggs and milk – affect a small minority, causing skin rashes and digestive disorders. Not all forms of food intolerance are caused by something in the food. For example, some people display adverse reactions when they eat something they believe does not agree with them. The symptoms are usually vague and commonly fluctuating, such as tummy ache, bloating, palpitations and nausea. But, unlike people with genuine food intolerance, they show no adverse reactions when given the food by stomach tube. This type of food intolerance probably results from an unpleasant experience such as gastric flu being linked with a food. Eating that food on future occasions causes unpleasant memories to flood back.

Eating should be a pleasurable activity because we spend enough time doing it. We're not asking you to become a puritanical health freak – there is no virtue in eating food that tastes awful. Nor do we want to blind you with science. If at any point you don't understand a particular term then look it up in the A-Z Directory at the back of the book. In Section IV we explain the particular dietary needs of your age group. But first we need to explain what the real hazards from food are and suggest how you can avoid them. We have divided them into five sub-sections:

- Getting the nutrients we need
- Diet-related diseases and how to avoid them
- Xenobiotics – hazardous materials in food
- Alcohol
- Food risks in perspective

In each of the first four sub-sections we explain the hazards associated with specific types of food, tell you about the latest research and summarize the key points. In the final sub-section we put the risks from food in perspective and tell you how to enjoy your food. In short, how to get away with it.

GETTING THE NUTRIENTS WE NEED

Key Points in selecting a nutritionally adequate diet:

> Make sure you eat a variety of foods.
> Avoid feeding bulky diets low in fat to young children. For example, diets containing high proportions of fruit, leafy vegetables and brown rice.
> If you are a woman, make sure you consume plenty of foods rich in iron such as red meat, wholemeal bread, dark green vegetables.
> If you are a vegetarian make sure you have a good dietary source of vitamin B_{12} such as milk, eggs, fortified soya milks, and yeast extracts such as Marmite.

ARE YOU GETTING ENOUGH?

This cheeky phrase came from a milk advert in the 1960s when the milkman allegedly brought more than just the milk. For the post-war generation, milk symbolized good nutrition. It came as a shock to many people that such a nourishing food was linked to heart disease. While milk plays an important part in the nourishment of children, a high intake of milk fat in adults is probably a major cause of heart disease. The moral is what is good for kids may not be so good for adults.

Human beings are known to require thirty-two different nutrients but, because most nutrients are present in all food, only a few nutrients ever go lacking. Getting an adequate intake of every nutrient may sound more complicated than it is in practice. Food provides a blend of nutrients. Some foods contain higher amounts of particular nutrients than others but when foods are combined, they supplement each other so that the lack of a nutrient in one food complements the abundance in another. For example, you can't live by either bread alone, meat alone or vegetables alone. But if you mix all three you get all the nutrients you need. Individual meals do not have to be balanced as some books claim. No one eats the same food at each meal day in day out and any shortfall in one meal is usually made up in another.

Nutrients provide the body with energy and the raw materials for growth and repair. The nutrients we need are protein, fat, carbohydrates, minerals and vitamins.

RECOMMENDED DAILY AMOUNTS

You may have noticed many breakfast cereals have a panel on the side giving the amounts of nutrients expressed as a percentage of the recommended daily allowance (RDA). Should you worry about them? Do you know what they are?

Governments publish tables of recommended daily amounts (RDA) of nutrients. These figures are for specific groups of people rather than for individuals, but they do tell you roughly how much of a particular nutrient you require. RDAs tend to be set on the generous side to make sure that everyone gets enough. RDAs are not set for all nutrients because deficiencies of those nutrients are unknown among people freely selecting their own diets.

The Food and Nutrition Board in the United States published revised RDAs in October 1989 and the British Department of Health is currently revising UK RDAs. RDAs are provided for males and females of different ages, since males require larger amounts of most nutrients than females (with the exception of iron). RDAs have been set very high in some countries for political reasons. In the days of the cold war the Russians vied with the Americans to see who could set the highest RDA, presumably to show that they were the more caring society! The British have traditionally been more conservative in setting RDAs and over the years journalists have accused the British government of having lower standards. But the latest US RDAs are much lower for several nutrients than in previous editions (*glasnost* works in mysterious ways). In fact, most nutritionists acknowledge that the UK RDAs are realistic and based on estimates derived from experiment and observation rather than guesswork. For example, the British carried out experiments on conscientious objectors in the Second World War to find out how much vitamin C was required to prevent scurvy, discovering that 10mg a day was adequate. The British RDA for vitamin C is 30mg a day and is the same as that recognized by the World Health Organization. The USA recommends adults consume 60mg/day and smokers 100mg/day. These recommendations are not based on the amounts needed to prevent any deficiency disease but to maintain maximum levels in the blood. It is a bit like insisting on driving a car around with a full tank of petrol.

The only accurate way to determine the level of nutrients in a diet is to collect duplicate portions of all the food eaten over a period of time, grind it up and then measure the nutrients in it. But dietitians assess the nutritional adequacy of a diet by measuring how much of each food is consumed over a period of a week. They then calculate how much of each nutrient is provided using food composition tables where the grinding has been done for them. (It is not good enough to make an estimate from one single day because some foods which are only occasionally consumed can make a big contribution to intake. For example, a portion of liver would provide all the vitamin A you need for a month). Dietitians can then compare the amount of nutrients provided by the diet with the RDAs. This sounds fine, but as accurate information isn't available on all the foods this method tends to underestimate the intake of several nutrients. Consequently dietitians tend to underestimate our nutrient intake, not overestimate it.

CAUSES AND EXTENT OF NUTRITIONAL DEFICIENCIES

Globally a lack of food or the money to buy it is the most important cause of nutritional deficiencies. An inadequate food intake is called 'protein energy malnutrition' and it contributes to the deaths of millions of children every year in developing countries and causes stunting of growth in those who survive. Even the poorest people in developed countries do not approach the levels of poverty in developing countries. After protein energy malnutrition, the two most widespread nutritional deficiencies in the world are of iron and iodine. Iodine is not a cause for concern in developed countries, but iron deficiency is.

Iron Iron deficiency affects most men, women and children in developing countries and causes anaemia. It is made worse by infectious diseases such as hookworm and malaria which cause blood loss and so increase the requirement for iron. Iron is needed in small amounts for the formation of haemoglobin, the red oxygen-carrying pigment in blood. Anaemia is the condition that results when the level of haemoglobin in blood is not sufficient to transport enough oxygen to the tissues. The symptoms of anaemia are tiredness, weakness and giddiness. It decreases work output and thus causes a vicious cycle by limiting a person's capacity to earn more money to buy better food.

Anaemia also occurs in developed countries such as Britain and the United States but it is less common and severe. Those most at risk are children under five, teenage girls and women of childbearing age because of blood loss during their monthly periods. In a recent survey the majority of women under the age of fifty had iron intakes below the RDA, but only 4 per cent were found to be anaemic. The highest incidence of anaemia was in women aged eighteen to twenty-four where about 6 per cent were anaemic. This group also had the lowest iron intake. The mild anaemia often seen in women does not impair work capacity. Symptoms of anaemia are usually tiredness and breathlessness.

It is only possible to diagnose anaemia by a blood test. If you think you are anaemic you should see your doctor. Foods rich in iron are red meat, wholemeal bread and dark green leafy vegetables.

Vitamin deficiencies Despite what you might read in the advertisements of the vitamin manufacturers, vitamin deficiencies are rarely encountered in developed countries and tend to be confined to the underclass of vagrants. Vitamin D deficiency – which causes rickets (bow legs) and osteomalacia (painful bones) – is thought to result from lack of exposure to sunlight coupled with a low availability of calcium from the diet. It was formerly common in Northern Europe but now is rare and mainly confined to Asian Indians.

In June 1990 the Department of Health published their *Dietary and Nutritional Survey of British Adults*. This survey measured the food intakes of over 2000 men and women who were examined by their own doctors and had blood samples taken to measure the levels of nutrients in their blood. The study found that with the exception of iron intakes of women under the age of fifty, the intakes of all the other nutrients met RDAs. The medical examination and blood tests failed to show that any of the subjects were suffering from nutritional deficiencies other than anaemia. This and many other studies carried out in Britain, Australia, Canada and the United States show that with the exception of iron deficiency anaemia *nutritional deficiencies are rare in adults in developed countries.*

How do nutritional deficiencies occur? The best way to convince yourself that your diet is adequate is to understand how nutritional deficiencies occur. Nutritional deficiencies in a developing country such as India are caused either by a lack of food or relying too heavily on one or two foods. As countries and people become more affluent they eat more and expand their repertoire of foods. In developed countries food shortage does not occur except in times of war. People are free to select their own diets and the range of foods available is great (except in Eastern Europe). Most developed countries are fortunate in that foods of all types can be obtained all the year round. For example, seasonal variations in the availability of fruit and vegetables are much less marked than they used to be since we are able to import foods from other parts of the world where they are in season.

Variety – the spice of life   Generally, the more variety there is in the diet the better the chances that the diet will provide all the nutrients required. But you can obtain all of the nutrients you need from just a handful of good foods – for example, bread, milk, meat or fish and fruit and vegetables. In fact, most people *do* obtain all the nutrients they need from basic foods such as milk, cheese, bread, biscuits, spreading fats, meat, fruit and vegetables. Where people differ is in how much they eat and how they prepare and cook these basic foodstuffs.

Fake foods and junk food   Our general celebration of variety may soon need some qualification because food manufacturers can now make foods that look nice and taste nice but have little nutritional value – these are sometimes referred to as 'fake foods'. Will it soon be possible to choose a diet with no nutritional value? Recently, food scientists have developed products that taste and have a mouth-feel like fat and these are likely to hit the market soon. These fat substitutes fall into two categories, those that imitate the mouth-feel of fat such as Simplesse and Nutrifat, and those which are chemically altered fats that cannot be digested such as Olestra.

Imitation fats (Simplesse, Nutrifat) are usually just made out of normal food ingredients such as potato, egg white and milk protein and have nutritional value. They are mechanically blended protein particles that fool the tongue into thinking that they are fat; the process doesn't bring about changes in chemical composition. It is possible to make a low-calorie ice-cream out of these products. This is good news for fatties who eat too much ice-cream because now they will be able to indulge themselves without putting on weight. In fact what is likely to happen is that these products will increase the overall sales of ice-cream just as low-calorie drinks led to a boom in the soft drinks market.

Chemically altered fats – such as Proctor and Gamble's Olestra, which is a sucrose polyester – have no nutritional value and cannot be absorbed from the gut. It is intended that these products be used in place of oils used for frying and fat spreads. The bad news is that they interfere with the absorption of fat-soluble vitamins from the gut and result in 'anal leakage'. The sucrose polyester passes through the gut and comes out the other end like vaseline – a novel way to oil the slipway! As yet none of the chemically altered fats have been approved for food use.

At present there are few 'fake foods'. Diet drinks might be regarded as such but we drink fizzy drinks as a pleasant way to quench thirst and give us the liquid we need, not to provide nutrients. Artificial sweeteners such as saccharin and aspartame have no significant nutritional value, are acceptable in moderation (see 'Artificial Sweeteners' in the Directory) and are also suitable for diabetics. What is referred to as 'junk food' – such as burgers, chips, crisps, corn snacks, hot dogs, ice-cream, pot noodles, etc – all have good nutritional value. *Even if you lived entirely on 'junk food' you would not suffer from any nutritional deficiencies. But it would certainly not be the same as eating a healthy diet.* Getting the nutrients we need is just one part of healthy eating, avoiding diet-related disease is the other part.

Children   There is a widespread myth that children are not properly nourished nowadays. Height is an excellent measure of how good a diet is. When diet and health are poor height is stunted. Five year olds are now almost three inches taller than their counterparts at the beginning of the century. Before the Second World War working-class children were smaller than those of the professional classes. Schoolchildren are taller now than ever before and class-related height differences have largely disappeared.

A good diet means that children sexually mature at an earlier age. The age at which girls start having their monthly periods has fallen from about sixteen years at the turn of the century to about twelve years. Some people have speculated that rapid growth might make you grow old faster. But we know for certain that poor growth in infancy is associated with poor health and increased risk of heart disease in adult life. There is clearly no alternative to a good diet in childhood.

Too much of a good thing   Just because small amounts of certain nutrients are essential, it doesn't follow that larger amounts will be better. Several nutrients can be poisonous if consumed in excess. Generally excess intakes of fat-soluble vitamins and minerals pose the greatest hazard. Every year children die from accidental overdoses of iron supplements prescribed for their mothers. In the United States, there are approximately 2,000 cases of iron poisoning each year among young children.

Cooking techniques can also lead to contamination of food with toxic levels of essential minerals. For example, people have suffered from zinc poisoning by using galvanized containers to make jam or beer.

As a rule of thumb, nutrients are not toxic unless they are consumed in amounts greater than ten times the recommended daily amounts (RDA). Generally, the levels of nutrients present in food are not great enough to cause poisoning. *The main hazard of overdosing with vitamins and minerals is with supplements.*

There is one famous exception and that is polar bear's liver. Some famished arctic explorers killed a polar bear and ate its liver and suffered from vitamin A poisoning – it caused their skin to peel, severe fatigue and headaches and some of them died. Eskimos have known for centuries that seals' and polar bears' livers are poisonous and bury them after killing the animals to prevent their huskies from being poisoned. Levels of vitamin A (retinol) are also high in calf, chicken, lamb, pig and ox liver, but not great enough to harm adults or children if only eaten occasionally (not more than once a week). The government has warned pregnant women and those intending to become pregnant to avoid eating liver because very high intakes of vitamin A can cause birth defects. However, no birth defects have yet been attributed to the consumption of liver in Britain.

CAUSES OF NUTRITIONAL DEFICIENCIES IN DEVELOPED COUNTRIES

As we have seen, simple nutritional deficiencies are uncommon in Britain, Europe and the USA. When nutritional deficiencies *do* occur they are usually due to one or a combination of the following:

- A restricted diet
- Loss of appetite
- An increased requirement for nutrients

Vitamin deficiencies are occasionally self-inflicted in people who have followed extremely restricted diets such as living off tea and biscuits or fruit or drinking too much alcohol to the exclusion of food. Vitamin B_{12} deficiency occasionally occurs in vegans and vegetarians.

The memorable term 'muesli-belt malnutrition' was coined by Professor Vincent Marks of the University of Surrey to describe the growth stunting in children caused by over-zealous parents restricting what their children could eat by feeding them large amounts of bulky food low in calories.

Loss of appetite is common with illness and can lead to decreased food intake and cause nutritional problems. This is particularly true of elderly people.

Nutritional deficiencies can arise because disease or some other adverse factor increases the requirement for nutrients. Many patients with cancer who are losing weight rapidly are often found to be suffering from nutritional deficiencies. In part this is caused by loss of appetite and in part by the effects of the tumour itself which is using up nutrients to support its growth. Heavy menstrual blood loss increases the need for iron and is the major cause of iron deficiency anaemia rather than poor diet.

Harmful effects have been noted with *excess* intakes of the following nutrients and minerals:

- Vitamin D – ideopathic hypercalcaemia in children (causes excess accumulation of calcium in the blood).
- Vitamin A (retinol) – death from prolonged overdosing and birth defects when consumed in early pregnancy.
- Vitamin B_6 (pyridoxine) – damage to the nervous system following the consumption of gram quantities.
- Vitamin B_3 (niacin) – death from liver failure in a man who took gram amounts in the hope that it would lower his high blood cholesterol level.
- Vitamin E – death after the repeated consumption of gram quantities.
- Boron – deaths have been reported in adults and children in the USA.
- Iron – deaths in young children accidentally consuming their mothers' iron supplements.
- Germanium – death and kidney failure.
- Tryptophan – death and eosinophilic myalgia syndrome.
- Zinc – vomiting and sickness, impaired copper absorption.

Great care should be taken when using vitamin and mineral supplements. They should be treated like medicines and the stated dose should not be exceeded.

DIET-RELATED DISEASES

– AND HOW TO AVOID THEM

The term 'nutritional imbalance' is used to describe the diet-related diseases that result from either consuming too many or an inappropriate ratio of nutrients in the diet. The major diet-related diseases are:

- Obesity
- High blood pressure
- Heart disease
- Cancer

Obesity results from an excess calorie intake. It affects almost 50 per cent of the adult population in Britain and its prevalence is increasing. High blood pressure affects about 15 per cent of the adult population and is decreasing. Heart disease affects about 33 per cent of the population and has become more common over the past fifty years. About one in three people will die from cancer. Although the number of people dying from cancer is on the increase this is partly because more people are living long enough to get it. Certain cancers, such as stomach cancer, have fallen, whereas others, such as breast cancer and colon cancer, have increased over the past fifty years. A good diet can reduce the risk of cancer.

OBESITY AND RELATED DISORDERS

Key Points if you are trying to lose weight:

- Cut out biscuits, cakes, chocolate, crisps, nuts, and deep fried foods.
- Avoid alcohol and sugary drinks including fruit juice.
- Change to skimmed milk.

Getting enough is one thing, getting too much is quite another. If you eat more than you burn up then you store the excess as fat. Obesity is the term used to describe the excessive accumulation of body fat. Different standards apply to men and women. Women are naturally fatter than men. A healthy woman contains about 20 per cent fat by weight and a man about 15 per cent. Most people put on weight as they get older and this tends to show around the midriff in men (apple shaped) and around the hips and backs of the legs in women (pear shaped). A recent survey suggests that 35–45 per cent of British adults are overweight and 8–12 per cent are obese. Obesity is less common in adolescents and primary school children, typically affecting between 1–3 per cent of children.

Being very fat is a hazard to health, but the health risks of being plump are much smaller. Nevertheless, it is well known to life insurance companies that overweight policy holders do not live as long as those who are of normal weight. Obesity in itself does not directly increase risk of heart disease, but in some people it causes high plasma cholesterol levels, high blood pressure and diabetes – all factors that increase the risk of heart disease. Obesity is a major cause of heart disease in women, particularly after the menopause.

Obesity results from an imbalance between energy intake and expenditure. It has been said that some people can eat what they like and not become fat while others just have to look at a cake to get fat! Most people who are fat do not have anything wrong with their glands nor is there any evidence that they use up energy at a slower rate. In addition, there is little support for the idea that diet in childhood causes obesity in adulthood. However, one thing is certain – if you are fat you have eaten too much in the past.

Fat people and fat dogs Professor Albert Stunkard has studied pairs of twins adopted by different families in order to see which was more important for the development of obesity – the home environment or heredity. He found that obesity was determined by inheritance rather than the home environment.

Another study overfed pairs of twins and found that one twin put on the same amount of weight in response to overfeeding as the other twin. Obviously this does not mean that what you eat does not matter, simply that some people have an inherited tendency towards obesity. The inherited defect may be a lack of control over what they eat because fat people tend to have fat dogs.

Pills, potions and miracle cures   A variety of untested and untried slimming cures are foisted on the unsuspecting public every year along with numerous slimming books. Yet it is known that the only way to lose weight is decrease your energy intake. Increasing the amount of exercise you take might be good for your health, but it isn't going to make you lose weight. Even if you ran a marathon all the energy you expended could be put back with just one meal.

At present the law does not protect the public from unproven slimming claims. A variety of pills and potions are sold claiming to promote weight loss, sometimes without even dieting. These pills are not covered by the laws governing medicines and so do not have to be shown to be effective and safe. They are covered by food laws which are much more lax and prosecutions rarely result because it is up to the local trading standards officers to take the company to court and show that the product does not work – the boot is on the wrong foot.

A trial of some of these slimming cures was carried out using volunteers from the BBC's *That's Life* programme and the results were published in *The Lancet* in 1990. Five hundred overweight volunteers were randomly divided into eight groups to receive different treatments for six weeks. We realized that because the volunteers were being watched on TV they were likely to change their diet spontaneously and lose some weight whatever treatment they were allocated. So we invented a placebo diet which consisted of eating half a carrot before the main meal. There is no reason why a carrot should make you lose weight – we chose the term 'carrot diet' because there have been popular diets like the 'banana diet' and the 'grapefruit diet' in the past. We didn't tell the viewers the carrot diet was a placebo until we announced the results. We decided before the trial that a treatment would be judged successful if the volunteers lost significantly more weight than those on the carrot diet.

Weight loss (kilograms) in the subjects following six weeks of treatment

Treatment	Average weight loss	Outcome
Placebo (carrot diet)	2.8	—
Bai-lin tea	0.9	Fail
Grapefruit pill	1.1	Fail
Natural vitality pill	2.9	Fail
Limmits	4.8	Success
1000 Calorie a day diet	5.5	Success
Slimming clubs	5.5	Success
Weightwatchers	6.3	Success

None of the magic cures for weight we tested worked. In fact the Bai-Lin tea which had been heavily promoted in one of the tabloid newspapers turned out to be an ordinary Taiwanese semi-fermented tea. Only those methods that lowered energy intakes were successful, such as meal replacement (Limmits) or a low-calorie diet. The most successful method was that promoted by the commercial slimming clubs. The key to their success is that they give continuing support to slimmers when their morale is flagging. Over 95 per cent of the volunteers who went to the slimming clubs lost weight successfully.

Losing weight effectively   There are no magic cures but you can lose weight by following a well-balanced 1,000 calorie a day diet. We give you advice on how to follow just such a diet that has been tried and tested later on. (*See* the Liberation Diet, p208.)

A few years ago very low-calorie diets (less than 600 calories a day, usually as powders in sachets) were fashionable because they led to rapid weight loss. Indeed they have been used successfully on a one-week-on, one-week-off basis. But they do not teach you how to change your eating habits. As soon as they stop dieting most people put the weight back on again. If you are trying to lose weight it is best to do it gently. Aim to lose 1–2lbs a week.

Some people think that certain foods are fattening. In fact, an excess energy intake whether from fat, carbohydrate or alcohol will lead to weight gain. There is no direct evidence to show that sugar is a cause of obesity. However, sugar does make many fatty foods extremely palatable – for example, doughnuts, cakes, Danish pastries and biscuits. Foods high in fat are more fattening because they are very high in food energy (calories). Even adding a little bit of fat to food can double its energy value. For example, a slice of bread provides 65 calories but spread with butter it provides 124 calories.

HIGH BLOOD PRESSURE

> **Key points** in avoiding high blood pressure are:
>
> Avoid excess alcohol.
> Maintain ideal body weight.
> Don't add salt to food.
> Avoid pickled foods which are high in salt or only eat them occasionally.
> Eat plenty of fruit and vegetables.

About 10–15 per cent of the population have high blood pressure. High blood pressure in itself causes no symptoms, but it does greatly increase the risk of stroke and heart disease. High blood pressure is less common than it used to be and this probably explains why deaths from strokes have been declining over the past fifty years in Britain and other Western countries. On the other hand, high blood pressure affects the majority of elderly Japanese and they also have the highest rate of strokes in the world. High blood pressure is common in communities where large amounts of salted and pickled foods are consumed.

Blood pressure tends to rise with age. Differences in salt intake between communities explain only a small fraction of the increase in blood pressure. Salt intakes are not particularly high in Britain compared with Japan. In a large study carried out by the Department of Health no relationship was found between high blood pressure and salt intake. In Britain men who drink too much alcohol (but not women) and those who are overweight (as opposed to obese) are generally at risk from high blood pressure. However, once people have high blood pressure they certainly do benefit from cutting down on the amount of salt in their diet. Most of the salt in the diet is added during cooking and at the table and a sizeable amount comes from processed foods such as bread. *Cutting down on salt intake is best achieved by not adding salt to food at the table or during cooking and avoiding pickled foods.*

Cutting down on salt intake does not lower blood pressure in everybody. The 15–20 per cent of the population whose blood pressure is lowered on reduction of salt intake are 'salt sensitive'. Some people with normal blood pressure may even show a slight rise in blood pressure, but this is nothing to worry about. However, there is currently no way of finding out who is salt sensitive. If you have a family history of high blood pressure then it does make sense to keep your salt intake low.

Blood pressure levels rise when men migrate from rural to urban areas. This has been carefully recorded in Kenya. It is also true that when people migrate to towns they eat fewer vegetables and more salt. Vegetables are a rich source of the mineral potassium and it may be that this mineral counteracts some of the harmful effects of salt. Indeed, some (but not all) studies have found that vegetarians who have high intakes of potassium have lower blood pressure than meat eaters. Supplements of potassium may lower blood pressure in people who eat a lot of salt but they do not affect those with low intakes.

Blood pressure rises with age in some people. A Dutch study found that the ratio of potassium to sodium in the diet was an important predictor of increases in blood pressure in children. So if we want our children to avoid high blood pressure we should be encouraging them to eat more potassium rich foods such as fruit and vegetables, as well as avoiding excess salt. Ordinary salt, consisting of sodium chloride, is often indicated by food labels which state the amount of sodium.

Key Points to help adults avoid heart disease:

Keep an eye on your weight.
Change to skimmed or semi-skimmed milk.
Use liquid vegetable oil for cooking instead of solid fats.
Change from butter or ordinary margarine to a low-fat
spread or margarine high in polyunsaturates.
Choose lean cuts of meat, discard excess fat.
Eat fish, especially oily fish, at least twice a week.
Eat a starchy food such as bread, pasta, rice or potatoes
with your main meal.
Eat at least one piece of fruit each day and have a salad or
coloured vegetable with your main meal.
Avoid excess coffee intake (not more than six cups a
day). Drink fresh filtered coffee rather than other types
of real coffee.

Coronary heart disease (CHD) is a major cause of premature
death, especially in men. Heredity plays a strong part in
determining risk of CHD. If either parent or a sibling (brother
or sister) has suffered from a heart attack under the age of
fifty-five years then the risk is ten times greater than average.
CHD is the result of an interaction between diet, environmental
factors and genetic make-up. Over 200 risk factors for heart
disease have been identified – including English as a mother
tongue! The major factors that increase risk are high blood
pressure, high blood cholesterol and cigarette smoking.
However, rates of CHD are low in Japan where high blood
pressure is common and they smoke like chimneys. But
when the Japanese migrate from Japan to the USA acquiring
a western life-style and diet, their blood cholesterol rises and
they suffer just as much from CHD as the Americans.

A high level of cholesterol in blood is almost certainly the
underlying cause of heart disease and smoking and high
blood pressure are things that make it worse. The British are
top of the league for CHD. The areas inside the country with
the highest rates correspond to the political map of the
country. Labour strongholds such as South Wales, Scotland

and the North East have the highest rates. Interestingly, Labour MPs also have a higher death rate from heart disease than Tories!

The blood vessels that supply the heart muscle with blood are called coronary arteries. With increasing age they become furred with a substance called atheroma which comes from the Greek word meaning porridge. This condition is called atherosclerosis, which means a lumpy hardening of the arteries. The rate of furring up occurs faster in some people than in others, especially in people who have a high level of blood cholesterol. Atherosclerosis of the coronary arteries develops silently over twenty to thirty years. Most men aged fifty already have quite badly furred up arteries. A heart attack occurs if one of the arteries supplying the heart muscle becomes blocked, usually by a blood clot. If an artery is badly furred up then it is much more easily blocked in this way. Atherosclerosis can affect arteries throughout the body. If it affects those supplying the brain it can cause a stroke. If it affects the arteries supplying the limbs, it causes peripheral vascular disease (PVD). PVD can lead to gangrene and might even result in the amputation of a limb.

A heart attack usually occurs suddenly and without warning but may be preceded by chest pain (angina pectoris). Angina and heart attacks result from an insufficient supply of oxygenated blood to the heart muscle. Whether the attack is fatal or not depends upon the position of the blockage in the coronary arteries. If it cuts off the supply of blood to a large area of the heart muscle it is likely to be fatal. Factors that decrease the tendency for blood to clot can protect patients with heart disease from future heart attacks. For example, aspirin taken in small amounts two to three times a week helps prevent second heart attacks by decreasing the tendency of blood to clot.

How is diet related to atherosclerosis? Atherosclerosis is common in all populations that have a high rate of heart disease. The development of atherosclerosis is related to the level of cholesterol in blood – the higher it is the more rapid the development of atherosclerosis. Scientists have found that monkeys fed on a typical Western diet high in saturated fat develop atherosclerosis in their coronary arteries. Generally, the damage caused by atherosclerosis is irreversible so changing our diet won't undo the damage (though it may stop it getting worse). This means that steps to prevent atherosclerosis must be started at an early age.

Post-mortems on young people killed in road accidents and in wars have found that many eighteen to twenty-one year olds show early signs of atherosclerosis. Blood cholesterol levels tend to be relatively low until the age of twenty and then rise with age plateauing at forty-five in men and fifty-five in women. This probably explains why women get heart disease on average ten years later than men. Consequently *it is important for a diet to prevent CHD to begin in early adult life.* Preventing atherosclerosis besides preventing heart attacks will help prevent strokes and PVD.

Some critics claim that the scientific evidence is inconclusive as some short-term studies show no benefit. However, it is indisputable that if you have high blood cholesterol and lower it you decrease your risk of suffering a heart attack. It is just that it may take at least five years before any benefit becomes apparent.

What determines the level of cholesterol in blood? High blood cholesterol levels can be inherited but are usually caused by our being overweight and eating a diet high in saturated fats (milk and meat fats). As we have seen, women up to the age of menopause have lower levels of cholesterol than men, and this may explain their lower risk of CHD. Women of this age seem to be protected by their sex hormones. After the menopause women often have higher blood cholesterol levels than men. Early menopause or removal of the ovaries increases their blood cholesterol, whereas hormone replacement therapy decreases it.

Weight loss in the overweight is usually accompanied by a fall in blood cholesterol level. It has also been found that *people who maintain their body weight from early adult life do not show the same age-related increases in blood cholesterol.* However, some people who have high blood cholesterol levels are not overweight and they may need to change the composition of their diets. Besides being overweight, the most important dietary influence on blood cholesterol is the type of fat in the diet.

Fat in the diet consists of mixtures of three types of fatty acids – saturated, monounsaturated and polyunsaturated:

- Saturated fats – solid at room temperature, such as butter, lard, meat fat, solid vegetable fat.
- Monounsaturated fats – liquid at room temperature, such as olive oil, rapeseed oil, peanut oil, fish oil.
- Polyunsaturated fats – liquid at room temperature, sunflower, safflower and soybean.

Saturated fatty acids increase the level of cholesterol in the blood. If the saturated fatty acids are replaced by either monounsaturated or polyunsaturated fatty acids then the level of cholesterol in the blood will fall. For example, when olive oil replaces butter and meat fats then blood cholesterol levels will fall. In countries that have high rates of heart disease, most of the fat in the diet comes from cow's milk and other animal fats – typically western developed countries. Saturated fats are believed to increase blood cholesterol levels by slowing down the rate at which cholesterol is removed from the blood stream by the liver.

Changing the type of fat in your diet can lower your blood cholesterol by up to 20 per cent.

The myth of cholesterol in the diet Most of the cholesterol in the blood is derived from cholesterol made in the body, only a small fraction is derived from that obtained in diet. It is true that cholesterol is present in foods of animal origin – in particular, eggs and organ meats such as liver. But eating cholesterol containing foods such as eggs only has a small effect on the level of cholesterol in the blood. It makes little difference to their blood cholesterol level whether people eat three or seven eggs a week. Only if large amounts are consumed (three to four eggs a day) do blood cholesterol levels rise substantially.

Exaggerated claims for the cholesterol lowering effects of fibre Most of the fibre in our diet comes from wheat bran and this has no effect on blood cholesterol. Soluble fibre, particularly the type found in oats and in beans and fruit, can help lower blood cholesterol levels. But you need to consume quite large amounts of these fibres to experience any measurable effects. Advertisements and packaging now claim or imply that eating oat bran will lower your blood cholesterol and reduce your risk of heart disease. But you have to consume in the region of 60-100g daily to show a small reduction (about 5 per cent) in blood cholesterol. Dr Swain from Boston found no effect on blood cholesterol levels with 40g of oatbran a day. *This is still greater than the average portion in a breakfast cereal.*

Some of the cholesterol-lowering soluble fibres such as guar gum, glucomannans and galactomannans are sold in tablet form in health food shops. These can be dangerous because they can swell up and get stuck in your gullet. One man who was eating 60g of oat bran a day had to have an operation to remove a two foot long impacted lump of oat bran from his intestines. The manufacturers also don't tell you that high intakes of bran reduce the absorption of several essential minerals such as iron, calcium and zinc. Neither do they tell you that races which traditionally eat large amounts of oats (eg, the Scots) have the highest rates of heart disease in the world!

We don't want to put you off eating fibre-rich foods, but most authorities suggest that you should get the fibre you need by eating real foods not fibre concentrates – wholegrain cereals, pulses and vegetables. These also provide minerals and vitamins.

Coffee and heart disease Several studies have found a relationship between heavy coffee consumption and risk of death from coronary heart disease. Even after allowing for differences in smoking habits, heavy coffee drinkers run three times the risk of dying from heart disease. The link between coffee and heart disease appears to be due to its blood cholesterol raising effect. The effects of coffee on cholesterol depend on how much is consumed and the way it is prepared. It is boiled coffee that raises blood cholesterol levels by about 10 per cent. By boiled coffee we mean pouring boiling water on to coffee grounds and leaving it to stew either in a thermos or on the stove as with a percolator. This effect has nothing to do with caffeine because both fresh filtered and boiled coffee provide the same amount of caffeine. The active substance is almost certainly in the fats that occur naturally in the coffee beans but the exact chemical identity of the substance has yet to be discovered. This advice does not apply to coffee that has been filtered through paper. However, there is much still to be learnt about coffee and it is sensible not to leave any sort of coffee to stew for long periods of time. Drink it freshly made.

The Cholesterol Mafia From the newspaper articles you read you might think that lowering blood cholesterol is the answer to heart disease. Professor Alex Leaf of Harvard University argues that the medical establishment has become 'infatuated with the role of cholesterol' to the neglect of other approaches.

Professor Dan Steinberg believes we need to understand why cholesterol causes atherosclerosis. In an article entitled 'Beyond Cholesterol' published in the prestigious *New England Journal of Medicine*, he suggests that cholesterol-carrying proteins in blood need to be modified before they can cause harm and suggests that anti-oxidant vitamins such as vitamin C, vitamin E and carotene may protect against atherosclerosis.

Several European countries have similar blood cholesterol levels but different rates of heart disease. The highest rates of heart disease have been found in the countries with the lowest blood levels of vitamins C, E and carotene (vitamins provided by fruit and vegetables). This could mean that eating fruit and vegetables may protect us from heart disease by stopping the modification of cholesterol-carrying proteins. This may explain why the Scots and Northern Irish – who have a very low intake of fruit and vegetables – top the world league for heart disease.

One reason for the excessive emphasis on cholesterol as a risk factor for heart disease has been the support of the drug companies who sell cholesterol-lowering drugs. Promoting the cholesterol/heart disease theory is in their interest. However, these drugs are very beneficial to a particular group of patients with 'familial hypercholesterolaemia'. They have very high cholesterol levels that do not respond to diet.

Is it worth lowering your blood cholesterol? High blood cholesterol levels predict risk of CHD up to the age of about fifty-five years in men. In the over sixties, slightly higher than average blood cholesterol is associated with longevity, probably because those who were at most risk have already died. It has been calculated on the basis of studies with young men with high blood cholesterol that each 1 per cent reduction in blood cholesterol decreases risk of CHD by 2 per cent. It is possible to lower blood cholesterol by about 20 per cent by changing what we eat. So this would decrease the risk by about 40 per cent. Medical opinion favours treating those with very high blood cholesterol levels whatever their age (*see* p216 for information about cholesterol levels).

Professor Hugh Tunstall-Pedoe from the University of Dundee believes that modest changes in diet would lower most people's blood cholesterol to an acceptable level. *Once again, small changes in our diet can revolutionize our long-term health.* It is probably only the small minority with very high cholesterol levels that do not respond to diet who should be considered for drug treatment because of the potential side-effects. Lowering blood cholesterol will not entirely prevent heart disease, but will defer its onset.

Diet and thrombosis   Diets high in fat increase the tendency for blood to clot, so cutting down on fat should also reduce your risk of suffering a heart attack. The type of fat in the diet also influences the tendency of the blood to clot. Fats high in saturated fatty acids such as butter, lard and coconut oil increase the tendency of the blood to clot, whereas monounsaturated fatty acids such as olive oil are neutral. The special type of polyunsaturated fats found in fish oil decrease the tendency of blood to clot. So partially replacing saturated fats with monounsaturated fats and eating more fish can also be helpful.

Vegetarian diets and heart disease   British vegetarians tend to have lower rates of heart disease than the average. However, as a group they tend to be non-smokers and health conscious so diet may not be the sole protective factor. A study on Seventh Day Adventists by Roland Phillips from Loma Linda University found that vegan men, but not women, had lower rates of heart disease than vegetarians and meat eaters. (Vegans are not people from the planet Vega, but strict vegetarians who exclude all food of animal origin from their diet.) Vegan men have much lower cholesterol levels than vegetarians and meat eaters because of their low intake of saturated fats. They also tend to be very lean.

Not all vegetarian groups are at low risk of heart disease. Indian Hindus are usually vegetarian and they have very high rates of heart disease. Like the white vegetarians they tend to be non-smokers and have lower than average blood cholesterol levels. It has been suggested Indians get more heart disease because of racial harassment but the West Indians in UK have lower rates of heart disease and also suffer from harassment. In fact, high rates of heart disease in Indians are common in other parts of the world such as Canada, the West Indies and Mauritius and it may be because they are more prone to diabetes which greatly increases the risk of heart disease. Heart disease and diabetes are also common in other Indian groups who are not vegetarians. The high rate of heart disease in Indians is perplexing because at first sight Indian diets conform to many of the current guidelines for healthy eating!

The protective effect of fish   Hundreds of studies have now been carried out over the last decade feeding people and animals large amounts of fish or fish oil. It seems that fish oil protects against heart disease by mechanisms that do not involve lowering blood cholesterol (fish oil supplements may even increase blood cholesterol levels in some people). Fish oil contains two polyunsaturated fatty acids which have profound effects on blood flow and inflammation. These polyunsaturated fatty acids are called eicosapentaenoic acid (EPA) and docosahexaenoic acid (DHA). In many respects the effects of consuming EPA and DHA are similar to those of aspirin which, as we have seen, reduces risk of heart disease.

Until recently it was thought you had to eat buckets of fish to get protection from heart disease. Then long-term studies from Holland, Sweden and the USA showed that people who ate fish as little as two or three times a week had lower rates of heart disease than those who ate none at all. More importantly, they weren't dying from other causes. A study from Norway published in 1990 found that fish oil lowered blood pressure in people who did not normally eat fish, but not in those who ate fish two to three times a week. It showed that small amounts of fish oil could favourably affect the cardiovascular system.

Another trial with patients who had suffered a heart attack showed that eating oily fish twice a week reduced the risk of dying over the next two years by 29 per cent. This fall in death rate was due to a reduction in fatal heart attacks.

A decline in the popularity of oily fish is one of the major changes in the British diet this century. It is interesting that heart disease was uncommon at the turn of the century in London when oily fish was a common food. It was allegedly responsible for the stench of London streets. White fish is also a good food and is low in saturated fat. It clearly makes sense to eat more fish, especially the oily varieties. It contains a rich source of nutrients that are scarce in other foods. A single portion of fish can make a major contribution to the intake of several nutrients such as iodine and vitamin D. But to eat more pickled fish or fish fried in animal fat would defeat the object of the exercise.

Falling rates of heart disease in Australia and North America
Since about 1968 rates of heart disease have fallen in Australia and the USA. Yet rates in Britain have been relatively static (although they are at last showing a falling trend). No one really knows why heart disease has fallen although many people would like to take the credit. Some experts suggest that it is because more Australians and Americans quit smoking. But many people in Britain have also given up over the past two decades yet CHD rates continued to rise into the 1970s. There is little evidence that Americans and Australians eat less fat than they used to. But the type of fat has changed. They now eat between 50 and 100 per cent more polyun-saturated fats. This change occurred in the 1960s with a change from solid to soft margarines and the use of liquid vegetable oils in place of solid cooking fats. According to the latest survey by the Department of Health, the British have also now increased their intake of polyunsaturated fats by 50 per cent in the last few years and heart disease has started to fall. Dr John Charnock and Professor Paul Nestel believe that the increase in polyunsaturates in the diet may have reduced the risk of cardiac arrhythmias developing in people who have already suffered a heart attack. Cardia arrhythmias,

which are irregular heart beats, can lead to a condition called ventricular fibrillation – the heart does not pump blood properly because the muscle surrounding its pumping chamber (the 'ventricle') does not contract and expand normally, instead it twitches irregularly. This is a major cause of death in patients following a heart attack. They found that marmosets fed sheep fat were more susceptible to arrhythmias and fibrillation than animals fed polyunsaturated fats, whether of vegetable or marine origin.

The olive oil connection   Olive oil is perhaps better known for its connection with the Mafia than heart disease. The southern Mediterranean countries such as Greece and Southern Italy, besides having a nice climate and gentle life-style, have very low rates of heart disease. The typical Mediterranean diet contains plenty of fruit and vegetables, starchy foods such as bread or pasta, along with meat, fish and cheese. But crucially, about 70 per cent of the fat in the diet comes from olive oil, which is low in saturated fats. Olive oil is regarded as neutral when it comes to heart disease, but when it displaces saturated fats such as butter and lard from the diet then it exerts a beneficial effect. Thus there can be no benefit to be derived from taking olive oil supplements.

CANCER

Key Points in decreasing the risk of cancer from diet:

Avoid obesity and maintain ideal body weight throughout adult life.
Avoid excess alcohol intake.
Eat plenty of fresh fruit and green, yellow and orange vegetables.
Eat less fat.
Only eat pickled and smoked foods occasionally.

WHAT IS CANCER?

Cancer is a disease which we all dread. In fact, it is not a single disease at all but a large number of related disorders. All tissues are made up of cells and, with the exception of brain cells, these cells are continually being replaced by new cells in an orderly manner. But sometimes the cells of a tissue begin to divide spontaneously and multiply in an uncontrolled fashion, thus creating a lump or tumour. The tumour may compress surrounding tissue or, if it is on the skin, appear as a growth. In most cases, the tumour is benign – that is, harmless. Malignant or cancerous tumours differ because they invade adjoining tissues and organs and can also spread through blood and lymph glands to remote organs where they can seed new tumours. These are known as secondary cancers or metastases.

Most cancers are believed to originate from a single altered cell and its development involves a series of steps. The first step is *initiation* which leads to an irreversible mutation in the cell's genetic make-up. The second stage is called *promotion* where the mutant cell grows into a tumour. There may be a gap between initiation and promotion of tumour growth of up to thirty years. Diet may be involved in both the initiation and promotion of cancer.

WHO'S AT RISK?

The risk of getting cancer increases with age, but some cancers are more common in young people than old people (eg, leukaemia and testicular cancer). Although it seems likely that malignant cells do occur by chance, a number of chemicals, viruses and other factors such as exposure to radiation (including sunlight) can increase the chances of a malignant cell forming. It is not certain whether all malignant cells develop into cancer. Some scientists believe that malignant cells are being formed all the time but are neutralized by the immune system. Some drugs that depress the immune response increase risk of cancer and this fits in with the idea of 'immune surveillance'. Also as we get older our immune system becomes less competent. Cancer is becoming more common as a far higher proportion of the population are living long enough to get it. However, the death rate from cancers in children and people under forty-five has dropped markedly and this is largely due to improvements in treatment such as chemotherapy.

WHAT CAUSES CANCER?

It is generally agreed that risk of cancer is mainly determined by exposure to environmental factors, although certain cancers – such as breast and colon cancer – do seem to be more common in some families. So the cause could either be hereditary or, in some cases, a common environmental factor.

In the UK about a third of cancers are caused by smoking. Of the established causes of cancer, alcohol is the second most important. Ethanol (ethyl alcohol) is the responsible factor so it does not make any difference whether wine, beer or spirits are consumed. The exception to this is an increased risk of large bowel cancer with certain beers. Those who smoke *and* drink are at greatly increased risk from cancer of the mouth, pharynx and oesophagus, compared with those who smoke but don't drink or those that drink but don't smoke. A high proportion of causes of cancer remain unexplained and diet could be a factor causing anything between 30 and 70 per cent.

The pattern of cancer varies quite markedly from country to country. In Japan, cancer of the lung and breast are far less common but stomach cancer rates are amongst the highest in the world. In most Western developed countries lung cancer is the main cancer, followed by large bowel cancer, breast cancer and prostatic cancer. Most developed countries have high intakes of meat, fat and low intakes of fibre. Comparisons between countries show strong associations between the rates of cancer of the breast, colon, pancreas, prostate and the intakes of these nutrients. These associations in themselves are not proof of a causal relationship.

Over the past fifty years stomach cancer rates have fallen dramatically in most Western countries and the lowest rates are in the USA. It seems that as countries get richer the site of cancer moves down the gut. The decline in stomach cancer has been attributed to the consumption of less pickled and smoked food, refrigeration and an increased intake of fruit and vegetables. The decline in stomach cancer also parallels the decline in peptic ulcers. People who suffer from peptic ulcers are also known to be at increased risk of stomach cancer. Peptic ulcers have recently been linked with infection by a bacterium (Helicobacter pylori). So the fall in stomach cancer and peptic ulcer could be a result of improved food hygiene.

The Seventh Day Adventist Church advocates a vegetarian diet and prohibits the use of tobacco, alcohol or stimulants such as tea or coffee. Adventists in America were found to have lower rates of cancer than the general population and this was initially interpreted as showing that vegetarians were less at risk from cancer. However, cancer rates are similarly low in Mormons who are not vegetarians but who also avoid tobacco, alcohol and tea and coffee. Later studies found that Adventist vegetarians had similar rates of cancer to Adventist meat eaters. So these studies do not support the idea that meat consumption causes cancer.

A study by Dr Hirayama in Japan found that cancer of the colon (large bowel) was less common in subjects consuming meat and green and yellow vegetables daily but was three to four times greater in those eating meat daily but not vegetables. Those subjects who ate vegetables only had a similar risk to those who ate meat only. Again this study shows there is little evidence to support the popularly held belief that meat causes bowel cancer. Perhaps what it suggests is that a balanced diet offers some protection. Here are Dr Hirayama's findings:

COLON CANCER RISK PER 100,000 POPULATION

Meat but not vegetables daily	18.4 per 100,000
Vegetables but not meat daily	13.6 per 100,000
Both meat and vegetables daily	3.9 per 100,000

Countries with high intakes of fat tend to have high rates of colon cancer and when people migrate to a country where the intake of fat is high their rate of colon cancer goes up. In experiments, a diet high in fat increases the growth and numbers of colon tumours in animals. High fat intakes are believed to promote the rate of growth of tumours by increasing the amount of bile acids secreted into the gut to digest the fat. Bile acids have been shown to stimulate tumour growth.

FIBRE AND CANCER

Fibre relieves constipation and its use should be recommended on these grounds, but there is insufficient evidence to be sure that a low intake of fibre increases the risk of colon cancer. Colon cancer is rare among Eskimos on their traditional diet which contains no dietary fibre whatsoever. Moreover, Adventist vegetarians have higher intakes of fibre than Adventist meat-eaters yet they have the same rate of colon cancer. It is well established that colon cancer rates are lower in peoples whose diet consists in the main of large quantities of white rice. Both their fat and fibre intakes are low but it is now known that some starches – like those found in rice and maize – are resistant to digestion and act like fibre.

Claims that fibre supplements may reduce risk of colon cancer have not been substantiated. Studies in animals have found that the soluble fibres such as guar, oatbran and pectin actually increase the growth and number of colon tumours in animals. This is probably because they increase the excretion of bile acids which, as we have seen, are known to promote tumour growth. On the other hand, the insoluble fibres such as wheatbran decrease the growth and number of tumours.

PROTECTIVE EFFECT OF FRUIT AND VEGETABLES

Several studies have shown a protective effect from fruit and vegetable consumption against colon and stomach cancer risk. Various theories have been advanced to explain the nature of this protective factor. Green leafy vegetables and carrots are rich in carotene. A number of studies in humans have found lower levels of beta-carotene in the blood of people who went on to develop cancer. Studies with animals have shown that beta-carotene does reduce the development of cancers in animals exposed to irradiation.

Cancer of the mouth is common in people who chew tobacco quid. One of the early stages in the development of this cancer is the presence of abnormal cells in the cheek. At least two studies have shown that it is possible to reduce the number of abnormal cells in tobacco quid chewers by giving them large amounts of beta-carotene. However, the obvious way to prevent this cancer is to stop chewing tobacco! Further studies are underway to see if beta-carotene can prevent cancer, but it may be ten years before the results are known.

It is interesting that protection from cancer is most strongly associated with green leafy vegetables from the cabbage family rather than with carrots, even though they are the major source of carotene in the diet. It could be that green leafy vegetables also contain other substances that are protective. It has been found that the characteristic pungent tasting compounds in these foods called glucosynilates in small amounts have a protective effect against some types of chemically induced cancers in animals. Similar sulphur-containing compounds in garlic have the same effect.

DIET AND BREAST CANCER

Breast cancer rates vary markedly between countries. Rates are very low in Japan but high in the USA. But when Japanese women migrate to the USA their risk of breast cancer increases. Rates of breast cancer have been rising in the UK over the past thirty years; currently about one in twelve women will get breast cancer. During this period there was a marked decline in breast-feeding. However, breast-feeding does not protect against breast cancer.

Risk factors for breast cancer include onset of monthly periods at an early age and a family history of breast cancer. Having a first child, especially a boy, under the age of twenty-three years and early menopause or removal of the ovaries gives some protection. The risk of breast cancer is mainly determined by high levels of ovarian hormone levels, particularly oestrogen and progesterone which are to a large extent inherited. There is not much one can do to alter these risk factors. But a large trial of a drug has begun to see if it is possible to prevent breast cancer in women at high risk. The drug is called Tamoxifen and it lessens the effect of the oestrogen naturally present in the body.

As far as diet is concerned, obesity and excess alcohol increase the risk of cancer. There is no truth in the allegation that meat consumption increases the risk because vegetarians are just as likely to get breast cancer as meat-eaters. Animals fed a high-fat diet are more likely to develop mammary cancer than those on low-fat diets. Thus it has been argued that a high intake of fat may increase risk of breast cancer, although the relationship between fat intake and breast cancer risk is certainly not clear cut. One study measured the dietary habits of 89,500 American nurses and then followed them over several years to see which ones developed breast cancer. Those on lowest fat intakes were just as likely to develop breast cancer as those on the highest fat intakes. However, even those consuming the lowest amounts of fat, were eating much more fat than people in low-risk countries like Japan. It is well established that a low-fat diet helps relieve cyclical mastalgia (painful breasts associated with periods) and it is believed to act by decreasing the production of oestrogen and progesterone (the hormones implicated in causing breast cancer). So it remains a possibility that a low-fat intake may decrease risk of breast cancer. *However, besides avoiding obesity and excess alcohol intake there is no firm evidence that any other changes in diet will help women avoid breast cancer.*

XENOBIOTICS – HAZARDOUS MATERIALS IN FOOD

Key Points to help avoid the hazardous material in food:

Always cook beans well.
Avoid mouldy food.
Avoid excess coffee intake (more than six cups per day).
Avoid eating sprouted or green potatoes.
Follow all the guidelines we give you for avoiding food poisoning (*see* Section V).
Eat raw fish and meat at your own risk.
Avoid frequent consumption of pickled, smoked and barbecued foods.
Always draw water from the mains supply.
Don't overconcern yourself about pesticides and food additives.

Food consists of material other than nutrients. The technical term for the substances in food that are not nutrients is xenobiotics (foreign compounds) – ie, the substances that cannot be used to provide energy or to make body tissues and are foreign to the body's normal *metabolic* pathways. They include naturally occurring toxicants, dietary fibre, drugs (including alcohol – *see* p328), some food additives, agricultural chemicals (pesticides, fungicides, herbicides) and chemicals formed during the cooking and processing of foods.

Xenobiotics occur in a wide variety of foods in at least as great a diversity as nutrients themselves and some may be useful in the diet. For example, a high intake of dietary fibre provides roughage and prevents constipation. However, under certain conditions others may cause disease. It's certainly worth remembering that naturally occurring toxicants pose a far greater hazard to health than food additives and agricultural chemicals (*see* the Risk Business table on Section 1, p92).

Most xenobiotics are poisonous if consumed in sufficient quantity. Fortunately, nature has equipped us with mechanisms to breakdown and eliminate them and providing we do not consume too much they cause no harm. However, the system for breaking down xenobiotics is immature in babies and children, which is why you have to be careful about giving certain drugs to children. The more varied the diet, the greater the chances of being exposed to xenobiotics. It is, therefore, advantageous for young children to eat a diet that seems monotonous to an adult. This point illustrates a general principle: *the risks posed to health from food vary throughout the life-cycle*.

NATURAL BUT NASTY

The term 'natural' is used to convey a sense of wholesomeness and goodness. Advertisements talk about foods being full of 'natural goodness' or foods being 'naturally flavoured'. The implication is that natural is good and that unnatural is bad, but this is not always true. Natural can be nasty.

Plants contain a number of naturally occurring toxicants and they can also be contaminated with toxins produced by moulds that grow on them. For example, apricot and plum stones release cyanide when cracked open – this killed a health food enthusiast who decided to eat apricot kernels. Butter beans, sometimes known as Lima beans, can also release quite large amounts of cyanide, but fortunately the cyanide is destroyed when the beans are cooked. Linseed, sometimes called flaxseed, which is sold in health food shops also contains a compound called linamarin that releases cyanide. It is well known to vets that large amounts of linseed meal cause cyanide toxicity in animals. Fortunately, we seem to be able to cope with the small amounts of cyanide found in apple pips.

Beans are a food with a very healthy image so you might be surprised to learn that they contain several naturally occurring toxicants. We do not want to discourage you from eating beans, but you do need to make sure that you cook them properly. Most of the naturally occurring toxicants in beans are destroyed in cooking. Some years ago a number of people fell ill from eating raw soaked kidney beans which contain a toxin that causes severe diarrhoea and sickness and can even be fatal. However, if the beans are boiled for twenty minutes the toxin is destroyed and the beans are safe to eat. Red kidney beans cooked in a slow cooker have also caused poisoning because the temperature in the slow cooker was not high enough to destroy the toxins.

ALKALOIDS

Many plants contain a related series of compounds called alkaloids which have drug-like properties. Caffeine – which is found in both tea and coffee – is a good example. Caffeine is a mild stimulant and in the amounts normally consumed poses no hazard to health. However, caffeine is addictive and withdrawal from coffee can lead to headaches. Small amounts of caffeine increase intellectual performance during low states of arousal (first thing in the morning) and obviously this is useful if you are trying to concentrate on driving. However, heavy caffeine consumption can cause anxiety. Caffeine is the component of coffee that keeps you awake and so beverages which contain caffeine are best avoided last thing at night. Herbal teas also contain alkaloids. Comfrey tea contains an alkaloid that causes liver cancer in animals, so there is no guarantee that herbal teas are going to be any better for you than tea or coffee.

Solanine and chaconine are two alkaloids found in potatoes. They occur in highest quantities in the above ground parts and in the sprouts. In the potato itself they are found mainly in the skin and eyes, so peeling potatoes reduces the alkaloid content. Acute illness and even death has resulted from the consumption of green, sprouted or blighted potatoes. These alkaloids cause drowsiness, difficulty in breathing and paralysis; they also inflame the gut leading to stomach-ache and diarrhoea. An outbreak of potato poisoning occurred in Lewisham in 1978. Seventy-eight school boys were taken ill after eating potatoes later found to contain high levels of the alkaloids. Seventeen children required hospital treatment of whom three were described as seriously ill. Poisoning is rare because the amount of alkaloids normally present in potatoes is not great enough to cause much harm. The current trend to consume potato peel (mistakenly considered to be a good source of fibre) may mean that many people are consuming quite large amounts of these alkaloids. Little is known about the long-term health consequences. (For advice on preparing potatoes, *see* Section V, p295.)

SPICES

A wide variety of spices have been used for centuries to enhance the flavour of food. Spices contain a number of components that would never get through the stringent toxicological testing carried out on food additives! Nutmeg and mace contain myristicin which has mild sedative and anaesthetic properties. The red star anise (an ingredient of Chinese Five Spice mixture) and sesame oil contain compounds known to cause cancer in animals. However, there is no direct evidence to show that spices cause harm in people in the amounts in which they are usually consumed.

MYCOTOXINS

Mycotoxins are toxins produced by filamentous moulds that grow on food, particularly in warm, humid conditions. Nuts and cereal grains are most susceptible to the moulds which are known to cause disease in both animals and people. Problems can result either from the direct consumption of mouldy food or by consuming meat from animals that have been fed on contaminated food. Animals are particularly at risk because their feed may not be stored under ideal conditions. Mycotoxins can be a major hazard because they can contaminate everyday foods such as cereals and thus can affect large numbers of people.

The harmful effects of mould-contaminated peanuts were discovered in England in the 1960s when there was a serious outbreak of disease in turkeys. In all the cases, peanut meal had been a constituent of the turkey feed. The toxic factors in the peanut meal were extracted and shown to be derived from the mould *Aspergillus flavus* and were called aflatoxins. Aflatoxins are known to cause liver damage and liver cancer when fed to animals. Aflatoxin is one of the most potent cancer-causing agents known to man, so it's not surprising that rates of liver cancer are high in parts of the world where exposure to aflatoxins in the diet is high – eg, Indonesia, Thailand and West Africa. The harmful effects of aflatoxins are made worse by a poor diet.

In Britain aflatoxin levels in imported nuts are controlled by law. The chances of consuming aflatoxins in pre-packaged peanuts is small as each nut is screened, but the risk is greater if you buy them in their shells. High levels of aflatoxins have also been found in a popular brand of 'health food' peanut butter. Dried fruit, particularly Turkish apricots, has also been found to be contaminated.

Several mycotoxins are produced by Penicillium mould which grows on rotting fruit. These mycotoxins are found in relatively high levels in rotting apples, apple juice, cider and mould ripened blue cheeses such as Stilton. Penicillin, the antibiotic, is also a mycotoxin produced from the same mould. It is now known that several of these Penicillium mycotoxins can cause cancer in animals, but there is no evidence to support a link between human cancer and the consumption of blue cheese or apple juice.

DODGY FOODS

Food of animal origin – meat, fish, eggs, milk and honey – is free from toxins unless the animal has fed on a toxicant. For example, quails fed on hemlock are both lethal and a novel way to make sure your dinner party-guests don't come again (and probably don't leave either). Honey from bees that have fed on rhododendrons and related species causes paralysis. Toxic honeys have been known since antiquity, the oldest record being the description by Xenophon of the mass poisoning of the expedition of Cyrus in 401 BC. A physician described poisoning by mountain laurel honey thus: 'Shortly after eating, within a few minutes to two hours, the person felt a tingling and numbness in the extremities and lost consciousness.'

Perhaps the most bizarre food is the Fugu or Puffer fish. This fish is a great delicacy in Japan but you have to be very careful how you eat it because parts of it contain a deadly poison called tetrodoxin. In Japan, there are licensed restaurants where the chefs are trained to eviscerate and remove the dangerous parts. Apparently the trick is to leave enough tetrodoxin in to give you a mild tingle! Every year in Japan there are a number of fatalities amongst amateurs who catch their own Fugu fish but don't prepare them properly.

Raw meat and fish can contain worms, worm eggs or bacteria, all of which can cause disease. In Iceland, the consumption of raw fish is a delicacy but unfortunately it also transmits a tapeworm called *Diphyllobothrium latum*. This formidable beast can grow up to several metres long in the intestines and cause vitamin B_{12} deficiency in the host. Raw fish consumed in Thailand transmits a parasite called *Opos-thorchis* which infects the liver and is linked to liver cancer. It's best to give raw meat and fish a wide berth if you don't want to get worms, although if you only eat it very occasionally the odds are you will get away unscathed. Pickled and smoked fish carry no risk of worms.

RED TIDES

Shellfish such as oysters, mussels and cockles are particularly susceptible to bacterial and toxin contamination. The hazards of eating contaminated shellfish have been known since biblical times and this may be why shellfish is not kosher. There is a biblical reference in the plagues of the Pharaoh where 'the rivers were turned to blood'. This was probably caused by a bloom of the protozoa Gonyaulux, a microscopic animal which grows in blooms when nutrients are abundant and turns the water red. Mussels are filter feeders and can accumulate these *protozoa* inside their filters along with bacteria. When *Gonyaulux* is infected with a particular bacteria it produces a deadly toxin called saxitoxin. If you are unfortunate enough to consume shellfish contaminated with *Gonyaulux* it could result in paralytic shellfish poisoning which can be fatal!

Outbreaks of paralytic shellfish poisoning have been recorded since 1934 down the north-east coast of Britain and as a result shellfish are routinely monitored for toxins in Britain (as they are in both Canada and USA). In May 1990, a ban was placed on the sale of shellfish by the British government following the discovery of high amounts of toxin in mussels first on the north-east coast and, later in the summer, on the north-west coast. Red tides and related blooms – such as the one that causes *Ciguatera* poisoning in the Indian Ocean – have been known to occur from time to time in many parts of the world, but are usually short-lived as the *protozoa* only thrive when the levels of nutrients in the water are high. There is little evidence to suggest that pollution is the cause as outbreaks are also common in the clean waters of the Pacific coast of America and those of Northern Canada.

BLUE AND BROWN FLAGS

The EEC has started looking at the safety of water for bathing around the UK and is awarding resorts 'Blue Flags' if there is not too much sewage in the sea (a brown flag might have been more appropriate in resorts like Brighton or Blackpool where 'Mersey goldfish' mix with the swimmers when the wind blows onshore!). In many parts of Britain raw sewage is pumped into the sea. To us it may be sewage but to mussels it is Cordon Bleu and they thrive on it. We warn you not to collect mussels or cockles for consumption because they can be contaminated with bacteria and viruses that can cause very unpleasant gastric upsets. However, it is safe to collect prawns, shrimps, crabs and lobsters because we do not eat their filters. Commercially farmed mussels are cultured in a special way and routinely checked for contaminants.

BACTERIAL FOOD POISONING

Food is an important means of transmitting disease. In the last century, milk was responsible for transmitting tuberculosis, brucellosis and a host of other bacterial diseases. But the introduction of pasteurization (a mild heat treatment of milk) killed the harmful bacteria and led to a marked fall in food-borne diseases.

The term 'food poisoning' is usually used to describe illness resulting from food contaminated with bacteria and is most commonly caused by contamination with salmonella, clostridium perfringens, camplyobacter, staphylococcus aureus and bacillus cereus. There are hundreds of strains of salmonella, one of which causes typhoid. In Britain and the USA the number of cases of salmonella food poisoning has risen dramatically over the past few years. Most cases are related to the consumption of poultry and eggs contaminated with salmonella. Fortunately, if you cook poultry and eggs properly you kill all the salmonella bacteria. Watch out for 'salmonella on a stick' – undercooked chicken legs at barbecues (*see* Section V, p315).

Some bacteria produce toxins that remain in food, the most common of which is produced by staphylococcus aureus and is not destroyed by cooking. Consumption of food containing the toxin results in diarrhoea and vomiting two to eight hours later. The deadly botulin toxin is produced by the bacterium clostridium botulinum, a bacteria that only grows in the absence of air and used to be a problem in canned and bottled food. Commercial tinned food is heated at a high temperature to kill the clostridium spores in a process called a Botulinum cook.

Botulism is very rare in Britain, in fact there have been only two outbreaks in the last ten years. In France and the United States, there are several cases of botulism every year resulting from the consumption of home canned food.

Bacterial food poisoning can be avoided by proper food handling and storage. We give you detailed advice about this in Section V.

NATURAL AND MAN-MADE CONTAMINANTS

The development of increasingly sensitive methods of analysis has focused attention on the presence of many harmful or potentially harmful substances in the environment, which may be present in minute amounts in foods. Recently, chemists in the US discovered by chance that Perrier water had levels of benzene above the permitted levels for drinking water. This led to the well known 'Perrier fiasceau' where Perrier water was temporarily withdrawn from the market. The benzene was a natural contaminant which now has to be filtered out.

Governments set guidelines to define upper limits of the levels of contaminants in foods. The term 'acceptable daily intake' (ADI) refers to the amount of substance which can be safely consumed every day for an individual's entire lifetime. The ADI is expressed in milligrams of the substance per kilogram body weight of the consumer. The ADI is usually calculated on the basis of 70kg body weight for men and is normally determined by dividing the dose of a substance which has no harmful effects in the most sensitive animal species by a huge safety factor of 100. Thus if the ADI for a contaminant is exceeded, this does not necessarily mean that disease will result.

HEAVY METALS

This has nothing to do with rock groups. Certain heavy metals, in particular lead, mercury and cadmium, can contaminate food and water. Water supplies can acquire lead from lead plumbing and lead solder, particularly in soft water areas. Glasgow is one of the worst affected areas. Unacceptably high levels have been found in drinking water especially when the water has been standing in the pipes. Contamination levels are reduced if water is run from the tap for a few minutes before it is used for drinking. Lead levels are greatest if water is drawn from the hot water supply rather than from the mains.

At one time high quantities of lead got into tinned food (particularly acidic foods) because lead solder was used to seal the tin. Nowadays, cans are treated with lacquer and lead solder is no longer used. Lead glazes are still used in some North African countries on earthenware – the type of thing tourists bring back from their holidays. Pewter mugs and plates contain lead and like the lead glazed earthenware will release lead if acidic foods and drinks are put in them. The same is true of whisky stored in lead crystal. Lead poisoning used to result from children chewing lead painted toys but now the majority of toys are painted with non-toxic paints.

The average daily lead intake is about 0.13mg/kg which is less than the ADI 0.2-2mg/kg. One source of such contamination is petrol – lead tetraethyl is used as anti-knock and the exhaust fumes of cars can contaminate the outer leaves of vegetables near roadsides. Hence the moves to encourage the use of lead-free petrol.

Acute lead toxicity causes severe stomach pain, damages

the nervous system, leads to muscle wasting and is fortunately rare. More insidious are the harmful effects of long-term exposure to lower amounts of lead which have been linked with behavioural problems and poor learning ability in children. One study looked at the level of lead in children's milk teeth to ascertain exposure to lead in early life. It was discovered that children with learning defects had higher levels of lead in their teeth. Other studies have not confirmed these findings but areas where lead intake is high often tend to be socially deprived, so it is difficult to separate the effects of poor housing and other aspects of poverty from lead poisoning.

Cadmium levels have been found to be higher in vegetation near smelting works and fungi, in particular, accumulate heavy metals. High intakes of cadmium can lead to kidney damage and high blood pressure. The average intake for cadmium is about 0.015-0.021mg compared with an ADI of 0.100mg. Some areas of the UK have high levels of cadmium in their soil (eg, Shipham in Somerset) and this leads to high levels in home-grown vegetables. Quite high levels of cadmium have also been found in shellfish products from the south coast of England (3.8mg/kg in dressed crab). If you ate dressed crab more than twice a week you might exceed the ADI. A more recent study has shown that as many as one in ten Belgians have levels of cadmium in their bodies that could adversely affect their kidney function.

Mercury is very toxic. As little as 100mg of mercuric chloride produces poisoning, 500mg is fatal and long-term exposure to mercury causes brain damage. Mercury salts used to be used to blacken top hats in the last century, which is the source of the expression, 'Mad as a hatter'. Although there have occasionally been scares about mercury in dental fillings, you may be relieved to know that mercury is not toxic when it is mixed with other metals (as it is in dental work). Mercury salts released into the environment can be converted into more toxic organic forms such as methyl mercury. Bacteria make methyl mercury which accumulates in the food chain. In the 1950s in the Japanese town of Minimata, fifty people died and many more were brain damaged and paralyzed from eating fish contaminated with methyl mercury which was discharged into the sea by a plastics factory.

In the late 1960s, fish were also contaminated in the Great Lakes of USA and poisoned the Indians who fished there.

Most countries have standards to establish acceptable levels of heavy metals in seafood which these days is routinely monitored. *So there is no need to worry about heavy metals in tinned seafood.*

RADIOACTIVITY

Since the Chernobyl disaster, many more people are aware of the potential hazard of radioactivity in the environment. Exposure to radioactivity is related to an increased risk of bone marrow cancer and other soft tissue cancers such as leukaemia and aplastic anaemia. Children are particularly at risk from the harmful effects of radioactivity because the tissues that produce their white blood cells are active and therefore vulnerable.

While it is hotly debated whether there is such a thing as a safe dose of radioactivity, there's no doubt that some forms of radioactivity are more harmful than others. The term 'ionizing radiation' is used to cover X-rays, gamma rays, alpha and beta emitters. Alpha emitters such as uranium 235 and plutonium 239 are potentially the most hazardous forms. However, we are exposed to natural radioactivity every day and this 'background radioactivity' varies depending on the geological strata. For example, it is high in granite areas and low in chalk areas. There is an abundance of naturally occurring radioactivity which far outweighs the amount derived from man-made sources. During the 1960s, the level of strontium 90 – which is known to accumulate in bone – rose in milk as a result of nuclear testing. This was viewed with some concern, because blood cells divide and mature in the bone marrow. Fortunately, since the ban on atmospheric nuclear testing the levels of such radioactivity have fallen.

Iodine 127 and 131 are short-lived isotopes originating from nuclear reactors. These isotopes pose the greatest hazard in the short-term from nuclear accidents because they are avidly taken up by the thyroid gland. Fortunately, their uptake can be blocked by taking potassium iodide tablets. This measure was taken by countries worst affected by the Chernobyl disaster.

Caesium radionuclides 134 and 137 lead to more long-term contamination of the food chain. In many parts of Europe, levels of caesium radionuclides were unacceptably high following the Chernobyl incident and lamb from North Wales was banned because radioactivity levels were greater than 1,000 Becquerels/kg. The Welsh flocks have now been de-restricted.

Nuclear power-stations pump relatively large amounts of waste into the sea on the assumption that it will be diluted. However, because some of it is particulate in nature, hot spots occur and this can lead to the contamination of certain fish. A 1986 study of fish caught off the Cumbrian coast near the Sellafield nuclear plant revealed that they were 200 times more radioactive than in non-contaminated areas. But the radioactive discharges from nuclear plants (both intentional and accidental) account for about 13 per cent of our total exposure to radiation. In other words, natural radiation poses a far greater risk to health than man-made radioactivity. But there's no room for complacency because a nuclear accident could change the situation very rapidly.

TOO MUCH AGGRO OVER AGROCHEMICALS?

Many people are concerned about the health effects of the chemicals used in modern agriculture. It needs to be acknowledged that agricultural chemicals have taken the risk out of agriculture for the farmer. They have led to increased yields in crops, decreased post-harvest losses and are responsible for the stability of food supply in the developed countries. But if you are going to use technology you have to use it responsibly.

Organochlorine compounds such as DDE and DDT can accumulate in the food chain. As pesticides are fat soluble they tend to accumulate in our fat stores, with the danger that weight loss can lead to their mobilization into the blood and result in poisoning. In the mid-1960s concern was expressed about the effects of pesticides on wildlife. Over the next decade, legislation was introduced which restricted the use of certain pesticides, particularly the organochlorine range. The use of pesticides that do not have long-lasting residues was also encouraged and as a result the amount of organochlorine compounds in human tissues has fallen quite dramatically. Pesticide residues in food have also been falling and this has been accompanied by improved breeding rates of wild birds which previously were affected by the pesticides.

In developing countries some of the pesticides which are now banned in the West are still used to prevent spoilage of crops and the spread of insect-born diseases such as malaria. But some foods imported from developing countries have been found to contain unacceptably high levels of the banned pesticides.

Several pesticides and herbicides can cause cancer and birth defects. They can be absorbed through the skin and lungs as well as from diet. *But pesticide poisoning rarely results from eating foods contaminated with pesticides. It is those working with the pesticides in agriculture who are most at risk,* particularly in developing countries where even the most elementary safety precautions may be ignored. There is no evidence to show that consumption of agricultural chemicals present in trace amounts in food actually causes cancer in man. The strict controls on pesticides and fungicides are a good thing and ensure that pesticides come *at the bottom* of the risk table at the beginning of this section. Foods from large, reputable suppliers are now tested very thoroughly to ensure residues are within the strict safety limits. Ironically enough foods from 'health food' shops – often imported from less reputable suppliers – are less reliable. In September 1990, the Ministry of Agriculture published the results of a pesticide monitoring exercise. They found residues in twice as many 'health foods' as non-health foods.

NITRATE

Large amounts of nitrates are used as fertilizers throughout the world and in some areas the geological strata are also rich in nitrate. The EEC has a directive that suggests that nitrate in drinking water should not be above 50mg/l, although several areas of Britain have levels higher than this, especially during droughts. However, it is food and particularly vegetables that are usually the main source of nitrate in the diet. Vegetarians have much greater intakes of nitrate than non-vegetarians and it doesn't seem to do them any harm.

Nitrate itself is not regarded as toxic but nitrite which is derived from it by bacterial action is. Nitrite can cause 'blue baby syndrome' in babies fed on milks made up with water containing high levels of nitrate (greater than 100mg nitrate/l). An infant does not produce much stomach acid and the particular bacteria which can grow there convert the nitrate into nitrite. The nitrite reacts with the red oxygen carrying pigment haemoglobin to form methaemoglobin and this starves the baby's tissues of oxygen and so the baby turns blue. No cases of 'blue baby syndrome' have been reported since 1972 and if tap water does contain high levels of nitrate then mothers are warned not to use it to make up infant feeds.

Nitrites can react with protein-breakdown products to form compounds called nitrosamines and nitrosamides, which are potent carcinogens. As we said nitrate can be converted to nitrite in the body and it reacts with food constituents to form nitrosamines. Nitrites are also used as food additives in the salting of meat and nitrosamines are found in bacon and ham. Some beers have been found to contain significant amounts of nitrosamines (up to 6mcg/litre), and it's thought they arise during fermentation. Since this discovery the level of nitrosamine has been reduced ten-fold in Canada's beers. Perhaps of even more concern is the high amount of nitrosamines found in certain fungi – particularly in that most delicious mushroom the cep (Boletus Edulis)! So perhaps it's not a good idea to eat ceps every day.

Nitrosamines cause stomach cancer in animals. However, there appears to be no relationship between nitrate in drinking water and stomach cancer in the UK. In fact, the consumption of vegetables which are the major dietary source of nitrate is associated with a lower risk of stomach cancer. According to the Department of Health, 'The incidence of gastric cancer is relatively low in regions where the nitrate concentrations are relatively high; and the overall incidence of gastric cancer has continued to fall in England and Wales over the last thirty years despite the increase in water concentrations over that period.' Nevertheless, it's clear that the government needs to continue to monitor this important chemical in our environment.

FOOD ADULTERATION

From the earliest times governments have made various efforts to stop their more respectable citizens from being poisoned or swindled by the less reputable food manufacturers. The Bakers' Assizes were set up 800 years ago to control the sale of bread. Laws and regulations and decrees of varying sense and effectiveness have been passed to prevent the addition of injurious substances to food and to stop all types of fraud from short weight to direct adulteration. The aims of government have been:

- the protection of consumers against damage to their health;
- the protection of consumers against exploitation through commercial or industrial malpractice;
- the protection of the honest trader from unfair competition by the poor quality producer.

The first general food law in this country was published in 1860 when adulteration of food was rife. Ferricyanate was added to beer, sulphuric acid to vinegar, water to alcohol and so on. This catalogue of contamination was revealed in a series of articles published in *The Lancet* between 1851-4. During the Parliamentary debate of the general food law one member told the House that the only article of food that could be bought unadulterated was an egg and this was because there was no means of introducing injurious substances into it – ironic in the light of the recent scares about eggs.

These days the adulteration of food and drink is fortunately uncommon, although even now the public must be on its guard against unscrupulous manufacturers. In 1985 diethylene glycol (anti-freeze) was added to Austrian wine to make it taste sweeter! In 1937, this substance had killed 105 people when it was used as a vehicle for the antibiotic sulfanilamide. The Austrian adulteration was stopped before anybody died from kidney damage but the wine marketing industry suffered from another scandal the following year. A group of Italian wine merchants added methanol to low alcohol wines to reduce their density, a property that governs the wholesale price. Up to 14 per cent methanol was found in these wines and as little as 4ml can cause permanent blindness. More than thirty consumers died and many more were permanently blinded.

Perhaps the most horrific story of food adulteration is that of the Spanish toxic oil syndrome. In the summer of 1981, an outbreak of a disease that caused muscular wasting and damage to the nervous system occurred in an area around Madrid. The outbreak was traced to a consignment of vegetable oil sold by local vendors 'off the back of a lorry'. The oil, which had been designated for industrial use and originated from France, had been dyed with aniline. It was imported into Spain, illicitly decolourized and refined and sold. More than 20,000 people were affected by the disease and 340 died. The exact causative agent has never clearly been established because the Spanish authorities offered a premium on all oil handed in. Consequently, warehouses were filled with bottles of oil and no one was sure which was the contaminated oil and which was not.

FOOD PROCESSING

Food processing is necessary to feed an urban population. It decreases waste and increases the choice and variety of foods. It has also led to convenience foods and played an important part in emancipating women from the kitchen (for the effect it has on food, *see* Section V, p230). It makes life easier for us but, as with all technologies, it sometimes creates problems.

TOXIC COMPOUNDS PRODUCED ON COOKING

The industrial processing of food and cooking leads to the chemical modification of food. Oils are hydrogenated to make margarines and hard fats. Sugars caramelize on heating, meat browns on grilling or roasting. These reactions give food their flavour. Many novel compounds are formed as a result of these processes and some can be shown to cause harm in animals when consumed in large quantities.

The smoking and barbecuing of food leads to polycyclic hydrocarbon residues in food at relatively high concentrations. There is quite good evidence to suggest that these compounds are capable of causing cancer in human beings.

A significant study was carried out in Holland to see if normal cooking of food also increased the risk of cancer in rats. The rats were fed the ingredients of the typical Dutch diet either raw or cooked for a lifetime. This study found more tumours in the animals fed the Dutch diet but it did not make any difference whether it was cooked or not. So cooking is all right, but perhaps we should think twice about emigrating to Holland!

E DOES NOT STAND FOR EVIL

As we have mentioned, much of the current concern over food additives is out of all proportion to the size of the problem. Additives are substances *intentionally added* to food during processing. They are added for a variety of reasons:

- To improve appearance, texture, taste, nutritional value;
- To prolong shelf life (preservatives, anti-oxidants);
- As processing aids (emulsifiers, acidity regulators, release agents).

Food additives have to be shown to be safe, necessary and technically effective before they can be used. Unlike natural ingredients, the use of food additives is strictly controlled by law. In order to harmonize trade between EEC countries it was decided to give all additives that were approved for food use throughout the community an E-number. However, as we have seen, instead of being helpful the introduction of E-numbers has caused panic amongst consumers.

Good Es In a perfect world, we might all shop for fresh food every day and cook all our meals using raw ingredients. Unfortunately life, and in particular urban living, is just not like that. In the modern context, additives have many functions that benefit the consumer: they make food safer and make it keep longer and therefore keep food prices down. The food industry relies upon the use of additives in order to manufacture and distribute foods. The price of food has been one of the most important factors influencing food choice. If foods become prohibitively expensive people won't buy them.

The additives that stop spoilage and make food safer are the preservatives and anti-oxidants. Preservatives such as salt, vinegar, wood smoke and alcohol have been used for centuries to preserve food. *It is the safety of these traditional additives that is most in question rather than the more recently approved ones, though you wouldn't know it from what you read in the newspapers.* For example, high salt intakes have been linked to high blood pressure (*see* p108) and wood smoke contains carcinogens.

Some additives are used to enhance the nutritional value of a food. For example, cornflakes have added vitamins and minerals; margarine is fortified with vitamins A and D; white bread is fortified with iron and B-vitamins; some yeast extracts such as Marmite are fortified with vitamin B_{12}.

Some additives are used as processing aids to make novel foods. For example, it would not be possible to make low-fat spreads or soft margarines without the use of additives to emulsify water and fat. Low-calorie drinks would not be possible without artificial sweeteners.

Some vitamins are used as food additives but not for their nutritional values. Vitamin C (ascorbic acid) is used as a flour improver and enables British wheat – which is more suitable for making biscuits – to be used for bread. This saves millions of pounds each year for the balance of payments. Vitamin C also stops fresh apple juice going brown. Beta-carotene (E160) is used as a food colour and vitamin E (alpha tocopherol) is used as an anti-oxidant to stop fats going rancid.

Bad Es The additives that have attracted the most controversy are those which are used to increase the water content of food or tart up shoddy products. H.G. Wells wryly remarked that it was the aim of the food industry to sell air and water at inflated prices. It has been argued that the crafty food manufacturer is using additives to pass off second-rate food.

Food processing and storage results in the loss of colour from food so the manufacturers add colour back. Consumers have become accustomed to expect foods to be certain colours. For example, the British expect butter to be bright yellow whereas on the Continent butter is pale yellow. Consequently butter substitutes (margarine and low-fat spreads) are more brightly coloured in Britain than across the Channel.

Colour preferences vary between countries. In the USA the consumer prefers white eggs with a pale yolk. In Britain brown eggs with a dark yellow yolk are popular. The yellow colour in butter and egg yolk used to come from carotene pigments present naturally in the feed. Farmers can now change the colour of the eggs by feeding the hens a diet containing more carotene. It is interesting that objections to this practice have been made while at the same time it is being suggested that we should be eating more carotene-rich foods to help prevent cancer!

Despite the high level of public concern about additives not one death has ever been definitely attributed to the consumption of food additives in Britain. The nearest attributable death occurred when a man suffered a fatal asthmatic attack brought on after inhaling sulphur dioxide from a bottle of wine. However, a small proportion of the population, probably between 1 in 1,000 and 1 in 10,000, do show adverse reactions to some additives. In particular, the food colour tartrazine (E102) and the preservative benzoic acid (E210). A range of studies have failed to show that food additives are an important cause of hyperactivity in children (*see* Section I, p27).

FOOD PACKAGING

Mass packaging is a recent development. Foreign bodies occasionally get into food – eg, bits of machinery and extra nuts (the hexagonal, metal variety) in muesli. Almost everything we buy is packed in plastic. In their early years plastics were regarded as essentially inert material, but over the last decade some chemicals in plastic have been found to migrate into food. It's for this reason that the government has warned people not to use ordinary cling-film in ovens and microwaves. The toxicological effects of packaging material remain largely unknown but are being monitored by regulatory agencies worldwide. But suffice it to say that all our packaged food is affected by the material in which it is contained. While research is continuing, no one is suggesting all packaging should be banned. And it is worth remembering that gin or whisky served in a plastic glass suffers far more from migration of plasticizers than any packeted material.

FOOD IRRADIATION

Food irradiation is being introduced in the UK to preserve food. It is already used in thirty-six other countries. Food irradiation is a method of food processing that does not make the food radioactive and it has been used for the preparation of sterile supplies for hospitals for many years.

Irradiation is an effective means of killing insects and moulds and is seen as a clean alternative to fungicides and insecticides which might leave potentially harmful residues. It can be used to reduce the bacterial load of food and is particularly effective in decreasing the number of salmonella in poultry. But very high doses are needed to sterilize food and these can lead to off-taints and chemical changes in the food. Irradiation can also be used to accelerate the ripening of fruits and inhibit the sprouting of potatoes.

While the government and food industry are in favour of irradiation public opinion appears to be against it, especially in the wake of Chernobyl. Opponents of food irradiation complain:

- It is an attempt to sanitize the nuclear industry (rather a feeble argument as radioactive materials and radiotherapy are widely used in diagnosis and treatment of disease).
- It can be used to reduce the bacterial load of food that otherwise would be deemed unfit for consumption. (Something which has already happened – condemned prawns were zapped in Holland and sold in Britain. Clearly strict controls are necessary).
- There are no means of testing whether or not food has been irradiated.
- Not enough is known about the long-term effects of food irradiation.
- It could lead to the sale of counterfeit food – ie, food that looks fresh but is not of the same nutritional value.

But the nutrient losses that occur with irradiation are comparable with other food processes. Food irradiation has been used in some hospitals to feed patients sterile diets and many countries have used irradiation to kill pathogens in animal feeds for many years. The toxicological safety of food irradiation appears to be good.

Following the outcry of several pressure groups, the majority of British supermarkets have said that they will not use irradiation. Those suppliers that do will have to label the food they have irradiated so, in principle, we will be able to choose whether or not to buy it.

ALCOHOL

Key Points about the consumption of alcohol:

One unit is 10ml of alcohol (8g) which is equivalent to a measure of spirits, a small sherry, a glass of wine, half a pint of beer, a quarter of a pint of strong beer or cider.

Know your safe limits – up to 14 units a week for women and 21 for men.
Never drink and drive or operate machinery.
Don't mix drugs and drinks.
Avoid alcohol in pregnancy.

Alcoholic beverages have been produced by a variety of cultures for many centuries resulting in various degrees of intoxication. In developed countries alcohol is a legal social drug, yet in other cultures it is taboo – for example, the Islamic religion forbids the consumption of alcohol. And for good reason: *Excess alcohol consumption is a major cause of death and disability among the population.*

Alcohol also causes social problems such as wife battering

and child abuse and is responsible for many accidents both at work and on the road. Alcohol abuse is the most common mitigating factor offered in courts for crime. In terms of human suffering, far more is caused by alcohol than by heroin. And yet in small amounts it gives pleasure and may even be good for us. What matters most is how much is consumed and by whom.

Ethanol or ethyl alcohol is the main pharmacologically active ingredient of alcoholic drinks. It is produced by yeast fermentation of starch or sugar. A number of other substances are formed during fermentation which give various drinks their characteristic tastes and aromas. These are often referred to under the blanket name of congener. These congeners may be responsible for some of the after-effects of excess consumption. For example, red wines but not ethyl alcohol cause migraines in some people. Much fuss has been made about additives used in brewing but *the main hazard to health from alcoholic drinks is the alcohol itself*. So don't be fooled into thinking that organic wines are going to be that much better for you.

A unit of alcohol is 10ml or 8gm of ethyl alcohol (*see* Directory, p328). An alcoholic has been defined as someone who drinks more than his doctor. In our questionnaire we asked you how much you drank. Ideally you should have at least two alcohol-free days a week, so weekly limits are 21 and 14 units for men and women. Excess alcohol intake which leads to long-term damage is a daily intake in excess of 8 and 6 units in men and women, which is 56 and 42 units a week. Women break down alcohol more slowly than men because they have smaller livers, more body fat and are usually lighter than men. There are times when even one or two drinks can be too much. For example, if you drink before driving or operating machinery or if you are taking certain drugs. Concentrated bouts of drinking are more harmful than spreading your drink throughout the week.

THE WORLD ALCOHOL LEAGUE

The Italians, Australians, Germans and French are the world's heaviest drinkers and have the highest rates of alcohol-related disease. Britain and Scandinavian countries drink less. The rate of liver cirrhosis is seventeen times higher in France than in Britain. Overall, alcohol consumption has increased markedly worldwide. There are several reasons for this but probably the most important factors are lower prices, better incomes and increased availability (such as in supermarkets).

HOW DOES ALCOHOL AFFECT THE BODY?

Alcohol is absorbed more rapidly on an empty stomach than with food and diffuses rapidly into all body tissues. Alcohol dissolved in blood can diffuse into air in the lungs and this is the basis of the breathalyser test. But very little alcohol is excreted this way. Most is broken down by the liver. It takes about an hour to break down 1 unit of alcohol. This means if you drink 14 units of alcohol in an evening, you would probably still have excess alcohol in your blood the next morning, possibly more than the legal limit for driving.

The acute effects of alcohol consumption were accurately described by Shakespeare as 'Nose painting, sleep and urine. Lechery, sir, it provokes and unprovokes: it provokes the desire, but it takes away the performance.' One or two drinks cause mild sedation, flushing, increase in heart rate and increased secretion of gastric juices. Intellectual processes are not impaired providing there is no time-limit imposed. But complex reactions involving rapid decision making are impaired. At higher doses co-ordination becomes markedly impaired and the secretion of several hormones is inhibited. This causes diuresis (ie, wanting to pee) and 'brewer's droop' followed by motor inco-ordination ('leglessness'), analgesia (loss of sensitivity to pain) and sleep. Death from respiratory depression occurs with very high intakes.

Hangovers resulting from dehydration and congeners in the alcohol are best remedied by drinking plenty of water before going to bed.

HEALTH CONSEQUENCES RESULTING FROM OF EXCESS ALCOHOL CONSUMPTION

Acute pancreatitis (inflammation of the pancreas) This may follow binge-drinking in susceptible individuals. This is a potentially fatal disorder.

Cancer Regular drinking definitely increases the risk of cancer of the mouth, throat, stomach and liver and possibly that of the breast. Drinkers who smoke are at greatly increased risk (*see* the table on p158). It is believed that the alcohol dissolves harmful material in the smoke. The type of alcohol does not make that much difference but spirits tend to be worse for causing cancer of the mouth and throat. Beer, but not lager, seems to be linked to cancer of the rectum amongst heavy drinkers.

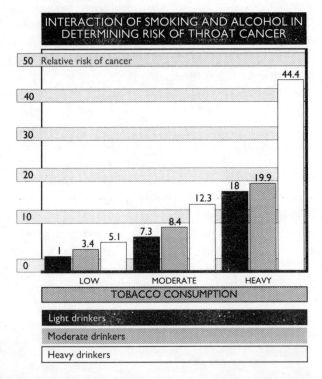

Cirrhosis The long-term effects of alcohol lead to liver damage. The liver first becomes infiltrated with fat and then

150

becomes scarred – this scarring is called cirrhosis. About 20 per cent of heavy drinkers develop cirrhosis and women are more susceptible than men.

Foetal damage   Heavy alcohol consumption (8 units a day or more) during pregnancy damages the foetus causing birth defects and gives rise to the characteristic foetal alcohol syndrome: the baby is of low birth weight, low intelligence and has a characteristic flattened face and cleft palate. All alcoholic drinks in the US now have to carry a warning about this.

Gout   There is good evidence that boozing can precipitate attacks of gout. Gout results from high levels of uric acid in blood and alcohol interferes with the excretion of uric acid by the kidney into urine.

Heart problems   Abnormalities in heart rhythm may be caused by bouts of heavy drinking and may lead to sudden death. Cardiologists call it 'holiday heart' because it often occurs when people have been drinking too much on holiday.

High blood pressure   Drinking more than two to three drinks a day raises blood pressure. High blood pressure is a major causative factor in strokes and heavy drinkers are known to have a high rate of strokes.

Obesity   Alcohol and, in particular, beer drinking causes obesity – the characteristic beer drinker's paunch. Beer is more fattening than wine or spirits (2 pints of beer provide 368 kcal, half a bottle of red wine 255 kcal and 4 single measures of whisky 200 kcal).

Vitamin deficiencies   Derelict alcoholics are often found to be suffering from nutritional deficiencies because they literally run on alcohol and eat little food. Thiamin and vitamin B_{12} deficiency cause damage to the nervous system leading to 'the shakes' and loss of sensation. Prolonged heavy drinking literally pickles the brain which shrinks in size. It also shrinks the testicles!

A TOT A DAY KEEPS THE DOCTOR AWAY

More than 2 million people in Britain drink dangerous amounts of alcohol. However, studies have found that people who drink two to three drinks a day have a lower death rate than the average and lower than even teetotallers. One explanation advanced by Professor Gerry Shaper is that the teetotallers are a sick population. That is, they are reformed alcoholics and people who are already ill. However, other studies have shown that moderate alcohol consumption protects us from coronary heart disease. It seems, therefore, that you can get away with up to two to three drinks a day. But remember, there are times when even one or two drinks can be too much. For example, if you are driving, pregnant or taking certain drugs.

FOOD RISKS IN PERSPECTIVE

At the beginning of this section we showed you how diet-related disease is a major risk and that problems relating to food additives and pesticides are relatively insignificant (*see* p126). But everything is bad for you if you eat too much of it. The Swiss sage and physician Paracelsus (1493–1541) said 'All things are poisons and nothing is without toxicity. Only the dose prevents anything not to be poisonous.' So the question is, what are the risks that should worry us and how do we work them out? First a few definitions:

- **Toxicity** is the ability of a substance to cause injury.
- **Hazard** is the ability of that substance to cause harm under the conditions in which it is used.
- **Risk** is a measure of hazard – it tells us how big the hazard is.

The risk to an individual depends upon the toxicity of the substance, how much is consumed (the dose), for how long (the exposure) and the age and health of the individual. For example, it is known that cigarette smoking is linked to lung cancer. Heavy smokers have a twenty times greater risk of dying from lung cancer than those who have never smoked. However, the risk is also determined by how many cigarettes are smoked a day, how long people have been smoking and their age and sex.

It is not possible to eliminate risk but it is possible to reduce risk. This involves identifying the number of people and any subsections of the population who may be at *increased* risk.

IDENTIFYING THOSE AT RISK

Enthusiasts for a particular food are sometimes at greater-than-average risk of harm. Every year in Europe there are a number of deaths caused by people picking and eating poisonous mushrooms by mistake. Deaths from fungi poisoning are rare in Britain because the pastime of picking wild mushrooms is less popular. Conversely, sometimes the consumption of an everyday food has an adverse effect on the health of a very small minority. When individuals at high risk can be identified dietary advice can be targeted at that group. For example, intolerance to the protein gluten (found in wheat, oats, rye and barley) causes coeliac disease. People with coeliac disease have to avoid bread, oats and flour.

Allergies   Some people react adversely to a number of foods. About 4 per cent of the population develop a rash when they eat strawberries. A high proportion of oriental people cannot tolerate cow's milk as adults and get diarrhoea. Some adverse reactions are allergies. Allergies are an exaggerated response of the immune system to certain substances, usually proteins. They typically result in skin reactions such as urticaria (nettle rash) and hives (bumps) or eczema. They also cause runny eyes and can lead to an asthmatic attack. The most common food allergies are to wheat, soya, corn, milk and shellfish. Allergies to food additives are far less common.

How severe allergic reactions can be is illustrated by this case reported in the *British Medical Journal*. A young man who knew he had a severe allergy to peanuts had carefully avoided peanuts and food containing peanuts. One day he ordered a burger. He was served a vegeburger which, unknown to him, contained peanuts. He died half an hour later of an acute allergic reaction.

The prevalence of allergies to peanuts is very low. Only four other cases are recorded in the world literature. Compare this with the number of deaths through choking on peanuts which averages about fifty annually in Britain.

Vulnerable groups   Often it is not possible to identify high-risk individuals so dietary advice cannot be targeted so accurately. However, experience tells us that certain groups of people are more at risk and we call these 'vulnerable groups'. They include the very young, pregnant women, the elderly and sick. For example, it is known that food poisoning has much more serious consequences in these groups than in healthy and unpregnant adults. Consequently advice is often targeted at these groups rather than the general population.

In 1989 a large number of cases of food poisoning were

linked with the consumption of eggs contaminated with salmonella bacteria. The strain of salmonella identified in the patients was the same as that found in the eggs (salmonella enteridis phage type 4). Outbreaks of salmonella had previously been linked to the consumption of uncooked eggs in foods such as mousse and ice-cream.

It was estimated that 1 in 40,000 British eggs might be contaminated with salmonella. As the average Briton consumes about three eggs a week then the probability of an individual consuming a contaminated egg was very small (1 in 13,300). But as about 150 million eggs were being sold every week, 3,000–4,000 of these would have been contaminated eggs. This could have lead to between 156,000 and 208,000 cases of salmonella poisoning a year.

Salmonella poisoning can be fatal in vulnerable groups, but in healthy adults the consequences are less dire (vomiting and diarrhoea). So the Department of Health warned us all not to eat raw eggs, but then subsequently warned the vulnerable groups not to consume lightly cooked eggs. It regarded the hazard to healthy people acceptable but unacceptable to vulnerable groups.

The population approach   When the whole population or a high proportion are at risk it is sometimes worthwhile treating the whole population. For example, where goitre is endemic adding iodine to salt drastically reduces the incidence of goitre. Another example is afforded by fluoride. In areas where the level of fluoride in drinking water is naturally 1mg/litre rates of tooth decay are much lower than where it is lower. Fluoride reacts with minerals in teeth to make them more resistant to bacterial decay. As a result of this finding fluoride is added to the water supply in many areas. The result has been a drastic fall in the prevalence of dental caries in those areas. At the time of fluoridation of water supplies objections were raised suggesting that the long-term effects of fluoride were unknown (which was not true). Also people saw it as adding chemicals to water and objected to it on 'moral grounds' suggesting the authorities would be putting sedatives or contraceptives in the water next! Similar unbalanced arguments have been made against other measures that clearly benefit the majority (eg, the wearing of seatbelts in cars).

A SENSE OF PROPORTION

Something that increases your risk of disease by a very small amount is not as important as something that does it by a lot. It is known that out of a million heavy smokers about a quarter will die prematurely from smoking-related diseases. That is 250,000 deaths. The estimated risk of cancer from exposure to the chemical Alar over a lifetime might result in forty-five cases per million. Cigarette smoking is a known hazard, whereas Alar is a hypothetical hazard. There is no evidence that anybody has ever died from cancer due to exposure to Alar. If you want to avoid disease and live longer what you need to do is identify the main avenues of risk and tackle them. It's not going to do you any good avoiding fruit and vegetables because you are worried about chemicals such as Alar, particularly if you smoke heavily.

Some people don't give up smoking because they are worried about putting on weight. However, the risk to health of being slightly overweight is less than that of smoking. Being very fat (ie, more than 80 per cent overweight) increases the risk of dying prematurely by about 50 per cent. But a very fat non-smoker is no more at risk than a normal weight heavy smoker. Fat smokers get the worst of both worlds and have at least a 100 per cent greater risk of dying prematurely.

People typically discount the adverse consequences of their actions, particularly when they bring pleasure – as with smoking, alcohol consumption and over-eating. They would rather focus on external causes of involuntary risks, tending to focus on involuntary risks they think they can 'see' – pollution, pesticide residues, food additives, nuclear power. As we shall see, these are not considered to be major factors in causing human cancer. *We suggest you act to change your lifestyle where the risk to health is well established.*

WHAT ARE THE MAJOR RISKS FROM FOOD?

Will I live longer? Will I have less disability? These are the key questions. Against this we have to consider the quality of life. We want to live longer – not just make it seem longer.

Any increase in life-expectancy is likely to result from preventing causes of premature death. Up until the age of forty-five, the main causes of death are accidents (a high proportion of which involve alcohol). In the forty-five to sixty-four age group the main causes of death are heart disease, cancer and stroke. As we have shown, diet is clearly linked with heart disease and stroke. We rest our case with the following table:

Major causes of death in England and Wales in men and women aged 45–64 in 1989

Cause	Men	Women
Coronary heart disease	18,561	5,388
Stroke	2,653	2,062
Lung Cancer	5,792	2,760
Colon Cancer	1,185	1,011
Breast Cancer	-	4,432
Prostatic Cancer	628	-
Other Cancers	9,608	7,685
Accidents	1,908	836
Food poisoning	2	5

Source: Office of Population, Censuses and Surveys

Nutritional imbalance is believed to play an important role in causing some cancers, as we have already discussed. Sir Richard Doll and Richard Peto estimate that diet may play an even bigger role than smoking in causing cancer. But as you can see below, they estimate that food additives account for less than 1 per cent of all cancers (and that certain food additives may even protect against cancer).

Although food poisoning is an acknowledged public health problem, it is not a major cause of death. We have attempted to pull together all the changes in diet that might reduce risk of disease and have given an indication of the degree of certainty of benefit. The following table should give you some idea of what you can get away with . . . which is what it is all about.

Proportions of cancer deaths attributed to various different factors

Per cent of all cancer deaths

Factor or class of factors	Best estimate
Diet	35
Tobacco	30
Infection	10
Reproductive and sexual behaviour	7
Occupation	4
Alcohol	3
Geophysical factors	3
Pollution	2
Medicines and medical products	1
Food additives	1

Source: Doll & Peto

Having studied the most likely causes of death for middle-aged people and having identified the most likely causes of cancer, we have now established the dietary modifications most likely to benefit us.

Reduction in Risk	Dietary modification	Certainty of benefit
Heart disease, diabetes, gallstones, cancer of gallbladder and uterus	Decrease calorie intake to reduce obesity	Certain
Cancer of colon, rectum, post-menopausal breast cancer		Possible
Cancer of mouth, throat, larynx, liver, cirrhosis of the liver, stroke	Less alcohol	Certain
Cancer of breast and rectum		Possible
Dental caries	Less sugar	Certain
Heart disease and stroke	Less saturated fat	Highly probable
Stomach cancer	More fruit and green yellow vegetables	Highly probable
Cancer of colon and rectum		Probable
Heart disease	More oily fish	Highly probable
Stomach cancer, stroke	Less salt-preserved food	Probable
Cancer of colon and rectum, diverticular disease	More starchy foods	Probable
Cancer of colon, rectum, breast, and pancreas, heart disease	Less fat	Possible
Many cancers	More carotene rich foods	Possible
Cancer	Avoid food additives	Unlikely
Cancer	Only eat organic food	Unlikely

So the main risks to health from diet are not getting a sufficient intake of nutrients, obesity and related disorders, coronary heart disease, dental caries (tooth decay) and certain types of cancer. Risks vary through the life-cycle. With children the main risks are not getting enough of the right type of food to support normal growth and development. With adults we should be concerned with avoiding diet-related disease.

In this section we have identified the main risk to health from food and told you what you can get away with. The lessons are:

- As far as the young are concerned, getting an adequate intake of nutrients is the priority.
- Dietary deficiencies are rare in adults.
- The average British diet is a major cause of ill-health leading to obesity and among the highest rates of heart disease in the world.
- Our national diet is unhealthily high in fat and sugar and low in lean meat, fish, fruit, vegetables and starchy foods.
- There are key factors which enable you to change your eating habits for the better.
- In most cases only small tweaks are needed to the typical diet, not radical changes.

Our requirements for food change throughout our lives. So in the next section we have put together practical advice for you, whatever age you are. Why not enroll in *The Food Revolution*?

SECTION IV
THE SEVEN AGES OF MAN

... One man in his time plays many parts,
His acts being seven ages. At first the infant,
Mewling and puking in the nurse's arms;
Then the whining schoolboy, with his satchel
And shining morning face, creeping like a snail
Unwillingly to school. And then the lover,
Sighing like furnace, with a woeful ballad
Made to his mistress' eyebrow. Then a soldier,
Full of strange oaths, and bearded like the pard,
Jealous in honour, sudden and quick in quarrel,
Seeking the bubble reputation
Even in the cannon's mouth. And then the justice,
In fair round belly with good capon lin'd
With eyes severe and beard of formal cut,
Full of wise saws and modern instances;
And so he plays his part. The sixth age shifts
Into lean and slipper'd pantaloon,
With spectacles on nose and pouch on side;
His youthful hose, well sav'd, a world too wide
For his shrunk shank; and his big manly voice,
Turning again towards childish treble, pipes
And whistles in his sound. Last scene of all,
That ends this strange eventful history,
In second childishness and mere oblivion;
Sans teeth, sans eyes, sans taste, sans everything.

Shakespeare, *As You Like It*, Act 2, Scene vii

In this section we look at each of Shakespeare's seven ages, since our food needs change dramatically as we go through life. Where necessary we have repeated information so as to make the study of each age complete. You can refer directly to the age group you currently belong to if you wish. But before the seven ages we have an eighth age that Shakespeare overlooked.

161

PREGNANCY AND LACTATION

Diet in pregnancy is very important both for the baby and the mother. The baby is most vulnerable to diet in the first four months of pregnancy. After that age it is less vulnerable and is more of a parasite on the mother. From the mother's standpoint, a good diet in pregnancy is necessary to protect her health and also to build up reserves to prepare for lactation.

There is no truth in the saying that women have to eat for two during pregnancy. A number of changes occur that make women use food more efficiently. Menstrual periods stop so iron is conserved in the body. The absorption of several nutrients from food is increased and the body squanders less protein and energy. Studies have looked at what women eat during pregnancy and found that they don't eat any more calories than normal.

The foetus is most vulnerable in the first four months of pregnancy. After that time it is more robust. *Exposure to drugs and excess alcohol in early pregnancy can cause birth defects. So you should avoid all drugs and alcohol during pregnancy.* Neural tube defects which lead to Spina Bifida are more common in Northern Ireland than in the rest of England and have been linked with a low intake of fruit and vegetables. Women who had one child with Spina Bifida are at high risk of having a second child with the disorder. It has been found that women at high risk of giving birth to babies with neural tube defects can be partially protected by vitamin supplements containing folate around the period of conception. The mothers who give birth to babies with Spina Bifida do not show any of the classical symptoms of folic acid deficiency and it is believed that the high intake of folic acid may be overcoming some metabolic defect. Although supplements may help prevent birth defects excessive intakes (more than ten times the RDA) of vitamin A should be avoided. As a portion of liver contains 20–40 times the RDA, the government has cautioned women who are pregnant or who may become pregnant to avoid eating liver.

Most women put on about two stone in pregnancy. A large proportion of this is the baby, the placenta and amniotic fluid. The rest – about 4kg (9lbs) – is body fat. Fat deposition in pregnancy is an entirely natural process and happens to all mammals. The fat acts as an energy store to help subsidize the energy cost of lactation. Each kilogram of fat deposited during pregnancy can be cashed in during lactation to yield 9,000 calories, which is sufficient to support the cost in energy of producing 10 litres of milk (16 pints). That's enough to support a baby for about twenty-five days. Mothers who put on a lot of fat while they are pregnant do not need to eat as much during lactation as those who put on very little. However, excessive weight gain is undesirable. If you don't breast-feed you are going to have to lose the fat you put on during pregnancy. This may be one reason why some women get fatter with each pregnancy.

The amount of breast-milk you produce is to some extent affected by your diet but also by your hormones and state of mind. If you do not produce enough milk it is generally due to these factors rather than an inadequate diet. (Frequent suckling stimulates milk production and some wet nurses have been known to produce up to 2 litres of milk a day!) However, the vitamin content of your breast-milk is definitely affected by your diet. If you have a vitamin deficiency it means your baby will get one too. The only vitamin likely to be low in breast-milk in developed countries is vitamin B_{12}, particularly in vegans and vegetarians. Some years ago we found that vegan mothers who were not taking supplementary vitamin B_{12} were producing milk with very low levels of vitamin B_{12}. A case of vitamin B_{12} deficiency resulted in a baby fed by vegan mother who herself had a deficient intake but showed no signs of deficiency. The baby was treated by giving the mother vitamin B_{12} supplements. Vegans and vegetarians who are nearly vegan must make sure they have adequate intakes of vitamin B_{12} in their diets (such as fortified soya milks and Marmite) or take a supplement.

It is important to have a good intake of calcium during pregnancy and lactation to ensure you replace the calcium lost to the foetus and to the baby during lactation. Most authorities recommend that pregnant and lactating women eat more calcium. Foods rich in calcium are:

- milk
- cheese (especially Parmesan)
- dark green leafy vegetables

Pregnant women should avoid soft rinded cheese (eg, Camembert, Brie and in particular goat's cheese) because of the risk of listeriosis.

Vegan women are advised to take calcium supplements during pregnancy and lactation. Many doctors prescribe iron and folic acid tablets to mothers (vegetarians and meat eaters alike) during pregnancy as a safeguard against anaemia. Supplementing your diet with iron during pregnancy also means that your baby will be born with greater stores of iron. It is important not to exceed the recommended dosage as excess iron intakes can be harmful (*see* Section III, p376).

Women can have strange passions for food when they are pregnant but this is not related to any specific dietary need. Some women have even been known to eat coal or clay! It is often said that stout beers (eg, Guinness) are good for pregnant women. There's no truth in this and current medical advice is to avoid all alcoholic drinks during pregnancy.

INFANCY

A newborn baby depends upon milk for the first few months of life. The milk has to support rapid growth. Human milk is sweet tasting (owing to its high content of milk sugar or lactose), high in fat and relatively low in protein. The fat supplies dietary energy, enables the absorption of the fat-soluble vitamins and supplies the essential fatty acids which are needed as structural components of all cells in the body.

At the turn of the century babies that could not be breast-fed seldom survived. If a mother fell ill and there was nobody to wet-nurse the baby then it would usually die. Cow's milk at that time was responsible for the transmission of diseases such as tuberculosis. The advent of sterilization meant that babies could be fed sterile milk. However, the sterilization of milk destroyed vitamin C and infants fed this milk developed scurvy and died.

The introduction of 'humanized' infant formula around about 1915 revolutionized infant feeding. Infant milk formulae attempt to imitate the composition of human milk. They are usually based on cow's milk and other ingredients are added to make the level of fat, protein, carbohydrate, minerals and vitamins similar to that of mature human milk.

It has been argued that the introduction of infant formulae was partly responsible for the sharp decline in infant mortality between the First and Second World Wars. However, artificial feeds for babies need to be made up carefully with sterile water. Exporting the practice of bottle-feeding to developing countries where hygiene conditions are poor and water is contaminated with bacteria has led to increased disease and malnutrition. The problem is so great that the World Health Organization wants to ban artificial feeds in developing countries. As we shall see, there are a number of reasons why breast-feeding is regarded as best, although it is possible to bottle-feed babies safely and mothers who choose not to breast-feed should not be made to feel guilty. Also there are times when a baby *has* to be bottle fed. For example, if the mother is ill or cannot produce enough milk.

Specially made milk formulae have enabled children who would otherwise have died to survive. For example, the inborn error of metabolism, 'phenylketonuria', affects about 1 in 10,000 babies. Babies with this defect cannot break down the essential amino acid phenylalanine. Consequently the level of phenylalanine in blood rises to very high levels and causes brain damage. Phenylketonuria is now diagnosed by the 'Guthrie' test shortly after birth and can be treated by giving a special milk formula low in phenylalanine. Special milks are also used for feeding premature babies and also for children with other inborn errors of metabolism such as congenital galactosaemia (caused by an inherited enzyme deficiency that prevents the infant metabolizing the sugar galactose normally).

Human milk does not contain enough protein and nutrients to support the growth of premature infants. Specially modified milks sometimes based on human milk are used to feed these babies.

Cow's milk contains about four times as much protein as human milk. Up to the mid-1960s artificial milk formulae had a higher protein content than human milk. This was believed to have led to accelerated growth rate in some infants. The bottle-fed babies tended to be longer than breast-fed children. If the high level of protein in infant formulae did increase adult height we might expect to see a decrease in adult height in the next ten years as infant formulae now have a similar protein content to human milk. But it is more likely that the increase in average height seen in children born in the sixties has more to do with better health than infant feeding practices. Diseases such as diarrhoea and respiratory infections cause growth faltering in young children. If growth faltering occurs at a critical stage of bone growth then complete catch-up growth may not occur. Improvements in housing conditions, general hygiene and immunization against childhood diseases (such as whooping cough and measles) may have been more important than changes in diet.

BREAST IS BEST

Besides providing all the nutrients required, breast milk also transfers some immunity to the baby. The first milk secreted, colostrum, has a different composition from mature milk and contains proteins called globulins that give the newborn infant some protection from infectious diseases. Milk also has a high lactose content and other substances that favour the growth of the bacteria *Lactobacillus bifidus* in the baby's gut. The colonization of the baby's gut with this bacteria helps exclude harmful disease-causing bacteria. Thus breast-feeding reduces the chances of gut infections in the newborn. In some cultures, colostrum is withheld from the infant. This practice is unwise as it prevents the transfer of immunity from mother to child.

Breast-feeding is certainly convenient for fathers. They do not have to get up in the middle of the night to feed the squawking brat. Indeed, many mothers find themselves becoming breast-feeding drudges. The newborn infant has to adapt from being dependent upon maternal blood for nutrients to obtaining food from the gut. A full-term infant has quite large stores of fat to tide her over the first few days of life while her gut gets used to digesting milk. Breast-milk is also much better digested than most artificial milks. The composition of breast-milk does depend to some extent on the mother's diet. However, the levels of protein, fat, lactose and minerals tend not to vary. The levels of vitamins in human milk depend on the amounts in the mother's diet. For example, cases of vitamin B_{12} deficiency have occurred in infants breast-fed by vegan mothers whose diets were deficient in vitamin B_{12}.

The composition of fat in human milk is also changed by diet. Mothers who consume larger than average amounts of polyunsaturated fats produce polyunsaturated breast-milk. For example, the breast-milk from vegetarian mothers contains about twice as much polyunsaturated fat as that from meat eating mothers. However, this seems to do no harm to the baby.

The full-term infant typically consumes 400–500ml of milk a day rising to about 850ml/day at about three to four months. One disconcerting thing about breast-feeding is that you cannot see how much the baby is taking. The best assessment of whether a baby is getting enough is whether she is putting on weight. Most babies gain about 110–140g (4–5oz) a week in the first three months and by the age of six months they should have doubled their birth weight. You should not be too concerned if a baby is a bit podgy. Most fat babies do not become fat adults. However, most fat adults were fat babies. To be slightly overweight is actually an advantage to health in the first few years of life. The growth of chubby babies is less severely affected by childhood infections because they have energy reserves to draw on. The table below shows the normal range of weights for babies of different ages and size. If your baby is not growing well, see your doctor.

NORMAL RANGE OF BABY WEIGHTS IN FIRST YEAR OF LIFE

Age in weeks	lbs and ounces	kilograms
0	6–2 to 9–0	2.8 to 4.1
4	7–4 to 10–10	3.3 to 4.8
8	8–12 to 12–14	4.0 to 5.9
12	10–2 to 14–12	4.6 to 6.7
16	11–8 to 16–10	5.2 to 7.6
20	12–10 to 18–4	5.7 to 8.3
24	13–14 to 19–8	6.3 to 8.9
28	14–10 to 21–0	6.6 to 9.5
32	15–8 to 22–0	7.0 to 10.0
36	16–4 to 22–14	7.4 to 10.4
40	16–12 to 23–8	7.6 to 10.7
44	17–4 to 24–4	7.8 to 11.0
48	18–4 to 24–12	8.3 to 11.3
52	18–8 to 25–10	8.4 to 11.6

BOTTLE-FEEDING

Although much is made of the psychological bonding between mother and baby with breast-feeding, it is also possible to develop the same relationship with bottle-feeding. People choose to bottle-feed for a variety of reasons – an inability to breast-feed, the mother returning to work or a decision to share the responsibility between parents more evenly. There is nothing wrong with any of these reasons.

Modified cow's milk formulae falls into two categories: those for young infants under six months and those for babies over six months. *You must not give formulae for infants over six months to younger babies.* Here are a few other dos and don'ts when making up feeds:

- Make sure you wash your hands before making up a feed. (You might be surprised how many people don't.)
- Make up the formula properly with boiled water. Do not use softened water to make up feeds because many commercial water softeners increase the sodium content of water, which puts a strain on the baby's kidneys.
- Never take water from the hot tap because it can be contaminated by lead and copper in your plumbing. Run the mains tap for about half a minute before drawing the water.
- Make sure that you fill the scoop provided exactly to the top. Never add an extra scoop for luck or a heaped scoop because it will make the milk too concentrated and put a strain on the baby's kidneys. (In the USA most baby feeds are now sold ready to feed in cartons and this practice is catching on in Britain. Besides being convenient it also ensures that the milk is not made up too concentrated or too weak.)
- Always check the temperature of the milk before giving it to the baby by squirting a little milk on to the back of your hand. It should be lukewarm. Some parents warm up milk in a microwave. The Department of Health does not recommend this practice but some manufacturers of baby milks do. You must be very careful to make sure the milk is well mixed and not too hot. *Heating milk in a microwave can lead to hot spots in the milk. Remove the cap, teat and disc before you heat the milk, make sure you shake the bottle well after heating and test the temperature.*
- Always clean out the bottle and sterilize the teats. Make sure there are no residual bits of milk dried out in the bottom of the bottle as these can harbour germs.

Newborn babies need about six to eight feeds a day, but as they get older they need fewer feeds. If the weather is hot they will need extra fluid. Boiled water is the best thing to give them. Don't give them sugary drinks because even at this age it can damage their tooth buds.

VOMITING OR POSSETTING

Many babies bring up dollops of milk shortly after a feed usually followed by large burp. Some babies posset more than others but providing they are growing normally there is nothing to worry about. Severe vomiting is a different matter and you should consult your doctor straight away.

DIARRHOEA

Loose stools are very common in breast-fed babies – it looks like mustard. Some babies have ten to twelve motions a day (if you're unlucky!). Diarrhoea is much more watery and is usually accompanied by lots of mucus. The most important thing to do if a baby has diarrhoea is to keep her fluid intake up. If the diarrhoea is profuse you will need to give her some oral rehydration solution such as Dioralyte: let the baby suck small amounts off a spoon. But seek medical help immediately. In an emergency you can make up your own from a level teaspoon of salt and eight teaspoons of sugar in 1 litre of water.

COT DEATH

Cot death – or sudden infant death syndrome (SIDS) – accounts for two-fifths of all deaths between one and twelve months in babies. Each year 1,500 babies die in Britain. It is more common in boys than girls and most cases occur between one and four months of age. Diet has been suggested as a possible cause but it seems to occur in both bottle-fed and breast-fed infants. The cause remains unknown and there is little parents or health professionals can do to predict risk.

Some experts now advise against babies sleeping on their fronts and all agree that an overheated room and a duvet that is too thick could cause respiratory problems.

WHEN TO INTRODUCE SOLIDS

Babies can be fed exclusively on breast-milk for up to one year. However, most parents choose to introduce other foods in the diet from about four months. The Department of Health recommends introducing other foods from about four months but some experts feel that six months is a better age because introducing foods too early increases the chance of food allergies. Milk needs to be the main food in the baby's diet until at least the age of one.

A biological sign that the child is ready to be weaned is the cutting of a tooth, which usually occurs any time after four months. Breast-feeding mothers may rapidly decide it is time to give solids to the little 'nipper'. Foods containing wheat are probably best avoided under the age of six months because of the risk of developing food allergies. The food should be a mushy gruel or a rusk. Gradually introduce a variety of foods into the diet. If you make your own baby food never add salt to it. And remember:

- Never force an infant to eat anything.
- Introduce new foods only one or two at a time.
- Don't try to introduce a new food when your baby is tired or unwell.
- Use a special drinking beaker to make the transition to drinking easier. Tuck a wedge of kitchen paper under the neck of the pip to stop the baby getting drenched by spilt drink.
- Encourage self feeding – it is wise to have one spoon for yourself and one for the baby. Give the baby food she can eat with her fingers – pieces of banana or bread soldiers are good. Only give peeled fruit without the pips.
- If the baby is about to sneeze get out of the way otherwise you will be splattered with food.
- Never leave a baby unattended with food because she can easily choke.

CHOKING

If the baby does choke put her face down over your knees and give her four gentle pats on the back. This should dislodge any food. If she stops breathing give mouth to mouth resuscitation by gently breathing into her mouth.

WEANING FOODS

The idea of weaning foods is to get the baby used to consuming foods other than milk. Commercial weaning foods are acceptable but you can make your own by liquidizing the food the rest of the family is eating. Make sure there are no lumps or bits that could cause choking. The more weaning foods a child eats the less milk she will take. Don't get upset if most of the food lands up on the floor or on the bib. Here is a list of suitable weaning foods:

- baby cereals
- mashed bananas
- scrambled eggs (cooked thoroughly not lightly)
- mashed potato with grated cheese
- mashed meat or fish (check for bones)
- puréed carrot
- mashed peas or lentils (but may make for a messy nappy)
- puréed pear or apple
- custard

Nutritional deficiencies in babies are rare in developed countries, but tend to occur when parents try to wean their babies too early. There is a macrobiotic food called kokoh, sold in some wholefood shops, that is a mixture of cereals, sesame and soya. This weaning food has led to severe malnutrition in babies because it is too dilute in nutrients. Babies aged between two and three months weaned on to this mixture have rapidly become emaciated.

Milk (breast-milk or milk formula) needs to be the main food in the diet of babies for at least the first year of life as we mentioned. After the age of one, infants can be given ordinary cow's milk to drink. *You should never give skimmed milk to babies* because it does not contain enough energy, vitamin A and essential fatty acids.

You can give the baby a drink of orange juice but dilute it one to one with water. This will give her some vitamin C. Don't give babies orange squash because it contains artificial colours and additives that are unsuitable for infants.

VITAMIN DROPS

As long as the baby is getting breast-milk or a milk formula there should be no need for vitamin drops. Some doctors recommend vitamin drops containing vitamin A, D and C. This is a good idea in winter months when exposure to sunlight is low. However, if you take the baby out for a walk in the sunlight or leave her out in the garden with her cheeks exposed she will make all the vitamin D she needs. Fluoride supplement will help protect your baby's teeth from dental decay in adult life if you live in an area where the level of fluoride in drinking water is low. If you want to find out whether the level of fluoride in your area is adequate, phone your local water company.

DUMMIES

Never give a child a bottle or comforter filled with fruit juice or syrup to suck because it will rot her front teeth.

RASHES AND ALLERGIES

Skin rashes can be related to food. Nettle rash (urticaria) can be caused by foods or contact with other things like carpets and pets. If it is food related it is pretty obvious because it happens quickly.

Eczema may affect as many as 5 per cent of children and is known to be caused mainly by food allergy. It is a red, itchy, scaly skin condition. Severe food allergies do occur in some children and the warning signs are:

173

- severe vomiting
- severe diarrhoea
- failure to grow
- itchy skin rashes

Normal children get lots of things wrong with them and food intolerance is still relatively uncommon. If they do suffer from it there is a good chance that they will grow out of it. *A proper diagnosis is essential so consult your doctor if you suspect your child has an allergy.*

FEEDING THE VEGETARIAN BABY

Most vegetarians and vegans breast-feed their babies well into the second year of life and then wean them on to their own respective diets. The growth of these children and their development are normal. If the supply of breast-milk is inadequate, infant milks based on a modified cow's milk formula can be used. There are special soya milks such as Ostersoy which have been developed for feeding babies who cannot tolerate cow's milk. These soya milks should only be used as complementary feeds for babies under the age of six months. *Never use them as the sole source of food for any length of time unless under medical supervision.*

Weaning foods such as puréed fruit and vegetables, baby cereals and rusks can be introduced at six months. There are now a number of well-balanced vegetarian weaning foods available from Robinson's and Heinz. When you begin to give more solids wholemeal bread is good to start with. Spread it with margarine and smooth peanut butter or a yeast extract. Do not fill your baby with bulky or watery foods like puréed green vegetables and fruit – these are not sufficiently concentrated forms of nutrition. These foods, of course, are part of a balanced diet but should not dominate it. Make sure the food is smooth and does not contain bits that could lead to choking. Never give unground nuts to young children. A variety of vegetarian weaning foods that are ready prepared are now available. If you are bringing your child up as a vegan you will need to give her supplements of vitamins D and B_{12}.

TODDLERS – AGED 1–5

Although toddlers have a lower rate of growth than infants, they are more prone to nutritional deficiencies. This is mainly because they have low stores of nutrients, small stomachs and, unlike older children, cannot forage for food in the kitchen when they are hungry. Children are the main victims of food shortages in developing countries. Low food intakes cause stunting of growth and decreased resistance to infection. Poor hygiene often causes diarrhoea in children and leads to further growth faltering. The combination of diarrhoeal disease and low food intake explains the high death rates in children under the age of five in Third World countries. Only 75-90 per cent of children born survive to the age of five. Fortunately malnutrition is a rare cause of death among children in developed countries and 98 per cent of children born survive to the age of fourteen. The main causes of death in children between one and five years in developed countries are congenital abnormalities and accidents.

The major nutritional hazards posed to children under the age of five are:

- A bulky diet which is too dilute in nutrients.
- A low iron intake which can result in anaemia.
- A low intake of calcium and vitamin D which can cause rickets.
- A low intake of vitamin A which can cause xerophthalmia (*see* Section VI, p419) and decreased resistance to infection.

Other hazards posed by diet are:

- Dental decay resulting from frequent exposure to sugars (as with dummies filled with undiluted syrup).
- Choking on food – nuts, fish bones, lumps of meat, fruit pips.
- Food allergies.

Obesity is not a significant problem in toddlers. Plumpness poses no hazard to health and it may even be advantageous as it can make them more robust. The main dietary risk with toddlers is not getting enough food rather than getting too much.

Toddlers have high demands for energy which they need to support their growth. Fruit and vegetables tend to be very bulky and are generally low in food energy. So a diet consisting mainly of fruit and vegetables will be low in energy. This may be desirable if you are an adult trying to lose weight but can be disastrous for a young growing child who needs plenty of energy to support growth. Strict vegetarian and macrobiotic diets can be very bulky and have been known to retard the growth of children under the age of five. On the other hand, grains, meat, fish and dairy products are high in energy and will promote growth. Consequently, when selecting a diet for young children great care should be taken to avoid giving the child a diet that is too bulky.

THE IMPORTANCE OF FAT

Fat is very important in the diet of children under the age of five years. It provides a concentrated supply of energy and thus reduces the bulk of the diet. The addition of small amounts of fat to food can double its food energy value. Decreasing fat intake drastically lowers the energy intake. A glass of skimmed milk contains 40 calories compared with 80 calories in a glass of full-cream milk.

Fat is also necessary for the absorption of the fat-soluble vitamins A, D, E and K. In parts of the world where the intake of fat is very low, vitamin A deficiency disease (xeropthalmia) is common in toddlers. The richest sources of vitamin A are liver and fish-liver oils. Good sources are butter, cheese, full-cream milk and eggs. Carotene, a substance that can be converted into vitamin A in the body, is found in large amounts in carrots and dark green leafy vegetables. Before the Second World War in Denmark vitamin A deficiency occurred in children because they were given unfortified margarine instead of butter. These days margarine is fortified by law with vitamin A so that it contains the same amount as summer butter. Skimmed milk, low-fat yoghurt and cottage cheese contain virtually no vitamin A since it is contained in the fat that is removed during processing. Although manufacturers are under no legal obligation, many low-fat spreads are also fortified with vitamin A.

Toddlers are more prone to vitamin A deficiency because they have a high rate of growth and low stores of the vitamin. Deficiency initially results in night blindness (an inability to adapt to light of low intensity) and decreased resistance to infection. But vitamin A deficiency is not seen in developed countries because the diet of pre-school children is high in fat and contains plenty of vitamin A. *More than half the vitamin A in the diet of toddlers comes from milk products.* If you fed a child on low-fat milk products and did not let her eat eggs, liver, butter and margarine you could cause vitamin A deficiency. However, as far as we know this has not yet happened. But this is another reason why *you should not put children under the age of five on a low-fat diet*.

Fat is also needed in the diet because it provides the essential fatty acids which are needed as structural components of all tissues in the body. The essential fatty acids are found in cereals, leafy vegetables, nuts, vegetable oils, meat and oily fish. Essential fatty acid deficiency was first shown to occur in babies fed exclusively on skimmed milk. The deficiency resulted in a scaly inflammation of the skin and poor growth rate.

The type of fat in our diet is important because of its relation to the risk of heart disease. Saturated fats such as those found in butter increase the level of cholesterol in blood. High levels of blood cholesterol in *adults* are linked to increased risk of heart disease especially when associated with high blood pressure and cigarette smoking. Many expert committees have recommended that we should cut down on our intake of saturated fats. However, the Department of Health in its report on Diet and Cardiovascular Disease specifically excludes children from these dietary recommendations. The reason for this is that the hypothetical risk of cardiovascular disease in later life resulting from consuming saturated fat in the first five years of life is regarded as negligible compared with the known risks of nutritional deficiency resulting from a reduction in total and dairy fat intake.

AVOIDING RICKETS

Vitamin D deficiency is probably the most common vitamin deficiency seen in Northern latitudes. It causes rickets (bow legs) in children and osteomalacia in adults. Rickets is caused by low exposure to sunlight in the winter months coupled with a low availability of calcium from the diet. But rickets is far less prevalent than in the past. Children affected with rickets have abnormally bowed legs because the process that leads to the deposition of minerals in the bone which gives it rigidity is impaired. Toddlers are prone to rickets because of the high rate of bone growth that occurs at this age.

Rickets and osteomalacia in the United Kingdom are now mainly confined to the Asian Indian population. But cases are also found in the general population from time to time. Vitamin D can be made in the body by the action of sunlight on the skin but in the absence of sufficient sunlight it is necessary to consume vitamin D in the diet. Vitamin D is needed for the absorption of calcium. There are few dietary sources of vitamin D except for oily fish, liver and fish oils – one indication that people who live in northerly latitudes need fish in their diet. But some foods – such as margarine and breakfast cereals – are also fortified with vitamin D.

People with pigmented skins such as Indians make less vitamin D on exposure to sunlight than the white population. They also accumulate less vitamin D in the summer months which they can store to tide them over winter. Lack of exposure to sunlight does not explain why rickets also occurs in some parts of the world where exposure to sunlight is high – for example in the Middle-East. It seems likely that rickets also results when the amount of calcium available from the diet is low.

Milk and milk products are a major source of calcium in Western diets. Calcium is often poorly absorbed from plants because of the presence of other compounds. For example, cereals, especially unrefined cereals such as oats, contain large amounts of a substance called phytic acid which binds with calcium and makes it unavailable to the body. The consumption of oatmeal in Northern Ireland and Scotland was formerly strongly linked with rickets. Rickets is occasionally seen in children fed vegan and macrobiotic diets. One large study of a macrobiotic community in Holland carried out by Dr Peter Dagnelie from the University of Wageningen found several cases of rickets. It seems likely that a high intake of unrefined cereals – particularly brown rice or chappatis – and a low intake of milk increases the chances of getting rickets.

There are several reasons for the decline in rickets in the UK: the introduction of 'smokeless zone' in the 1950s which allowed more ultra-violet light in sunlight to penetrate cities; an increased intake of calcium from milk products and the fortification of foods such as margarine with vitamin D.

GETTING ENOUGH IRON

Iron deficiency leading to anaemia is a potential hazard in toddlers because the iron content of milk is low, the body is growing rapidly and body reserves of iron are low.

About ten years ago a study in the United States found that a high proportion of black toddlers suffered iron deficiency anaemia. More recent studies suggest that it is now less common. The reason for the decrease is believed to be the supplementation of many foods with iron.

Iron is best absorbed from the diet in the form that is found in red meat. Iron from plant sources is less well absorbed and, like that of calcium, is inhibited by substances such as phytic acid. Whole wheat is a good source of iron and in Britain white bread is fortified with iron. Rice, on the other hand, is a poor source of iron. Dark green vegetables are a good source but the iron is poorly absorbed. (In addition, most toddlers loathe dark green vegetables!) Many breakfast cereals (such as cornflakes) are fortified with iron, but ironically many of the 'health food' type cereals such as muesli are not.

It is not known how common iron deficiency anaemia is in British toddlers. Anaemia can only be diagnosed by a blood test and it is regarded as unethical to take a blood sample from a random selection of toddlers to see if they are anaemic. Iron deficiency anaemia has been found in toddlers fed macrobiotic diets in Holland but British toddlers fed vegan or vegetarian diets do not appear to be particularly prone to anaemia. But iron deficiency is not uncommon in toddlers of Asian vegetarians.

AVOIDING TOOTH DECAY

The term 'fruit-juice caries' is used by some dentists to describe the tooth decay in babies and toddlers caused by undiluted fruit juices or other sugar solutions in a bottle or comforter which a child sucks for *prolonged periods of time*. It causes the erosion of tooth enamel of the front teeth and can even result from prolonged demand breast-feeding in children aged about two! Caries occurs because sugar is fermented by bacteria in the mouth to produce acids which dissolve the enamel of the teeth. Prevention of caries involves making sure that sugary solutions do not remain in the mouth for long periods of time (as with sucking a boiled sweet), ensuring an adequate intake of fluoride in childhood and good oral hygiene – in other words, brushing teeth after a meal.

ALLERGIES

Allergies to food can arise in the first few years of life and are largely inherited (eg, asthma). The chances of food allergies are increased by the premature introduction of foods in an infant's diet. This is because a gland called the thymus (it makes the white blood cells that control hypersensitivity) is particularly active at this age. However, well over a third of young children stop reacting to the offending food before they reach the age of three.

The term 'allergy' is used to cover a whole range of different conditions – typical signs are failure to thrive, skin rashes and runny eyes. The term 'failure to thrive' is used to describe children who are not growing properly. There are many causes but one frequently overlooked is whether or not the child is eating enough.

Failure to thrive can result from digestive disorders some of which may be caused by allergies. Any parent should first seek advice from their general practitioner rather than attempt self-diagnosis. The most common food allergies are to wheat, milk, eggs, soya and shellfish. Allergies to meat are relatively uncommon. Food additives are not used in baby foods but if your children are eating the same food as the rest of the family they may be getting some additives which are best avoided in childhood. Two additives have been identified as causing adverse reactions in children – tartrazine (E102), which is a yellow food colour added to many foods, and the preservative sodium benzoate (E211). Sunset yellow (E110), another food colour, was also found to cause adverse reactions but is now little used. If, as a family, you have a history of allergic reactions (eczema, asthma, aspirin intolerance) you should avoid giving toddlers foods containing these additives. Allergies to egg have also been known to occur after children have been vaccinated with a vaccine raised in egg.

Treatment of the allergy simply involves avoiding the food in question. If a child is allergic to a food then it is important to ensure the nutrients that were provided by that food are replaced. For example, in a child with an allergy to cow's milk, goat's or ewe's milk could be used. This is probably preferable to soya milk as allergies to soya are common. Also soya milk is nutritionally inferior to goat's or ewe's milk and has been found to contain high levels of aluminium. In any case if you suspect that your child is allergic to a food get a proper diagnosis from your doctor.

VEGETARIAN DIETS

Toddlers reared on vegan or the more restricted vegetarian diets are at risk of vitamin B_{12} deficiency. However, there are sources of vitamin B_{12} acceptable to vegans such as fortified yeast extract and soya milks as well as meat substitutes. Meat substitutes also have iron and zinc added to them by law. Provided care is taken to avoid the known pitfalls of too much bulky food, rickets and vitamin B_{12} deficiency, children can be successfully reared on vegan diets.

CHILDREN – AGED 5–11

Children should be encouraged to acquire a love for bread.
Nelson 1750.

There are several reasons why children of this age are much less at risk from nutritional deficiencies than younger children. Their requirements are lower as they grow more slowly. If they are hungry they can fill up on food by a foray into the kitchen, usually to the biscuit tin! One child of our acquaintance can hear the rattle of the biscuit tin from the other end of the house and appears expectantly like Pavlov's dog waiting for a biscuit. It is at this stage that parental control over what children eat declines. Children of this age start to assert their own preferences and dislikes for food. Some of these assertions are ways of expressing their individuality. Parents should persist in offering a variety of foods rather than giving in to the fickle whims of a child. Tooth decay is the major diet related disorder in this age group. Obesity is not very common – fewer than 3 in 100 are obese.

TOOTH DECAY

Children are most susceptible to dental caries at an age when their permanent teeth are erupting and they are guzzling lots of sweets. Fortunately, the rate of dental caries has fallen dramatically over the past twenty years. This is mainly due to fluoridation of water supplies and better oral hygiene. Confectionery consumption has not changed. The Germans now have worse teeth than the British. But dental caries is still much more of a problem in the economically deprived parts of Britain. It has been said that 80 per cent of the caries is in 20 per cent of the population. The frequent consumption of sugary foods such as biscuits, sweets, sugary drinks (including fresh fruit juices) as well as fruit between meals is strongly linked with caries. Children with an inherited disorder that prevents them eating sugars have teeth free of caries. Some foods rot teeth more than others, notably toffee and biscuits. Chocolate is less cariogenic. Sugar eaten during a meal has little effect because other food and drink carry it away with them when swallowed.

Sweets Now here we have a real problem. There is little doubt that the frequent consumption of confectionery causes tooth decay. There are two approaches. First you prohibit the consumption of all sweets (only to find that Granny or the next-door neighbour is undermining your attempts and providing them with sweets). The second is a damage limitation approach. This involves only letting them have sweets once or twice a week or on special occasions. Also try to discourage them from eating the type of sweet that gets stuck in their teeth like toffees and boiled sweets – chocolate is better. Make sure they brush their teeth after eating sweets. Explain to them why you won't let them have sweets every day and they will start to take responsibility for their own teeth. Offer a graphic description of toothache!

DOES IT MATTER WHAT THEY EAT?

We should be concerned about what children eat at this age because some diseases that occur in later life have their foundations in childhood and also because eating behaviour is learnt in early life.

Many parents fear that, left to their own devices, children would subsist on a diet of sweets, fizzy drinks, crisps, biscuits and cake. However, measurements of what children actually eat show that they do not select a nutritionally deficient diet. Most primary school children eat three meals a day and a couple of snacks. Typically these are a cereal breakfast, a snack at break, a packed lunch or school lunch, a snack when they get home and high tea.

Breakfast Cereal breakfasts have replaced the traditional English breakfast of bacon, eggs and fried bread which has been described as a heart attack on a plate. Parents are often blackmailed by children into buying cereals because of the 'frees' inside them, usually a plastic toy or sticker. Indeed TV advertising of breakfast cereals is often targeted directly at school children. Most households must have suffered from the distorted cereal packet caused by the hand thrust down to the bottom of the packet to get a plastic dinosaur or a mutant hero turtle.

The nutritional value of a breakfast cereal is increased by the milk added to it. Many popular brands of cereals have added minerals such as iron and zinc and vitamins (thiamin, riboflavin, niacin, folate, vitamin B_{12}, vitamin D) and a single serving of these does make a substantial contribution to the total intake. Some cereals (porridge, muesli, granola, All-bran) are a good source of dietary fibre but others such as cornflakes and puffed rice cereals are poorer sources (*see* Section V, p256). But as far as children are concerned, fibre is not critical. Most breakfast cereals are high in sugar even those ones that claim that they have no added sugar (dried fruit is high in sugar and so is honey). The sugar in the cereals does not matter if it is part of a meal but don't let children regularly eat cereals like sugar-coated cornflakes between meals.

It has often been claimed by the manufacturers of breakfast cereals that children who do not eat breakfast perform worse at school than those who do. However, Dr Nigel Dickie of the University of London carried out a study in which he showed that a child's performance at school was determined by what he was used to. If a child had breakfast regularly and then missed it he performed badly. On the other hand, if a child was used to not having breakfast and was given it then his performance deteriorated!

Staff of life Bread is a very good food and children should be encouraged to eat plenty of it. However, it's important to consider what you allow them to spread on it. It is probably better to encourage the use of low-fat spread in place of ordinary butter or margarine. Children of this age don't need as much fat as the under-fives. Letting them have jam or whatever they like on that will make them eat it but don't put the jam or low-fat spread on too thickly. Bread and peanut butter are nourishing mixes for kids. So is Marmite and bread. It is best to encourage them to eat wholemeal bread which is nutritionally superior to white bread. But if they are fussy you might have to compromise and get them to eat white bread with added vitamins and fibre such as Mighty

White. Most kids find it difficult to eat wholemeal bread cut in thick slices like doorsteps. They hate the way it falls to bits. Sliced wholemeal bread is generally much more acceptable to them.

White bread is a good food even though it contains less fibre and vitamins. The famous nutritionist Dr Elsie Widdowson studied the growth of children in German orphanages at the end of the Second World War. She showed that the normal growth and development of children could be supported on a diet containing plenty of fresh vegetables but minimal amounts of meat and milk providing they had an unlimited supply of bread. It didn't matter whether the bread was white or wholemeal.

Packed lunches Many children take a packed lunch to school with them. The following makes a perfectly healthy lunch:

- A sandwich, preferably made with wholemeal bread, filled with one of the following: cheese, chicken, ham, peanut butter, Marmite, tuna.
- A piece of fruit (a satsuma is easy to peel).
- A biscuit or a small packet of crisps.
- A small carton of fruit juice.

Many schools prohibit nuts because so many children have choked on them. While on the subject of choking, *never let children throw food into their mouths or take nuts to school.*

Snack foods Potato crisps have been much maligned by people involved in health education. But a packet of crisps can provide two-thirds of the recommended dose of vitamin C and is an important source of dietary fibre and potassium in the diets of school children. And although crisps are high in fat it is not usually the type linked to heart disease. In fact, the average consumption by school children of crisps is about three bags a week which only supplies about 2 per cent of their total dietary energy intake. However, there are some children who eat two to three bags a day. Crisps are all right as part of a balanced diet, but you can have too much of a good thing. We suggest you limit them to not more than three *small* bags (28 grams) of crisps or similar snacks (corn chips) a week. Remember that corn snacks often come in bigger packets! (*See also* Section V, p234.)

Biscuits are another *bête noire* of the health educators – usually those who don't have children themselves. Most mothers will realize that there is a price for peace. Like all foods, in moderation they are fine. The problem as far as biscuits are concerned is the fat and sugar content, especially as they tend to be eaten between meals. Chocolate digestive biscuits have the highest amount of fat (about 25 per cent by weight) and ordinary biscuits a bit less (about 20 per cent by weight). The biscuit industry is trying to improve its image with a series of health-orientated biscuits claiming 'all natural ingredients' or 'no artificial colours'. Unfortunately, many of these biscuits contain high amounts of saturated fat. The muesli bars and chewy bars are even worse for teeth than ordinary biscuits. In this respect crisps are a healthier between meal snack because they do not damage teeth. Here is a list of snackfoods that are kinder to teeth drawn up by Martin Curzon, who is Professor of Child Dentistry at Leeds University:

- Potato crisps
- Corn snacks
- Savoury biscuits – Ryvita, water biscuits, sesame biscuits
- Savoury spreads – any cheese spread, cold meat, meat and fish paste, Marmite
- Bread – brown, wholemeal or white
- Fruit – oranges, bananas, pears, plums, apples, but avoid very frequent intake (ie, continuous munching at fruit)
- Vegetables – carrots, tomatoes, celery

Soft drinks In hot weather children need to drink more fluid. Orange juice is a good source of vitamin C, but remember fresh orange juice contains about 10 per cent sugar – the same as fizzy drinks – so should be consumed in moderation. Given the opportunity, most kids would rather drink pop than water. It is better to encourage them to drink the low-calorie soft drinks than the sugar-sweetened drinks. It is also probably better to choose drinks sweetened with aspartame than saccharin. A recent report by the Ministry of Agriculture found that children were consuming more than the acceptable daily intake of saccharin. Aspartame is an intense sweetener and even if a child consumed 1.5 litres a day, the acceptable daily intake would not have been exceeded. Also, its safety is well established despite a succession of well-orchestrated scares.

Milk Children over the age of five do not need as much fat as toddlers. It is quite acceptable to give them semi-skimmed or skimmed milk like the rest of the family. This will cut down their intake of saturated fat which is linked to the development of heart disease. Milk and yoghurt are excellent sources of calcium but cheese is even better. Children should be encouraged to eat small amounts of cheese as this is an excellent source of calcium needed for growing bones and teeth.

Meat Children need little encouragement to eat meat – often it is the only thing they will eat. Meat is an excellent source of protein, iron and vitamins but it can be high in saturated fat. Meat products such as hamburgers and sausages tend to be particularly high in fat (*see* Section V, p262). Encourage children to eat real meat rather than meat products because real meat contains less fat. However, ready prepared foods like chicken escalopes in breadcrumbs are fine if they are grilled. Most kids love sausages. Buy them lower-fat sausages instead of the ordinary high-fat variety and *grill them*. Chunks of lean meat grilled on kebab skewers are popular with kids and quick to prepare.

Fish Care needs to be taken when giving fish to children because of the danger of choking on the bones. Fish fingers are excellent in this respect because they are boneless. Cartilaginous fish such as dogfish (rock salmon or huss) are also good because they have no bones. Tinned fish such as tuna, sardines, pilchards and mackerel is also good because the bones dissolve in the canning process. It is also very cheap. Fish fingers are a great way of getting kids to eat fish, but you should grill them rather than fry them to help keep the fat content down.

Vegetarians Some children decide they do not want to eat meat and become vegetarians. This can be exasperating for a non-vegetarian parent as the child does not appreciate the need to eat a balanced diet. However, there are now a large number of vegetarian meat substitute products available, made from nuts and soya (such as tofu) or a fungal protein, Quorn. Many are good nourishing products and have been fortified with vitamin B_{12} and iron. Baked beans on toast provide an excellent source of high quality protein. You may have read that baked beans have sugar added to them and now there are brands that claim they have no added sugar. The sugar in baked beans does no harm to teeth so there is no reason to avoid ordinary baked beans – we think they are a jolly good food.

If you have the patience, you can also make a mouth-watering variety of vegetarian dishes but you might find your offspring does not take to your lentil bake or timbale of mushrooms. As a general rule, *the more time you spend preparing food for children the less likely they are to eat it!*

Yellow and orange foods For some reason unbeknown to us, children prefer yellow and orange food – sausages, fish fingers, baked beans, carrots, chips, crisps, cheese, etc.

Most kids love chips and it seems a shame to deny them the pleasure of eating them. Oven chips cooked in sunflower oil are a healthier alternative to ordinary chips: they are low in total fat and saturated fat. They also have the advantage in that they don't stink the house out and don't have the fire and safety hazards of deep fryers (*see* Section V, p236–8).

Baked potatoes are popular with kids but if you wallop a great lump of butter in it then it is as bad and possibly worse than chips fried in beef fat. We're not saying don't eat butter but don't overdo it. Ordinary pizzas are also a good food for kids but not the deep-pan varieties which are glorified fried bread.

Introduce variety Encourage children to eat green vegetables or salad. Don't give up because they leave most of it behind, persist. Introduce them to foods like pasta and rice. *But don't force them to eat anything.*

Puddings Make sure they eat some fruit every day. Persuade them to eat a piece of raw fruit for pudding. There is a wonderful variety of different fruits available such as kiwi fruit, mangoes, rambutan, sapodilla, guava as well as the more traditional fruits. Many fruits such as plums, blackcurrants and apples need to be stewed with a little sugar to make them edible. The benefit of getting them to eat the fruit is far greater than any hazard from adding sugar.

Few kids will settle for fruit alone as pudding. Custard made with low-fat milk or yoghurt is a good accompaniment. Another way of getting milk into your children is to prepare a pudding containing milk – rice pudding, bread-and-Flora-pudding, instant whip, etc. *Remember food is not going to do them any good if they don't eat it.* Ice-cream is a favourite with most kids but it contains anywhere between 6 and 15 per cent fat and most of that fat is saturated. But a single scoop of ice-cream once or twice a week would do them no harm – it only contains as much fat as a pat of butter. Yoghurt is a healthy pudding. Don't worry about whether it contains sugar or not as it is part of a meal.

The puddings to avoid except on special occasions are those that contain the most fat such as cheesecake, Black Forest gateaux, sponge puddings, pastries and pancakes.

Obesity Obesity is relatively uncommon in this age group. However, if your child is getting podgy then it's time to cut back on the foods that are least important in the diet such as biscuits, crisps, ice-cream and sugary drinks.

ADOLESCENCE

Adolescence is an awkward age for both parents and children. It is the age at which parental control over what children eat is finally lost. Kids of this age have higher energy requirements than at any other time of life. It is quite normal for a teenager to be eating twice as much as an adult.

The main nutritional problems encountered among teenagers are iron deficiency in girls and inadequate energy intake that leads to growth stunting and delayed maturation. Poor bone growth in adolescent girls can lead to difficulties in childbirth in later life. Women with large body frames give birth to bigger babies. Big babies tend to be healthier and develop into brighter adults than small ones.

MILK

Milk is the major source of calcium in the diet. The minerals, and in particular calcium, that give bone its strength are largely deposited in adolescence. Bone mineral density increases up to the age of about twenty-five years then it gradually declines. Osteoporosis is the term used to describe the condition where bones have a low mineral density. Osteoporosis is a major cause of hip and leg fractures in the elderly. Consequently, the foundations for healthy bones are laid down in adolescence. A high intake of calcium in adolescence is thought to protect against osteoporosis in later life.

Vitamin D is needed for the absorption of calcium. Vitamin D deficiency (rickets) is rare in British adolescents but used to be common before the Second World War. Rickets, still occasionally seen in the Asian population, is caused by a combination of a lack of exposure to sunlight and a low availability of calcium from the diet. The decline in rickets in the population is probably due to the high consumption of milk, an excellent source of calcium. It thus makes sense to encourage teenagers to drink milk. However, ordinary milk is high in saturated fat which is linked to causing heart disease in later life, so instead they should be encouraged to drink semi-skimmed or skimmed milk.

GETTING ENOUGH IRON

Girls often have low intakes of iron and may suffer from mild iron deficiency anaemia. Liver and red meat (beef, lamb, pork) are very good sources of iron – far better than poultry or fish. The iron from meat is much better absorbed than from other sources. Bread is also an important source of iron in the diet. Other sources are dark green leafy vegetables, haricot beans and lentils. If menstrual blood losses are particularly heavy a combined iron, folic acid and vitamin B_{12} supplement can be taken.

SPORT

Teenage boys and girls play a lot of sport. Adverts often imply that certain foods are associated with prowess at sport. Food companies seem to be taking over sports sponsorship from the tobacco and alcohol industries. Drinks and sweets containing sugar or glucose are promoted by famous sportsmen as giving you extra energy. It is true that they provide energy but it is a half-truth. You don't need to consume these products to perform well at sport. Pasta would do just as well. Marathon runners find they can increase their endurance by bingeing on pasta a few days before the run. Pasta is a rich source of starch which is broken down into glucose. Glucose is the preferred fuel for exercise but you can only store small amounts as a substance called glycogen. It is possible to increase glycogen stores by eating a high carbohydrate diet for a couple of days before a marathon.

CHANGING SHAPE

As girls mature they become fatter. This is quite natural – a certain amount of body fat is needed for normal hormonal functioning. It is known that the age of menarche – the age at which girls start having their monthly periods – is related to the amount of body fat. When the level of body fat reaches about 18 per cent, menarche strikes. If the level of body fat drops below about 15 per cent then girls stop having their periods. This is common in gymnasts and ballet dancers who are very figure conscious. The expression of female sexuality is strongly associated with body shape and eating disorders such as *anorexia nervosa* are sometimes a way of suppressing this sexuality.

Anorexia nervosa is a condition that leads to loss of appetite in adolescent girls and can lead to severe under-nutrition. It is a psychiatric disorder that arises from preoccupation with desirable body shape. Terrific pressure is placed on girls through advertising to have a slender figure. An early sign of anorexia nervosa is an unhealthy interest in food books and slimming. Adolescent girls need to be reassured that the changes in body shape that occur during puberty are quite normal.

Slimming Obesity affects a small proportion of teenagers and it is more common in girls. Many adolescent girls go through a podgy stage and many grow out of it by the age of eighteen. This 'puppy fat' stage may result because it takes time to re-adapt to a lower food intake after the growth spurt.

If a child is overweight then it is the most dispensable foods that should be cut out of the diet – eg, sugary drinks, confectionery and snack foods. Overweight teenagers should be encouraged to drink low-calorie drinks instead of sugary drinks. It is surprising how much fizzy pop a teenager can drink. Three cans of ordinary sugared fizzy drink supplies about 400 calories. It takes about 10,000 calories to put on 1kg (2.2lbs) of weight. If a kid is regularly drinking three cans of pop a day and eating normally then he could be putting on roughly 1kg of fat a month or 12kg a year! They should also be discouraged from hogging snack foods such as crisps, nuts and chocolate bars (a 28g packet of crisps provides about 130 calories, a 50g packet of peanuts 280 calories and a 50g bar of chocolate about 265 calories).

It is a bad idea to encourage teenagers to follow crash diets. If they do need to slim down, they should follow a standard reducing diet (*see* p207). Once they have lost weight they need to change their eating habits to avoid putting it back on again, otherwise there is a danger of entering the cycle of dieting and bingeing. Tell-tale signs are large fluctuations in body weight and irregular periods.

TEENAGE DRINKING

A frightening number of teenagers are becoming alcoholics. The increased availability of alcohol is a major reason. Parents who prohibit everything encourage revolt in their children. The difficulty is treading the thin line between encouraging drinking and teaching them to drink sensibly. It seems quite reasonable to allow teenagers to have a drink on special occasions but it should never become a habit. You need to explain to them the hazards of excess alcohol and how much you can safely drink without damaging your health. Stress the responsibility they have towards other people and explain the dangers of drinking and driving. It is tempting for a gang of teenagers to raid your booze cabinet while you are out of the house. So make it clear that they cannot drink in your absence. If you don't trust them, lock up your drinks. It is rather like medicines – you should keep them out of the reach of children.

VEGETARIAN TEENAGERS

Teenagers generally don't want to be like their parents, they want to be different and to be individual. There is a lot of pressure on school children to become 'Green' and 'environmentally friendly'. Vegetarianism is strongly tied up with environmental groups and other more radical movements and thus very much in vogue at the moment. The usual reasons given are the belief that it is cruel to eat animals, that it is environmentally more economical to live on plant foods than animal foods and that vegetarian diets are more 'natural' and 'wholesome' than ordinary mixed diets. We are not going to enter that debate – the point is that it is quite possible to select a well-balanced vegetarian diet for teenagers. But it is probably easier to select a bad vegetarian diet than a bad meat diet. The quality of a vegetarian diet depends upon what foods are included.

In the typical diet, meat provides important quantities of energy, iron, protein, B-complex vitamins and vitamin B_{12}. Energy, protein and B-complex vitamins are unlikely to be lacking in a vegetarian diet. But vitamin B_{12}, while found in milk, cheese and eggs, is not found in plant foods unless they are fortified.

So parents need to make sure that children are eating:

- At least half a pint of milk or an ounce of cheese or an egg (daily to make sure they are getting enough vitamin A and B_{12} and calcium).
- Plenty of wholemeal bread and salads (for energy, protein, fibre and B-complex vitamins and vitamin C).
- At least one piece of fruit a day (for vitamin C and folate).

On a vegetarian diet it is important to consume wholemeal bread to ensure an adequate intake of iron and B-complex vitamins. It will also ensure they eat plenty of fibre.

Some children decide they want to become vegans and exclude all food of animal origin. It is possible to choose a healthy vegan diet too, but much more care is needed and the diet needs to be supplemented with vitamins B_{12} and D. There are now many meat substitutes either made from soya or Quorn and these are of good nutritional value. But because they do not contain dairy products, vegan diets can be very low in calcium. This problem can be overcome by using fortified soya milks like Plamil or Granogen. Another way to increase calcium in the diet of vegans is to add chalk to flour in home baking. Children can grow and develop quite normally on vegan and vegetarian diets providing care is taken.

YOUNG ADULTS – AGED 18–30

Young adults think they are immortal. Problems like heart disease and cancer at this age seem remote to them. However, the foundations for these diseases are probably laid down in early adult life. It has been said that you pay for a wild life in your twenties in middle age. Excess alcohol intake is a major contributory cause of death in this age group, particularly in accidents on the road. This is why insurance companies load the premiums on young drivers. Two-thirds of all male deaths in this age group involve accidents or violence.

The majority of teenagers are not overweight but many start to put on weight in early adult life. Ideally you should maintain the weight you are in early adulthood throughout life. The best way to do this is to *weigh yourself regularly*. Also keep an eye on your waistband. If you are having to buy trousers with a bigger waistband that is a sure sign you are getting fat. Many men claim that their paunches are solid muscle. This is rubbish. What they don't realize is that most of the fat is stored inside the abdominal cavity.

Preventing weight gain means keeping an eye on your weight and cutting back on food and drink when your weight goes up. Don't wait till you get very fat before taking action. It is much harder to lose 2 stone than half a stone. On a 1,000 calorie per day diet it will take you about four months to lose 2 stone if you are a man, and about six months if you are a woman. *If you keep your weight down you will also look and feel better.* (For advice on losing weight, *see* p104 and Section IV, p207.)

At this age, most people are concerned about how they look. Some women in particular can become obsessive about what they eat and enter a cycle of dieting followed by feeding frenzies. A sense of guilt often results after the feeding frenzy and they make themselves sick. This condition is called *bulimia nervosa*. If you suffer from this condition then you really need to seek professional advice. We suggest you discuss your problems with your doctor and he will refer you to a specialist.

No one is really sure what causes bulimia nervosa, but it

does seem related to the extreme pressure exerted on women to be slim whatever their biologically determined shape. It is assumed that women can squeeze into tight jeans. If they can't do this they are encouraged to diet to attain the desired shape. Coming to terms with bulimia nervosa means accepting one's body shape.

Many young adults don't have access to decent cooking facilities and live on a lot of pre-packaged and takeaway foods. What many people don't realize is that convenience and takeaway foods are expensive.

Much of the food eaten away from home also tends to be high in fat. For instance, you don't know what type of spreads are used in sandwiches. In our experience, catering establishments use whatever is cheapest and usually the worst for you (ie, a spread high in saturated fats). However, you can easily make your own sandwiches or rolls that will keep you going through the day. And fresh fruit requires no preparation and yoghurts are convenient.

If you have limited cooking facilities, some of the ranges of ready-cooked frozen foods are easy to prepare and good value. But be careful to read the labels to check they are not high in fat. It doesn't take much effort to cook vegetables – all you need is a saucepan (for the best methods *see* Section V, p301). Failing that you can always have a salad. Preparing your own food requires some planning of your shopping and it is often much cheaper to buy in bulk than piecemeal. You land up paying a hefty premium for your food in small 'convenience' corner shops. Bulk buying food when you are sharing a flat has its disadvantages: you come home to find that someone else has gone and polished off your food! However, on balance the advantages in terms of cost far outweigh the disadvantages.

It is important under the age of twenty-five to have a good intake of calcium, so you should aim to drink at least half a pint of milk a day but drink semi-skimmed or skimmed milk, not full cream.

Many people of this age group, particularly women, become vegetarians. That's fine but remember you need to compensate for the lack of meat in your diet. If you are a vegetarian you should be eating:

- Wholegrain cereals rather than refined cereals.
- One piece of fruit a day.
- A salad or coloured vegetable at least once a day.
- At least one portion of cheese/beans/nuts/eggs daily.
- Half a pint of milk (semi-skimmed or skimmed) or fortified soya milk daily.

If you are living on beer, chocolate bars, chips, crisps and nuts then that is not a healthy vegetarian diet.

MIDDLE AGE

There are five main hazards associated with middle age:

- Obesity
- Excess alcohol
- Heart disease
- Stroke
- Cancer

If you are eating healthily you should be doing all of the following:

- Base your meals round a starchy food such as bread, rice, pasta, potatoes, beans, breakfast cereal.
- Drink a third to half a pint of skimmed or semi-skimmed milk a day.
- Eat lean meat.
- Eat fish at least twice a week, especially the oily variety.
- Eat at least one piece of fruit a day.
- Eat at least one portion of green, yellow and orange vegetables every day and usually have a salad once a day.
- Cook with liquid oils rather than hard fat.
- Use a low-fat spread or margarine high in polyunsaturates.

Most people in their thirties and forties don't like to be called middle-aged but they are. By this age most adults are settled down and have the facilities and usually the money to buy the food they want. If they have families, this introduces another dimension – eating as a family.

If you have to prepare food for other people, especially young kids, it is very easy to eat up the scraps. Phrases like 'Better belly bust than let good food go to waste' or 'Leave a clean plate' or 'Think of all the people starving in Ethiopia' come to mind. But you will help nobody by scoffing the leftovers. If you are on the plump side, whether it goes into your stomach or the dustbin makes little difference except that if you eat the scraps you're asking for trouble.

Remember you don't have to leave a clean plate. As you get older your need for food energy gets less and so it is easier to put on weight. Most people put on the most weight in their thirties. *If you keep your weight down then you will stay fit and look younger for longer*.

Weight gain isn't something that is inevitable. To prevent weight gain you have to learn to know your limits. You can only do this if you *regularly weigh yourself*, say once a week. If you are putting on weight, then you are eating and drinking too much and you will need to cut back. Many people put on weight in phases, particularly around Christmas or on holiday. Consequently weight gain tends to be in steps rather than gradually. If you are going to keep your weight down you have to change your eating habits so avoid those situations that lead to overeating. We give some practical advice on p207.

Gall-stones are common in middle-aged people and can be extremely painful. They are made out of cholesterol which the body excretes from the liver. The typical candidate is 'fair, fat, female and forty'. Keeping your weight down is also known to reduce your risk of gall-stones, as well as other disorders such as diabetes (*see* p218 for advice on diabetic diets).

BRITTLE BONES

Women are particularly prone to osteoporosis (brittle bones) which is caused by a loss of calcium from the bones after the menopause. Regular exercise such as walking can help stop the rate of loss of calcium from bones and so can hormone replacement therapy. An adequate intake of calcium helps prevent the loss of calcium. Most women have adequate intakes of calcium but still lose calcium from their bones. Taking extra calcium in the diet has not been shown to be of any added benefit.

HEART DISEASE CAN BE PREVENTED

The importance of preventing heart disease, although advocated by British experts for many years, has only recently received support from the government. This tardy response may have something to do with revenue gathered by the Treasury from taxes on cigarettes and alcohol. For every 1,000 middle-aged men, four to six will die every year from heart disease. Many deaths could be prevented by simple lifestyle changes such as stopping smoking, changing the type of fat and avoiding obesity.

Many general practices are running 'well person clinics' where they check your blood pressure, weight and blood cholesterol level in order to identify people at high risk of heart disease. Chemists and health-food shops are also offering blood cholesterol tests, but the results obtained may not always be reliable. You also need to make sure that you are not fobbed off with quack remedies. In the USA, some health-food shops have been selling large amounts of the vitamin niacin to lower blood cholesterol. This led to liver failure and death in one customer. Our advice is, if you want your blood cholesterol checked, get it done by someone you can trust – your doctor. For some years cholesterol testing has been fashionable in the USA and one's cholesterol rating is a topic of conversation almost as popular as house prices.

Most health centres routinely check your blood pressure but not all do cholesterol tests. If you have a family history of heart disease it is worth getting your blood cholesterol checked by your doctor. Remember, prevention is more effective than cure – if you have a high blood cholesterol level and it is treated it can stop you having a heart attack in your fifties. Changing your blood cholesterol once you've had a heart attack is not as effective (that is, of course, if you survive), but can help prevent a second heart attack.

Most middle-aged men and many women have cholesterol levels high enough to put them at risk from heart disease. Consequently, almost everyone needs to keep their blood cholesterol level down. Here is a list of the main dietary changes needed to lower your blood cholesterol:

- Change to skimmed or semi-skimmed milk.
- Change from butter or ordinary margarine to a low-fat spread or a margarine high in polyunsaturates.
- Choose lean cuts of meat.
- Change from hard fats to oils.

If you are overweight, then losing weight will bring down your blood cholesterol level. We have specialized advice on cholesterol lowering for people with high levels or with a family history of heart disease (*see* p215).

BLOOD PRESSURE

Many people develop high blood pressure in middle-age. Nobody knows why and it occurs in thin as well as fat people. You should have your blood pressure measured every two years. If you develop high blood pressure it can be treated. This can reduce your risk of dying from a stroke. Detailed dietary advice for people with high blood pressure is given on p217.

Although the precise causes of high blood pressure are not known, current opinion suggests that the following should help avoid it:

- Watch your weight – if you gain weight eat less.
- Eat plenty of fruit and vegetables.
- Avoid excess alcohol.
- Avoid adding salt to food.

LATE MIDDLE AGE

Heart disease, cancer and stroke are the major causes of death. Most people of this age have had friends who have dropped dead of a heart attack or who have died of cancer. The death of a friend or relative could act as an emotional cue to change your lifestyle. Even at this age it is not too late to change your diet. It is important that changes in diet accompany other changes in life-style, such as giving up smoking and taking regular exercise.

Avoiding obesity is very important, particularly for women. In post-menopausal women being overweight increases the risk of both breast cancer and heart disease. Women beyond the menopause lose the protection against heart disease provided by their hormones. If you have high blood pressure (*see* p217) or high blood cholesterol (*see* p215) then you must be more careful about what you eat and drink.

DIET FOLLOWING A HEART ATTACK

If you have suffered a heart attack then you must stop smoking. The following changes in diet may help prevent you having a second heart attack:

- Eat two good size portions of oily fish twice a week.
- Watch your weight.
- Change from full-cream to skimmed milk.
- Change from ordinary margarine or butter to a low-fat spread or a margarine high in polyunsaturates.
- Only eat lean meat – avoid fatty meats and meat products.
- Avoid eating heavy meals last thing at night.

CANCER

Many people with cancer look for special diets hoping they will cure this dreaded disease. Although diet may be able to prevent cancer, unfortunately there are no diets that can cure cancer. But diet can improve the quality of life and make treatment more bearable. The type of diet for a person with cancer may be very different from the type of diet advised to prevent cancer. For example, a diet low in fat and containing plenty of fruit and vegetables may help prevent cancer but it is often the wrong type of diet to give a patient with cancer of the stomach or large bowel.

The type of diet needed will depend on where the cancer is and whether the patient is losing weight. Weight loss is an early sign of many cancers. If you find you suffer from any of these symptoms seek medical advice straight away:

- Unexplained weight loss.
- Blood in faeces or urine.
- An abnormal discharge.
- Difficulty in urinating (men).
- A lump or growth.
- A mole that bleeds or changes in shape or size.

These symptoms can result from a variety of disorders. For example, blood in faeces can result from piles (haemorrhoids). However, never delay getting proper medical advice, whatever your fears. Many cancers – particularly those of the colon, breast and prostate – can be successfully treated if they are caught early enough.

Loss of appetite is common in cancer and can be caused by the disease itself or the drugs used to treat it. Consequently many patients with cancer become malnourished. It is important to keep food intake up to improve the quality of life. Many cancer patients receive chemotherapy and one of the unpleasant side-effects can be nausea and vomiting, although drugs are available to help prevent this. Chemotherapy is often given in cycles of two to three weeks' duration and it usually involves an intravenous infusion of drugs once a week. Some changes in diet can reduce the risk of nausea and vomiting and thus make the treatment more bearable.

The day before chemotherapy Avoid consuming smoked or barbecued foods the day before chemotherapy because they contain compounds that interfere with the metabolism of certain drugs used in chemotherapy and can cause vomiting.

The day of chemotherapy Avoid fatty food which stays in your stomach longer. Just eat sugary and starchy foods like toast or crackers. Sipping a sugary, fizzy drink is a popular remedy for overcoming the feeling of sickness.

THE ELDERLY

The main dietary problems for the elderly are:

- Not eating properly.
- Eating too much fried food.
- Not eating enough fruit and vegetables.

As we age, our need for energy gets less so we don't need to eat so much. But it is still more important to eat a good-quality diet. Eating properly can keep you fit. Some people in their mid-seventies can be as healthy as somebody in their fifties. Most of the advice about healthy eating for someone in their fifties applies to the sprightly seventy year old.

Beyond the age of sixty your level of blood cholesterol is not a good predictor of risk from heart disease. In fact, a person over sixty with slightly higher than average blood cholesterol level tends to live longer! It has never been shown that lowering your blood cholesterol over the age of sixty prolongs life. At this age, you should not be over-concerned about your blood cholesterol.

The main danger to the elderly is not eating properly – eg living on tea and biscuits. Most people by the time they have reached their sixties have well-established eating patterns. Retirement can alter these patterns, particularly if the main meal of the day was taken at work. The loss of a husband or wife can also change the eating habits of the surviving spouse, especially if it is a man who has not usually prepared the food. It is vital that a regular eating pattern continues. Large changes in diet at this age are undesirable and can cause problems. If you have survived into your sixties, your diet can't be that bad. You must ensure that you don't let your diet deteriorate. Most important of all you should enjoy your food.

Physical disabilities can also restrict what many elderly people can purchase and eat. Loss of mobility from arthritis or stroke or a heart attack makes shopping difficult. It may also be hard to prepare and cook certain foods. For example, opening a tin can be a problem for someone with arthritis. Loss of teeth and ill-fitting dentures can make it difficult to eat certain foods such as fruit. Being housebound reduces exposure to sunlight and so increases the risk of vitamin D deficiency. Loss of mobility also leads to osteoporosis which in turn can lead to hip and leg fractures following a fall. Low food intake coupled with low mobility can also lead to hypothermia.

Cooking is a chore for many old people and they often choose foods that can be rapidly prepared such as pre-packaged convenience and fried foods. Ready prepared frozen meals and microwave ovens are a boon for the elderly, but many old people often have difficulty in coping with new gadgets. It may need a young person such as a grandchild to show them how easy they are to use. And making the effort to cook can be a useful way of taking some exercise and developing an interest. Meals-on-wheels are also another way of making sure that an elderly person living alone gets properly fed. For the elderly who are still active but living alone, lunch clubs are run by WRVS in the community centres of many towns.

In many ways catering for the very old (the over eighties) can be similar to feeding the very young – they like mushy food and the meat chopped up for them and they like sweet foods. This is because of loss of teeth and a reduced sense of taste and smell. Milk is a particularly good food for the elderly. Because many old people suffer from constipation, it is a good idea to get them to eat wholemeal bread. Many old people would probably benefit from taking a multivitamin and mineral supplement.

Hypothermia is a problem in many elderly people and is made worse by being sedentary. Eating small meals frequently helps keep the body temperature up. Foods with a high carbohydrate or protein content increase heat production more than foods high in fat.

DIETING – SENSIBLY AND EFFECTIVELY

Diet is a four letter word to most people who are overweight. Ideally, you should never have to diet but most people are human and do over-eat and put on weight. Dieting is the only safe way to lose body weight – there are no miracle cures. Various drugs are being developed that stimulate the metabolic rate, but as with all drugs they have side-effects (such as nausea, vomiting and hypertension). It is unlikely that they will ever do away with the need for dieting.

If you are overweight you must change your basic eating habits because they probably caused the problem in the first place. This means recognizing the situations that led you to over-eat or eat the wrong type of foods. You need to learn which foods are most fattening for you. It may be

- sugary drinks or cakes or chocolate bars;
- that you just have portions that are too big;
- that you just can't bear to see food go to waste;
- that you drink too much beer.

Having identified the problem, you can then set about finding ways of avoiding those situations that lead to this behaviour.

The diet we recommend will make you lose weight at a sensible rate and is nutritionally well-balanced. To find out how much weight you need to lose, refer to the chart on p64. If you don't want to put weight back on again then you have to discover your limits. The only way you can do this is to weigh yourself regularly. If you start to put on weight then you have to cut back on what you eat.

Dieting properly involves eating at regular times. *A regular meal pattern is essential*. If you skip meals you are more likely to fill up on snack foods which tend to be very high in calories. Losing weight requires will-power and it is easy to be tempted. Remember will-power is soluble in alcohol. Try to avoid situations where you will be tempted to nibble – keep away from bowls of nuts and crisps.

The diet we describe provides about 1,000 calories a day and has been shown to work. If you are a woman you will lose about 1.5–2lbs of fat a week, if you are a man you will lose 2–2.5lbs of fat a week. In the first week you may lose more than 5lbs but a lot of this will be water. The rate at which people lose weight decreases the longer they are on a diet. So after about three months most people are only losing 1–1.5lbs a week. There may be weeks when you lose no weight at all. But don't despair, the diet works and it is fat that is being lost. *If you lose weight at a higher rate on a crash diet you are likely to lose muscle as well as fat and this lowers your metabolic rate so that when you stop dieting it is easier to put on weight.* Remember, regular exercise is important as it uses up any energy and helps keep you fit. Swimming, cycling and walking are excellent forms of exercise. Walk or cycle rather than take the bus or car.

THE LIBERATION DIET

Instead of telling you what you can't eat we are telling you what you can eat. *Losing weight means reducing the intake of those nutrients that provide most of the calories that is fat, carbohydrate and alcohol (if you drink a lot).* There is no need to be obsessive and count the calorific value of everything you eat. More than 80 per cent of the calories we eat come from fat and carbohydrate and alcohol (if you drink). If you look after the fats, alcohol and carbohydrates, the calories look after themselves.

The list of foods we are going to give you will provide the nutrients you need and will not make you fat. You can eat as much fruit, leafy and root vegetables, lean meat and fish, and drink as much skimmed milk and sugar-free drinks as you like. You can even eat bread, rice, potatoes and pasta but not in large amounts. When we say as much as you like, we don't expect you to go bananas and eat twenty pieces of fruit a day or dive in at the deep end and eat five mackerel a day.

The foods you can eat freely and those you need to watch the portion sizes of are listed. We also give you a list of foods which you should avoid so there is no misunderstanding. Read through these lists carefully.

Having told you about the foods you can eat freely and the ones to avoid here are some tips to help you keep to the Liberation Diet.

Ready prepared meals   Controlling portion size is one of the big problems people have when slimming. Ready prepared meals take the choice away from you. You may find it convenient to buy ready prepared meals – there are many now available. But check the label to make sure that they do not provide more than 300–350 calories.

How to cope with eating out   It can be difficult to control what you eat when you are eating out because of the social pressures put on you. We have assembled some tips that may help you:

- Keep out of the kitchen in a friend's house or you will be tempted to nibble.
- Say no to second helpings.
- Eat slowly.
- Don't be the first in the queue for food. For example, if you are at a party where there is a help-yourself buffet you can choose a small plate to stop you taking too much food. And make sure that you are not up at the table to get food first. This prevents you getting second helpings.
- Leave food on your plate. It is a false economy to imagine that all the food on the plate must be eaten.
- Avoid alcohol except on special occasions because after a few drinks you won't care what you eat! Drink fizzy mineral water instead of alcohol.
- Don't eat bread rolls or bread sticks when you are out to a meal in a restaurant. Enjoy the food from the cook instead. Always be the first to order, that way you won't be tempted to eat something piggy.
- Choose fish and poultry dishes with a side-salad. And have fruit for desserts.
- Because a meal is being paid for by someone else you don't have to make a hog of yourself.

Food	Eat Freely	Eat in Moderation	Best Avoided
Dairy	Skimmed milk, cottage cheese, quark, low fat yoghurt	Full fat cheese (cheddar, edam, brie) 1 oz/serving Egg (1/day), full fat milk (⅓ cup/day)	Ice-cream, cream, condensed and evaporated milk
Meat and fish	Lean meat, ham, poultry, fish, shellfish but not fried		Sausages, meat pies, fatty meat products (salami, garlic sausage, bacon), meat and fish fried in breadcrumbs or batter
Cereal foods		Bread (wholemeal) 1 slice/serving pasta (½ cup cooked/serving) rice (½ cup cooked/serving), sweetcorn (½ cup cooked/serving), breakfast cereal (1oz portion)	Biscuits, cakes, pastries, pancakes
Fats	Small amounts only see next column	Vegetable oil for cooking 1 dessert spoon/day 4 teaspoons low fat spread or 2 teaspoons butter or margarine/day	All other fats
Spreads	Meat and yeast extracts – Bovril, Marmite, Vegemite	Peanut butter (1 teaspoon/serving), jam or marmalade (2 teaspoons/day)	
Fruit	All types of fresh fruit		Dried fruit, tinned fruit in syrup

Food	Eat Freely	Eat in Moderation	Best Avoided
Vegetables	All leafy vegetables, asparagus, aubergines, runner beans, carrots, cauliflower, celery, chicory, courgettes, cucumber, leeks, mushrooms, okra, onion, parsley, peppers, parsnips, pumpkin, radishes, sauerkraut, swede, tomatoes, turnips	Boiled or baked potato (1 medium) Oven chips (3oz serving) Pulses – peas, lentils, beans (½ cup cooked/serving)	Fried vegetables – bubble and squeak, ordinary chips, samosas, avocado
Snackfoods			Nuts, crisps, Bombay mix, corn and wheat snacks, chocolate, sweets
Drinks	Tea, coffee, sugar free drinks, water	Fruit juice (1 small glass/day)	Sugar-containing fizzy drinks and squash alcoholic drinks
Miscellaneous	Herbs, spices, soy sauce, tomato ketchup, clear soups	Sugar (1 tablespoon/day)	Mayonnaise, oil-based salad dressings, cream sauces, gravy

COOKING HINTS

- Do not fry food in deep fat.
- Trim the excess fat off meat.
- With poultry only eat the meat not the skin.
- Grill or steam fish in a microwave or cook wrapped in foil in the oven.
- You can stir-fry meat, fish and vegetables using vegetable oil from the allowance.
- Salad dressings – use fresh flavours such as basil, mint and lemon juice or flavoured vinegars or low-calorie dressings.

A sample meal pattern follows for meat eaters and vegetarians. And remember – *you will only lose weight if you stick to the diet*.

SAMPLE DAILY MENU

Breakfast 1 slice bread with low-fat spread and marmalade
from allowance
or
1 small glass fruit juice
or
½ grapefruit
1 boiled egg
or
1oz breakfast cereal with milk from allowance
or
4oz porridge with milk from allowance
Coffee or tea (no sugar) with milk from allowance

Break Coffee or tea (no sugar) with milk from allowance
or low-calorie drink

Lunch   Clear soup
Sandwich made from 2 slices of bread with meat, fish or cheese filling
Side salad
1 piece of fruit

Mid-afternoon   Coffee or tea (no sugar) with milk from allowance or low-calorie drink

Supper   1 serving meat or fish or cheese
Salad or boiled vegetable
1 small boiled or baked potato
or
½ cup of rice
or
2 slices of bread
or
½ cup sweetcorn
or
½ cup pulses
1 low fat yoghurt
or
1 piece of fruit
Coffee or tea with milk from allowance

Drink plenty of water with meals and throughout the day.

SAMPLE VEGETARIAN MENU

Breakfast   1 slice bread with low fat spread and marmalade from allowance
and
1 small glass fruit juice
or
½ grapefruit
1 boiled egg
or
1oz breakfast cereal with milk from allowance
or
4oz porridge with milk from allowance
Coffee or tea (no sugar) with milk from allowance

Break	Coffee or tea (no sugar) with milk from allowance or low-calorie drink

Lunch	Clear soup Sandwich made from 2 slices of bread with cheese, peanut butter or yeast extract filling Side salad 1 piece of fruit

Mid-afternoon	Coffee or tea (no sugar) with milk from allowance or low-calorie drink

Supper	Vegetarian dish Salad or boiled vegetable 1 small boiled or baked potato or ½ cup of rice or 2 slices of bread or ½ cup sweetcorn or ½ cup pulses 1 low fat yoghurt or 1 piece of fruit Coffee or tea with milk from allowance

Drink plenty of water with meals and throughout the day.

CUTTING YOUR CHOLESTEROL

BLOOD CHOLESTEROL LOWERING DIET

If you are overweight first lose your excess weight (*see* p208) then follow the dietary advice below:

- Change to skimmed milk.
- Change from butter or ordinary margarine to a margarine high in polyunsaturates (Flora, Vitalite) or a low-fat spread (Gold, Flora light, Outline).
- Choose lean cuts of meat and trim off excess fat. Beef and pork are suitable *providing the excess fat is removed.* Lamb tends to be high in fat and is best avoided. Chicken and turkey are low in fat but don't eat the skin. White fish are low in fat when grilled or steamed. Oily fish are low in saturated fats and so are acceptable. Avoid fatty meat products such as sausages and meat pies.
- Use liquid vegetable oil for cooking in place of hard fats such as lard, white fat or solid vegetable fat. Sunflower oil, olive oil or ordinary blended cooking oil are suitable.
- Avoid deep-fried food.
- Don't eat more than 1oz of cheese a day. Cottage cheese can be consumed freely.
- Avoid filling up on biscuits, cakes and pastries which are high in fat. Fill up on fruit, vegetables, potatoes and cereals such as bread (preferably wholemeal), rice and pasta.
- Avoid excess alcohol. Drink no more than 2–3 units/ day (*see* p147).
- Avoid excess coffee consumption (more than six cups/day) and drink filtered in preference to percolated coffee.

Doctors are now measuring blood cholesterol levels if they suspect you have a family history of early heart disease or if they think that you might be at increased risk from heart disease. If you want to get your blood cholesterol measured ask your doctor. We don't recommend you get it done in a chemist or a health food shop. If it is high you will need proper advice which they are not qualified to give. Also they exist to sell you pills and potions. In the UK, we measure cholesterol levels in units called millimoles/litre or mmol/l for short. Here is what the levels mean:

Cholesterol level	Risk of heart disease
less than 5.2 mmol/l	Low
5.2–6.5 mmol/l	Increased risk
6.5–7.5 mmol/l	Moderate risk
greater than 7.5 mmol/l	High risk

If your blood cholesterol level is above 6.5–7.5 mmol/l then you have a three times higher risk of heart disease. But if you smoke and have high blood pressure as well as a high blood level your risk of heart disease is eight to ten times higher. *The majority of middle-aged men have cholesterol levels above the desirable level.* The average blood cholesterol level in middle-aged men is about 6.1 mmol/l. Most women under the age of about forty-five have levels below 5.2 mmol/l but after this age it rises to be as high or even higher than in men.

If you have been told you have high blood cholesterol, remember it's not the end of the world and it can be treated and can help prevent you having a heart attack. If you smoke and have high blood cholesterol you greatly increase your risk of a heart attack and it is essential to stop smoking (don't think that you can get away with lowering your blood cholesterol without stopping smoking).

Some people have a high blood cholesterol level that does not respond to diet alone. Drugs can be used to lower cholesterol levels in these people, but they can have side-effects. Drug treatment seems to benefit most those patients with very high levels of blood cholesterol rather than those with moderately raised levels. Drugs should not be seen as an alternative to diet. Drug treatment of high cholesterol usually needs to be accompanied by a change in diet as the two work together. Remember, the risk of heart disease from high blood cholesterol is much less if you don't smoke.

LOWERING YOUR BLOOD PRESSURE

DIET FOR LOWERING BLOOD PRESSURE

- Keep an eye on your weight.
- Avoid excess alcohol.
- Avoid adding salt to food at the table.
- Cook vegetables without adding salt to the cooking water.
- Avoid salted and pickled foods.
- Eat more fruit and vegetables.

Blood pressure increases with age and many people develop high blood pressure in middle-age. Two readings are recorded by the doctor when measuring your blood pressure – the first is called the systolic and the second the diastolic. Blood pressure measurements are expressed in the following way: systolic/diastolic in millimetres of mercury. For example, 120/80 means a systolic blood pressure of 120 and a diastolic blood pressure of 80. The diastolic blood pressure is the most important and it is this that is raised in hypertension. The systolic blood pressure is increased on exertion.

- Normal blood pressure is about 120/80.
- Mild hypertension is greater than 140/90.
- Severe hypertension is greater than 160/110.

Patients with severe (but not mild) hypertension benefit from drug treatment. Blood pressure falls following weight loss in people with mild hypertension. So if you are overweight then losing weight will lower your blood pressure (*see* p207). Excess alcohol intake causes high blood pressure in some people. Cutting down on salt and eating more fruit and vegetables help lower blood pressure.

ALL ABOUT DIABETES

- Keep your weight under control.
- Aim to eat several small meals a day rather than two large meals.
- Eat more complex carbohydrate rich food like pasta, rice, beans, muesli without added sugar.
- Avoid sugary foods, especially biscuits and sugar soft drinks. Use artificial sweeteners such as acesulfame, aspartame and saccharin in place of sugar.
- Avoid drinking large amounts of fruit juice or fruit. Limit your intake to one small glass of fruit juice a day.
- Use a low-fat spread or margarine high in polyunsaturates instead of ordinary margarine or butter.
- Use liquid oils for cooking not hard fats.

Diabetes is probably the most common metabolic disorder in developed countries. It affects about a million people in Britain. Diabetes can affect young people and this is usually caused by an inability to produce the hormone insulin. This form of diabetes is called juvenile onset diabetes or insulin dependent diabetes mellitus. These diabetics have to have regular injections of the hormone insulin.

A second type of diabetes occurs more commonly in people from middle-age onwards and is called maturity onset diabetes or non-insulin dependent diabetes mellitus. This is caused by an inability to respond to the effects of insulin rather than by an inability to produce insulin. In fact, patients with maturity onset diabetes produce larger than normal amounts of insulin. Diabetes is easily detected by the presence of sugar in urine. The risk of getting maturity onset diabetes is increased by being overweight, especially if you are apple-shaped (waist bigger than hips). Diabetics have to be careful about what they eat. Often it is possible to control the diabetes by diet alone without recourse to drugs. Diabetes greatly increases the risk of heart disease and many diabetics have high blood cholesterol levels. So some of the dietary advice is the same as that given for lowering blood cholesterol. There are a number of diabetic products such as diabetic jams and chocolate but you don't have to buy these. However, you should avoid chocolate (diabetic or ordinary) and sweets except on special occasions. You don't have to avoid sugar altogether but you have to restrict how much you eat.

SECTION V
THE CONSUMERS' GUIDE

If you have analysed your diet using the questionnaire in Section II you know how well you eat. Sections III and IV are the antidote to the health puritans – they tell you what you can get away with, whatever your age and without the merest hint of a hair shirt. Having discovered which foods you should eat to avoid diet-related disease, the important question is how you can put it into practice. That is what this section is all about.

How do you judge the nutritional quality of food? How do you judge its microbiological quality? And will it taste good? Those are surely the three most important things about the food we eat.

In this Consumers' Guide we take you through the whole cycle of food handling:

- Buying food
- Storing food
- Food preparation
- Cooking
- Eating out

Throughout this section our concern is to explore how you can end up eating food that tastes good, that does you good and, by golly, that doesn't give you food poisoning!

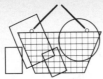

BUYING FOOD

In this subsection we look at how you can judge the standards of a shop, how to judge the quality of both fresh and packaged foods, how to read a label to advantage and whether organic produce is worth buying. You will find that we have devoted quite a few pages to our simple labelling guide – if you understand labels properly you can revolutionize your diet.

When food is produced on a mass-market scale then food bugs can spread very easily. The few chickens containing the salmonella bacterium are processed alongside thousands of others which can easily become contaminated. The lettuces washed by a supermarket for a delivery of prepared salads will soon contain listeria only if only a few did to start with. Intensive rearing of animals makes the spread of bacteria between them much easier than in the past. The five massive supermarket groups who sell us the bulk of our food are now making efforts to tackle the prevalence of food-poisoning bacteria. Two supermarket groups claim to have drastically reduced the incidence of salmonella in their fresh chickens. The Ministry of Agriculture has announced some twenty measures to clean up the egg industry alone. But the problem will remain with us for the foreseeable future.

Countless surveys have found the standards of our shops lacking. We buy 75 per cent of our groceries from five supermarket groups whose standards are, on the whole, quite high. But they are by no means perfect, corner shops are worse and garages (who are now in on the act) can be awful. Here are some tips to help you judge the standards of a shop:

Staff should be wearing clean clothes and should not wipe their hands on their clothes.

Staff should not touch their face while serving food and their hair should be tied back.

Their hands should be clean and any wounds, particularly on the hands, should be covered with a waterproof plaster.

Chiller and freezer cabinets should not be overloaded and should not look too old or damaged.

Dirty floors and shelves are a helpful warning to shop elsewhere.

Chilled and frozen food needs to be kept at particular temperatures. Some shops now display a thermometer so you can check that this is the case. New laws are being introduced to regulate what temperatures chilled food may be kept at. But broadly:

Chilled foods should be kept between 0°C and 3°C (listeria can multiply above that).
Frozen foods should be kept at or below −18°C.

Many chiller display cabinets have red 'load lines' on the inside – food should not be stored above these. Frozen food in which the individual pieces of food have become stuck together suggests that poor transit has allowed the food partially to thaw before re-freezing. A brief word in defence of cheese: real cheese needs to ripen and it cannot do so at 3°C. As long as those at risk obey the rules about listeria set out on p377 then there is little to fear.

Packaged food should always be examined. Packages which are dented are sometimes sold off cheaply. Don't buy them, since a broken internal seal can allow metals to leach into the food. Do not buy tins that are swollen – this indicates that the food is reacting with the metal and giving off a gas. The food will be poisonous. Where the external packaging of dry goods is damaged there may be no problem but look carefully to ensure that the inner bag remains sealed. Many goods now have 'tamper-free' packaging. In a sorry age in which a malign few deliberately spike foods check all tamper-free packaging is intact.

Meat products put on display outside shops in unchilled cabinets should be avoided like the plague. This habit is unfortunately still widespread. Bacteria love meat products and they should always be kept chilled once they have cooled after cooking. Beware market traders who offer a cut price bargain – you may be buying more than you bargained for. Here are some tips about buying raw meat:

Beef should be pink to red. (Well-hung beef will have dark red flesh and yellow fat.)
Lamb should be bought red, firm and have white, brittle, flaky fat.
Pork should be pale pink and firm and its fat should be white and hard.
There is now enormous choice as to how lean or fatty meat is. Butchers will trim fat off for you if you wish.
Offal, like all meat, should never have an unpleasant 'off' odour.
All meats should smell fresh and be free of the stickiness due to food spoilage bacteria and decomposition.
Chicken should have firm, glossy, white flesh and unbroken skin free of bruising or blood spots. Corn-fed birds will have yellowish flesh.

Fish is safer than meat, microbiologically speaking. The chief danger of food poisoning comes from shellfish as we explain on p287. Here are some tips about buying fresh fish:

The colour should be bright and clear.
The skin should have a shiny, glistening appearance.
The eyes should be bulging with a clear black centre – not opaque or misty.
Inside the gills should be pink to red in colour and free of slime. They should smell fresh and 'seaweedy'.
The scales should be firm and not easily rubbed off.
The odour should be fresh with no trace of rankness or ammonia.
The texture should be stiff and rigid, not floppy and loose.
Fish fillets should be firm and elastic, not crumbly.
Oysters, mussels and clams should still be alive and their shells tight. (If they are open they should shut when you touch them.)

Fruit and vegetables that look 'tired' should be avoided. If leaf vegetables have gone limp, for instance, then they will have begun to suffer considerable vitamin loss. Apples and other fruits with stalks will be fresh and not woolly if the stalk is flexible and green. Heavy oranges and lemons with withered skins will contain more juice. Ripe galia and canteloupe melons should give slightly when pressed at the stalk end. Ripe honeydew melons should give when pressed at the opposite end to the stalk. Pineapples smell fruity when they are ripe and the inner leaves should come out fairly easily. Fruit and vegetables with mould or soft rot are not only nutritionally inferior but may contain poisons.

Bread Check use-by dates on bread and, in particular, pitta breads (for more on use-by dates, *see* p245). Ensure they do not have mould spots growing on them.

ORGANIC PRODUCE

What does the label 'organic' mean? Is the food so labelled healthier or better tasting? Is organic food worth the extra money? The plain truth is that while there are some excellent philosophical reasons for buying organic produce there is no evidence that the actual food is better for you.

Until the 1980s organic farmers were a tiny minority regarded as amiable romantics not living in the real world. They were known as the 'muck and magic brigade'. Then, in 1983, one of the Archers on Radio 4 went organic. That did it. Now more than 800 supermarkets stock organic produce and countless health-food shops besides. Although at present less than 1 per cent of British farmers are organic, their ranks are swelling all the time and there are some astute farmers who are making a good living at it. We compared a shopping basket of ordinary food with an identical basket of organic food, both at Safeways. The baskets contained fruit, vegetables, tinned food, spreads and preserves, eggs, cereals and meat. The organic food cost around 45 per cent more – a result born out by other surveys carried out recently by *Which?* and the *Sunday Telegraph*. The higher prices can be justified for a number of reasons. There is a high demand for a restricted supply, organic farming takes longer, has higher labour costs and lower yields. In addition, more of the crop is discarded because it is diseased or misshapen.

Before we look at the different labels, what they purport to guarantee and whether there is a genuine difference between organic and non-organic, let's try to answer an equally basic question. Why do people buy organic produce and pay all that extra money? In November 1989, *Which?* questioned 325 people who bought organic food:

- 1 in 2 said they bought it because it is better for health.
- 1 in 3 bought it for a similar but more specific reason – that they believed it to be free of pesticide and fungicide residues.
- 1 in 5 preferred the taste.
- 1 in 6 said organic farming was better for the environment.
- 1 in 25 said that in the case of livestock it was kinder to animals.

So the majority buy organic food because they believe it to be healthier. Only a minority say that they do it out of concern for the environment and animal welfare. Let's examine what evidence there is to support these different reasons.

Health – pesticides and fungicides There is obviously plenty of evidence that pesticides and fungicides consumed in large quantities would be injurious to our health. The key questions – as we explored in relation to Alar in the Introduction – are not only how potentially toxic it is but also how much of it we are exposed to and how often. In the case of Alar, it has been argued by many scientists that there is no real risk. So little of it has been used in such small quantities that we simply did not come into contact with it often enough.

So how great is the danger? To find out we have commissioned a detailed analysis to discover what sort of levels of insecticides, herbicides and fungicides exist in apples sold in our shops. We asked a respected firm of analytical chemists, Dr Angus-tus Voelcker and Sons Ltd, to test for around half the commonly used sprays, including Alar. The results are there-fore not exhaustive, but they are highly indicative of whether we have much to worry about. Twelve samples of apples from street markets, greengrocers, supermarkets, corner-shops and health-food shops were tested for twenty sprays – 240 individual tests in all. There were five apple varieties from England and France. *In not one single test was any spray detected, although most would have been permitted within levels laid down by the Ministry of Agriculture.*
Privately, the technical directors of the large supermarkets

will admit they are happy to sell organic fruit and vegetables if that is what people want, but that they believe there is no real difference between them and their cheaper, non-organic counterparts. None of this means that the strict controls on pesticide use should be relaxed – clearly none of us wish to ingest large quantities of these chemicals. But on health grounds it is very difficult to argue in favour of organic foods.

Indeed, there is evidence that organic produce is itself not always free of residues. Between 1985 and 1988 the Ministry of Agriculture found that eleven out of forty-one examples of organic food had pesticide residue. And Trading Standards Offices in Birmingham found the growth inhibitor, tecnazene, on 'organic' potatoes in 1989. None were at dangerous levels and there are several possible reasons for it – spray drift from a non-organic farm to an organic one, cross-contamination in storage or plain, old-fashioned fraud. In any event, there was no danger to the public and the unscrupulous suppliers are certainly in a minority. But it proves that you should never take a label at face value.

The least regulated area of 'organic' produce is wine. There is no generally agreed definition of what an organic wine is in Britain or France. The basic idea, of course, is to grow the grapes without artificial fertilizers or sprays and to make the wine with a minimum of additives. A recent test of wines sold as organic wines in Britain showed that ascorbic acid had been added to a Muscadet and that a German tafelwein had levels of sulphur dioxide just as high as non-organic wines. Neither deserved to be described as organic. Yet organic wines command a premium of around 50 pence a bottle.

Although it is hard to prove that organic food is genuinely healthier might it be nutritionally superior? A 1983 study concluded:

> There are few significant differences in the proximate composition of a wide range of foods between organic and intensive agriculture and the scientific evidence for difference in nutritional composition is almost non-existent.

Dr David Southgate from the Institute of Food Research has compared the nutritional difference between potatoes in 1934 (effectively organic) and 1987 (grown with all the help of modern agricultural methods). He found little difference between them. The results, he said, 'do not support the conclusion that intensive methods have altered composition in such a way as to make the present crops nutritionally inferior.'

Taste Taste is a very subjective yardstick by which to assess any food. A number of blind tastings have been carried out with inconclusive results. Organically grown carrots have tended to come out well. And there are some fruit and vegetables produced in a highly modern, intensive way that are remarkably flavourless. Tomatoes are the classic example. There is no doubt that tomatoes grown traditionally (at a reasonable pace in soil and not water troughs) are markedly superior. But produce can be grown in a reasonably traditional way with chemical fertilizers. So the growing method is probably the key factor here.

Better for the environment and kinder to animals This is where organic produce scores heavily. There is no doubt that organic farming is more sympathetic to the environment. The loss of woodland, hedgerows and wild flowers, the destruction of the natural habitat of wild animals, the dire effect on insects such as butterflies – traditional farming with its revolutionary changes to the countryside and its sprays has harmed our environment. If that is something that concerns you then you have a strong motive for buying organic produce. Organic farms treat nature much more gently.

Likewise, the public's concern about animal welfare is growing rapidly. Battery farming, antibiotics and growth promoters, animal protein fed to herbivores – none of these are allowed on organic farms where strict codes of practice are enforced for livestock. (But even with the advent of BSE there is still no hard scientific evidence that organic meat is better for us.)

So the conclusion must be that there are very good reasons for buying organic food but that the food itself is no better and no worse for our health than non-organic produce.

Organic labels There have been many cases of unscrupulous traders passing non-organic produce off as the real thing in order to rake in extra cash. Trading Standards Offices were growing increasingly frustrated because there was no entirely reliable definition of what 'organic' means. So the United Kingdom Register of Organic Food Standards (UKROFS) was set up to co-ordinate organic labels and lay down standards enforceable in court. To be an organic farmer you must subscribe to one of five organizations, all of whom are registered with UKROFS. Here are the symbols to look out for:

Soil association – awarded to food from British farmers and foreign schemes conforming to the strictest organic standards. Man-made chemical fertilizers, pesticides and chemical feedstuffs are banned. Crops have to be rotated regularly to protect the soil. Annual inspection of farms. Several hundred farms subscribe and farmers wishing to go organic have to wait three to five years while their land 'cleanses' itself.

Demeter – awarded by the Bio-dynamic Agriculture Association (BDAA) to farmers meeting the most far-reaching organic standards in UK. Not only are chemical treatments banned, but farmers use 'special herbal and other biodynamic preparations' as they term them, to nourish the soil. They aim for 90 per cent self-sufficiency in fertilizers and animal feedstuffs. They also take account of lunar and planetary influences in timing planting and harvesting. Only twenty UK farmers have the symbol – but it is common on imports.

Biodyn – also awarded by the BDAA to farmers taking a holistic approach but it is not strictly organic since it relates to food produced by farms in the three to five year conversion period to Demeter status.

Organic Farmers and Growers – they are registered with UKROFS but are essentially a marketing group. Until two years ago farmers were allowed to use the fertilizer sodium nitrate to enhance crop yields. That is now banned but the Soil Association is apparently unhappy with other aspects – their rotations are apparently more exhaustive of the soil and they allow use of broiler chicken manures.

UKROFS – launched in May 1989. Standards are roughly the same as Soil Association. Annual inspections. It is the official UK standard but is voluntary. You may see 'produced to UKROFS standards' or a UKROFS registration number, or the symbol.

There is also a sixth label you may see:

 Conservation Grade – not organic by any common definition. Farmers use selected synthetic fertilizers and pesticides alongside typical organic methods like crop rotation. Annual inspections.

One final word of warning – don't be taken in by 'organic honey'. A beekeeper would have to have very well-trained bees to be able to restrict them to organic land only!

IS PROCESSED FOOD BAD?

If you listened to some of the more self-appointed pundits you would conclude that all processed food is bad. But the same pundits will frequently sing the praises of traditional cheeses which are, of course, highly processed. Indeed, the food we cook at home is processed too.

But the unavoidable truth is that we live in an age of convenience – many people have neither the time nor the inclination to spend hours in the kitchen preparing food. To them processed food is a great blessing and, as a result, 75 per cent of our housekeeping is spent on processed foods. In the subsection on food labelling we outline some of the tricks food manufacturers get up to. But here the question is whether processed food is nutritious or not. We know the manufacturers 'add value' to the product, but do they add goodness as well?

Well, some manufacturers do just that, often because they are required to by law. Iron, thiamin (vitamin B_1), niacin (vitamin B_3) and calcium must be added to white bread. And vitamins A and D must be added to margarine. Breakfast cereal manufacturers have always boasted of a range of vitamins on their packets. They are nearly all added. And incidentally, the milk poured on to cereal is as important nutritionally as the cereal itself.

Food is processed either to preserve it or to render it edible in one of three basic ways:

- **By physical agents** – ie, heating, chilling, freezing, drying, evaporating and so on.
- **By chemical agents** – ie, preservation by acid, salt, sugar, smoking, pickling and a variety of other additives, the safety of which we discuss elsewhere. One common process is the hydrogenation of fat (the conversion of liquid, unsaturated oil into a more solid saturated form – *see* Trans-fatty Acids, p361).
- **By biological agents** – ie, the use of micro-organisms to turn milk into yoghurt or yeast to turn carbohydrates into alcohol for a drink like beer.

The chief methods of commercial processing and preservation are:

Freezing   Freezing created one of the greatest revolutions in food technology when it was developed seriously after the war. It gives us the likes of New Zealand lamb and garden peas all the year round and virtually our own butcher's shop at home. But remember that freezing can only stop bacterial growth. It cannot kill bacteria. So observe all the food safety rules relating to frozen foods (*see* p292). Remember also that frozen foods when fried take up much more fat than fresh foods. Most vitamins are well preserved by freezing.

Chilling   This more recent technology involves suspending food, raw or cooked, just above freezing. It has given rise to many fears about food poisoning because so many so-called 'cook-chill' ready-cooked dishes have been found to contain potentially harmful bacteria. Most nutrients are retained by this method. It is a beneficial technology that we are not yet using carefully enough.

Sous-vide   (literally 'under a vacuum') is a process whereby food is cooked or partially cooked and sealed in a plastic pouch with all the air removed. It is then kept cool. Sous-vide preserves fresh flavours and textures better than any other method. But the food is not heated to a level at which it would be pasteurized and this method in inexperienced hands could prove a disaster. The botulism bug loves exactly the conditions sous-vide creates of airlessness with moisture. Albert Roux, the distinguished French chef, has called for its use to be strictly licensed, but at the moment anyone who wishes can sell sous-vide food.

Drying   This method of preservation is particularly good for cereal foods – eg, breakfast cereals and pasta and starch-based foods like instant mashed potato and instant puddings. Packet soups are another example.

Smoking, salting and pickling   All these ancient methods evolved because they inhibited bacterial growth. With the advent of modern techniques such as freezing and with modern distribution of fresh fruit and vegetables, the original reason for these methods of preservation has disappeared. Now we eat such foods because we like the taste, whether it is smoked salmon, ham or pickled onions. All three methods have a question mark over their safety if people consume them heavily and regularly (*see* 'Getting Away With It', p143). Pickled food is at its best eaten within two months of being processed. Smoking of food destroys vitamin A and pickling increases the salt content. Much vitamin C is lost in pickling but some still remains in pickled cabbage.

Preserves   Just as salt is a powerful preservative, so is sugar. Thus the original purpose of jam was to preserve fruit. Now we have many better ways of preserving fruit so we eat jam because we like it. However, you shouldn't kid yourself that it is particularly good for you. The fruit in jam is so highly processed that all its water-soluble vitamins have escaped before you spread the luscious stuff on your bread.

Canning and bottling   Canning involves sealing the food and sterilizing it with heat. It may sound an over-technical description for one of our staples, baked beans. But the can is not heated for long and so tinned food retains its nutritional qualities well. The key to preserving nutrients is processing the fruit and vegetables within hours of harvesting. Indeed canning factories are often placed in the middle of the agricultural areas which grow the vegetables so that the produce only has to be transported a few miles and can be processed the same day. The principle is the same with freezing. In North America, where home canning is quite common, cases of botulism are relatively high. The airless conditions favour this dangerous bug in much the same way as sous-vide does. Processes not to be undertaken unless you know what you are doing. The same applies to bottling which relies on the same principle as canning – heating and sealing food.

UHT (Ultra Heat Treatment) Food is heated rapidly to between 135°C and 140°C. It is held there for just one second and then cooled rapidly and put into sterilized containers. It is most often used with liquids such as milk and fruit juice. 'Long-life' milk is usually UHT. Vitamin losses are minimal. Liquids treated in this way usually have a minimum shelf life of three months.

Pasteurization Unlike canning and UHT, pasteurization does not sterilize the food. But it does kill off a significant number of the bugs and thus make the food safer. Again, it is mostly used on milk and fruit juices and also pickled food where the acid (vinegar) is already a good inhibitor of bacteria. Food is heated to 71.7°C, held at that temperature for fifteen seconds and then cooled rapidly. Vitamin losses are minimal.

Ohmic heating This is a sterilizing process whereby an electric current is passed through food as it is pumped along an electrically insulated pipe. This heats the food and sterilizes it. It is then cooled to 25°C and sealed in aseptic containers. Up to now this method has generally been used by bulk caterers for such foods as pasta in sauce, rice pudding, pie fillings and soups. But ready-prepared meals rather similar to cook-chill are beginning to be marketed. They will be safer than cook-chill.

Extrusion This process produces many of the light, airy packet snacks you can now buy. A cereal or starch mixture is moistened with steam or water, fed into a barrel and heated as high as 200°C. Pressure in the barrel extrudes the mixture out of the end greatly expanded for a hollow, airy texture. Because of the high temperatures many of the vitamins that originally existed in the mixture are eliminated and such snacks have little nutritional value except energy. Unfortunately, many of the extruded snacks are marketed directly at children. Our advice would be to stick to crisps or corn snacks.

Irradiation   This involves bombarding food with gamma rays to kill bacteria. So it can give fruit and vegetables a longer shelf life and sterilize such salmonella-carrying foods as chicken. It does not make the food radioactive and has been used to sterilize the food of astronauts and some hospital patients for some years. Now it is legal but opposition to it is so vocal that, at the time of writing, only one British supermarket has said it will sell irradiated food. Irradiated food has to be labelled as such. For arguments for and against this process, *see* Section III, p145. Vitamin losses are minimal.

Our conclusion must be that 'processed' is not a dirty word and that processed foods yield us many benefits. We are arguably at more risk (whether bacteriological or nutritional) from handling fresh food badly at home than we are from the products of the food industry. But, as with all elements of our diet, balance is the watchword. A diet omitting all fresh foods would be a poor one. A kitchen where no cooking takes place would be a dull one. Let us not forget that we cook and eat for enjoyment as well as sustenance.

Vitamin losses in processing   The Campden Food Preservation Research Association carried out some experiments in 1987. This was the vitamin C content of garden peas under different conditions:

	Vitamin C content mg per 100g
Fresh and raw	**130**
Cooked (12 mins, minimum water)	**116**
(12 mins, in equal volume of water)	**84**
Stored in pod for 1 day and then cooked 12 mins in minimum water	**90**
Stored 4 days in pod and then cooked 12 mins in minimum water	**57**
Frozen then cooked for 4 mins	**65**
Frozen for 3 months then cooked	**61**
Frozen for 6 months then cooked	**58**
Canned then cooked for 5 mins	**50**
Canned for 3 months then cooked for 5 mins	**40**
Canned for 6 months then cooked for 5 mins	**37**

It is interesting to note how prolonged storage of fresh peas had as great an effect as cooking. Whereas frozen peas, once frozen, lost nothing to speak of in storage. If we did not freeze peas we could only eat them during their short season so frozen peas have their advantages (not least because they do not need shelling and cook more quickly). A fresh garden pea has the best flavour of all and the most vitamin C. But there is still a goodly quantity of vitamin C left in frozen peas along with minerals, protein and soluble fibre. Canned peas – and even 'mushy peas' – may be more of an acquired taste, but even they are by no means devoid of nutrition.

The vitamin C content of potatoes is lower than peas. But potatoes are still the most important source of vitamin C for most of us. We have prepared a table showing how much vitamin C potatoes contain after different methods of processing and cooking:

	Vitamin C content mgs per 100g
Old potatoes – raw	20
– boiled	14
– mashed	12
– baked	16
– roast	16
Chips (deep fried)	16
Frozen chips	6
Frozen shallow fried chips	4
McCains Oven chips (oven cooked)	14
Oven chips (grilled)	10
Oven chips (shallow fried)	7

	Vitamin C content mgs per 100g
Oven chips (deep fried)	**11**
Oven chips (microwaved)	**12**
New potatoes – boiled (for 15 mins)	**18**
– canned	**17**
Instant potato powder	**12**
Instant potato powder (made up as per instructions)	**3**
Crisps	**17**

(*Source*: McCance & Widdowson, McCain's)

What can we conclude from this? That processed potato products like oven chips, canned new potatoes and crisps retain their vitamin C very well. Instant mashed potato, once prepared, is the exception. Personal likes and dislikes are just as important here. As far as we're concerned, canned new potatoes taste and have the texture of old blotting paper. Instant mashed potato bears as much resemblance in flavour to fresh mashed potato as processed cheddar does to farmhouse cheddar. But, as we say, these are matters of taste.

The table also shows that crisps and chips are by no means the 'junk food' they are often held up to be. Their vitamin C retention is very good. The only exception to this is when chips are cut a long time in advance. As you can see the frozen chips have the lowest levels of vitamin C. And while we are on the subject of chips, their take-up of fat during cooking is also an important nutritional factor. Let's now look at the fat take-up of different sorts of chips and crisps once cooked:

	Fat gms per 100g
Chips (deep fried)	11
Frozen chips (deep fried)	19
McCain's Oven chips (oven-baked)	5
Crisps	36

Note that once frozen, the chip takes up more fat on cooking. This is true of most frozen foods, including fish. Another important factor is what sort of oil the chips or crisps have been fried in. If it was an animal fat such as beef dripping (still widely used in the north of England and also used – until recently – by McDonald's) then the fat would be highly saturated. Crisps, while clearly high in calories, are usually not fried in saturated fats. Nor are oven chips. In fact McCain's have not only managed to achieve a low level of fat, their product also contains a very low level of saturates too. Below we have analysed two samples of their oven chips bought at two London supermarkets. They vary slightly but the picture is clear:

McCain's Sample	Saturated	% of Fat' Monounsaturated	Polyunsaturated
Tesco	12.7	24.1	63.2
Co-op	13.5	24.7	61.8

Chips, and in particular processed oven chips, do not seem to be the junk we took them for. Whether you like their taste is up to you.

Most processed foods provide all the nutrients we need. The danger comes from high levels of fat, salt and sugar –

convenient ingredients which improve the palatability but which we need to keep an eye on. Always look at the label.

THE LABELLING CODE

Food labelling has gone through a complete revolution since the last war. Historically food manufacturers had always been reluctant to reveal the ingredients of their products. Partly this was because the villains did not wish to be discovered adulterating food with all manner of cheaper, bulkier materials – why sell food when you can sell water instead? The other reason was that they liked to boast of secret recipes and mystery ingredients.

So when the law changed and manufacturers were obliged to come clean many regretted it. None more so than Lea and Perrins – the veil was lifted on their Worcestershire Sauce revealing that its much vaunted secret recipe used anchovies to achieve that distinctively pungent flavour.

Now, of course, there is a massive amount of information on packets. The purpose of this subsection is to help you identify what really matters on a label and pinpoint the things you can safely ignore or of which you should be sceptical. In the course of doing this we will explain everything that you might see on a product. But we emphasize that our purpose is to help you be selective and gather the information that will be beneficial to you. After all, you cannot shop in a busy supermarket with a computer in the trolley to analyse all the data. Nor can you spend your life reading small print when all you want to do is eat. But buried amidst all the detail and the small print are one or two crucial details. Once you crack the labelling code you can start to make many of the small changes that will revolutionize your diet.

There is plenty of evidence that the sheer weight of information now available causes us problems, either because we do not understand it or because we get sidetracked by things which seem important but are in fact trivial. In 1990, Professor Donald Naismith of King's College, London, published the results of a survey he had carried out for Dairy Crest. Altogether 1,200 shoppers from London, the

Home Counties, the Midlands and Wales were asked whether they read labels and, if so, why. The great majority said they read labels frequently or occasionally, which is very positive. It is more difficult to be positive about the confusions and misapprehensions that were then revealed. Among them:

- Six out of ten read the label to check for additives (as we have seen, additives are simply not the threat they are perceived to be).
- Eight out of ten always read sell-by dates but seven out of ten thought food was still safe beyond this point (we will help clear up this confusion later).
- Only five out of ten realized that ingredients have to be listed in order of weight (so the biggest ingredient in volume or weight is always listed first – this can be a useful indicator).
- Everyone thought the total fat we consume is the most important factor for health (an encouraging response, but the truth is that it is more the sort of fat we eat that matters, ie how much of it is saturated).
- Six out of ten thought polyunsaturated fat promotes weight loss. (All fats can make us put on weight but only saturates seem to lead to heart disease.)
- When asked how much fat there is in a packet of crisps, one out of four gave an answer which exceeded the weight of the whole packet. (Nutritional labelling which shows how much fat there is in every 100g of a food is obviously difficult to relate to packets and portions.)
- One out of two thought salt was an important health factor, but only one out of five thought the same about sodium. (Salt *is* sodium chloride.)
- Only one out of four knew that kilocalories are what we popularly call calories and only one in eight knew the difference between kilocalories and kilojoules. (Read on – all will be revealed.)

Meanwhile another survey (*The National Health Survey*, Jones Rhodes Associates) revealed that half their respondents found information on food packaging unclear. Jones Rhodes

Associates had talked to 300 women between sixteen and sixty-four. But it was encouraging to note that the most frequently consulted items of information were the sell-by date and the fat content. You could do worse than that, as we will explain later.

The purpose of food labelling is both to help us regulate our own diet and also to ensure that the manufacturer is not up to any tricks. But before we look at the regulations in detail there are general laws which apply to food which are well worth knowing about. The Food Act lays down that food must be

'of the nature, substance and quality demanded by the purchaser'

and makes it an offence to sell

'food unfit for human consumption.'

'Of the nature' means you should get a Cox's Orange Pippin when you ask for one, not a Golden Delicious. It means that a butcher labelling pigs' liver as calves' liver is breaking the law. 'Substance' means that things should not be there that do not belong – eg, sand in curry powder or glass in milk. 'Quality' refers to foods that quite simply do not come up to standard. For example, if they are stale or mouldy. Food which is 'unfit for human consumption' is that which is microbiologically contaminated – eg hazelnut yoghurt contaminated by the botulism bacterium. (No supermarket has ever been prosecuted for selling a chicken with salmonella in it, but it would be an interesting judgement for a court to be asked to make.)

There are a massive number of regulations which govern how particular foods must be labelled. But in general terms it is an offence to have a false or misleading label on a product. This offence is enshrined in a whole range of national laws across the world. The interesting thing is that labelling laws are coming closer and closer together. Members of the EC will have agreed common rules by 1992. Australia's laws are almost identical (barring the odd difference in terminology and size of lettering). And even in the US we would have no difficulty understanding the more important parts of a label – so long as we had mastered the basics already – so read on!

Later on in this subsection we will look at the specific regulations for particular foods, concentrating on the ones where fats and sugars are most likely to be hidden. But before that, we have prepared a guide to what you find on packets – everything you wanted to know about labelling but no one would tell you . . .

What must appear on a label?

At Ackroyd's – the well-known speciality food manufacturer – the staff are in a state of high excitement. Old Mr Ackroyd has perfected a new technique for rendering a product of nature into powdered form. The resultant food will be of incontestable benefit to Ackroyd's profits (as well as to the human system). The name and slogan have now been settled upon and the packet designed.

But the work on the packet has only just begun. There are at least seven legal requirements for a food package and, increasingly, manufacturers are including much more than that.

- The name or description of the food.
- Exactly what it's made from – the ingredients.

- How long it can be kept and under what conditions.
- Its weight, volume or the number in the pack.
- Its place of origin, if relevant.
- Preparation or cooking instructions where necessary.
- The name and address of manufacturer, packer or seller.

These rules sound simple enough, but they actually cover a huge range of complex requirements which have developed over the years, all designed to prevent the likes of Mr Ackroyd pulling the wool over the eyes of his customers.

THE NAME OR DESCRIPTION

A product's name must reveal what the food actually is. Brand names are fine, but on their own are no substitute for a proper description. Thus 'Dinkies' must be accompanied by 'a hot chocolate drink'. In our case, the name will suffice unless, of course, the powdered moonbeams are, in fact, merely sherbet. In which case it should say so.

If food has been processed, this should be acknowledged in the description – eg, *smoked* cheese, *UHT* cream or, indeed, *powdered* moonbeams.

If a strawberry yoghurt genuinely derives its flavour from strawberries then it is allowed to be called '*strawberry yoghurt*' or '*strawberry flavoured yoghurt*'. If its flavour is an artificial one then it can only be called '*strawberry flavour yoghurt*'. Yes, we know, it is ridiculous ('When I use a word,' said Humpty Dumpty, 'it means just what I choose it to mean – neither more nor less'). To complicate matters further, it is legitimate for the manufacturers to illustrate a 'serving suggestion' with real strawberries even when there is not a shred of real strawberry flavour in the product!

INGREDIENTS

Pre-packed foods must have a complete list of ingredients, listed in descending order of weight. So the ingredients list for sweet biscuits will always begin with sugar, flour and fat because they contain little else. This is a very good guide as to the nature of the predominant ingredients, but very few of us seem to know about it.

There are moves afoot in the EC to introduce 'quantitative' labelling so that we can see more precisely how much of each ingredient there is in a product. This could be in force by 1992 and would relate only to the 'main characterizing ingredients'. It would be difficult, after all, to attach a meaningful percentage to a pinch of paprika or (more likely) a pinch of monosodium glutamate. Under the proposed rules, the ingredients of a packaged potato and haddock pie would read like this:

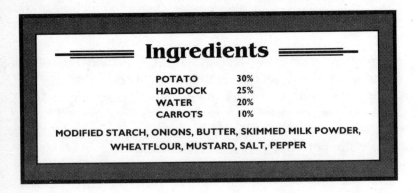

══ **Ingredients** ══

POTATO	30%
HADDOCK	25%
WATER	20%
CARROTS	10%

MODIFIED STARCH, ONIONS, BUTTER, SKIMMED MILK POWDER, WHEATFLOUR, MUSTARD, SALT, PEPPER

So-called 'reserved description foods' – cheese and chocolate, for example – do not have to reveal their ingredients. Nor do they need to be broken down when declared as an ingredient in another product.

All additives have to be declared on ingredients lists. They may be shown by their E number (denoting their *approval* by the EC) or by name. They should be preceded by a description of their function (eg, preservative, colour, emulsifier). The use of flavourings must be declared but they need not be named individually. Finally, although alcoholic drinks do not have to declare their ingredients, it is thought that there will soon be changes on this front too (if they are low-alcohol drinks under 1.2 per cent then they are classified as a soft drink and must declare ingredients anyway). The brewers have made a song and dance about declaring ingredients but if they can do it for low-alcohol drinks they can do it for *all* drinks.

DATEMARKS

Most foods must carry a datemark to tell when it should be consumed by. 'Sell-by' dates were phased out before the end of 1990 because of the confusion they caused (how many days after that could the food be consumed?). 'Use-by' dates are now in force which let us know by when the food should be eaten.

However, there are also problems attached to use-by dates. What if a highly perishable product like a cooked, chilled chicken in sauce is kept at too high a temperature in the store, left in a hot car for several hours after purchase and then put into a fridge that is too warm before being eaten? It should have a much earlier use-by date than an identical dish which has been kept properly chilled. There is a new invention which solves this problem. It is called a Time Temperature Indicator. It amounts to a use-by dot which reacts to the temperature of the food and changes colour accordingly. The colour code is simple to understand and the sooner this ingenious invention is widely introduced the better. The good news is that the Ministry of Agriculture is currently assessing the value of these indicators.

From 1 April 1991, it has been an offence to sell food after its 'use-by' date has expired. It is also an offence to re-date the use-by label unless you are the person or company who put the label on in the first place – ie, the manufacturer.

Another common datemark is the 'best before'. If food is to last longer than three months then only the month and the year need be shown. There are a number of foods which are currently exempt from the datemark rules:

- some canned food (though rotating the cans on a first-in, first-out basis is still a good idea)
- most alcoholic drinks (beer is an exception)
- vinegar
- salt
- sugar and sugar-based foods
- chewing-gum
- some cheeses
- some breads and pastries
- fresh fruit and veg

- frozen foods (although these have a voluntary system of stars indicating how long the product will last at three different temperatures)

The laws on food labelling change constantly. It is likely that before long datemarking will be required for cheese, frozen foods and all canned foods.

WHAT ELSE MUST THE LABEL SHOW?

What else must Ackroyd's come clean about before they launch their powdered moonbeams on the public? Well, first they have the unenviable task of weighing a moonbeam.

The Weights and Measures Law says that most foods must state the quantity either by net weight (ie, minus the packaging) or by volume. You'll often see the letter 'e' beside the weight. This denotes that an EC system of quantity control is being adhered to which allows the actual quantity to be slightly above or below the stated figure.

The name and address of the manufacturer, packer or seller must appear on the packet. The place of origin must be included if the name might otherwise be misleading. Ackroyd's may genuinely harvest their moonbeams from the moon but 'Devon Recipe Fudge' from Humberside would have to admit its origin. Storage instructions must be given if they are necessary to keep the food in good condition. And alcoholic drinks are obliged to state their strength in percentage by volume. For example, whisky is 40 per cent by volume – ie, 40 per cent of it is alcohol.

Loose foods are exempt from many of the legal requirements we have listed, but they *must* display category names (such as Webb's Wonder or King Edward) and they should declare additives – eg, salami containing preservatives. This remains something of a pious hope, however, since you rarely see loose foods labelled properly.

NUTRIONAL LABELLING

Nutritional labelling is the most recent and most dramatic information to appear on packets. Potentially, it gives us enormous control over our diet and it could be the key which enables us to reduce the amount of fat we eat. In most cases, nutritional labelling is voluntary and, after a recent EC decision, will remain so. But all the supermarkets are now putting it on their packets and supermarkets sell us the bulk of our food these days. Food manufacturers who still do not display detailed panels of nutritional information (biscuits and confectionery makers in particular) can only be assumed to have something to hide. Perhaps they would prefer us not to discover how high their products are in saturated fat and sugar. Up to now, they have given as their excuse the uncertainty surrounding what the law will be on nutritional labelling. This will no longer wash, since most food producers have *voluntarily* implemented a standard way of displaying the information. *If you understand nutritional labelling then you understand your diet. The nuts and bolts of good nutrition are all contained on that small panel.*

At its simplest, nutritional labelling breaks a food product down into four constituents (known as the 'Big Four'):

Energy   Food is essentially fuel and provides us with energy via the fat, protein and carbohydrate it contains. This energy is quantified by a unit of measurement we are all familiar with – the calorie. The average adult requires around 2,000 to 2,500 calories a day and would lose weight when restricted to 1,000 calories a day. What we popularly call a calorie appears on the packet as a 'kilocalorie'. Technically, it is defined as the energy needed to raise one kilogram of water from 15°C to 16°C. Most foods now express kilocalories in 'kilojoules' as well. Don't be confused by that. A kilojoule is a metric calorie and is approximately four times smaller in value. So a 1,000 calorie-a-day diet would be around 4,000 kilojoules. Since we derive most of our energy from fat, protein and carbohydrate those are the other three of the 'Big Four'.

Fat   Fat provides our most concentrated source of energy and eating too much means that we store it as body fat. We rely on fats and oils for many absolutely vital nutrients affecting everything from our reproductive system to our brain function. On average, 42 per cent of our energy – our calories – comes from fat. The government's COMA report on heart disease (Diet and Cardiovascular Disease), published as long ago as 1984, recommended that no more than 35 per cent of our calories should come from fat and no more than 15 per cent from saturated fat. Saturated fat is one of the three 'fatty acids' that makes up a fat or an oil. Saturated fat is usually hard at room temperature and of animal origin. The other two fatty acids are called monounsaturated and polyunsaturated. They are usually soft or liquid at room temperature and are generally of vegetable origin.

Fats and oils contain these three fatty acids in varying amounts. It is the saturated fat that we should eat less of because it can raise the level of cholesterol in our blood. We are still a long way from achieving the COMA target for fat and saturated fat in our diet. But if we can see at a glance the fat content of our food then we can begin to reduce the amount we eat.

Protein Protein provides the building blocks for our bodies, being essential for growth and tissue repair. It should provide us with 10–15 per cent of our calories. Deficiencies in protein do not occur in Britain. This is because protein can be derived from such a wide range of foods – bread, potatoes, cereals, eggs, nuts, peas, beans and pulses as well as meat and dairy products.

Carbohydrates All starchy and most sweet foods contain carbohydrate. Carbohydrates are very high in calories and if eaten to excess can be fattening. But carbohydrate is a less concentrated source of energy than fat and it does not carry the health warning that fat does. Along with a range of sugars starch is the other common form of carbohydrate. Starchy foods include bread, potatoes and rice. Starch is broken down by our digestive system into glucose. So those of us who need to cut down on fat should replace it with starchy carbohydrate to ensure we are still getting enough energy. It is a mistake to follow the slimming advice widely given in the fifties and sixties to cut down drastically on bread and potatoes to lose weight. By doing so we deprive ourselves of much-needed fibre and ignore what really matters – fat.

These Big Four – energy, fat, protein and carbohydrate – are a good foundation for nutritional labelling, but they are only a starting point. The Department of Health has a permanent committee of experts called the Committee on Medical Aspects of Health (COMA). COMA appoints sub-committees to investigate particular subjects. In 1984 it published its report on Diet and Cardiovascular Disease to which we referred earlier. In 1990, it published its report on sugars. The 1984 report pointed to the particular importance of saturated (mostly animal) fats and their link to heart disease (recommending, as we said before, that we should only get 15 per cent of our energy from saturated fat and less than 10 per cent if we are at high risk of heart disease). And the 1990 report said that if we managed to reduce the amount of 'added sugars' we eat (whether it is sugar added to breakfast cereal by a manufacturer or to a cup of tea by ourselves) we would see a significant improvement in our dental health. The Big Four are only a starting point because fat is not broken down into saturated and unsaturated fats and carbohydrate is not broken down into starch and sugars. To be useful to us nutritional labelling needs to include both the constituents highlighted by the two COMA reports. To be really useful to us it should include one or two other elements as well.

FULL NUTRITIONAL LABELLING

There is a range of information which must be added to the Big Four to make nutritional labelling genuinely of value. The more forward-thinking supermarkets are already doing it. Some food manufacturers (the ones who have to be dragged screaming and kicking into the nineties) are not.

Fat The most common addition here is to specify how much saturated fat there is in a product. Polyunsaturated and monounsaturated fats might also be specified (*see* Section VI, p362–4 for more information about them). Animal fats (whether in hamburgers, milk, butter, cheese or some margarines) are mainly saturated and raise the level of cholesterol in our blood. A high level of blood cholesterol is one of the risk factors for heart disease.

Carbohydrate   As we have already explained, the two types of carbohydrate are starch and sugars. There are a range of sugars that occur naturally in food – eg, fructose in fruit, lactose in milk and sucrose in sugar cane and sugar beet. However, it has been estimated that only about 10 per cent of the sugars we eat are the ones which occur absolutely naturally in food. The other 90 per cent are added by us or are more concentrated than they would otherwise have been because of the way we have processed the foods. In other words, the bulk of the sugars we eat we add to tea, coffee or breakfast cereals ourselves; or they are added to products such as cornflakes, soft drinks or confectionery by manufacturers; or they are contained naturally in foods we have processed, such as fruit juices. These sugars are sometimes described as 'extrinisic'. Remember, a glass of apple juice might well have the same sugar content as a glass of cola.

The 1990 COMA report on dietary sugars recommended that we cut down on extrinsic sugars in our diet for the sake of our teeth. So a label which breaks carbohydrates into starch and sugars is a helpful one. Some manufacturers are now doing this despite opposition from the sugar producers (the companies which process sugar beet and cane into the refined white sugar we buy in packets).

Incidentally, studies have shown that sugary foods eaten within the body of a meal are far less of a threat to teeth than they are when eaten on their own as a snack. But do remember that a banana (an excellent fruit with a range of nutrients in it) is also high in sugar. It is not just boiled sweets that can rot teeth.

Fibre   Dietary fibre – often referred to as 'roughage' – is the indigestible, fibrous parts of fruit, vegetables, cereals, beans and pulses. Most of us only eat around 20g of fibre a day and 30g is recommended. A low intake of fibre is linked to constipation and bowel disease. However, you can overdose on fibre (particularly neat bran), since 'insoluble' fibre like this can prevent you taking in other nutrients from your food. So a range of fibre is preferable, including the 'soluble' sort found in potatoes, beans and pulses. Because of its importance, the amounts of fibre are often specified on the nutritional panel.

Vitamins and minerals Important vitamins and minerals may be included expressed as a percentage of the government's Recommended Daily Amount (RDA). All the recent surveys of our diet have shown that the vast majority of us get all the vitamins and minerals we need. The only deficiencies shown up are those of iron (particularly in women) and vitamin B_{12} (particularly in vegans and strict vegetarians). *See* Section III, p95 and Section VI, p376 and p413.

WHAT IS THE LAW ON NUTRITIONAL LABELLING?

Before we look at how to read a nutritional label in detail, a brief word about the laws applying to nutritional labelling:

- The EC has decided that nutritional labelling will remain voluntary.
- But if any of the Big Four are specified then all must be shown.
- From 1996 onwards if any added sugars, saturated fat, fibre or sodium are specified then, again, all must be shown.
- Any claims on the packet (such as 'low fat', 'high fibre' or 'rich in vitamin C') must be substantiated specifically in the nutritional labelling.
- The standard way to indicate quantity is to list how many grams there are of a given constituent per 100g of the food (100g is around 3½ ounces). The label may also show how many grams of the constituent there are in a typical serving.

HOW DO YOU USE A NUTRITIONAL LABEL?

Computer programmes can calculate nutrient intakes. You can enter what you have eaten in a meal and the computer gives you a breakdown in terms of calories, fat (including saturates), protein, carbohydrates (including added sugar), fibre, salt, vitamins and minerals. All these can be expressed as percentages of the RDA so that you can judge whether you have had too much saturated fat that day, or too little fibre.

Since gizmos are not yet built into shopping trolleys to allow you to work this out, it is important to use nutritional labelling selectively so as to get something out of it without trying to turn into a walking computer. These are the critical factors:

- **Fat**   We should aim to get no more than 35 per cent of our daily calories from fat – that's around 90g for a man and 70g for a woman. Saturated fats should account for no more than 38g for a man and 30g for a woman. For example, three typical pork sausages contain around 40g of fat (half of a man's allowance) of which 16g is saturated fat (again, half of a man's allowance).

- **Carbohydrate**   We should be trying to eat more starchy foods and fewer ones with added sugar. Kellogg's Crunchy Nut Corn Flakes, for instance, will provide you with plenty of starch (48g in every 100g – or 16g per bowl), but also contains a lot of sugar (35g per 100g – or 11.5g per bowl). There is nothing wrong with the sugar in itself, but a helpful comparison such as Kellogg's give us on their nutritional labelling panel helps us begin to assess how many foods high in sugar we are buying.

- **Fibre**   Most of us need to eat more fibre, from a range of sources such as fruit, vegetables and bread. Wholemeal bread (medium sliced) will provide 6.3g per 100g and 2.3g per slice. So two slices of wholemeal bread can provide almost ⅙ of the daily fibre we need (30g a day). All this information is now available on bread wrappers.

- **Salt**   Salt is not a problem for most of us, but no one should live exclusively off highly salted foods and if you have high blood pressure you need to control your salt intake. Any food that shows salt at more than 3 per cent (ie, 3g per 100g) is highly salted.

- **Vitamins and minerals**   As long as your diet is varied (and even if it isn't) you have little to worry about here. If you are a vegetarian look out for foods supplemented with vitamin B_{12}.

- **'Per 100 grams' and 'per serving'**   Most nutritional panels say how much of a particular nutrient there is per 100g of the food and in a typical serving. You should use the 'per 100g' information to compare the food with other foods to judge how high or low it is in a particular nutrient. You should use the 'per serving' information to work out how much of a particular nutrient you will be consuming each time you eat the food.

The real value of nutritional labelling does not lie in adding up exact quantities of nutrients to make up the ideal amount for each day from a range of foodstuffs. That way lies madness – particularly if you are in a crowded supermarket on a Saturday morning, exhausted and irritated by your screaming children. The enormous benefit of nutritional labelling is that it allows us to develop a feel for foods that are *high* in fat, sugar, fibre and so on and for foods that are *low*. In this way we can begin to balance our diet with a variety of foods none of which are 'good' or 'bad' except if eaten to excess.

You will find a helpful summary on the following page of how to interpret a nutritional label. It draws on the information contained on a typical label of a breakfast cereal from Tesco:

Number of Calories (kcal) in the food. As a guide an average man consumes 2300 calories per day & an average woman 1700 calories. (A kilojoule is the metric equivalent of a Calorie. One Calorie is about 4kJ.)

Protein, needed for growth and repair. Aim for about 65g per day.

Fibre, needed for a healthy digestive system. Aim for about 30g per day.

This shows how much salt is in the food's ingredients. Aim to eat less than 5g per day an average.

The Government recommends how much of each mineral and vitamin we need each day (Recommended Daily Amount). The table tells you how much of your needs you get from one portion of the food.

The middle column tells you how much a portion of the food contains.

Use the 100g column to compare one food with another.

This shows the amount of fat in the food. As a guide an average man should eat no more than 90g total fat per day & an average woman no more than 70g.

Fat is often split into saturates and polyunsaturates. These are different types of fat. Aim for products with the least saturates.

Made up of two types of carbohydrate: starches and sugars. Go for the fibre-rich starchy foods like cereals, bread and potatoes.

This shows how much sugar, syrup, glucose, etc. is in the food's ingredients. It might help to think of it in teaspoons: 1 teaspoon = 4g.

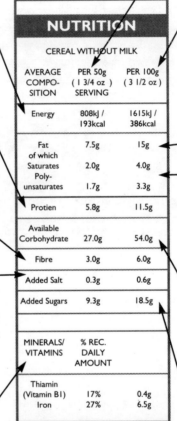

NUTRITION

CEREAL WITHOUT MILK

AVERAGE COMPO-SITION	PER 50g (1 3/4 oz) SERVING	PER 100g (3 1/2 oz)
Energy	808kJ / 193kcal	1615kJ / 386kcal
Fat	7.5g	15g
of which Saturates	2.0g	4.0g
Poly-unsaturates	1.7g	3.3g
Protien	5.8g	11.5g
Available Corbohydrate	27.0g	54.0g
Fibre	3.0g	6.0g
Added Salt	0.3g	0.6g
Added Sugars	9.3g	18.5g

MINERALS/ VITAMINS	% REC. DAILY AMOUNT	
Thiamin (Vitamin B1)	17%	0.4g
Iron	27%	6.5g

INFORMATION

To help us develop our skill at assessing which foods are high in certain nutrients and which are low, Tesco have published some comparative lists of food products. Although the lists only contain their 'own-label' foods they do not differ markedly from their 'branded' equivalents. The tables that follow can also be used as a handy reference and rough guide to the breakdown of a whole range of similar foods from other companies. Let's look at them in nine categories, beginning with foods that can be a good source of fibre.

1. BREAKFAST CEREALS

TYPICAL COMPOSITION PER 100G (3½oz)	Energy kJ	kcal (Calories)	Fat (g)	Protein (g)	Carbohydrate (g)	Fibre (g)	Added Salt (g)	Added Sugar (g)
Bran Breakfast Cereal	1055	252	3.5	13.0	44.0	28.0	3.4	15.5
Bran Flakes	1376	329	2.0	9.3	71.5	15.0	1.9	17.0
Bran Flakes with Sultanas	1293	309	1.5	7.3	69.6	13.0	1.4	12.4
Bran Muesli	1185	283	5.9	11.4	48.3	19.5	0	0
Cocoa Puffs	1590	380	4.0	4.8	85.0	2.0	1.1	40.6
Corn Flakes	1331	318	1.0	8.0	72.4	7.0	2.8	6.9
Crisp Puffed Rice	1435	343	1.0	6.0	81.0	4.0	1.6	12.3
Crunchy Oat – Raisin, Honey and Almond	1615	386	15.0	11.5	54.0	6.0	0.6	18.5
Fruit and Fibre	1459	348	3.1	8.0	75.5	5.2	1.9	13.0
Honey 'n' Nut Corn Flakes	1599	382	3.1	7.0	85.3	–	1.1	30.2
Iced Flakes	1556	372	0.2	6.1	90.3	2.2	1.1	34.7
Instant Hot Oat Cereal	1668	398	8.0	12.0	73.0	6.6	0	0
Jumblies	1559	372	5.6	4.7	79.5	4.0	1.3	29.6
Multigrain Crunchies	1439	344	1.4	9.1	77.0	9.0	1.0	28.0
Scotch Porridge Oats with 20% Bran	1460	349	8.0	12.0	60.0	14.0	0	0
Scotch Porridge Oats	1598	382	8.5	11.5	68.0	7.0	0	0
Swiss Style Breakfast Cereal	1468	351	7.0	9.0	66.0	7.0	0.4	8.0
Toasted Oat Cereal Bran and Apple	1618	386	12.9	10.6	60.0	12.6	0.5	18.2
Unsweetened Swiss Style Muesli	1412	337	6.3	11.0	62.0	9.5	0	0
Wheaties	1362	325	2.1	8.7	71.0	8.6	1.5	12.3
Whole Wheat Flakes	1321	316	2.0	10.5	66.8	12.9	0.8	5.2
Whole Wheat Cereal	1321	316	2.0	10.5	66.8	12.9	0.8	5.2
Whole Wheat Muesli	1452	347	10.0	10.0	57.0	12.0	0	0

When you compare all the products in one table like this you can see that Bran Breakfast Cereal is by far the highest in fibre, but also by far the highest in added salt (bran is pretty unpalatable stuff without something added to it). You can also see that the only breakfast cereal which mentions fibre in its name – 'Fruit and Fibre' – is in fact below average in its fibre content. (It may be none the worse for that, but it would certainly provide you with less of your daily fibre than some of the others.)

You can also see that the cereals which are high in added sugars (Cocoa Puffs – 40 per cent and Iced Flakes – 35 per cent) are correspondingly low in fibre. In fact these two products are the highest in added sugars and the lowest in fibre on the whole list!

2. BREADS

TYPICAL COMPOSITION
PER 100G (3½oz)

	Energy kJ	kcal (Calories)	Fat (g)	Protein (g)	Carbohydrate (g)	Fibre (g)	Added Salt (g)	Added Sugar (g)
Malt Loaf	1203	287	2.6	7.8	60.9	–	0.4	6.0
Multigrain	915	219	2.3	7.6	43.8	4.2	1.3	0
Oatmeal	914	218	2.8	8.3	41.8	4.9	1.7	1.8
Premium White	954	228	2.4	9.0	44.5	2.3	1.4	0.3
Rye and Barley	954	228	3.7	10.8	39.6	5.1	1.0	0.2
Rye and Caraway	953	228	3.0	8.0	44.1	3.3	1.1	0.1
Soft Grain	1027	245	1.9	8.1	51.2	3.3	1.0	0.3
Soft White Batch	1054	252	3.2	8.0	50.0	3.0	1.3	0
Stoneground Wholemeal Batch	884	211	2.0	10.0	40.0	8.0	1.2	0.5
Stoneground Wholemeal	1075	257	2.6	9.4	51.2	8.5	0.8	0
Wheatgerm	1017	243	3.0	10.0	46.0	5.0	1.2	0
Wheatgerm with Added Bran	1005	240	3.6	10.6	43.2	6.8	1.8	0.2
White	1010	241	2.0	8.0	50.0	3.0	1.1	0
White Farmhouse	1010	241	2.0	8.0	50.0	3.0	1.2	0
Wholemeal	1012	242	2.0	10.0	48.0	9.0	0.9	0
Wholemeal Sliced Fruit Loaf	1034	247	3.9	10.0	45.0	5.3	0.7	5.7
Brown	1042	249	2.0	8.0	52.0	5.0	1.2	0
Crust Bread – All Types	1081	258	1.3	9.0	55.0	3.0	1.3	0
Danish Loaf	1010	241	2.0	8.0	50.0	3.0	1.2	0
Fruit Loaf (Sliced)	1199	286	4.3	8.3	56.2	2.0	0.7	3.5
Fruited Batch	1179	282	4.0	7.0	57.0	–	0.6	4.8
Garlic and Herb Bread	1624	388	24.0	7.5	38.0	–	1.8	0
Garlic Bread – Soft Grain Brown	1568	375	21.5	7.4	40.4	5.0	1.4	0
Garlic Bread – White	1711	409	22.3	7.5	47.4	2.0	1.5	0.1
High Fibre White	1150	275	4.0	9.7	52.3	3.0	0.9	0
Hovis	1017	243	3.0	10.0	46.0	5.0	1.2	0

This table confirms what you will already know if you have ever looked at bread closely. 'Wholemeal' bread has the most fibre (7 per cent), 'brown' breads (such as 'Granary' and 'Hovis') come next (between 4 and 7 per cent) and white breads have the least (2–4 per cent). Incidentally, to find out what happens to bread when you put butter on it look at the three Garlic Breads. Other breads contain around 2 per cent fat, Garlic Bread is up to 24 per cent and most of that is saturated!

3. BEANS

TYPICAL COMPOSITION PER 100G (3½oz)	kJ	kcal (Calories)	Fat (g)	Protein (g)	Carbohydrate (g)	Fibre (g)	Added Salt (g)	Added Sugar (g)
Bean Salad	295	70	0.5	4.0	13.0	4.6	1.0	4.0
Beans (50% Less Added Sugar and Salt)	252	60	0.4	5.0	9.5	7.3	0.5	2.2
Beans and Burgers	405	97	3.7	5.4	11.0	5.0	1.4	4.6
Beans in Tomato Sauce	392	94	0.5	5.0	18.0	7.3	1.0	4.3
Beans with 4 Pork Sausages	426	102	3.1	4.5	14.7	2.3	1.3	4.0
Beans with 8 Pork Sausages	426	102	3.1	4.5	14.7	2.3	1.3	4.0
Chilli Beans	471	112	0.7	5.5	22.0	5.0	1.0	4.3
Red Kidney Beans	505	121	0.5	6.0	24.0	7.0	0.9	3.5

This table shows how beans are an important source of protein, carbohydrate and fibre. Red kidney beans and baked beans are the highest in protein and fibre.

4.   SWEET BISCUITS

TYPICAL COMPOSITION PER 100G (3½oz)	Energy kJ	kcal (Calories)	Fat (g)	Protein (g)	Carbohydrate (g)	Fibre (g)	Added Salt (g)	Added Sugar (g)
BISCUITS								
Fig Rolls	1414	338	6.3	4.5	69.0	6.6	0.5	24.0
Fruit Shortcake	1961	468	20.0	5.0	71.0	–	0.8	19.0
Garibaldi	1633	390	9.0	4.0	77.0	–	0	11.0
Ginger Nuts	1872	447	16.0	5.2	74.5	–	0.6	36.0
Lemon Crisp	1940	463	19.0	5.0	72.0	–	0.8	32.0
Lincoln	2016	482	21.0	7.0	70.0	–	0.8	21.0
Malted Milk	1975	472	19.0	8.0	71.0	–	1.0	17.0
Marie	1869	446	14.0	7.0	77.0	–	0.4	19.0
Morning Coffee	1853	443	14.0	7.0	76.0	–	1.0	19.0
Nice	1911	456	16.0	7.0	75.0	–	0.8	28.0
Rich Shortie	2020	482	22.0	6.0	69.0	–	0.6	22.0
Rich Tea	1890	451	15.0	7.0	76.0	–	0.6	17.0
Rich Tea Fingers	1816	434	13.0	7.0	76.0	–	0.8	20.0
Shortcake	2016	482	21.0	7.0	70.0	–	1.0	18.0
Snowballs	2044	488	22.6	3.0	72.3	–	0.3	54.6
CHOCOLATE BISCUITS								
Milk Chocolate Digestive Sweetmeal	2078	496	24.0	6.0	68.0	–	0.5	27.0
Milk Chocolate Digestive	2105	503	26.0	7.0	64.0	–	0.5	9.3
Milk Chocolate Orange Sandwich	2030	485	24.0	6.0	65.0	–	0.2	24.0
Milk Chocolate Sandwich	2063	493	24.0	7.0	66.0	–	0.2	24.0
Milk Chocolate Shortcake	2104	503	26.0	6.0	65.0	–	0.3	11.0
Milk Chocolate Teacakes	1812	433	19.0	5.0	64.0	–	0.2	41.0
Milk Chocolate Wafers	2177	520	31.0	6.0	58.0	–	0	44.5
Plain Chocolate Country Oat Bakes	2029	485	23.6	6.8	65.0	4.0	0.6	31.0
Plain Chocolate Digestive Sweetmeal	2078	496	24.0	6.0	68.0	–	0.5	26.0
Plain Chocolate Half Coated Ginger Rings	2015	481	21.3	4.7	71.7	1.5	0.3	30.6

This table shows only about half the sweet biscuits Tesco sell under their own label. They are a popular product. And, as you can see from the table, they are all high in fat and sugar. When dried fruit is introduced into a biscuit like the Fig Roll the fat drops because there is less actual biscuit by comparison. Of course, there is nothing wrong with biscuits, it's simply a question of how many of them we eat to the exclusion of other foods.

5. MEAT PRODUCTS

(a) Sausages
TYPICAL COMPOSITION PER 100G (3½oz)

	Energy kJ	Energy kcal (Calories)	Fat (g)	Protein (g)	Carbohydrate (g)	Fibre (g)	Added Salt (g)	Added Sugar (g)
SAUSAGES: Chilled (when cooked)								
Barbecue Pork	903	216	12.7	15.8	10.3	0	1.7	0
Beef	1043	249	15.5	10.2	18.5	0	0	0
Beef Sausages (Traditional)	1071	256	14.8	16.1	15.6	0	2.2	0
Beef Skinless	1041	249	17.2	9.5	15.2	0	1.7	0
Cumberland	1162	278	19.2	14.3	13.0	0	1.9	1.5
Cumberland Ring	1162	278	19.2	14.3	13.1	0	1.8	1.3
Economy	1271	304	22.0	11.0	16.9	0	1.4	0
Economy Sausage Meat	1294	309	23.7	10.5	14.9	0	1.2	0
Lincolnshire Pork Chipolata	1194	285	21.7	13.3	10.3	0	1.7	0.3
Lorne Sausage	1230	294	19.0	15.0	17.0	0	2.7	0
Low Fat Pork	772	184	9.3	15.2	10.6	0	1.5	0
Low Fat Pork and Beef	853	204	8.1	14.4	19.3	0	1.4	0
Low Fat Pork and Beef Chipolatas	853	204	8.1	14.4	19.3	0	1.4	0
Low Fat Pork Chipolatas	772	184	9.3	15.2	10.6	0	1.4	0
Low Fat Sausage Meat	804	192	11.4	12.7	10.4	0	1.4	0
Mini Pork Skinless	1170	279	20.2	10.2	15.6	0	2.5	0.3
Pork	1400	334	25.7	15.0	12.1	0	2.2	2.2
Pork and Beef	1094	261	16.2	12.5	17.6	0	1.9	2.2
Pork and Beef Chipolatas	1107	264	15.4	12.4	20.4	0	1.9	2.1
Pork and Beef Skinless	1160	277	19.4	10.4	16.6	0	1.9	2.1
Pork Chipolatas	1395	333	26.8	14.2	10.1	0	2.1	0
Pork Sausages (Traditional)	1335	319	23.2	16.0	12.8	0	2.2	0
Pork Skinless	1179	282	24.1	11.6	5.6	0	1.9	0
Premium Lincolnshire Pork	1194	285	21.7	13.3	10.3	0	1.7	0.3
Premium Pork	1229	294	23.3	12.1	10.1	0	0	2.0
Premium Pork and Onion	1273	304	25.2	12.4	8.1	0	2.2	2.1
Prize Winner Sausages	985	235	14.1	15.0	13.0	0	2.3	0

Beef sausages are considerably lower in fat than pork sausages. 'Low-fat' sausages are lower still with approximately ⅓ the fat of pork sausages. 'Premium' sausages, with more lean meat in them, are marginally lower in fat. Overall sausages are very high in fat, high in saturated fat (although this table doesn't show that) but high in protein.

(b) Pies

TYPICAL COMPOSITION PER 100G (3½oz)	Energy kJ	kcal (Calories)	Fat (g)	Protein (g)	Carbohydrate (g)	Fibre (g)	Added Salt (g)	Added Sugar (g)
Beef and Onion Pasty	1180	282	15.1	6.7	31.7	0	1.4	0
Beef and Onion Pie (Individual)	1306	312	18.5	6.7	31.7	0	1.4	0
Chicken and Leek Pie	1082	258	16.0	8.4	21.7	0	0.8	0
Chicken and Mushroom Pie (Individual)	1151	275	18.7	6.7	21.6	0	0.7	0
Chicken and Vegetable Pie (Individual)	1269	303	17.0	9.4	30.0	0	1.5	0
Chicken and Vegetable Pie (Family)	1198	286	16.4	9.0	27.4	0	1.3	0
Chunky Vegetable Pasty	1083	259	14.0	5.0	30.0	2.0	1.4	0
Chunky Vegetable Roll	1089	260	16.5	6.0	23.5	0	1.2	0
Cornish Pasty (D-Shaped)	1286	307	20.0	8.4	25.2	0	0.8	0
Cornish Pasty (Large)	1066	255	13.0	7.1	29.0	0	1.3	0
Cottage Pie	619	148	8.0	6.3	13.5	0	1.1	0
Cottage Pie (Large)	619	148	8.0	6.3	13.5	0	1.0	0
Cumberland Pie	621	148	6.4	7.9	15.6	0	0.8	0
Minced Beef and Onion Pie (Large)	1040	248	15.5	7.3	21.4	0	1.1	0
Minced Beef and Onion Roll	1224	292	16.9	9.8	27.0	0	0.8	0
Mini Cornish Pasty	1096	262	14.7	6.1	28.0	0	0.8	0
Ploughman's Pasty	1213	290	14.0	7.0	36.0	0	1.3	0
Roast Turkey and Ham Pie	1125	269	16.7	11.0	20.0	0	1.1	0
Scotch Pie	959	229	12.4	7.6	23.2	0	1.3	0
Steak and Kidney Pie (Large)	1047	250	15.3	9.3	20.2	0	0.9	0
Steak and Kidney Pudding (Small)	1021	244	12.0	8.5	27.0	0	1.0	0
Vegetarian Sausage Roll	1144	273	17.4	3.9	27.1	2.5	1.2	0
Melton Mowbray Buffet Pork Pies	1668	398	28.0	8.0	31.0	0	1.3	0
Melton Mowbray Pie (Large)	1549	370	26.0	11.0	25.0	0	1.1	0
Melton Mowbray Pork Pie (Individual)	1621	387	28.0	9.0	27.0	0	1.7	0
Mini Sausage Rolls	1576	376	24.4	11.9	29.4	0	1.5	0
Ploughman's Pie	1536	367	25.5	14.5	21.6	0	1.2	2.2
Pork and Egg Pie	1436	343	23.0	9.0	27.0	0	1.4	0
Pork and Gammon Pie with Pineapple	1300	310	19.9	10.4	24.2	0	1.2	0.4

This table shows a selection of Tesco pies. All are high in fat because even the vegetarian and poultry pies use pastry which contains a lot of fat. As usual, pork products are the highest in fat.

(c) Frozen

TYPICAL COMPOSITION PER 100G (3½oz)	Energy		Fat	Protein	Carbohydrate	Fibre	Added Salt	Added Sugar
	kJ	kcal (Calories)	(g)	(g)	(g)	(g)	(g)	(g)
Beefburgers	1216	290	25.3	14.3	2.3	0	1.0	0
Beefburgers – Low Fat	830	198	12.6	18.3	3.3	0	1.4	0
Cheesburgers	1115	266	18.5	15.6	10.3	–	1.6	1.3
Economy Burgers	1152	275	17.5	14.6	16.0	0	1.9	0
Faggots in Rich Sauce	721	172	12.3	6.2	10.0	0	1.2	0.3
Grillsteaks	863	206	12.3	24.0	0	0	1.0	0
Grillsteaks – Low Fat	745	178	8.0	25.0	1.5	0	1.0	0
Quarter Pound Beefburgers	1036	247	16.5	25.0	0	0	0.7	0

Beefburgers range from 12 per cent fat (low-fat beefburgers) to 18 per cent fat (cheeseburgers). The 'Economy' products, bulked out with potatoes or cereal, are correspondingly higher in carbohydrates.

We have information about the laws governing meat products at the end of this subsection.

6.   DAIRY PRODUCTS

(a) Milk & Cream
TYPICAL COMPOSITION
PER 100G (3½oz)

	kJ	kcal (Calories)	Energy Fat (g)	Protein (g)	Carbohydrate (g)
MILK: Fresh					
Semi-skimmed Milk	199	48	1.7	3.4	4.9
Skimmed Milk	142	34	0.1	3.4	5.0
Whole Milk	279	67	4.0	3.3	4.7
CREAM: Fresh					
Cornish Clotted Cream	2306	551	61.0	1.0	2.0
Devon Clotted Cream	2417	577	64.0	1.0	2.0
Double Cream	1847	441	48.0	1.7	2.6
Extra Thick Double Cream	1847	441	48.0	1.7	2.6
Half Cream	559	134	12.0	3.0	4.0
Single Cream	810	193	19.0	2.6	3.9
Soured Cream	810	193	19.0	2.6	3.9
Whipping Cream	1525	364	39.0	2.0	3.0

Whole milk is 4 per cent fat whereas semi-skimmed is 1.7 per cent and skimmed 0.1 per cent. Whole milk may look low in fat compared to butter and cheese. But it really depends how much we drink of it. We actually drink enough for it to provide as much as a quarter of the saturated fat in our diet. The calories in whole milk are the highest, but skimmed milk still has 34 calories per 100g. They are derived from the protein and carbohydrate. Amongst the creams you can see that single is 19 per cent fat, double is 48 per cent fat and Devon Clotted Cream is 64 per cent. Naughty but nice . . .

(b) Cheese
TYPICAL COMPOSITION
PER 100G (3½oz)

	kJ	kcal (Calories)	Energy Fat (g)	Protein (g)	Carbohydrate (g)	Fibre (g)	Added Salt (g)	Added Sugar (g)
Blue Stilton	1686	403	35.0	23.0	0	0	2.3	0
Brie	1211	289	24.0	19.0	0	0	1.8	0
Caerphilly	1538	367	31.0	23.0	0	0	1.3	0
Cambozola	1718	410	40.0	14.0	0	0	1.8	0
Camembert	1211	289	24.0	19.0	0	0	1.8	0
Cheddar, All Types	1700	406	34.0	26.0	0	0	1.8	0
Cheese Singles	1183	283	23.0	19.5	0	0	1.8	0
Cheese Spread, Triangles	1131	270	22.0	13.0	6.0	0	1.5	0
Cheshire	1555	371	31.0	24.0	0	0	1.4	0
Chevre (Goats Milk Cheese)	1299	310	25.0	22.0	0	0	1.8	0
Danish Blue	1433	342	30.0	19.0	0	0	3.6	0
Danish Blue (Mature)	1678	401	38.0	16.0	0	0	3.2	0
Derby	1666	398	34.0	24.0	0	0	1.4	0
Dolcelatte	1359	324	28.0	19.0	0	0	2.4	0
Double Gloucester	1683	402	34.0	25.0	0	0	1.5	0
Edam	1276	305	23.0	25.0	0	0	2.5	0
Emmental	2034	486	30.0	28.0	0	0	1.2	0
Gouda	1276	305	23.0	25.0	0	0	2.5	0
Gruyère	1867	446	33.0	38.0	0	0	1.3	0
Half Fat Cheese (Blue Type)	1056	252	17.5	24.0	0	0	2.0	0
Half Fat Cheese (Cheddar Type)	1045	249	14.0	31.0	0	0	1.0	0
Jarlsberg	1418	339	25.0	29.0	0	0	2.3	0
Lancashire	1583	367	31.0	25.0	0	0	1.5	0
Low Fat Processed Cheese Slices	824	197	10.0	26.5	0.2	0	2.0	0
Lymeswold	1668	398	37.3	16.2	0	0	1.1	0
Melbury	1424	340	28.4	21.7	0	0	1.3	0
Red Leicester	1666	398	34.0	24.0	0	0	1.6	0
Red Windsor	1648	394	33.0	25.0	0.1	0	1.7	0
Sage Derby	1631	390	33.0	24.0	0.1	0	1.4	0
Vegetarian Cheddar	1698	405	33.0	25.0	3.0	0	1.2	0
Wensleydale	1575	376	32.0	23.0	0	0	1.2	0
White Stilton	1487	355	31.0	20.0	0	0	2.3	0

Hard cheeses tend to have 50 per cent more fat and protein than soft cheeses and processed cheese, but they contain less water. As this selection shows, cheese is an excellent source of protein.

(c) Yoghurt
TYPICAL COMPOSITION
PER 100G (3½oz)

	Energy kJ	kcal (Calories)	Fat (g)	Protein (g)	Carbohydrate (g)	Fibre (g)	Added Salt (g)	Added Sugar (g)
Natural Set	193	46	1.0	4.7	4.6	0	0	0
Nectarine and Apricot	425	102	0.9	4.6	19.6	0	0	13.4
Orange	360	86	1.0	4.6	15.3	0	0	8.7
Passion Fruit and Melon	388	93	0.9	4.7	17.2	0	0	11.0
Peach	408	97	0.9	4.8	18.3	0	0	10.3
Peach Melba	425	102	0.9	4.6	19.6	0	0	13.4
Pineapple	360	86	1.0	4.7	15.2	0	0	9.1
Raspberry	424	101	0.9	4.8	19.3	0	0	11.6
Rhubarb	390	93	0.9	4.8	17.2	0	0	9.8
Rich and Creamy French Style (All Flavours)	419	100	3.3	3.8	14.5	0	0	9.4
Strawberry	395	94	0.9	4.7	17.6	0	0	9.7
Strawberry and Lychee	372	89	0.8	4.6	16.5	0	0	9.8
Strawberry and Mango	369	88	0.8	4.6	16.3	0	0	9.8
Strawberry and Peach	358	86	0.8	4.7	15.5	0	0	9.8
Strawberry and Vanilla	392	94	0.9	4.6	17.5	0	0	12.0
Toffee	443	106	1.3	4.7	19.7	0	0	14.0
Tropical Fruit	446	107	0.9	4.6	20.9	0	0	14.8
Very Low Fat Set Yoghurt (All Flavours)	160	38	0.1	4.5	5.0	0	0	0
Whipping Yoghurt	735	176	10.6	5.3	15.8	0	0	8.5
YOGHURTS: Healthy Eating								
Apricot and Mango	158	38	0.1	3.7	5.7	0	0	0
Banana	158	38	0.1	3.7	5.7	0	0	0
Black Cherry	156	37	0.1	3.7	5.6	0	0	0
Mandarin	158	38	0.1	3.6	5.8	0	0	0
Melon	151	36	0.1	3.7	5.3	0	0	0
Natural	217	52	0.2	6.3	6.4	0	0	0
Peach Melba	158	38	0.1	3.8	5.6	0	0	0
Pineapple	161	38	0.1	3.7	5.9	0	0	0
Raspberry	158	38	0.1	3.7	5.7	0	0	0
Rhubarb	153	37	0.1	3.7	5.4	0	0	0
Strawberry	150	36	0.1	3.7	5.2	0	0	0

Yoghurts are generally low in fat and the 'low-fat' ones have a negligible fat content. It is worth keeping an eye on the added sugar as well – toffee and tropical fruit are 14 per cent added sugar. The yoghurts with no added sugar are correspondingly low in carbohydrates.

7. SOFT DRINKS

TYPICAL COMPOSITION
PER 100G (3½oz)

DRINKS: Carbonated	kJ	kcal (Calories)	Fat (g)	Protein (g)	Carbohydrate (g)	Fibre (g)	Added Salt (g)	Added Sugar (g)
Cherryade	98	23	0	0	6.1	0	0	6.1
Cola	176	42	0	0	11.0	0	0	11.0
Cola (Can)	141	34	0	0	8.8	0	0	8.8
Cream Soda	102	24	0	0	6.4	0	0	6.4
Diet Cola	1	0	0	0	0	0	0	0
Diet Lemonade	1	0	0	0	0	0	0	0
Lemonade	91	22	0	0	5.7	0	0	5.7
Lemonade Shandy	69	16	0	0	4.3	0	0	4.3
Lemonade Shandy (Can)	107	26	0	0	6.7	0	0	6.7
Limeade	102	24	0	0	6.4	0	0	6.4
Low Calorie Traditional Lemonade	2	0	0	0	0.1	0	0	0
Orange Crush	138	33	0	0	8.6	0	0	7.9
Orange Juice and Low Calorie Lemonade	104	25	0	0.4	6.1	0	0	0
Orange Juice and Low Calorie Pineappleade	103	25	0	0.4	6.0	0	0	0
Orangeade	98	23	0	0.1	6.0	0	0	6.0
Orangeade (250ml Bottle)	114	27	0	0	7.1	0	0	7.1
Traditional Lemonade	195	47	0	0	12.2	0	0	12.2
Tropical Fruit Crush	203	48	0	0	12.7	0	0	11.2
DRINKS: Dilutables (Undiluted)								
Apple and Blackcurrant Drink	480	115	0	0	30.0	0	0	27.5
Hi Juice Blackcurrant Squash	1216	290	0	0	76.0	0	0	70.0
Hi Juice Lemon Squash	618	148	0	0	38.6	0	0	33.5
Hi Juice Orange Squash	640	153	0	0	40.0	0	0	34.0
Lemon and Lime Drink	394	94	0	0	24.6	0	0	23.0
Lime Juice Cordial	407	97	0	0	25.3	0	0	22.8
Orange, Lemon and Pineapple Drink	421	101	0	0	26.3	0	0	23.8
Whole Lemon Drink	432	103	0	0	27.0	0	0	27.0
Whole Orange Drink	397	95	0	0	24.8	0	0	23.6

Sweet fizzy drinks are generally high in sugar. Their benefit is that we like drinking them and our bodies need a good quantity of liquid every day. The squashes are diluted one in four with water and contain about the same amount of sugar as diet drinks.

8.   SANDWICHES

TYPICAL COMPOSITION PER 100G (3½oz)	Energy kJ	Energy kcal (Calories)	Fat (g)	Protein (g)	Carbohydrate (g)	Fibre (g)	Added Salt (g)	Added Sugar (g)
'Triples': Beef and Horseradish, Egg; Poached Salmon	1129	270	17.9	10.2	18.3	3.7	0.8	0
'Triples': Chicken and Ham; Cheese and Celery; Prawn	1329	317	23.8	9.8	17.6	3.7	0	0
'Triples': Cheese and Onion; Egg and Bacon; Corned Beef and Pickle	1351	323	21.7	13.2	20.2	1.5	1.3	1.7
Bacon, Lettuce and Tomato	1315	314	25.5	8.1	14.6	3.3	0.9	0
Cheese and Celery	1362	325	24.0	10.2	18.8	4.0	0	0
Chicken Salad	1169	279	22.0	8.0	13.7	2.9	0	0
Chicken Tikka	1179	282	19.0	12.0	17.0	3.3	1.2	0.2
Chicken, Ham, Mayonnaise and Lettuce	1300	310	24.5	9.0	15.0	3.0	0	0
Chicken, Smoked Ham and Mayonnaise	1222	292	21.0	11.4	15.7	2.2	1.2	0
Coronation Chicken	1347	322	23.7	9.1	19.7	3.8	0.7	0.5
Crunchy Cottage Cheese	694	166	6.3	10.8	17.3	2.7	1.0	0
Egg Mayonnaise and Cress	1162	278	19.5	8.4	18.6	3.9	0	0
Egg, Bacon and Mayonnaise	1137	272	18.7	11.7	15.4	3.2	0	0
Garlic Sausage and Cream Cheese	992	237	16.0	7.6	16.9	2.4	1.0	0
Mature Cheddar Cheese and Pickle	1246	298	16.7	11.9	26.6	4.5	1.5	0
Prawn and Mayonnaise	1335	319	22.6	10.5	20.0	4.1	0	0
Roast Beef, Tomato and Mustard	769	184	7.3	9.4	21.2	1.8	0.8	0
Smoked Ham, Mature Cheddar Cheese and Mayonnaise	1355	324	22.7	12.8	18.6	3.8	1.1	0
Smoked Mackerel Pâté with Onion and Salad	926	221	14.0	7.8	17.2	2.7	1.0	0
Stilton and Salad	1270	303	21.6	9.6	19.2	2.5	1.0	0

This table illustrates how a sandwich can almost be a meal in itself with a balance of fat, protein, carbohydrate and fibre. One thing though – if you want a low-fat sandwich don't put mayonnaise in it.

9.   FRESH FOOD

The next table is not published by Tesco, but we have assembled it to allow you to compare fresh produce with the processed foods we have already looked at.

TYPICAL COMPOSITION PER 100G (3½oz)	Energy kJ	kcal (Calories)	Fat (g)	Protein (g)	Carbohydrate (g)	Fibre (g)	Added Salt (g)	Added Sugar (g)
Potatoes new boiled	324	76	0.1	1.6	18.3	2.0	0	0
Carrots boiled	79	19	0	0.6	4.3	3.1	0	0
Lettuce	51	12	0.4	1.0	1.2	1.5	0	0
Cabbage	109	26	0	3.3	3.3	3.1	0	0
Broccoli spears boiled	40	9	0	1.6	0.8	2.1	0	0
Lentils split and boiled	420	99	0.5	7.6	17	3.7	0	0
Peanuts roasted	2364	570	49	24.3	8.6	8.1	0	0
Apples	196	46	0	0.3	11.9	2	0	0
Pears	175	41	0	0.3	10.6	2.3	0	0
Bananas	337	79	0.3	1.1	19.2	3.4	0	0
Grilled cod	402	95	1.3	20.8	0	0	0	0
Grilled plaice	392	93	1.9	18.9	0	0	0	0
Grilled mackerel	784	188	11.3	21.5	0	0	0	0
Roast beef sirloin	806	192	9.1	27.6	0	0	0	0
Roast leg of lamb	800	191	8.1	29.4	0	0	0	0
Roast pork lean only	777	185	6.9	30.7	0	0	0	0
Roast chicken meat	621	148	5.4	24.8	0	0	0	0
Rump steak fried	797	190	7.4	30.8	0	0	0	0

Don't be put off the mackerel because it is higher in fat than the meat. Fish oil, high in monounsaturates and polyunsaturates, is good for you. Peanuts are very high in fat and thus very fattening. But the fat itself is mostly monounsaturated. There is no added sugar or salt to record, of course. But a lot of sugar occurs naturally in some of the items – bananas (around 20 per cent), pears (around 10 per cent) and carrots (around 4 per cent). But the very high level of carbohydrate in potatoes is mostly accounted for by starch, not sugar.

DON'T BELIEVE EVERYTHING YOU'RE TOLD

Jo Grimond, the distinguished Liberal politician, has always argued that for every law Parliament passes it should be made to repeal one first. Nowhere is the nightmare of one complex law piled upon another being realized more quickly than in the field of food labelling. Many laws – whether from Westminster or Strasburg – are helpful and effective. But seen as a whole they make up a hostile jungle which even many food manufacturers cannot find their way through. So pity the poor consumer.

A recent survey of confectionery found several examples of illegal labelling from leading companies. And when an instant pudding (from one of our biggest manufacturers) was shown to food technologists at a lecture they spotted two infringements on just that one packet. None of these companies were setting out to mislead us, they just got it wrong.

Those areas of labelling that are covered by the law are covered inadequately and, in any case, are highly complex. Those areas not governed by law can be downright misleading. You should be as sceptical of labels as you are of advertisements – don't believe everything you're told.

Negative claims Batchelor's Small Processed Peas had a prominent label on the tin boasting 'No preservatives'. As a contribution to the sum of human knowledge about food this deserved a minus score. Of course there are no preservatives in their tinned peas. Tinning is *itself* a method of preservation. So while doing nothing to help us understand how food processing works Batchelor's continued to encourage our overplayed obsession with food additives. They will eventually be hoist by their own petard because the same product used artificial colour to keep the peas green. While they encouraged us to beware of preservatives they could have made us more wary of the artificial colours in the same product.

One major retailer's fish finger packets proclaims 'No artificial additives'. There is a colouring used in the breadcrumbs but it is allegedly 'natural'. The colour in question – annatto (E160b) – is not chemically created but extracted from a tree seed. As we have said before, only a tiny number of us might possibly suffer an allergic reaction from colourings. But research shows that for that tiny minority annatto is itself capable of causing adverse reactions! So there is no benefit in its naturalness.

Our advice is to ignore all negative claims, read the small print on the rest of the label and make up your own mind about the product.

Natural So that retailer's colouring is 'natural' because it derives from a tree seed. It might equally be argued that it belongs 'naturally' in a tree seed as nature intended and not in a fish finger. Tesco sold free-range chickens from South West France which 'grow to maturity on a natural diet'. In fact the feed of the birds was medicated with an anti-parasite drug for the majority of their short lives. This may be a very good thing but in what sense was their diet 'natural'? A Bovril product boasted until recently, 'the natural way to bring out the real flavour of your food'. This natural way in fact relied on the monosodium glutamate in the cube.

Some voluntary guidelines for the food industry state that foods claiming to be natural should be made with a 'minimum of processing' and with 'natural ingredients'. Try defining those two phrases. Well, as you might have guessed, an army of Eurocrats is actually attempting that but their proposed rules are not yet published. If they are adopted there will be yet another complex piece of labelling law. Meanwhile products continue to claim 'natural goodness' as well as such dubious merits as 'real', 'pure' and 'wholesome'.

We have a simpler solution than the EC's. Ignore the word 'natural' whenever you see it and look at the small print.

Cholesterol Sales of oats and oat bran have boomed in the US and, to a lesser extent, in Britain since research was published suggesting oats can lower the levels of cholesterol in our blood. But the amount you would have to consume every day to see a significant effect is so great that, on their own, oats are by no means the solution to high cholesterol. But in the meantime the marketing men have gone to town. At the time of writing Kellogg's oat cereal had 'the heart of a good breakfast' and a heart-shaped bowl to match. Quaker had a strip saying 'can help reduce cholesterol as part of a low fat low cholesterol diet'. Jordans had a similar claim too, but had gone one stage further – their cereal itself was heart-shaped! Such health claims are not quite covered by the law because the Medicines Act only governs foods which make claims for particular organs of the body. Suffice it to say that these manufacturers are guilty of a good deal of hype – that's hype for hyperbole.

Our advice is to eat oats (if you like them) as part of a balanced diet including other grains and pulses. But don't think because you eat a large bowl of oats in the morning you can eat pork pies for the rest of the day.

Some foods claim to be 'low in cholesterol'. To do this they must be no more than 0.005 per cent cholesterol. In addition, the label must tell you the food's polyunsaturated fat content as, for example, 'Pura Light Touch' cooking fat does. But in any case, the claim is not a particularly significant one. The level of cholesterol in our blood is governed much more by how much saturated fat we eat and how our body functions than the amount of cholesterol we consume in food.

Low fat Manufacturers are to be congratulated for developing lower fat products for those of us who wish to eat less fat (and, as we have seen, most of us should eat less fat). If the food is lower in fat than its normal equivalent then it seems reasonable enough to say so on the packet. The confusion arises when you look at what 'low fat' actually means. A low-fat sausage (with 8.3g per 100g) may have 80 times more fat in it – gram for gram – than a low-fat yoghurt (with 0.1 g of fat per 100g). A low-fat spread (typically 40 per cent fat) will be much lower in fat than butter (typically 80 per cent fat). Remember that this claim is comparative not absolute. The EC is considering the 'low-fat' problem and will probably decide that whenever such a claim is made a nutritional label panel must be published as well.

Our advice is to use low-fat labels only as a general guide. Look at the nutritional label to find out what the fat content really is.

Margarine has a legal definition and must be fortified with vitamins A and D but the new generation of 'yellow fat' spreads do not (although the Government is to recommend that such fortification is a good idea). In fact, there is a bewildering variety of yellow spreads now on sale, and not a week goes by without a new brand or even an entirely new product category appearing. Yellow spreads have been developed to give us a healthier and more convenient alternative to butter. So they tend to emphasize one of three benefits:

- They spread straight from the fridge.
- They are particularly low in saturates.
- They are lower in fat.

The spreads which are 'high in polyunsaturates' are usually made from soya or safflower oils. The low-fat spreads are made by emulsifying a lot of water into the product so that overall the fat is less concentrated.

There is nothing definitely 'good' or 'bad' about any of these spreads. Indeed butter is a most delicious food. It is merely a question of how much we eat and how often. If you discovered that you tend to eat too much saturated fat when you analysed your diet in Section II then you should consider changing either to a margarine 'high in polyunsaturates' or a low-fat spread. Choose a spread that contains less than 15g saturates per 100g. If you discovered that you are overweight then a low-fat spread will enable you to cut your calories.

There are so many yellow spread products now that it would be counter-productive to list them all. What we have done is divide them into seven categories in the table below. With the help of Tesco's nutritionist and various other manufacturers we have listed a Tesco spread and a well-known brand equivalent in each category. We show the total fat of each product along with how much saturated and polyunsaturated fat it contains. When you are choosing a yellow spread you can use this table to help you decide what category of product you want. Then, when you are shopping, double check with the nutrional label that the spread has the fat content you are after.

Two other points to note: first, the word 'Light' has no legal meaning. 'Light Philadelphia' has less fat and fewer calories than ordinary 'Philadelphia', but it still contains a lot of fat and quite a lot of saturated fat. Even 'Flora Extra Light' is 39 per cent fat, though relatively high in polyunsaturates. Secondly, the cheaper the spread the more likely it is to have a variable fat content. To be able to make cheap spreads the manufacturers switch the oils and fats they are using depending on current market prices. They call this 'blend flexibility'.

Category	Product	Total Fat	Grams per 100 grams Saturates	Polyun-saturates
1. Butter	Butter	80	54	3
2. Dairy Spreads: Made from a blend of vegetable oils and dairy fat for a buttery taste	Clover	75	32	10
	Tesco Golden Blend	75	26	16
3. Margarine Spreads: Blended from a variety of oils which may change	Krona	70	29	8
	Stork SB	81	26	12
	Tesco Soft Marg	80	23	15
4. Cooking Margarine: Made from a variety of oils for cooking and baking	Stork	80	28	6
	Echo	81	29	6
	Tesco Cooking Marg	80	26	7
5. Polyunsaturated: Usually made from sunflower oils high in polyunsaturates	Flora	80	14	40
	Blue Band	82	18	38
	Tesco Sunflower	80	15	42
6. Low Fat Spreads: A creamy taste but half the fat of butter	St Ivel Gold	37	10	6
	Delight	40	12	7
	Tesco Creamy Low Fat Butter	40	17	5
7. Low fat spreads higher in polyunsaturates	Flora Extra Light	39	7	19
	Shape Sunflower	37	9	16
	Tesco Half Fat Sunflower Spread	40	7	18
8. Very Low Fat Spreads: For those on low-calorie diets but unsuitable for cooking	Gold Lowest	25	6	3
	Delight Extra Low	20	4	6
	Outline	27	6	5
	Tesco Very Low Fat Spread	25	5	11

(These figures – current in December 1990 – should be used as a guide only. All products may be subject to revision from time to time. In particular, manufacturers are gradually reducing saturated fat where possible.)

High in polyunsaturates This claim can only be made if the oil contains more than 50 per cent of its fatty acids as polyunsaturates. Below is a table of liquid vegetable oils showing what proportions they contain of polyunsaturated, monounsaturated and saturated fats.

OIL	POLYUNSATURATED	MONOUNSATURATED	SATURATED
Almond	31	59	10
Blended Vegetable	33	58	9
Coconut Oil	2	7	91
Corn Oil	57	29	14
Grapeseed	73	17	10
Groundnut (peanut)	34	49	17
Hazelnut	24	68	8
Olive Oil	11	75	14
Olive Oil (Virgin)	7	79	13
Palm Oil	9	44	47
Pinenut	61	30	9
Pumpkin Seed	58	24	18
Rapeseed	32	59	8
Safflower	76	14	10
Sesame	48	38	14
Soyabean	59	25	16
Sunflower	66	22	12
Walnut	72	18	10

Compared to animal fats, vegetable oils are uniformly low in saturates. Coconut and palm oils are the exceptions – they are relatively high in saturates. Coconut oil is widely used in West Indian cuisine and gives a delicious flavour to rice. It should be eaten in moderation, though. Remember that oils high in polyunsaturates and monounsaturates may be better for you but they are still high in calories and can lead to your putting on weight if consumed in large quantities.

Low calorie and diet 'Low Calorie' does have a legal meaning – there must be no more than 40 kilocalories in one serving. Nor must there be more than 40 kilocalories in 100g of the food (or 100ml if it is a liquid). 'Reduced calorie' has a less strict meaning – the food must have no more than 75 per cent of the kilocalories of its normal equivalent. But 'diet' has no legal definition. At the time of writing, Diet 7UP had fewer than 3 kilocalories per can but Diet Ribena had more than 60 kilocalories a can. *Again, remember to read the small print.*

The Ministry of Agriculture's Food Advisory Committee wants quantitative limits set on all claims relating to 'high' and 'low' contents. Either the British government or the EC may thus pass yet further laws defining what a low-fat sausage is or a high fibre breakfast cereal. But the best way to frustrate all the excesses of manufacturers is for us to read the nutritional labels and apply our common sense.

Sugar 'No added sugar' is a negative claim of which we should all beware. While it is true that a COMA Report recommended that we cut down on added sugars their absence does not guarantee a low-sugar product. 'Robertson's Pure Fruit Spread' and 'Prewett's Fruit and Nut Bar' both announce 'no added sugars'. So no sucrose has been added. But they are still both very high in naturally occurring sugars which are quite capable of rotting our teeth. By the same token, if you ever see that a bar contains concentrated apple juice then it is just as capable of rotting your teeth as toffee. (Not a reason for avoiding such products altogether, but a good reason for not eating such products too often between meals.)

'Sugar-free' is also a highly abused phrase. Manufacturers of soft drinks which are high in glucose or dextrose are claiming the product is sugar-free. They may not have added sucrose but this claim is simply not true. It needs an enterprising Trading Standards Officer to prosecute them under the Trades Descriptions Act. Meanwhile, don't be taken in.

Hitherto labelling on baby foods has been particularly inadequate. Sugary foods, while beloved by babies and toddlers, have to be used with caution not only because of the danger to milk teeth but also because they have enough of a sweet tooth anyway. There is no need to increase it (for further advice *see* the Seven Ages of Man, p175).

Water Water occurs naturally in foods in varying amounts. Water can also be added to food and the more that is added the better the deal for the manufacturer and the worse for us. But we should add that added water can yield benefits such as lowering the fat content of yellow spreads.

Unfortunately it is difficult to legislate about water since factors such as the method of processing, the weather and cooking can all alter the level considerably. However there are laws governing various foods and processes:

- It is generally an offence to mislead consumers and this could include adding water to deceive.
- If it is used as an ingredient, water must be listed in the normal way – in its place by descending order of weight. But if the added water is less than 5 per cent of the total weight or volume it need not be listed.
- Many uncooked meats have nevertheless been processed using water. Most bacon is 'wet cured', which either means inserting brine or giving it a salt bath (hence the many complaints there have been about sodden bacon). Water that has been added during processing must be declared but only when it is more than 10 per cent of the total weight or volume.
- Most frozen chickens are put through a chlorinated bath as part of the process. There is an EEC regulation which lays down that no more than 7.4 per cent of a frozen chicken should be water. It is very expensive to test chickens for this but a recent investigation revealed a number of chickens that exceeded this limit. (Fresh chickens and dry-cured bacon may be more expensive but are dryer and more traditional in texture.)
- Added water in cooked meats must be expressed to the nearest 5 per cent – eg, 'not more than 10 per cent water'.

Fish   It is quite appropriate that we should look at fish after water. Frozen, glazed fish and shellfish are a very controversial area since there are no regulations covering their water content. What is there to stop us buying water at fish prices? The quoted weight on the packet includes the ice but reputable companies also list a 'minimum defrosted weight'. If you cannot see that on a packet of frozen prawns our advice is to buy other products. Trading Standards Officers point out that 40 per cent of the weight of a packet of glazed prawns is often water!

Fish fingers are a very nutritious food and incredibly convenient to feed to children. There are no laws in force as to what their minimum fish content should be though laws have been promised forcing manufacturers to declare how much of their fish fingers are fish and how much breadcrumbs. A rough guide would be that the cheaper the product the more breadcrumbs and the less fish you will get for your money. In addition, some fish fingers are made of highly processed minced fish and simply do not taste as good. The more reputable retailers now declare whether minced or whole fish has been used and the nature of the fish content. So, as ever, read the labelling closely and compare the products. We should warn you that fish fingers are not as cheap as they seem – some work out more expensive, pound for pound, than farmed salmon.

Meat   The Meat, Meat Products and Spreadable Fish Regulations govern what is and what isn't meat. The truth is that these rules are incredibly complicated, often quite bizarre and frequently unenforceable. But we now offer a brief guide to the slightly surreal world of the meat manufacturer:

- **Sausages**   Pork sausages must be a minimum of 65 per cent meat but half of that can be fat. So in fact pork sausages must only be 32.5 per cent lean meat and may contain a lot of fat. All other sausages (mainly beef ones) must be at least 50 per cent meat. Again, half of that can be fat leaving 25 per cent lean meat. Any similar product that does not use the name 'sausage' can have as little meat as its manufacturer wishes. (Other names that have been suggested from time to time include 'hydrogenated meat and cereal tube' and 'meat and cereal breakfast stick'!)
- **Burgers**   The law recognizes three sorts of burgers – the 'burger', the 'hamburger' and the 'economy burger'. The burger must be at least 80 per cent meat and 65 per cent of that meat must be lean (the rest can be fat). In fact, most burgers sold are made of beef. But the hamburger may contain beef, pork or a mixture of the two and must obey the same rules as a burger. The economy burger need only be 60 per cent meat and 65 per cent of that must, again, be lean.

- **Meat Pies** Cooked meat pies must have a minimum of 25 per cent meat but only half of this need be lean meat – that is 12½ per cent. So pies can contain a lot of pastry, fat and other fillers. Cooked and uncooked meat pies weighing less than 200g are allowed to contain even less meat.

There is a different set of rules for sausage rolls and pasties but we will not try your patience by delving into them. The joke is that a legal case in the 1960s (Skeates v Moore) concluded that it was impossible to take a properly representative sample of a pie to test it to see whether it complied with the law!

The moral with meat pies, as it is with all meat products, is to read the nutritional label carefully paying particular attention to fat and saturated fat. Meat pies are full of the stuff.

And what is 'lean meat'? we hear you cry. Well, it is flesh and 'fat, skin, rind, gristle and sinew in amounts naturally associated with the flesh used'. That can include heart, kidney, tongue, tail meat and some head meat. But since the measures brought in to combat BSE, no meat products can contain 'specified offal'. That is defined as brain, spinal chord, spleen, thymus, tonsils and intestines.

Meat products may still include 'Mechanically Recovered Meat' (MRM) about which there has been much controversy. MRM, which does not need to be labelled, is produced by sucking tiny pieces of muscle, connective tissue and often bone off the bare carcass at very high pressure. It is mostly recovered from poultry and pigs (it can account for as much as 5 per cent of the total meat from a pig's carcass). Very little MRM is derived from beef or lamb carcasses and the practice is in decline. The major supermarkets are steadily phasing out MRM in their products altogether because of consumers' apparent dislike of it. In the light of BSE, some experts believe the process should certainly not be allowed at all with cows but it remains legal at the time of writing.

Orange drinks All families drink large quantities of orange squash and orange juice. But there is a bewildering variety of descriptions on the label governed by a number of rules set out in a 1964 law. Let's look at the 'squashes' first – all drinks high in added sugar designed to be diluted:

- 'Orange flavour' means it may have no orange in it at all.
- 'Orange flavoured' means that some real orange must have been used.
- A 'whole orange drink' has minced whole oranges in it (so-called 'comminuted' orange). It must be a minimum of 10 per cent comminuted orange.
- 'Orange juice' must be a minimum of 25 per cent orange juice, although some of the 'high-juice' squashes have a higher precentage (Sainsbury's put in more than 50 per cent).

Cartons of already diluted drinks have become very popular:

- Any 'orange drink' must have at least 5 per cent real orange whether juice or minced fruit, peel and pith.

Juices, which are drunk without dilution, also have a number of categories:

- 'Orange juice' should be just that. However, sugar can be added to get it to the normal level of sweetness (any more than that and sugar must be declared on the label). All such orange juices are made up from concentrates and pasteurized. They must declare the fact that they are made from a concentrate on the carton. It is this process which makes them taste inferior to 'freshly squeezed' (see below).
- 'Premium' orange juices, so-called, are more expensive, but are a mixture of concentrated and unconcentrated juice with a better selection of oranges to give a better flavour.
- 'Freshly squeezed' must be just that. Look carefully at the 'use-by' date as the quality and flavour deteriorates rapidly after twenty-four hours.

Apple juice Brown apple juice made from concentrates is markedly inferior to freshly pressed apple juice (pale gold in colour). The concentrate, once again, must be declared. The freshly pressed apple juice can include ascorbic acid (E300 – vitamin C) which stops it oxidizing and going brown.

Mineral water   The basic truth about mineral water is that it is no better for you than tap water. However, it may taste better and you may prefer your water carbonated. Such a preference comes with a considerable price tag – mineral water is six or seven times the price of petrol and massively more expensive than tap water. (Incidentally, if you do not like the aroma of chlorine in tap water if you leave it to stand it will largely evaporate within a few minutes.)

The labelling and marketing of mineral water is all aimed at promoting a healthy image for which there is no basis in fact. That is why some of us took a certain malicious pleasure from Perrier having to withdraw their water in 1990 when an American analyst discovered relatively high levels of benzene in it. There are EC rules governing mineral water. Broadly, the waters need to be free of contamination with a consistent mineral content. The most stringent rules apply to those calling themselves a 'natural mineral water'. The basic idea behind them was that such a water should be pure enough to be drawn out of the ground and not treated in any way. However, in a classic EC fudge, the rules were actually written so as to include Perrier. Perrier now draw the water and the gas that carbonates the water separately. They then filter the gas to remove benzene. They then recarbonate the water. Not exactly what we would call 'natural'. And in fact they had to agree to change the way they label their water in 1990 when word got around they were arguably being economical with the truth. Perrier no longer describe their water as 'naturally carbonated' on their label.

Alcohol   Some of the general laws about labelling apply to alcoholic drinks in Britain. The manufacturer, the manufacturer's address, the volume and the alcoholic strength all have to be declared. But ingredients do not have to be. A lot of additives are used in the production of alcoholic drinks but the producers do not have to come clean about them. Whether ingredients labelling would have deterred the

Austrians and Italians who put highly illegal substances into their wine recently is an open question. But when the additives normally used (such as sulphites in wine) are compared to the effect alcohol itself has on our health they are, in truth, much less important. 'Low-alcohol' drinks (which must not exceed 1.2 per cent alcohol by volume) do declare their ingredients because they come under soft drinks regulations. 'Alcohol-free' drinks must not exceed 0.05 per cent alcohol by volume.

In the US all alcoholic drinks now have to carry these two warnings:

- According to the Surgeon General women should not drink alcoholic beverages during pregnancy because of the risk of birth defects . . .
- Consumption of alcoholic beverages impairs your ability to drive a car or operate machinery and may cause health problems.

Tesco have now decided to include an extra measure of strength on their alcoholic drinks – they now indicate how many 'units' (*see* Section III, p148) each glass contains. For further information on alcohol, *see* Section III, p147 and Section VI.

There are a number of rules and regulations for other foods which we have not included – chiefly so as not to try your patience. Here, by way of summary, is a list of the key elements on a food label.

WHAT'S IMPORTANT ON A LABEL?

Use the weight to compare value-for-money with other products.

Obey use-by dates to minimize the risk of food poisoning.

Read the ingredients list to find out which ingredients are there in greatest quantity – the ones mentioned first.

Don't worry about E-numbers unless you have been clinically diagnosed as allergic or intolerant. But keep an eye out for the additives that help dress up cheap (particularly fatty) ingredients as quality ones.

Always look at the panel of nutritional information and use it to compare products. The key elements of nutritional labelling are energy, fat and saturated fat content.

Don't worry too much about vitamins and minerals – a balanced diet will nearly always bring you enough of these.

Ignore all 'health' claims unless validated by a reliable source. And be sceptical about 'negative' and 'natural' claims.

STORING FOOD

As we step through the door of your house to consider how food should be handled there, perhaps the first thing to beware of is food poisoning. We have already referred to food suppliers and how their practices can put us at risk. But what food suppliers do is beyond our control – what we can do is handle food sensibly in the home to protect ourselves from their mistakes and from the dangers that are inherent in food.

In 1989 there were 54,000 confirmed cases of food poisoning. But most food poisoning incidents are not reported – we tend to sit out most stomach upsets rather than go to the doctor. For this reason the experts in Britain multiply the official figure by a factor of 10 to get a more realistic estimate. In the US they use a factor of 100. So we can only say that the number of cases of food poisoning in 1989 was somewhere between 540,000 and 5.4 million. While food poisoning is a definite risk we should keep it in perspective – we suffer from it less than people in warmer countries with lower standards of hygiene. But it is a definite risk that we can do much to avoid.

Comparatively few of us now learn how to cook or master the basic rules of hygiene that go hand in hand with food preparation. With our increasing reliance on convenience foods this problem is likely to get worse. An analysis carried out by the Department of Health in 1985 of 463 incidents of food poisoning found that 259 occurred in the home and only 64 in restaurants. That should not let restaurants off the hook, but it underlines that we have much to learn.

WHAT ARE THE HIGH-RISK FOODS?

Poultry Much poultry is contaminated with salmonella. It should be cooked thoroughly to the bone – no blood should emerge when it is pierced. Frozen chickens are more contaminated than fresh. Tesco and Sainsbury's are now claiming to have reduced incidence of salmonella in fresh poultry to much lower levels than hitherto.

Eggs There is a small but proven risk from salmonella in chicken eggs. Government advice continues to be that no one should eat raw eggs (whether in ice-cream, mayonnaise or whatever) and that young children, the elderly, the sick and pregnant women should avoid semi-cooked eggs. More than a million infected hens have been slaughtered since March 1989 but salmonella enteritidis phage type 4 is still poisoning large numbers of people. Some blame our poor handling of food, others blame imported eggs and everyone blames Edwina Currie. But the prevalence of salmonellosis under-lines the need for careful handling of food.

Meat and meat products Bacteria like meat and thrive in it given the chance. Beef and lamb can be eaten rare but pork should always be cooked thoroughly because of the danger of worms. Meat pies and pâtés are a perfect breeding ground for bacteria if cross-contaminated.

Shellfish Shellfish are one of the most common causes of stomach upsets, particularly because many British shellfish feed in waters polluted with sewage. You should be entirely confident of the source of shellfish such as oysters which are to be eaten raw and therefore cannot be heated to kill any bacteria present. Some shellfish, such as oysters and mussels, are 'filter-feeders' and actually extract nasty bugs (both bacterial and viral) from sea water which they then harbour. That is why – where possible – all shellfish should be thoroughly cooked. In a 1987 report, the Communicable Disease Surveillance Centre said that gastroenteritis viruses had been found in British cockles and oysters and they cannot be guaranteed free of contamination. The same report says that shellfish have also been the source of hepatitis A infections. Since sewage pollution is still a problem on British coasts shellfish, especially cockles and mussels, should be approached with extreme caution.

Soft cheeses The term 'soft cheese' covers soft, rinded cheeses such as Brie and Camembert as well as all goat's cheeses (Chevre). Such cheeses have a lower level of acidity than hard cheeses like Cheddar or Stilton and listeria can multiply in them. To do so it has to be introduced first by contaminated raw ingredients or unhygienic methods of production. It is therefore possible to make safe cheese with unpasteurized milk and contaminated cheese with pasteurized milk (in fact in the worst ever outbreak of listeria poisoning which killed thirty-seven people in Switzerland they had been eating a pasteurized cheese). Current government advice is that all those particularly at risk from listeria (see above) should avoid soft cheese. In this context 'soft cheese' does not include cream cheeses such as fromage frais or Philadelphia, nor does it include semi-soft cheeses such as Roquefort.

Cooked chilled foods   Ready-to-eat meals which have been cooked and then chilled have been found to contain a variety of nasties. Many analyses have found listeria in a variety of dishes (whether the levels constitute a genuine danger experts cannot say, but the levels were certainly much, much lower than those found in soft cheeses). A survey by *Which?* in April 1990 found E. coli in nine out of twenty-nine fish dishes, four out of eighteen chicken dishes and one out of twenty lasagnes. It was not enough E. coli to make you ill but if you had stored the food in a warm place allowing the E. coli to multiply and then eaten the food without subsequent reheating you would have soon known all about it. While the food manufacturers and retailers are trying to improve the hygiene standards of their cooked dishes we should ensure that we reheat them very thoroughly.

Vegetables   Vegetables should always be washed thoroughly because much soil contains listeria. Prepared and pre-washed salads have also been found to contain listeria and should always be kept in a cool place, thoroughly washed and consumed quickly. Rice may contain bacillus cereus and should be thoroughly washed and eaten soon after cooking. If it is to be used in a cold rice dish then keep it cool in the fridge. Keeping it warm or at room temperature for any period of time could be tempting fate beyond endurance.

HOW TO AVOID FOOD POISONING

Before we look at the best way to store particular foods, a word or two about the conditions bacteria like best and how easily they can multiply. Food-poisoning bacteria need four things to multiply:

- **Food**   In particular, meat, fish and dairy products. Foods high in sugar or salt are generally unsuitable.
- **Warmth**   Bacteria love warm conditions, ideally our own body temperature of 37°C. But they can multiply at any temperature between 5°C and 63°C. This range is often referred to by Environmental Health Officers as 'the danger zone'. The importance of storing high-risk foods in the fridge and cooking them thoroughly is brought into sharp relief by the diagram below.

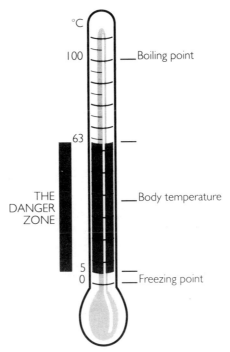

- **Moisture**   Only a little is required. But dehydrated and dried foods last so long precisely because there is not enough moisture for the bugs to get busy.

- Time   If the food is a good host and the bacteria have got into it, if the temperature is pleasantly warm and there is also some moisture present then all a bug needs is time. A hundred salmonella bacteria introduced into a meat pie by a dirty knife at 1 p.m. could multiply to more than 26 million by 7 p.m. the same day. Bacteria reproduce much like amoebas by dividing into two. Normally this would happen every twenty minutes, but in absolutely ideal conditions it happens in as few as ten minutes.

Use-by dates and storage instructions. We have already looked at the importance of use-by dates (*see* p245). They should always be obeyed. Storage instructions on packets are also important. Here is a table of recommended storage times – it is a guide, not a set of inviolate rules:

RECOMMENDED STORAGE TIMES

TYPE OF FOOD	DAYS IN THE REFRIGERATOR	MONTHS IN THE FREEZER
Raw meats		
Beef	4	8–9
Pork	4	6–7
Lamb	4	6–7
Veal	4	6–7
Mince	1–2	3
Sausages	3	3
Poultry	2	6–9
Bacon	7	1
Cooked meats		
Ham	2–3	3
Pâté	2–3	1
Poultry	2–3	1–2
Casseroles	2–3	2–3
Fish		
White fish	1–2	4
Oily fish	1	2
Shellfish	1	3
Dairy products		
Milk (pasteurized)	3–4	
Cream	2–3	
Eggs	6–8	

Fridges The refrigerator is a marvellous modern convenience and generally a very sub-standard piece of equipment. To keep its price down manufacturers have skimped on quality and most fridges have been unable to supply the more precise temperatures demanded of them by such developments as chilled food. We have all suffered the numbered dials that are different from make to make, that give you little clue as to which end is for higher temperatures and which for lower, and which give you no idea of the actual temperature in your fridge. Recent surveys have shown that few of us ever check whether our fridge is working properly and that most of our fridges do not. The temperatures a properly working fridge will register inside are lowest at the bottom and highest at the top (on the principle that hot air rises):

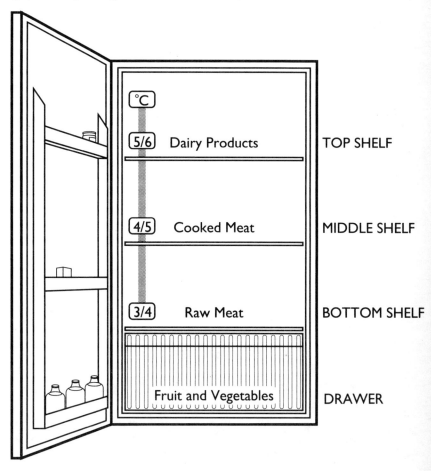

°C

5/6	Dairy Products	TOP SHELF
4/5	Cooked Meat	MIDDLE SHELF
3/4	Raw Meat	BOTTOM SHELF
	Fruit and Vegetables	DRAWER

The theory of storage is that fruit and vegetables go in the enclosed drawer at the bottom where cool air is not constantly circulating around them (this can damage green leaf vegetables such as lettuce). Then raw meat is stored on the bottom shelf – if it was high up the danger is that it would drip into cooked food below transferring bacteria. So cooked food is found above raw food.

If you are unsure as to the temperature in your fridge then buy a fridge thermometer (they are widely available and cost only a pound or two). Place it on the top shelf for two hours. It should then reach no more than 6°C. A new generation of refrigerators is now appearing in the shops. They have enclosed compartments which promise a constant temperature of −1°C to +1°C for chilled foods. Needless to say, they are more expensive.

Here are some points to watch if you wish to ensure your fridge is working properly:

- Don't overcrowd the interior. This prevents cool air circulating properly.
- Don't put warm dishes in it.
- Don't leave the door open longer than is necessary (ie, no more than ten seconds). It can take a fridge hours to recover its proper temperature otherwise.
- Defrost regularly. Heavily iced fridges don't work efficiently.
- Check the rubber seal on the door is not broken.
- Remove dust from the housing at the back. This can prevent warm air being removed from the fridge.
- Don't place the fridge next to the oven, radiator or washing-machine where the temperature is higher than average.

Finally, remember to keep the fridge clean and prevent cross-contamination between cooked and uncooked foods.

Freezers by comparison, work better and are less of a hazard. As in shops, freezers should be kept at −18°C or below. It is a good idea to use freezer bags labelled with the date the food was put in and consult the table we showed you earlier for advice on storage periods. Remember that freezers can make bacteria lie dormant, but they cannot kill them. So once defrosted food needs to be handled as carefully as any other (*see* Food Preparation, p297).

Only freezers carrying a four-star symbol are capable of freezing fresh food. Models with fewer stars can store ready-frozen food. This is what the number of stars signifies:

> * for I week
> ** for I month
> *** for 3 months

If you suffer a power cut, put a rug over your freezer to improve its insulation but do not open it. Food in a freezer without power should last around thirty hours and up to thirty-five hours if the cabinet was completely full (upright freezers do not last as long as chest freezers). When the power is restored switch on 'fast freeze' for a couple of hours.

If you are freezing fresh food yourself in a four-star freezer remember that:

- Small quantities will thaw more quickly.
- Seal food thoroughly.
- Never put warm food in.
- Label foods clearly with dates so that you know later whether they have passed their 'use-by' dates.
- Some foods are appropriate for freezing, others are not. Here is a list of foods that do not freeze well:

  salad ingredients ie, lettuce, watercress, onions, tomatoes, radish, cucumber; mayonnaise; salad dressings; single cream; sour cream; eggs (in their shells); hard boiled eggs; whole grapefruit; bananas; marzipan; strawberries; hard cheese (grated is all right); carbonated drinks; whole chestnuts. As to cooked dishes – generally if the individual ingredients freeze well then so will the dish.

Food containers   There have been scares about chemicals in cling-film migrating into oily foods like cheese and fish. As a result cling films are now less oily (and less clingy, unfortunately). The danger is not great because of the tiny amounts of migration involved. But current advice is to store food in a bowl and cover the top with cling film so that food and film do not touch. This is particularly advisable for oily foods such as cheese or fish.

Metal poisoning can result from storing food in an opened tin. This is particularly true of acidic foods like tomatoes because once opened the presence of oxygen accelerates the acid's attack on the can's interior. In March 1990, the Ministry of Agriculture announced that 2 per cent of tinned food was exceeding the amount of tin permitted in food. This under-lines why damaged cans also represent a small danger. When the inner coating of the can is broken migration is more likely. We emphasise the importance of rotating canned foods in the cupboard. Shops selling very old cans have been known to cause poisoning – a sure sign is an escape of gas when the tin is opened. If you hear this take it back to the shop and complain.

Lead   Lead can cause both acute and chronic poisoning. You should never drink water from the hot tap – this water is often delivered by lead piping where it has been stationary for a while. Earthenware containers are sometimes glazed with lead oxide and acidic foods should not be stored in them. The Ministry of Agriculture warned us in the mid-1980s to wipe the necks of wine bottles with lead foil tops since lead tartrate crystals form that can contaminate the wine. However, nowadays most wines have plastic or aluminium foil. It is not a good idea, either, to store whisky in a lead crystal decanter. What you end up with is the opposite of unleaded fuel.

Aluminium   One other warning is a point of practicality rather than safety: if acidic fruit or vegetables (eg, tomato pizza) are stored in aluminium foil then the aluminium will dissolve and the damn thing will leak over the rest of your fridge or freezer! The same has been known to happen with heavily salted foods like bacon.

Moulds   There are thousands of different moulds that can grow on food. Some are quite harmless. But the best advice we can give you is not to eat mould-infected food (for more information, *see* Section III, p129). There is some evidence that a regular intake of moulds containing aflatoxins might cause liver cancer. What can we do about it? Largely, we have to rely on the efforts of the food industry to protect us. But we should not eat nuts that are discoloured, decayed or obviously mouldy because they might contain aflatoxin. We should particularly beware of small independent suppliers like health-food shops who may have less than stringent standards. Storing soft fruit such as peaches in the fridge will inhibit the growth of mould. Incidentally, if manufacturers and suppliers heed our growing hostility to preservatives and fungicides and remove them from our food, then moulds are likely to be far more in evidence in the future.

KEEPING FOOD AT ITS BEST

- Obey all 'use-by' and 'best before' dates.
- Rotate tinned and packet foods on a first-in, first-out basis, ie put newly bought products at the back.
- Keep storage areas clean. This is important for cupboards as well as the fridge.
- Store fruit and vegetables with care. Don't over store them because the older they are the more vitamin loss they will have suffered. Below is a table showing how vitamin C content of potatoes diminishes over time:

	Vitamin C mg per 100grams
Potatoes freshly dug	30
Stored 1–3 months	20
Stored 4–5 months	15
Stored 6–7 months	10
Stored 8–9 months	8

- If possible, keep fruit and vegetables in a cool, shady, well-ventilated place. More particularly:
  Potatoes should be stored away from sunlight or they will turn green (the effect of a poison called solanine). When preparing cut off green parts as well as eyes and sprouts.
  Onions should not be stored touching potatoes since they can make them deteriorate.

Apples   cheek by jowl with carrots can make the carrots bitter.

Green vegetables   benefit from being stored in the cool compartment at the bottom of the fridge.

Lettuce   keeps best in the fridge in a moist plastic bag.

Mushrooms   should be kept cool and dry.

Peaches and Nectarines   should be stored in the fridge to inhibit the growth of mould.

- Keep foods out of direct sunlight. Leaving milk out on the doorstep for long periods will not only turn it into yoghurt, the sunlight can also destroy its vitamin B_2 (riboflavin). Sunlight will destroy vitamin E in cooking oils causing them to go rancid.

- **Flour**   should be stored in a cool dry place. Whether open or unopen plain flour should be used within thirteen months and self-raising within nine months (it is at its best within three months).

- **Dried beans, pulses, rice and pasta**   should also be kept dry and cool and will easily last for a year.

- **Dried fruit**   is best kept in a sealed container and will last up to three months.

- **Canned food**   should be consumed within a year though tinned ham is best eaten within six months.

- **Tea and coffee**   lose their flavour quite rapidly (within weeks) but instant or ground coffee that has been vacuum packet will last for up to a year.

- **Herbs and spices**   will suffer considerable flavour loss after time and should be used within six months.

The Larder may be a thing of the past in most modern homes but the following points apply to store cupboards just as well:

Rotate stock. Put newly bought foods at the back.
Prevent insect infestations by cleaning up spillages and keeping flour and other dried goods in sealed containers.
Look out for signs of rodents – gnawed packets, droppings, etc and call your local authority if you have a problem.
Throw away any foods which are growing mould.

 # FOOD PREPARATION

Much poultry contains salmonella, pets can carry E coli and humans may well be carriers of listeria and staphylococcus. All that and more can be present in the kitchen for, as we have seen, food-poisoning bacteria are all around us. It is only when we give them the chance to multiply that food poisoning occurs.

Personal hygiene is critical. You should always wash your hands before preparing food. If you visit the lavatory, blow your nose or empty the rubbish while cooking you should wash them again. And you should always wash your hands after handling raw meat and vegetables. Any cuts, sores or spots on your hands should be covered by a waterproof dressing. They all harbour bacteria. Wiping your hands on your apron will help spread whatever is on your hands further afield. Tasting food with your fingers will transfer thousands of bacteria to the food. Smoking involves putting your fingers to your mouth and is not a good idea while cooking.

Kitchens are unhygienic places, particularly since most houses now have 'kitchen-breakfast' rooms which are both cooking and living areas. Stroking pets while cooking and allowing them to lick plates are not good ideas. An ideal kitchen would be designed according to the principle of 'dirty through to clean'. That is, the kitchen areas would progress in the following sequence:

- Rubbish bins by the door
- Surface where raw, dirty foods are prepared
- Sink for washing up and cleaning
- Surface for cooked foods to be served up

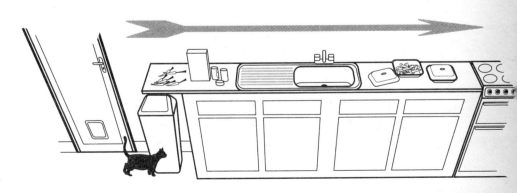

This basic sequence is designed to minimize the risk of cross-contamination by keeping raw and cooked foods apart. Bacteria can spread (with our help) from a raw chicken or vegetable to cooked food. If that cooked food is warm and moist, if it will not be cooked again but not eaten just yet then the circumstances are ideal for a case of food poisoning. Common sources of cross-contamination are:

Hands   Wash them frequently.

Knives   Never use the same knife for raw and cooked food without washing it in between. Some people keep separate colour coded knives for these different tasks.

Chopping boards   Wooden chopping boards harbour all manner of bugs and should be scrubbed down after use. Plastic chopping boards are easier to clean. It is a good idea to have different boards for different functions.

Cloths and sponges   Unless regularly disinfected, dishcloths spread more bacteria than they collect. A kitchen disinfectant such as Detox is a useful addition. Disposable paper towels are only used once and are preferable to dishcloths.

Tea towels   A classic source of contamination. Allowing dishes and glasses to dry is preferable. Dishwashers are ideal. If you wash up by hand use very hot water and a washing-up liquid. A nylon brush is less likely to harbour nasties than a dishcloth.

Keep floors and surfaces clean.

Pets can be carriers of bacteria, particularly campylobacter. Here are some sensible precautions:

- Don't let dogs, cats or any pets lick plates or utensils from which people eat.
- Make sure pets have separate feeding bowls.
- As far as possible, keep pets out of the kitchen and certainly don't let cats walk over work tops and work surfaces.
- Clean up pets' faeces and urine immediately and disinfect the area using bleach.
- Maintain good standards of pet hygiene by cleaning out bedding, boxes, cages, etc on a regular basis.

- Don't allow pets to lick your face and particularly the faces and fingers of children.

Many wild birds carry salmonella quite naturally. Food poisoning has been known to be caused by milk contaminated after being attacked by birds. Birds often peck through foil tops in winter and you would be well advised not to drink milk that has been contaminated in this way. If you insist on being intrepid, then for heaven's sake keep it well refrigerated.

Here are a few useful tips on defrosting food:

- The most convenient method is in a microwave, turning the food if you have no turntable.
- Otherwise the best way to defrost food is slowly in the fridge. Ensure that all the ice has gone before cooking (otherwise you are likely to undercook the food).
- Loosely cover the food (particularly cooked food) with aluminium foil or greaseproof paper during defrosting to help prevent cross-contamination.
- Avoid continual freezing, thawing and re-freezing of food. At home the thawing/freezing process is slow and this inevitably means that food stays in the danger zone for long periods.
- Throw away thawed liquids from meat and poultry and watch out for cross-contamination (eg, thawed liquids dripping on to other foods or leaving a wet surface after thawing which you later put cooked food on).
- Don't re-freeze food after a freezer breakdown or power cut. Most home insurance policies offer cheap cover for the contents of a freezer. If you do have a power cut leave the lid closed as this helps keep the cold in.
- Only freezers with a four-star rating are suitable for home freezing of fresh foods. Freezers with fewer stars can only be used for storage.
- The star ratings on frozen food packets tell us how long the food should be kept. They are as follows:
  * one week
  ** one month
  *** three months

•   Never re-freeze food once defrosted unless it is re-cooked in between.

When you see how long it is recommended you leave frozen poultry to thaw and when you consider that frozen birds are inferior in quality to fresh then it really does not seem worth buying frozen chickens and turkeys. The extra price of fresh is well worthwhile on grounds of convenience, quality and safety. That is why sales of fresh birds have risen rapidly while the demand for frozen has contracted. However, if you remain unconvinced the following times are recommended for thawing. It is best done slowly in the fridge. But we have also included a column for thawing in cold water which takes less time, particularly if the water is changed every now and again.

Weight	Thawing time	
	In the fridge (4°C)	In cold water
3lbs	24 hours	8 hours
4lbs	36 hours	11 hours
5lbs	42 hours	13 hours
6–8lbs	2–2½ days	16–18 hours
8–10lbs	2½–2¾ days	18–20 hours
10–12lbs	2¾–3 days	20–22 hours
12–14lbs	3–3½ days	22–24 hours
14–16lbs	3½–3¾ days	24–26 hours
16–18lbs	3¾–4 days	26–28 hours
18–20lbs	4–4½ days	28–30 hours

You are advised against thawing at room temperature. But if you ignore this advice, never thaw a bird in a sunlit or centrally heated room. Make sure it is a cool room.

COOKING

Later in this subsection we look at different methods of cooking and the effect they have on food. But before that we want to complete our advice about avoiding food poisoning.

The government's Communicable Disease Surveillance Centre at Colindale in North London has analysed the food poisoning statistics and compiled a list of the ten most common causes of food poisoning. The first three repeat points made in the previous subsection about food preparation. The rest relate to cooked food and how we handle it:

- **Preparing food in advance and storing it too long at room temperature, allowing bacterial growth.** The classic example is that of a summer wedding. So be warned!
- **Inadequate defrosting of frozen food, particularly poultry.** If the centre of a chicken is frozen the normal cooking time will not be sufficient to cook the bird thoroughly.
- **Infected food handler.** Any cook who does not observe basic rules of personal hygiene is asking for trouble.
- **Undercooking food.** Food generally needs to reach 75°C to ensure all bacteria has been killed. A meat thermometer can tell you when this temperature has been reached. Poultry is only cooked when no blood flows from the flesh when pierced through to the bone.
- **Failure to keep food properly hot, at above 63°C.** Keeping food merely luke warm is not a good idea.
- **Cooling cooked foods too slowly.** This allows any bacteria which have survived cooking, or any others that have subsequently been re-introduced, to multiply.
- **Cross-contamination from raw food to cooked food** whether via a dirty knife, hands or surface.
- **The use of cooked food which has been cross-contaminated.** It only takes a momentary piece of carelessness to allow this to happen.

301

- **Inadequate reheating of food.** All foods, particularly meat-based ones, must be thoroughly reheated before being eaten. Warming a pie is not enough.
- **Re-use of leftovers.** Continual heating, cooking and reheating of food, while destroying vitamins, also keeps the food at the mild temperatures that aid bacterial growth.

Cooking and reheating Even if you cook a chicken very thoroughly it is unlikely that all the bacteria will have been killed. When the chicken returns to room temperature ('the danger zone') the bacteria can begin to multiply again. But it takes them about one and a half hours to get into their stride. So if you want to cool, say, a roast chicken before putting it in the fridge you should not leave it for longer than one and a half hours. (And if you put it in the fridge too early, remember, then you will warm the fridge up.) Food cut into pieces or slices will cool more quickly as will food in a saucepan the base of which has been immersed in cold water.

Inadequate reheating of food is one of the ten most common causes of food poisoning listed above. In truth, it is a practice that Environmental Health Officers would prefer we didn't do at all – each time food is reheated it is taken up through the danger zone and then down through it once more as it cools. But none of us wish to waste food so the key thing is to reheat thoroughly until the food is piping hot. It is generally not a good idea to reheat food more than once. It should never be done when it may have been left for more than one and a half hours at room temperature or handled by unwashed hands.

Ovens and microwaves The manufacturers may not enjoy reading this paragraph, but the truth is that ovens can be unreliable and microwaves often are. Like fridges, these are generally cheap, inexact pieces of equipment. Food ought to reach a temperature of 75°C throughout to kill off the majority of the bacteria it contains (of course, this advice only applies to the high-risk foods we have already identified). Many of our ovens are old and do not cook at the temperature we instruct them to. Others, quite possibly new models, have thermostats that respond slowly – the food being cooked may descend some way below the temperature instructed before the thermostat cuts in. It is thus easily possible to undercook without knowing it. One answer is a meat thermometer which, like the fridge thermometer, is now widely available in kitchen shops. But there is no substitute for using your senses – checking to see no blood comes out of a chicken or turkey when pierced, for instance.

Microwaves are another story again. Our basic misconceptions about microwaves are the fault of the manufacturers. It is they who in the early days marketed their products as ideal for cooking meat which they weren't. But microwaves are undoubtedly faster for some types of cooking and do steam vegetables and fish beautifully. Half the households in Britain now own a microwave. They are a considerable blessing if we use them properly which we can only do if we understand how they perform. Here are some basic points about microwave technology:

- **Heat penetration is not as good as we have been led to believe.** The hottest point in microwaved food is only 1 or 2 centimetres from the surface – this is caused by the microwaves agitating the water molecules and making them 'boil'. But the centre of the food has to cook by conduction of heat in the same way as an ordinary oven operates. This takes time.
- **Different foods behave differently.**
  – *Thick soup* absorbs microwaves very quickly and heats intensely at the edges but remains cool at the centre. It has to be stirred.
  – *Sponge mixes* may not cook evenly.
  – *Mince pies* and other pastries stay cool on the outside (pastry has few water molecules to be agitated) while cooking on the inside.
  – *Meat joints* cook quickly below the surface but need time for the heat to be conducted to the centre.
  – *Chicken joints* and other irregular shapes have a greater surface area than regular shapes and they heat irregularly. Chicken legs heat more quickly than the breast.
- **Microwaves have 'hot spots' and 'cold spots'.** Microwaves are not evenly distributed. One part of a

dish may be burnt while another remains undercooked. This is particularly true of cheap models.

- **Defrosting can be inadequate.** The surface and just below can defrost quickly leaving the centre frozen. The danger here is that you do not notice and then put the food in the oven – with a frozen centre it will remain seriously undercooked after a standard cooking time.
- **Some timers are unreliable.** The mechanical 'clockwork' timers, usually on the older models, are unreliable and often do not give you the time you asked for.
- **Cheaper microwaves are not so effective.** Some ovens have a wattage as low as 400. In some cases they are so slow to cook food you might as well have used a conventional oven.
- **Microwaves cannot take standard metal containers.** Not relevant to food hygiene but mentioned for safety's sake.

If you have one of the older microwaves, you use it for single tasks and you do not want to buy another, then here is some advice for you:

- Don't use it for cooking high-risk foods (such as chicken or chilled, prepared meals that might contain listeria) for vulnerable members of your family – the sick, the elderly, young children and pregnant women.
- Instructions which specify standing times after the microwave has finished are very important. These allow the heat to be conducted evenly throughout the food thereby cooking it.
- Turning the food every now and again helps to distribute the microwaves more evenly across the food.
- Round dishes also help even distribution.
- Turn clockwork timers right round to the maximum time before returning them to your chosen time. This makes them more reliable.

If you are thinking of buying a microwave for the first time or replacing your existing one, go for these three features, even though they add to the cost:

Electronic 'touch-pad' digital controls.
Turntable.
Wave stirrers (you will have to ask about these rotating antennae which help distribute the microwaves more evenly since the manufacturers do not see fit to advertise them).

In addition, you can now buy 'combination ovens' with grills which can not only brown the food but also boost the cooking power.

Both consumer organizations and the government have been highly critical of both the clarity and the efficacy of cooking instructions on microwave food products. In November 1989, the Ministry of Agriculture announced that one in three microwaves they had tested failed to take chilled, prepared meals to a temperature which would be sure to kill food-poisoning bacteria. One of the chief reasons for one in three microwaves failing to heat food properly was that they were not being given long enough to complete the task. The instructions on the food packets were completely inadequate. Microwaves vary in power from 425 watts to 875 watts. Yet there was only a standard cooking time recommended on products such as cook-chill meals. Since 1991, a new system of power rating has been put into practice. Now different cooking times are given for ovens with different power ratings. The ratings are simply expressed according to the following table:

POWER RANGE (watts)	425–475	500–575	600–675	700–775	800–875
POWER RATING	1	2	3	4	5

If you are unsure what the wattage of your oven is most say on the back. Failing that look at the instruction booklet. If you no longer have that telephone the suppliers who will be able to tell you.

Do remember, above all, to observe the microwaving instructions closely with particular reference to cooking and standing times.

Advice about microwaves is not all doom and gloom. They preserve the vitamin content of foods better than any other cooking method as we will now discover.

In the remainder of this subsection we look at how the nutritional value of food – protein, vitamins, minerals and so on – can best be preserved in the home. It could be argued that we need not worry about such things because vitamin and mineral deficiencies are not a problem for most of us. But the truth is that food in which the nutrients have been destroyed will usually taste bland as well. *Good nutrition and tempting cooking go hand in hand*.

Why do we heat foods? To kill poisonous bacteria, to render food edible and to give it additional flavours and textures. But the basic rule with cooking is that the longer it lasts the greater the loss of nutrients. Some foods, though – notably pork, poultry and some beans – must be cooked thoroughly as a matter of safety. Once cut and peeled, do not leave vegetables standing in water or exposed to the air for prolonged periods. This will hasten vitamin loss. All foods intended to be eaten should be consumed as soon as possible after cooking. Keeping them hot thereafter leads to loss of nutrients. How do the different methods of cooking affect food?

The tissues of both plants and animals consist of cells. Many of the nutrients in raw foods are packaged up in these cells. Cooking foods causes the cell walls to break down and liberate the nutrients. It also makes the food more digestible. The raw starches found in plants such as potatoes are poorly digested unless cooked. Cooking liberates the starch from the granules in which they are stored. The availability of beta-carotene from vegetables is actually improved by cooking. Above about 60°C heat causes proteins to change shape and coagulate. For example, eggs coagulate when heated. The heating of food inactivates many naturally occurring tox-icants – this is particularly important with pulses. Several vitamins can be destroyed by heat. How much is lost depends on the temperature and duration of heating. At temperatures up to 100°C vitamin losses are low. Chemical changes such as browning occur at the higher temperatures used in grilling, baking and frying. Some of the materials produced by cooking food at high temperatures are potentially harmful and are similar to the constituents of smoke.

Boiling Boiling vegetables leads to a severe loss of water-soluble vitamins such as vitamin C. You throw them away with the water. The volume of water should thus be kept to a minimum. For leaf vegetables use only half an inch to an inch of water in the bottom of the saucepan and let the steam do most of the work. Do not cut vegetables up too much as this releases protective enzymes that help retain vitamins. Adding salt is also a bad idea – it extends the cooking time required because the plant cells break up less readily. It also makes beans tougher in texture. Leaf vegetables cooked until very soft will have less nutritional value and little flavour either. If you can persuade your family to eat them *al dente* you will be doing them all a favour.

Boiled potatoes lose vitamin B_1, vitamin C and folic acid for three reasons – heat, exposure to the air and leaching into the water. Not an argument against boiled potatoes or one in favour of half-cooked ones. But don't overcook them so they become floury. And consider baking and frying them as well (see below). Kidney beans, soya beans and lentils must always be boiled for a minimum of twenty minutes to destroy the poison they contain. A final warning – NEVER add bicarbonate of soda to vegetables. It destroys vitamins.

Pressure cooking Great for stews, ghastly for cabbage. The very high temperatures achieved inside a pressure cooker can dramatically increase nutrient loss. But that depends on how vulnerable the food is and how long it is left in. Pressure cooking is very convenient for the quick cooking of dried beans and pulses.

Steaming This is incomparably the best way to cook green vegetables. They retain more of their colour and flavour as well as nutrients. You can buy saucepans in two parts which are dedicated steamers. But a cheaper option is an adjustable steamer which fits inside an ordinary saucepan. And in extremis a colander inside a saucepan with a lid over it will do the job adequately. Steaming is also a good way to cook fish and poultry.

Stir-Fry   A stir-fry actually relies on steaming more than frying to cook the ingredients. Only a small amount of oil is used and a good stir-fry leaves the vegetables *al dente* and thus less exhausted of their nutrients. Groundnut oil is probably best for this purpose because of its high smoke point. A tip is to try to ensure that the different ingredients are cut into similar sizes so they cook at the same pace. Also, put such ingredients as meat in first because it takes longer to cook than vegetables. Stir frying really depends on the wok which is designed so you can toss the vegetables in the steam preventing a large uptake of oil. To keep cooking time to a minimum the wok should always be very hot before the food is put in.

Shallow frying   Frying has got itself a bad name but in many cases it is no worse than grilling, the method with which it is often compared. Frying enables meat and meat products to shed as much fat as grilling does – just look at the pan after frying sausages. And some foods – such as steak – do not take up much fat from the pan as long as they are not finely chopped. Meat and fish coated in breadcrumbs will absorb quantities of fat (we explore this in more detail below).

Vegetables also tend to be very absorbent of fat but who would deny us the pleasures of occasional bubble and squeak (fried in polyunsaturated oil, of course).

Deep frying   A deep-fried chip, cut chunkily rather than thinly, will retain more vitamin C than a similar quantity of boiled potato. Chips have been given a terrible reputation by the food puritans, but we still eat vast quantities of them and that is no bad thing. Deep frying in polyunsaturated oil is vastly preferable to a saturated beef fat. Many chip eaters in the North of England swear by their chips cooked in saturated beef dripping. But the practice is not a healthy one – McDonald's have reformulated their cooking oil to remove its beef fat content. You can minimize the uptake of fat by frying at 180°C – if the temperature is too low the food is not sealed and it takes up more fat. Removing the excess fat with kitchen paper also helps reduce the fat content.

Polyunsaturated oil for deep frying should only be used once. Not only does it lose its vitamin E rapidly but the fierce heat makes the oil go through a chemical change which is potentially harmful in the long run. Only using the oil once, though, does make this an expensive cooking process.

Grilling   Grilling, like steaming, is a cooking method where the food is not immersed in water or oil. So it maintains its nutrient value well.

Baking   Another non-immersion process which preserves the integrity of the food well. But it often involves relatively prolonged exposure to heat so that vitamin loss (while not extreme) can be slightly greater than with boiling. Baked potatoes have a marginally higher vitamin C content than boiled potatoes.

Roasting   The modern method of roasting – on a tray – allows fat to drip off a joint. A hook or spit has the same effect. The skin of a chicken (delicious though it is) is the part highest in fat. We eat meat for protein and this is not materially affected by heat. Roast vegetables have a very high take-up of fat.

Barbecues   Charcoal barbecues can form cancer-causing substances on meat or fish, particularly if the food sits directly in the flame caused by fat igniting on the charcoal. We do not have barbecues that often in Britain and the risk is minimal. But it is a good idea to keep the food out of direct flames and not to expose it to smoke for very long periods.

Microwaving   Ill-informed publicity about microwaves used to claim that they cooked food 'from the inside out'. This is nonsense. Microwaves agitate the water molecules in the outer 10 per cent of the food. Then the rest of the food cooks by conduction of the heat to the centre, much as other methods do but more quickly. In essence, microwaving is equivalent to steaming but rather more random because the microwaves are not as evenly distributed as steam. Hence the concern about undercooked foods. Turning the food several times during cooking and observing recommended standing times afterwards (to allow greater conduction) go some way to overcoming this problem.

Because of the similarity to steaming, microwaves are ideal for vegetables and fish. When they were first heavily advertised they were always shown cooking poultry and meat joints. This was entirely inappropriate and the results were often disgusting. Now combination ovens are able to use the microwave to hasten the meat along and then brown it conventionally.

Because microwaving is quick and, like grilling, does not involve immersion of the food, it is particularly good at preserving vitamin C and folic acid. When compared with conventional boiling of vegetables in tests reported by the British Nutrition Foundation microwaving was able to:

- preserve more than twice as much vitamin C in parsnips;
- preserve twice as much vitamin C in cauliflowers;
- preserve almost twice as much vitamin C in broccoli.

You should not use metalware in microwaves – sparks will fly. You should only use microwavable plastic dishes, pyrex or ceramics without a metal glaze. Reheating take-away pizzas on a plastic base can leave you eating more plastic than pizza as it melts into the food. Current advice from the Ministry of Agriculture is that we should not use cling film in microwaves because the plasticizers it contains can leach into the food. A few foods will explode in the microwave – whole eggs are a spectacular example. A good precaution with baked potatoes is to spear them first with a fork and then wrap them in kitchen towel. That way you won't end up with potato all over your oven.

COMPARING DIFFERENT COOKING METHODS

We have already indicated that microwaving and steaming (both similar processes) are best for preserving vitamins in vegetables. Let us put that in context. We took samples of broccoli and potato and cooked them in the following pieces of equipment for the same amount of time:

1. A microwave
2. A dedicated saucepan steamer
3. A bamboo steamer
4. A pressure cooker
5. A convection cooker
6. A saucepan of boiling water

We tested samples of the broccoli and potato for vitamin C content when raw and then again when cooked by each of the above methods. The table below shows what percentage of the original vitamin C was retained after cooking.

Method	Broccoli % vit C retention	Potato % vit C retention
Microwave	82	82
Saucepan steamer	72	41
Bamboo steamer	68	47
Pressure cooker	67	37
Convection cooker	62	26
Saucepan – boiled	35	40

Vitamin C is a water-soluble vitamin that is easily lost in cooking water. It is often used as a way of gauging the probable loss of other water-soluble vitamins as well. Most vitamin losses occur because the vitamins are thrown away with the cooking water. These results show that microwaving and steaming are the best cooking methods for vitamin retention and boiling is the worst.

Then we compared grilling and frying on samples of rump steak each trimmed of excess fat and weighing 100g. These were the four cooking methods:

- **Non-stick frying-pan** The pan was wiped with sunflower oil and preheated for two minutes. Each side of the steak was shallow fried for three minutes.
- **Grilling** The grill was preheated for five minutes. The steak was then cooked for three minutes each side.
- **Dry fry pan** with 4g of sunflower oil: The pan was preheated for one minute and each side of the steak was cooked for one minute on a medium flame.

- **Dry fry pan** without oil: The pan was preheated for one minute and the steak was cooked on each side for two minutes.

We then took samples of the cooked steak and extracted and weighed the fat still present in the meat. This we compared to the fat content of the raw steak:

Method	Total fat in the steak
Raw meat	9.1 grams
Frying pan wiped with oil	7.5
Grilling	7.3
Dry fry with oil	7.0
Dry fry without oil	6.2

So there was no statistical difference between shallow frying and grilling while the dry-frying method led to the greatest fat loss. The amount of fat taken up by food from a pan with oil in it depends on the surface area of the food – large surface areas take up more fat. And as we have seen above, grilled and fried foods lose approximately the same amount of fat. So grilled sausages have just as much fat as fried sausages. This is contrary to our general assumptions about grilling and frying. Grilled bacon, however, will lose more fat than fried bacon and no fat at all is lost from micro-wave bacon.

Meats that are easy to fry already have an appreciable fat content, such as sausages, beefburgers, pork, steak and lamb. When heated they release fat into the pan and thus can be drained off. But foods with a relatively low-fat content – such as white fish and chicken breast – require the addition of fat for frying. Eggs contain fat but it is in the yolk and does not escape during cooking. Eggs, bread, tomatoes and mushrooms soak up quite large amounts of fat when fried. Ah, the glories of an English breakfast!

Fat, of course, adds flavour and 'mouth feel' to food. It would be awful to remove it from our diet altogether. Here and elsewhere we are merely discussing how we can lower our intake, not eliminate it.

Cooking utensils Acidic foods (chiefly fruit and any recipes containing vinegar) should never be cooked in brass or copper saucepans. The chemical salts that form are poisonous. Small amounts of aluminium will leach from saucepans into food, particularly if it is acidic. Cooking in iron pans can also increase the iron content of food – this is one way to boost your iron intake! It is probably best to cook acidic foods in Pyrex, anodized aluminium, Teflon-coated, enamel coated or stainless steel pans.

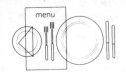

EATING OUT

Many more of us eat out than used to. There are correspondingly many more people – many untrained – preparing the sandwiches and other takeaways that account for so much food eaten away from home. The 1990 Food Safety Act requires all food premises to register with the local authority and all food handlers to undergo minimum hygiene training.

The pressing need for such a law was reinforced shortly afterwards. In June 1990, the Audit Commission and the Institution of Environmental Health Officers published a very damning report. They had surveyed more than 5,000 food premises and concluded that 12 per cent posed a significant health risk and that 4 per cent ought to be closed down. The survey covered cafes, restaurants, canteens and the kitchens of schools and hospitals.

We could, of course, ask to inspect the kitchens of a restaurant before we eat there, although we have no legal right to do so. But short of mice or cockroaches how could we tell how hygienic the place is? Although it is now a matter of law that all food handlers should have basic hygiene training the restaurant trade depends on so much casual labour that the enforcement of this new law will probably be impossible. The problem is that restaurants, caterers and cafes are responsible for nearly all the large outbreaks of food poisoning – if we get it wrong at home we only poison ourselves and our families.

In reality, the best thing is to take a good look at the dining area (and the cooking area if it is visible) and decide whether it is the sort of place we would trust our stomachs to. In particular:

> Are the cutlery and glasses clean?
> Do the staff show any evidence of having been near a bath recently?
> Are their hands clean?
> Is the hot food properly hot and served on a hot plate (the more lukewarm the more bacteria)?
> Is the food cooked thoroughly, except when you asked for it rare?
> Is there a pudding trolley and do its contents look old enough to be a museum exhibit?
> Are the lavatories clean?

The answer is probably 'no' to all these questions in your favourite greasy spoon cafe. But you would still walk a million miles for one of their breakfasts. All we can say to that is *caveat gustator*.

Takeaway foods are massively popular. Many amateurs are moving into this burgeoning market. So buy sandwiches from a source you trust. Or, to put it another way, don't buy high-risk sandwiches such as chicken and egg from a source you do *not* trust. Standards of hygiene in fast-food chains are generally high and deep-fried food (while a heartstopper) is the least likely to harbour bacteria. Once again, if you buy takeaway food from independent vendors keep an eye on the standard of their cleanliness (ice-cream dispensed from those small vans has been found to be widely contaminated by E-coli). If you ever see a barman or barlady pouring the beer slops back into glasses report them to your Environmental Health Office. Some drinkers do not wash their hands after going to the lavatory. Their hands contaminate the sides of the glass. The beer spills over the side of the glass into the tray – we need not tell you the rest.

By 'eating out' we also mean eating outside. Food poisoning at barbecues is unfortunately all too common. The food to be cooked is left waiting in a warm room or in the sunshine. Raw chicken is left next to other meats, bread or salad allowing cross-contamination. And then, as soon as the chicken looks done to a cinder it is eaten. Unfortunately, it may still be raw at the centre and seething with millions of friendly salmonella only too anxious to hit your stomach. Hence the famous barbecue speciality 'salmonella on a stick' (i.e. chicken). A useful tip is to partially cook the chicken in a microwave first and let it stand to allow the heat to permeate.

The other classic opportunity for salmonella *et al* to do their worst is at weddings. They normally take place in the summer when it is warmer, they are often catered for by amateurs, the bride is always late leading to a late arrival at the reception, there is invariably one of those infuriating receiving lines which keeps you from the booze and once everyone finally gets to the booze they don't eat till even later. Meanwhile, whatever is lurking in the food has run riot. If you are a pessimist by nature, then our advice would be to avoid high-risk foods at weddings.

For most of us eating out in a restaurant is an expensive and relatively infrequent treat. What we choose to eat at such occasions does not have much bearing on the quality of our overall diet. But overweight executives who have business lunches every day obviously need to be more careful. A number of local authorities are now subscribing to the Heartbeat Award organized by the Look After Your Heart campaign. Local restaurants and canteens get a rosette to display if they are providing healthy choices on their menus.

However, we have a much broader interpretation of 'eating out' in mind. Fast food now accounts for one in four catering outlets. In this subsection we will take a close look at different fast foods and their nutritional value. But we will also be looking at the other places we eat out:

- At work
- At school
- In hospital

FAST FOOD

In 1989 Britons spent around £4 billion on fast food and takeaways. This is how it broke down:

	£billion
Sandwiches	1025
Hamburgers & chips	750
Fish & chips	635
Pizza & pasta	530
Chinese	470
Chicken & chips	295
Indian	215
Other	95

There is nothing wrong with any one of these fast foods. But there would be if we ate just one sort regularly to the exclusion of other foods. One of the authors is particularly partial to Big Mac and chips but only every now and again – it has a very high saturated fat content. Let us show you what we mean. Here is a comparison of a Big Mac (a double burger, relish, mayonnaise and a bun) and chips, an ordinary hamburger and chips and a couple of filled bread rolls:

Food	Energy–kcals	Fat-grams
Big Mac & chips	950	40
Hamburger & chips	541	26
Bread roll with cottage cheese, celery & walnuts	362	32
Bread roll with tuna & tomato	414	20

We look at the nutritional breakdown of sandwiches in detail on p270. Here is it worth noting how versatile rolls and sandwiches are – you can pick the filling you want and vary your fat and calorie intake considerably. Whereas with a standard hamburger product the nutritional balance never changes. But there are some marked differences between different hamburger chains. We analysed the chips of three such companies.

Company	Fat grams	% sats	% polyunsats	% monounsats
Wimpy	10	16	29	55
McDonald's	12	53	7	40
Burger King	18	55	7	38

These figures, from an analysis carried out in November 1989, tell quite a story. Look at the column for saturated fat – Wimpy is low, the other two are very high. Look at the column for polyunsaturates – Wimpy is high, the other two are very low. You do not need to be an expert to deduce that Wimpy fried its chips in a polyunsaturated oil and the other two were using a saturated one. In fact, McDonald's and Burger King's oil contained a good deal of beef tallow – the same sort of oil that is generally used to fry fish and chips in the North of England.

Nutritionists had long been far from happy with McDonald's and Burger King's production methods. Not only did they use highly saturated oils but McDonalds, in particular, cut the chips very thin thereby increasing their fat take-up (gram for gram thin-cut chips present more surface area of potato to the fat, than thick-cut ones do). Reacting to health concerns, McDonald's and Burger King had produced leaflets about healthy eating for their customers. Burger King suggested asking for a Whopper without mayonnaise if you were dieting. They didn't highlight the saturated fat elsewhere at the same time. McDonald's said 'We believe food should do you good as well as taste good. That is why we have based our menu on good nutritious foods.' But they did not explain that their 'own shortening blend' included highly saturated beef tallow. Some people, particularly eighteen to twenty-four years olds, eat fast food very regularly and so the nature of its fat content is very important.

In 1989, a vociferous campaign started in the US to get McDonald's to change their cooking oil. It was a brief and successful campaign. By mid-1990, McDonald's in the US had switched to vegetable oil high in polyunsaturates. By the end of 1990, both McDonald's and Burger King in the UK had done the same.

The British Nutrition Foundation is concerned that those who eat snacks and fast food regularly may not know enough about nutrition to achieve a balanced diet – one that has a good variety and does not include too many calories. *However great your appetite for fast food we suggest you consult the Liberation List on p86 of Section II. There you can find the food you ought to be eating and how regularly.* The Foundation published a piece of analysis comparing a traditional meal with a snack meal and a fast-food meal. They then made an apparently small change to the fast-food meal.

	Energy (kcal)	Carbohy-drate g	Protein g	Fat g	Fibre g
Traditional Meal: Roast lamb, roast potatoes, peas & canned peaches & custard	650	82	26	27	12
Snack: 2 rounds of cheese, lettuce tomato sandwiches & coffee with milk	680	67	25	36	4
Fast food 1: Beefburger & chips & fruit pie & can of cola	1450	190	39	66	7
Fast food 2: Beefburger & baked potato & apple & coffee with milk	764	89	33	32	8

By far the two most important factors that emerge from this table are that the first fast-food meal is much higher in fat than all the rest, even a traditional roast lunch. And by substituting a baked potato for chips, an apple for the fruit pie and coffee for the cola the fat and carbohydrate are more than halved in the second fast-food meal.

AT WORK

Nearly all canteens and staff restaurants now have a very good choice of foods on offer. Many go further. Gardiner Merchant and Compass are the UK's two largest contract caterers. Gardiner Merchant alone serves lunches to 4 per cent of the UK's workforce. Both companies have a commitment to healthy eating which involves training for their cooks, point-of-sale information about healthy options on the menu and a good choice (chips *and* baked potatoes, whole milk *and* skimmed milk).

But wherever you work, it is up to you – the caterers cannot force you to eat one thing or another, nor should they. Once again we refer you to the Liberation List on p86 of Section II. Make a conscious effort to vary your diet and include all the important foods.

AT SCHOOL

The state of school lunches is a less positive story. During the Second World War the government required local authorities to provide all school children with a lunch and all but paid for the service. In the mid-1960s nutritional guidelines were introduced which laid down that a school lunch should give children one third of their daily nutrients.

The quality of school meals was a longstanding joke – glutinous stews, over-cooked cabbage, puddings smothered by custard or chocolate sauce the consistency of river mud . . . whatever they were they were not gastronomy. So in 1980, when the new Education Act abolished nutritional guidelines, price controls and even the local authorities' obligation to provide them, school meals were ripe for decline. And decline they did – dramatically. In 1979, 65 per cent of children ate the cooked school meal provided. By 1987, it was only 37 per cent. Where were the others eating? Some took packed lunches to school. Others joined the gaggle of school children you can find outside any fish and chip shop at midday.

In 1987, the National Association of School Meal Organizers debated the growing crisis and a campaign called 'FEAST' (Fun Eating At School) came out of it. A group of catering managers decided to spruce up their menus and the way their food was presented as well as applying modern nutritional ideas. They wanted to 'market' the food to the children, very often with the burgers and pizzas that they love eating.

FEAST has now been superseded by a number of local initiatives where local authorities and catering companies (where the service has been privatized) are marketing their lunches to the parents. If the parents believe the lunches are worthwhile and good value for money then they will cease to send their offspring to school with packed lunches.

There are many bitterly fought political battles taking place over school lunches. Should they be privatized? Should new nutritional guidelines be imposed? Should they be subsidized to encourage more children to eat them? Are enough children included in the safety net that pays for the lunches of the poorest families? Should schools be trying to make as much money as they can out of tuck shops and – more likely these days – vending machines? These issues will be debated until the cows come home and the outcome depends on the political persuasion of the government at any particular time. What can parents do? This is our advice:

> If you wish to send your child to school with a packed lunch that is fine. *See* Section IV, p185, for advice as to its composition.
>
> If you wish your child to eat at school go and see what the lunches are like and ask to see a week's menus to check the variety. You have every right to.
>
> If you are not happy with the lunches challenge what the nutritional policy of the local authority or catering company is. Make them state it. If it is not adequate get other parents on your side and campaign for improvements. If it is adequate but not being put into practice then, having mustered your evidence carefully, complain long and hard.
>
> If possible make friends with the cooks who are usually very positive if treated sympathetically. They will be able to tell you from the inside the training they have had and what their instructions are.
>
> Don't assume that all so-called 'junk food' is bad.

IN HOSPITAL

The most important office of the nurse, after she has taken care of the patients' air is to observe the effects of his food.

Florence Nightingale, 1859

We observed in Section I that most doctors are under-trained in nutrition and rely on the media for what up-to-date knowledge they do have. As for nurses, who have to serve most of the food to patients, their knowledge of nutrition is just as limited. Florence Nightingale's precept is, at the moment, no more than a pious hope.

A study in 1984 at the John Radcliffe Hospital in Oxford (*What Patients Eat in Hospital*) looked at fifty-five patients in four different wards over several days. Of the fifty-five:

- all had intakes below the RDA for iron, folic acid and vitamins A and D;
- 24 per cent had an energy intake below the RDA;
- 16 per cent had protein intakes below the RDA.

In 1985, a year-long study was undertaken by Mike Nelson of King's College, London looking at patients in a variety of wards (and therefore suffering from a variety of complaints). He found that:

- 45 per cent of the energy intake was accounted for by fat (way above the COMA recommendation of 35 per cent and comfortably above the national average);
- daily intake of fibre was only 14–15g a day compared with a recommended level of 30g and a national average of 20g.

In 1988, *Which?* surveyed the food choice in 557 NHS hospitals:

- 75 per cent of the hospitals claimed they had a healthy eating policy;
- 40 per cent of the hospitals were adjudged to have unhealthy menus.

322

Furthermore, recent surveys have confirmed that many RDAs are still not met. Indeed two dietitians have reported discovering quite a high level of sub-clinical scurvy (caused by a lack of vitamin C) amongst elderly patients. One American expert, commenting on the situation in the US, which is not dissimilar, once put it more forcefully. He reported to a conference that he thought as many as 5–10 per cent of patients were 'dying of starvation'.

On the face of it, the situation seems appalling. What are the causes? Here we must proceed carefully. The first point to make is that patients in hospital are ill – they have diseases which affect their bodies and they lose their appetites and fail to eat properly. Drug treatments are an additional factor that can both affect appetites and destroy nutrients. But are we doing all we can to ameliorate these unavoidable problems? No, we are not.

In some hospitals, the old system of cooking lunch by 10.30 a.m., 'plating' it and putting it in a heated trolley for as much as two hours still persists. Food heated in this way is not only ruined in a gastronomic sense (thus patients will not want to eat), but the vitamin loss is horrific (thus patients will derive little from the food if they do eat it). More modern systems depending on frozen or chilled meals with microwaves on the wards are now being introduced. But, as we have seen, those dispensing the food (usually the long-suffering nurses) need to understand the technology well for it to yield benefits rather than cause further problems such as food poisoning.

The money spent on meals for patients differs around the country, but it averages £1.40 per head per day. Wielding this generous budget are catering staff who are not very well paid and not always highly motivated. The cost restrictions mean that some health authorities buy cheap, surplus animal fats from the EC. Not exactly what the doctor ordered. While low motivation sometimes leads to poor presentation which fails to tempt the appetite of patients who may already be disinclined to eat.

There are no detailed nutritional guidelines for the caterers who work in the National Health Service (though there is a recipe guide). Although each hospital has a qualified dietitian, they often restrict themselves to supervising special diets for particular patients rather than helping implement a good policy for all patients. They do not always have a good relationship with the kitchens. All this explains the letters from patients complaining about the quality and appropriateness of the food they received in hospital – the Coronary Prevention Group receives a regular trickle from heart patients who emerge from intensive care on to a general ward and are immediately served with bacon, eggs and white bread and butter. Again, not exactly what the doctor ordered. Indeed, it is a missed opportunity. Elsewhere in this book we have shown how much disease is diet-related. Hospital could be the place where heart attack victims are shown how to eat properly thereafter.

This long litany of problems should not give the idea that all hospital food is terrible. There are health authorities with carefully drawn-up healthy eating policies, staffed by highly motivated catering managers and knowledgeable nurses. But it is clear that, as at work and at home, we can only be sure of eating well in hospitals if we make sensible choices for ourselves. That means watching fat intake; eating a reasonable amount of fibre; fresh fruit, vegetables or salad every day and eating fish every week.

One final point – there is no excuse for a dirty kitchen. Patients are particularly vulnerable to food poisoning and now that hospital kitchens have lost their Crown Immunity they can be prosecuted by Environmental Health Officers just like any other catering establishment. You should report any evidence of bad hygiene.

SECTION VI

A–Z DIRECTORY

Acetic acid   This is the main component of vinegar. It is produced when alcohol is exposed to air. It is used as a preservative – eg, in pickling and bread-making. Acetic acid is also produced naturally in the body and can be used to provide food energy.

Acid   This is a substance that will corrode metal. The strength of an acid is measured on a pH scale of 1–14. Strong acids have a pH of around 1, and weak acids around 4. Water is neutral – pH7. Anything above pH7 is alkaline.

Weak acids exist in many foods: acetic acid in vinegar, citric acid in fruit, malic acid in apples and lactic acid in yoghurt. They are also produced naturally in the body. Foods and drinks high in acid (eg, lemon juice) can corrode tooth enamel. Weak acids are used as acidity regulators and preservatives to stop food spoilage.

Strong acids such as sulphuric and hydrochloric are very corrosive and poisonous when undiluted. The stomach produces hydrochloric acid to aid digestion. Too much stomach acid leads to heartburn and indigestion. The small amounts of strong acids found naturally in food pose no threat to health.

The balance of acid and alkali in the body is maintained constant by the amount of carbon dioxide dissolved in blood. This balance is not affected by diet. There is no need to worry about balancing acid and alkali in the diet as claimed by some health drinks.

Ackee   This is an extremely popular fruit in the West Indies and Nigeria and can now be obtained in some supermarkets and street markets in London. Poisoning can occur if the fruit is consumed unripe, even after cooking. The unripe fruit contains a substance called hypoglycin that causes 'vomiting sickness'.

Additives   Food additives are substances intentionally added to food during processing. They are not contaminants. They are added:

- to make food safer and keep longer – they stop the growth of bacteria and mould and stop food going rancid;
- to improve the quality of food in terms of colour, taste, texture and nutritional value;
- as processing aids – emulsifiers, release agents, anti-caking agents, raising agents (eg, baking powder).

Food processing would not be possible without the use of additives. All additives have to be shown to be safe, effective and necessary before their use is permitted. There are permitted lists of all additives, except for flavours. If the additive has been approved by the EEC then it is given an E number. Approval of food additives is a lengthy procedure and involves reviewing evidence of safety based on toxicological studies carried out on animals. Many additives are also natural constituents of food. For example, vitamin C (ascorbic acid) and phosphate salts.

Benefits to the consumer

- Increasing the variety of food available and keeping food prices down.
- Enabling the safe delivery of food to an urban population.
- Enabling the creation of healthy alternatives to traditional foods. For example, meat substitutes, low-fat spreads and diet drinks.

Objections to additives

- Can be used to pass off second-rate food. Colours and flavours can disguise fatty meat products.
- Can be used as a means of selling air and water at inflated prices.
- A few individuals show adverse reactions to certain additives – eg, tartrazine (E102) and benzoic acid (E210).

Adulterant   This is a substance which is added to food or drink with the intent to defraud. Examples of adulterants in drinks are diethylene glycol in Austrian wine (*see* p140), starch in spices and water in milk.

Agar-agar   This is used as a food thickener and has properties similar to gelatine. It is a form of dietary fibre and, being extracted from seaweed, is acceptable to vegetarians. It dissolves in boiling water and then sets as a gel.

Acquired Immune Deficiency Syndrome (AIDS)   People with AIDS or carrying the HIV virus cannot transmit the disease to other people via food or drink. As they are at increased risk of infection they must avoid eating food contaminated with bacteria – eg, shellfish, raw eggs and soft rinded cheese such as Brie and Camembert. Further advice on avoiding food poisoning is given in Section V.

   Diet can influence the immune system but there is no good evidence that dietary supplements can boost the immune response. There have been several cynical attempts to foist supplements on these desperately ill people (*see* Germanium). Most of these are of no value and some may be harmful. High intakes of zinc should be avoided as they depress the immune system (*see* Zinc).

Alar   Alar is the trade name of the chemical daminazide made by Union Carbide. Daminozide has been used for over twenty years to make fruit trees produce more fruit – it acts as a sort of fertility drug. At one stage it was sprayed on apple trees to synchronize the dropping of fruit ar.d to make red apples develop a uniform colour. It has never been widely used in the UK. At the time of the Alar scare in March 1989 it was used on about 7 per cent of British apples. It is not used in New Zealand. The US Food and Drug Administration in 1989 announced its intention for a phased withdrawal of Alar. This decision was reached on the basis of new animal toxicity tests which showed that a breakdown product – called unsymmetrical dimethyl hydrazine – caused an increased number of angiosarcomas (a type of cancer) in mice but not rats. On the basis of these animal studies the Food and Drug Administration estimated that a life-time exposure to Alar might result in 45 cases of cancer per million which was above the acceptable level of 1 per million. Studies of individuals exposed to Alar during its manufacture and use and other individuals who have been exposed to huge amounts of Alar (one man fell in a tank of it) showed no increased risk of cancer or other diseases.

Unlike other agrochemicals Alar cannot be washed off the fruit and may be present even if the tree was sprayed the previous season. Studies found measurable amounts of Alar and its breakdown product in apple juice and apple products in the USA. This caused concern because apple products and puréed apple products especially are given to children. It was argued that children may be more susceptible to any toxic material. An American pressure group claimed that as many as 1 in 4000 children may develop cancer as a result of exposure to the chemical. The Food and Drug Administration denied this pointing out that the pressure group had used discredited data for their estimates. The scientific establishment generally does not consider exposure to Alar a significant hazard to health. Its use is permitted in the UK but hostile consumer pressure has meant that it will almost certainly be phased out.

Alcohol   Over-indulgence in alcohol is harmful to health and causes accidents and social problems (*see* Section III, p147). Moderate alcohol consumption is not harmful providing you are not pregnant, taking drugs or operating machinery.

What is a moderate intake?

The amount of alcohol in a drink is measured in units:

- One unit is 10ml or 8g of ethyl alcohol.

This is equivalent to:

- Half a pint of ordinary beer, lager or cider.
- One glass of wine.
- One small sherry or fortified wine.
- One measure of spirits.

These are only rough measures, as beer, wine and cider vary

328

in strength. Alcohol drinks are labelled by per cent volume. A wine that is 10 per cent by volume contains 10ml of alcohol in 100ml – ⅒th of it is alcohol. Safe intakes are:

up to 21 units a week for men;
up to 14 units a week for women.

Nutritional value

Alcoholic drinks have little nutritional value besides the calories they provide:

	kcal	Units
Half pint beer ordinary	90	1
beer – strong	204	2
lager	82	1
stout	205	1.5
cider	100–120	1–1.5
cider – vintage	286	3.5
One glass white wine (9% by volume)	82	1
red wine (12% by volume)	85	1.5
dessert wine (12% by volume)	118	1.5
One small glass of sherry or vermouth	56–72	1
glass of port	75	1
One measure gin, vodka, whisky	51	1
sweet liqueur	72	1

Allergy   Allergy refers to an acute over-reaction by the immune system, usually to a protein. Allergies may be mild, as with eczema, or severe, as with asthma or anaphylactic shock which can lead to collapse and death. Allergies arise for a variety of reasons but are frequently inherited. Allergic individuals show responses to a variety of substances present in the environment besides food – eg, animal fur, dust, furnishing material, etc. Many children under the age of three suffer from mild food allergies but they usually grow out of them. Coeliac disease affects about 1 in 2000 children and is caused by an allergy to a protein called gluten which is found in wheat, oats, barley and rye. Other common allergies are to maize, eggs, milk, soya, shellfish, coffee, tea and chocolate. Allergies to some food additives (tartrazine, benzoates, BHT and BHA) also occur but are less common.

Allergic reactions usually appear within a few minutes but may be delayed for hours.

Immediate reactions:

Lip swelling
Tingling of the mouth or throat
Vomiting
Pain or burning sensation in the stomach
Difficulty breathing
Runny eyes

Delayed reactions:

Diarrhoea
Bloating – abdominal distension
Constipation

A proper diagnosis is essential. If you think you or your child has an allergy, don't attempt self-diagnosis, and don't visit an 'allergy clinic' without seeing your own doctor first. Nowadays, people are quick to believe that they or their children may have some kind of allergy when, in fact, genuine allergies are relatively uncommon (*see* also food intolerance, p180).

Aluminium   Our diet typically provides about 0.1g of aluminium every day which is about a 10 to 100 times greater than the amount provided by drinking water. The maximum limit in water proposed by the EEC is 0.2mg/litre. Aluminium is very poorly absorbed from the diet because most aluminium salts are insoluble. Aluminium cooking pots can also contribute aluminium to the diet when they are used to cook acidic foods like fruit. But 40 per cent of our intake comes from drinks such as tea. Many commonly used medicines contain quite large amounts of aluminium such as aluminium hydroxide. This is used as an antacid in the treatment of indigestion. It is also present in toothpaste.

Aluminium is harmful if it gets into the blood stream. It was discovered that patients undergoing early types of dialysis developed damage to their brain that was linked to aluminium in the dialysis water. However, this disorder is quite different to Alzheimer's disease which has been linked with aluminium. It is clear that Alzheimer's disease is not caused simply by exposure to aluminium. While there is no hard evidence for a link, however, it might be a sensible precaution to use non-aluminium or anodized aluminium or Teflon-coated aluminium in place of ordinary aluminium pans to cook acidic foods. In 1988, the residents of Camelford in Cornwall had large quantities of aluminium sulphate introduced into their drinking water by accident. Many became ill at the time, and it is still not known what the long-term consequences may be.

Alzheimer's disease   Alzheimer's disease is a type of dementia (a term used to describe the progressive loss of mental function). It leads to loss of memory, confusion and personality and behavioural changes. In severe cases it leads to loss of control of bodily functions – eg, control of bladder and of bowel. It affects about 7 per cent of people over the age of 65, rising to about 20 per cent of people aged 80 and over. It is the main cause of dementia in the elderly.

No one really knows what causes Alzheimer's disease. It appears to be due to the loss of a substance in the brain called acetyl choline, and the cells that make acetyl choline in the base of the forebrain die. Without this chemical messenger – or 'neurotransmitter' – other brain cells die. This leaves the brain scattered with characteristic plaques and bundles of dead nerve cells and fibres. There is a parallel here with Parkinson's disease, in which the ability to produce a different neurotransmitter called dopamine is impaired. It has been suggested that giving patients choline supplements might be of benefit, but controlled trials have shown no benefit.

Early onset of Alzheimer's disease appears to run in families. But there seems to be little risk of inheriting the disorder if a relative developed it over the age of seventy.

Aluminium is currently being investigated as a potential cause of Alzheimer's disease. One recent survey found that Alzheimer's disease was more frequent in areas with high levels of aluminium in the water than in areas where levels were low. But this theory remains unproven.

Amino acid   This is the basic building block of proteins. There are over twenty different amino acids in food proteins. When proteins are digested they are broken down into constituent amino acids which are in turn absorbed. The body then makes new proteins from these amino acids (*see* Proteins p396).

The sulphur-containing amino acid cysteine is used as a food additive to improve the bread-making quality of flour. Aspartame (Nutrasweet) consists of two amino acids linked together (phenylalanine and aspartic acid). Glutamic acid and its salts are used as flavour enhancers (*see* Monosodium Glutamate p383).

Several amino acids are essential to health and are abundant in foods. The amounts of amino acids consumed as food additives are only a trivial fraction of our total intake. This is mainly provided by food proteins.

Amino acid supplements such as tryptophan, ornithine and arginine, are sold in health-food shops with claims suggesting they will build up your muscles and help you lose weight. There is no good evidence that this is the case. In excess they may even be harmful (*see* Tryptophan, p408).

Anaemia   Anaemia is a deficiency of the haemoglobin levels in your blood. Haemoglobin is the oxygen-carrying pigment in blood. Mild anaemia is accompanied by few symptoms except perhaps tiredness and weakness. Severe anaemia involves more marked weakness and shortness of breath. It is misleading to diagnose anaemia by pallor. Anaemia may occur for a number of reasons:

- Excessive blood loss.
- Red blood cells breaking down faster than they can be replaced.
- The production of new blood cells being impaired.

Excessive blood loss is common in women with heavy monthly periods. Sickle-cell disease, which occurs frequently in black people, can lead to increased breakdown in blood cells.

Iron, vitamin B_{12} and folate are three nutrients involved in the production of blood cells and a deficiency of any of these can lead to anaemia. Iron deficiency is the most common cause of anaemia but a combination of folate and vitamin B_{12} deficiency is a major cause of anaemia amongst Asian Indians.

Pernicious anaemia results from an inability to absorb vitamin B_{12}. It usually develops in mid-life and treatment involves regular injections with vitamin B_{12}.

Anaemia can only be diagnosed properly by a blood test. If you think that you are anaemic, you should seek medical advice rather than attempt self-medication.

Anorexia nervosa   This literally means 'lack of appetite through nervousness'. The problem has nothing to do with food itself but the fears people have about what will happen when they eat food. This eating disorder is mainly a female problem affecting girls and younger women. But it has also been recorded in men who are concerned about food for health or ethical reasons – for example, vegans. The excessive preoccupation of the media with slimming and food-scares is probably a contributory factor.

The main features of anorexia nervosa in women are:

- excessive preoccupation with body weight and shape;
- fear of eating;
- marked interest in food and cooking;
- abnormal menstrual cycle (periods normally stop);
- loss of interest in sex and growth of facial hair.

Weight loss can be so severe that the victim can look extremely emaciated. Interestingly, many sufferers of anorexia are good cooks. The disorder is also surprisingly common among students studying nutrition and dietetics. People with anorexia nervosa need specialized help, and medical advice should be sought.

Anti-oxidants   Anti-oxidants are used to stop food oxidizing – eg, to stop fats going rancid and to stop browning reactions in fruit juices. Several nutrients act as anti-oxidants in the body preventing fat from going rancid. Vitamin E, vitamin C, beta-carotene and selenium are sometimes called the anti-oxidant nutrients. They help mop up oxidation agents called 'free radicals'. Free radicals cause damage to the fats in cell membranes and harm the proteins in the body. They are generated naturally in the body but some chemicals drastically increase their rate of production – eg, the agroche-mical, paraquat, and the solvent, carbon tetrachloride. Smok-ers have lower levels of the anti-oxidant nutrients in their blood and it has been suggested that they need higher intakes of vitamins E, C, beta-carotene and selenium.

Apricots Apricots are a rich source of beta-carotene. Dried apricots, particularly those from Turkey, have occasio-nally been found to contain aflatoxins (*see* p129). Imports are now quite carefully monitored by both the Ministry of Agri-culture and the more responsible food companies. Surveys have shown that dried fruit in health food shops is the most likely to be contaminated.

Artificial sweeteners Artificial sweeteners are a class of food additives that fall into two categories:

- **caloric sweeteners** – eg, manitol, sorbitol, xylitol, hydrogenated glucose syrup;
- **non-caloric sweeteners** – eg, acesulfame K, aspartame, cyclamate, saccharin and thaumatin.

Cyclamate is banned in Britain but is freely available elsewhere in the EC. Cyclamate was banned in Britain following a scare in the late 1960s which suggested that it caused cancer in rats.

Saccharin is about 200 times sweeter than sugar. It has been used for over fifty years and has a good safety record. When it is fed to rats in huge amounts it causes bladder cancer, but there is no evidence to show that saccharin causes cancer in man. Studies of diabetics who have used saccharin for many years show no increased risk of bladder cancer. However, the increased popularity of soft drinks means that many more people are consuming saccharin. A study carried out by the Ministry of Agriculture in 1990 suggested that some people are exceeding the acceptable daily intake for saccharin (*see* p187).

Aspartame, also marketed as 'Nutrasweet', is probably the most extensively tested food additive. It was licensed for use in the USA in 1981 and allowed into soft drinks in 1983. Britain and other countries subsequently approved it for use. Like saccharin, aspartame is 200 times sweeter than sugar. It has a mouthfeel similar to sugar and, unlike saccharin, does not have a bitter after-taste. Aspartame consists of the two amino acids – aspartic acid and phenylalanine – which are linked together. On digestion, aspartame breaks down into methanol, aspartic acid and phenylalanine. The amount of methanol produced is trivial, similar to the amounts found naturally in fruits. Its constituent amino acids are absorbed and metabolized like other naturally occurring amino acids. People with the inborn error of metabolism phenylketonuria have to avoid aspartame (they also have to avoid milk and other foods that are high in phenylalanine).

Advantages of sweeteners

- Can be used as substitute for sugar in the diet – important for diabetics and slimmers.
- Enable the development of soft drinks and sweets that are neither harmful to teeth nor fattening.
- An alternative to alcoholic drinks.

Objections to sweeteners

- Long-term effects of high intakes in man unknown.
- May cause adverse reactions in small minority (never satisfactorily demonstrated).
- May stimulate appetite (never satisfactorily demonstrated).

Atherosclerosis   This is the term used to describe the lumpy fatty growths that occur on the inside of arteries. Arteries throughout the body are affected but those most susceptible are at junctions where the blood flow is turbulent. Atherosclerosis starts in early adult life, gets more severe with age and affects men earlier than women. In the early stages it causes no symptoms. But when it is severe it can block the artery. Atherosclerotic growths (plaques) can also rupture and cause blood clots. Atherosclerosis of the vessels supplying the heart muscle (coronary atherosclerosis) is a major cause of heart attacks. Atherosclerosis of vessels supplying the brain is the major cause of strokes in the elderly. Atherosclerosis of the vessels supplying the limbs can cause gangrene and necessitate the amputation of the limb. A high level of cholesterol in blood accelerates the development of atherosclerosis. Consequently a diet that lowers blood cholesterol levels will help prevent the disease (*see* Section II p86, Section IV, p215).

Bacon and ham   These are traditionally prepared by salting pork with a mixture of salt and saltpetre (potassium nitrate). Nowadays sodium nitrite is more commonly used. The nitrite reacts with the haemoglobin and myoglobin in the meat to produce a pink colour. The meat may also be smoked. While this treatment stops the growth of harmful bacteria it does also load up the meat with nitrosamines and polycyclic hydrocarbons (chemicals which have been shown to cause cancer in rats). Yet there is no evidence to show that people who eat bacon and ham are more likely to get cancer than those who don't.

Lean ham is low in fat (about 5 per cent). However, chopped ham can be high in fat (about 24 per cent). Spam, which is vaguely related to ham, is certainly high in fat. A slice of ordinary lean ham only provides 34 kcal and 1.5g of fat. So ham is fine as part of a low-fat or low calorie diet.

Bacon is high in fat, particularly streaky bacon. But you can reduce the fat content of bacon by grilling rather than frying. Although bacon is high in fat we don't eat much. An average rasher only weighs 25 grams and if you just eat the lean will only supply about 75 kcalories and 5 grams of fat of which 2 grams will be saturated. So even bacon can be part of a healthy diet.

- Choose lean ham, avoid cheap imitations like spam.
- Choose lean bacon, grill and don't eat the fat if you want to reduce the saturated fat or the calories in your diet.

Bananas   A typical banana provides 80 kcal, 16g of sugar and useful amounts of vitamin C, potassium and fibre. Bananas also contain small amounts of substances that can cause blood vessels to constrict giving rise to headaches. This may be why they cause migraines in some people. Banana skins contain quite high levels of the neurotransmitter dopamine – but our brains manufacture this substance anyway.

Barbecues   Charbroiling meat and fish leads to the formation of compounds called polycyclic aromatic hydrocarbons (PAH). These have been shown to cause cancer in animals and are similar to the compounds in smoke. It is possible to reduce the amounts of PAH formed by keeping the food out of direct flames. People who eat charbroiled meat regularly switch on the system in their bodies that breaks down xenobiotics. This means they break down drugs at a much faster rate. There is thus no direct evidence to suggest that barbecues are linked to cancer risk in man.

Bacteria   Bacteria are ubiquitous in the environment. Some are useful and others are harmful. Bacteria make yoghurt and vinegar and ripen cheeses. In animals with rumens (cows, sheep and goats) they help digest food, such as grass, which is indigestible by man. Bacteria are also responsible for food spoilage – it makes food go wet and slimy. Some bacteria cause disease and food and water can be the means by which the disease is transmitted. For example, tuberculosis, listeriosis (*see* p377) and cholera. The term bacterial food poisoning is used to describe the acute inflammation of the gastrointestinal tract caused by ingesting food containing a large number of bacteria or toxins produced by them. It typically results in diarrhoea and/or vomiting between one and forty-eight hours after eating contaminated food. Bacterial food poisoning is most commonly caused by infection with campylobacter or salmonella. Raw eggs, raw meat, milk products and shellfish are the foods most strongly linked with bacterial food poisoning. For more information *see* Section V, p286.

Bean curd   Bean curd is often called Tofu and it is made from a purée of soya beans. Proteins in the soya are precipitated by adding a salt mixture. It has a texture like firm junket and can be diced, cubed or sliced. The mineral content of bean curd depends upon the type of salt used to precipitate the protein. It is a good source of protein and, unlike soya beans, doesn't cause flatulence.

Beef   When you buy a piece of beef it usually comes from bullocks which have been slaughtered around the age of two years. Old cows are used to put in meat products such as pies and pasties because they tend to be tough as old boots and can be bought cheaply by manufacturers. Beef is an excellent source of protein, iron, B vitamins and vitamin B_{12}.

Lean beef is low in fat (about 4 per cent or less) but mince can be quite high (10-25 per cent). A 5oz grilled rump steak provides 150 kcal and less than 10g of fat. A typical portion of stewed minced beef provides about 350 kcal and about 23g of fat.

There is no health reason for avoiding beef but you can choose lean cuts of meat and discard the fat. For more about beef, *see* BSE (p341).

It makes little difference to the fat content whether you fry or grill steak providing of course you don't consume the juices left in the frying pan. So you can fry steak in oil with garlic if that's how you like it. When you cook mince you can drain off the excess fat.

Beta-carotene   Beta-carotene is the orange pigment found in green, yellow and orange vegetables. Carrots and dark green vegetables (such as spinach) contain the highest amounts. Beta-carotene can be converted into retinol in the body and so is a form of vitamin A. Strictly speaking beta-carotene is the essential nutrient rather than retinol. Beta-carotene is insoluble in water and needs fat for its absorption. Thus, it is easily absorbed from milk where it is dissolved in the fat, but less easily from plant sources.

Besides acting as an important source of vitamin A, beta-carotene may also offer protection against damage caused by free radicals (*see* Anti-oxidants) in the body, and may help prevent cancer. Beta-carotene is used as a food colourant and is responsible for the yellow colour of butter and egg yolk. High intakes of beta-carotene, usually in excess of 15mg/day, cause the skin to turn yellow (like a corn-fed chicken) but this is quite harmless. Pregnant women should get most of their vitamin A from foods rich in beta-carotene such as carrots and dark green vegetables rather than by eating liver. Carotene unlike retinol does not cause birth defects if consumed in excess.

Bicarbonate of soda   Bicardobonate of Soda is often called Sodium bicarbonate or baking soda. This is an alkaline substance which gives off carbon dioxide gas when mixed with an acid. It is used as a raising agent in baking powders. It is also secreted naturally into the intestines to neutralise stomach acid. It can be used to relieve acid indigestion. It is very good for removing the smell of vomit from carpets if mixed with lemon juice.

Biscuits   Biscuits are made from flour, fat and salt with or without added sugar. They typically contain about 20 per cent fat by weight. Hydrogenated fats, lard or butter are those most commonly used to make biscuits so they are high in saturated fats. Chocolate biscuits, shortbread and sandwich biscuits contain the most. Savoury biscuits such as matzo or crispbread are low in fat. Biscuits keep extremely well and this is why they were popular with armies and navies. Children derive a high proportion of their energy from biscuits. The frequent consumption of sweet biscuits between meals is a major factor contributing to tooth decay. So-called 'healthy biscuits' made with apple juice and wholemeal flour, differ little from ordinary biscuits in nutritional composition. Biscuits should be eaten and enjoyed but not too frequently and not in great quantities. Sweet biscuits are best avoided if you are trying to lose weight. Typical calorie values are:

•	One chocolate digestive	99 kcal
•	One shortbread finger	76 kcal
•	One matzo biscuit	31 kcal
•	One crispbread	32 kcal

Boiling   Water boils at 100°C under normal atmospheric pressure, at 90°C under reduced pressure as in an aircraft, and at 115°C in a pressure cooker. Boiling is a gentle method of cooking leading to little chemical change in the composition of food and yet killing most bacteria. It does, however, lead to the leaching out of water-soluble vitamins into the cooking water. This is of no importance if you consume the water (as with soup) but if, for example, you discard vegetable water, you will lose those vitamins. Loss of vitamins can be minimized by only using a small volume of water or steaming. (*See* Section V, p307). Boiling also renders inactive many harmful substances in raw food (*see* Pulses p399, and Section V, p307). Adding salt to the cooking water prolongs the cooking time.

Bottle Feeding　　Artificial formulae for feeding children are modelled on the composition of human milk and support the normal growth and development of infants. Ordinary cow's milk should not be given to babies under one year. You should never give a baby skimmed milk. Special care needs to be taken in preparing bottle feeds hygienically. (*See* Section IV, p168).

Never mix infant formula too strongly because it will make the milk too concentrated and put a strain on the baby's kidneys. Artificial milk formulae based on soya should only be used under strict medical supervision.

Botulism　　Botulism is an illness – usually fatal – that results from the consumption of botulin, a toxin produced by the bacterium clostridium botulinum. This bacterium only grows in the absence of air, and not in salty conditions. It is an extremely rare disease. Outbreaks have been traced to unhygienically canned or bottled foods. The toxin is destroyed by heating at 100°C for fifteen minutes but the bacterial spores are exceptionally heat resistant. Faults in canning, such as leaks, under-processing or overpacking, and in the concentrations of curing salts, are usually responsible for botulism. The most recent case in Britain was caused by the bacterium growing in hazelnut purée low in sugar.

Bread　　Bread, along with potatoes, is a major source of starchy carbohydrate in our diet. It is also an important source of protein, fibre, iron and B-complex vitamins.

The law recognizes five types of bread:

- Wholemeal – containing the whole, unrefined grain.
- Brown – which is equivalent to 80 per cent extraction flour. It can be made by blending wholemeal with white flour (70 per cent extraction).
- Wheatgerm – which contains 10 per cent added wheatgerm.

340

- Soda – if sodium hydrogen carbonate has been used as an ingredient.
- White – all other breads.

White bread has been much maligned, although it is true that the sliced variety may indeed lack flavour. Nutrients are lost during the milling of white flour but calcium, iron, thiamin and niacin have to be reinserted, by law, for the purposes of bread-making. Wholemeal bread contains more folate and vitamin E, and twice as much fibre than white bread primarily because the wheatgerm is high in vitamin E and folate. The refined white flour used for white bread has had the wheatgerm removed.

Breast feeding   Besides providing all the nutrients required, breast milk transfers immunity from the mother to the baby. The composition of breast milk does depend upon the maternal diet. Vegan and vegetarian mothers need to make sure they are consuming vitamin B_{12} in their diets so that they don't cause a deficiency in their babies. Certain drugs also pass into breast milk and can affect the baby. Always check with your doctor if it is safe to take medicines when you are breast feeding. Breast milk can support the growth of a human infant up to one year if the supply is adequate. Most babies need supplementary foods from beyond six months.

Broccoli   Broccoli is an excellent source of vitamin C. One 2oz (50g) serving (properly cooked) provides about twice the recommended daily amount and about 7.5mg beta-carotene.

Bovine spongiform encephalopathy (BSE)   Bovine Spongiform Encephalopathy (BSE) – 'mad cow disease' – is a slowly progressive and ultimately fatal disease of adult cattle. It affects those between three and five years. It generally does not affect beef cattle because they do not live long enough to get it. There is no evidence that BSE can affect humans. The current epidemic appeared in 1986 but BSE is believed to have occurred pre-1986 as a result of cattle eating offal from sheep that had scrapie. Scrapie is a similar disease to BSE, contracted by sheep, and has been endemic in Britain for centuries. Scrapie can be transmitted to mice, cats and mink through feeding scrapie-infected offal. Brain and spinal cord are the most effective means of transmitting scrapie to other animals. Organs of the immune system such as the spleen can also transmit the disease but less effectively. It cannot be transmitted via meat.

BSE is regarded as a 'dead-end disease', ie – there is no transmission of the disease between cattle. It is uncertain whether it can be passed on from cow to calf, but it is already known that scrapie can be transmitted from ewe to lamb. There are at least a couple of suggested causes of the current BSE outbreak:

- The national sheep flock has increased since 1980. Consequently, there may have been an increase in scrapie-infected flocks, and thus, more infected sheep offal may have been given to cattle who were normally fed animal protein.
- There was a change in the temperature used in processing the animal feed and this may have reduced the chance of the infective agent being destroyed.

The causative agent in BSE is almost certainly the same as that which causes scrapie. It is believed to be a particle called a prion. There are a number of encephalopathies that affect man – eg, kuru and Creutzfeld-Jakob disease. Kuru is a spongiform encephalopathy that, at one time, was common in certain tribes in New Guinea. It resulted from eating human brains! There are about fifty confirmed deaths a year from Creutzfeld-Jakob disease in the UK. Rates of this disease are similar in countries that don't have scrapie or BSE, and a case has also been found in a life-long vegetarian. Recently, it has been claimed that there may be under-reporting of Creutzfeld-Jakob disease and the incidence may be up to a hundred times higher. This has yet to be investigated.

Creutzfeld-Jakob disease has been transmitted from person to person by transplant operations, but takes up to twenty years to develop. High rates of Creutzfeld-Jakob disease are found in North African and Middle-Eastern people. There have been a number of studies trying to link the consumption of sheep's eyeballs and brains to the incidence of Creutzfeld-Jakob disease. They have failed to show any link between the disease and diet.

It is perhaps surprising that BSE has not been reported elsewhere in Europe as they also feed cattle on sheep offal. Possibly it exists, but may be diagnosed as a different ailment. A similar disease called 'Downer cow syndrome' has been reported in America in cows fed scrapie-infected offal. Animals with symptoms of BSE are destroyed in Britain and do not enter the food chain. Brain, spinal cord and 'specified offal' from all cattle and sheep are banned from the human food chain. And now, the feeding of offal to all animals, including pets, has been stopped.

Our advice is avoid eating brains.

Bovine Somatotrophin (BST)   This is a hormone naturally produced by the cow that stimulates lactation. Normally peak lactation is maintained for a short period and then declines. By giving cows injections of BST, peak lactation can be maintained. A trial of BST was carried out in Britain and the milk from the cows was pooled with milk from untreated cows. Despite claims made to the contrary, BST does not alter the composition of milk. It merely maintains maximal milk yield. But the Ministry of Agriculture has decided not to approve BST for use on animals because of concerns about animal welfare – it puts an additional strain on an already overstretched animal.

Bulimia nervosa   The main symptom of bulimia is binge-eating. It can occur in both fat and underweight people, but is more common in women than men. Typically there is rapid consumption of large quantities of food and drink consisting mainly of 'forbidden foods' eg, biscuits, cakes, chocolate, nuts and crisps. It is then followed by a period of remorse. The individual then induces vomiting by putting a couple of fingers down her throat, but the experienced bulimic can induce vomiting at will. The whole episode is then followed by a strong feeling of guilt.

It typically affects women in their twenties and thirties. It is surprisingly common in industrious and ambitious women including doctors, possibly because they are more concerned with their body image.

Large fluctuations in body weight are quite common in bulimics.

When vomiting is frequent the teeth may become eroded because of the acidity of the vomit and sometimes the salivary glands become enlarged so the face is puffed up as in mumps. There may also be vomiting marks on the knuckles from when the hand is raised to the mouth.

Preoccupation with body shape and 'healthy eating' probably have something to do with causing bulimia, and it is not surprising, therefore, that bulimia is on the increase. Treatment is usually through psychotherapy.

Butter   This is made by churning cream. Butter typically contains 81 per cent fat and the rest is mainly water. Salt is often added (1½–2 per cent). Butter is a good source of vitamin A. The yellow colour of butter is due to the pigment carotene and varies with the diet of the cow. Cows fed on grass give dark yellow cream and those fed on hay give pale cream. Concentrated butter has most of the water removed and is more suitable for frying. Butter, like hard margarines, is a saturated fat and should be eaten in moderation.

Cabbages   A medium serving of cabbages will meet the recommended daily intake for vitamin C and half that for folate. Dark green cabbage leaves are rich in beta-carotene compared with the inner white leaves. A medium serving of cabbage provides about 2g of fibre. Cabbages contain sulphurous substances called glucosynilates. In small amounts they may help protect against cancer. The consumption of absurdly large amounts of raw cabbage is not to be encouraged because glucosynilates interfere with the uptake of iodine by the thyroid gland and can lead to goitre (*see* p372). The sulphur-containing compounds in cabbage are responsible for the flatulence it sometimes causes.

Caffeine   Caffeine belongs to a group of stimulants called 'methyl xanthines'. It is provided mainly by coffee and tea. Caffeine stimulates the heart and central nervous system increasing mental performance during low states of arousal. It also increases the output of acid in the stomach and dilates the airways in the lungs. Caffeine is relatively non-toxic but can result in tremor, sweating, palpitations and rapid breathing and sleeplessness. It is also a potent inducer of migraine. Stopping drinking coffee often reduces the attacks of migraine but sudden withdrawal may lead to a reaction characterized by a severe headache, irritability and lassitude.

A fatal dose of caffeine for a human would be anything between 3 and 10g; that is, 50–160 cups of coffee drunk in half an hour!

Studies have shown that women who drink a lot of coffee may take longer to get pregnant but it has not made them infertile. Foetuses absorb caffeine and expel it more slowly than the rest of us so they can suffer withdrawal symptoms after birth. The advice of doctors (whether for health or simple comfort) is not to drink more than six strong cups of coffee a day. Those with high blood pressure, heart problems or kidney disease should drink less than that. Pregnant women and those breast-feeding should restrict themselves to a cup a day.

Sources of caffeine

Coffee is the best-known source of caffeine, but tea, chocolate of all sorts, and some cold and headache remedies also contain it. Here is a table comparing caffeine levels in a single, 150ml cup:

Ground coffee	115mg
Instant coffee	65mg
Tea	40mg
Cola	18mg
Cocoa	4mg
Drinking chocolate	3mg
Decaff coffee	3mg
Decaff tea	3mg

By comparison a 4oz bar of dark chocolate will contain around 80mg of caffeine, milk chocolate has 20mg, and two painkiller tablets might have as much as 60mg.

Decaffeinated drinks

Decaffeinated drinks are now big business – we either fear

caffeine more than we used to or we genuinely do not like its stimulating effects. 'Decaffeinated' must mean that the product has no more than 0.3 per cent caffeine (instant coffee has about 3-4 per cent). 'Low-caffeine' usually means 0.1 per cent or 0.2 per cent. Since concerns emerged about the level of caffeine in some colas drunk by children legal limits of 125mg per litre have been set. There are three methods of decaffeinating tea or coffee: via a chemical solvent, the use of pressurized carbon dioxide, or the 'Swiss Water Process' (which uses hot water and charcoal filtration). From June 1991 there are EC residue limits for the chemical solvent of 5 parts per million. It is usually only 0.1 parts per million at the moment (the US Food and Drug Administration said in 1985 that the solvent residue at 10 parts per million would cause less than one case of cancer per million amongst people drinking six cups of coffee a day for seventy years).

Cakes and pastries   Cakes are made from flour, sugar and fat. Eggs are usually also used to help emulsify the fat but soy flour can be used instead. Pastries are made from flour and fat. Bakery fats are generally high in saturated fats otherwise you do not get the correct mouthfeel (*see* Taste, Flavour and Mouthfeel, p406). Both cakes and pastries are high in calories. They are to be enjoyed but because of their high fat and energy content should be eaten in moderation.

Calcium   Mature bone is about two-thirds mineral salts and one-third protein (cartilage). Mineral salts give bone and teeth their rigidity. The bones of babies contain more cartilage and are soft and malleable. The bones of children continue to lengthen and harden until the age of about nineteen years when they account for one-sixth of the total body weight. Calcium, phosphorous, fluoride and magnesium are all needed to harden the bones and teeth.

The skeleton of a new born baby contains about 30g of calcium and that of an adult about 1200g. In the passage from childhood to adulthood the child must accumulate 1170g from the diet. During early life the child will obtain sufficient calcium from her mother's milk. Besides animal milk and tinned fish there are few other foods of animal origin that are rich sources of calcium. Calcium can also be provided by drinking water especially in hard water areas. Calcium is more easily derived from food by people with sufficient stores of vitamin D.

In teenage children a shortage of calcium stunts growth and in girls may affect pelvic growth causing difficulties in pregnancy and childbirth in later life. Women who have had repeated pregnancies and who breast feed their children for prolonged periods may be at increased risk developing osteoporosis (*see* p390). The supply of calcium to the foetus and to the infant in breast milk is maintained at the expense of the mother – calcium is mobilized from the mother's bones to meet these requirements.

Vegetarians who consume milk and milk products in their diets are likely to have adequate intakes of calcium. The calcium intakes of vegans may, however, be very low. In Britain, white bread contains more calcium than wholemeal bread because it is supplemented with calcium carbonate (chalk). The proportion of calcium that is available in wholemeal bread may be low because the higher fibre content interferes with the absorption of calcium. An easy way for vegans who bake their own bread to increase their calcium intakes is to add one level teaspoon of calcium carbonate (chalk BP) to each pound of flour.

Campylobacter   Campylobacter is a bacterium that probably causes more cases of food poisoning than any other in Britain. The bacteria themselves inflame the stomach wall. The symptoms can include severe stomach pains and the passing of blood with diarrhoea. The incubation period is between two and five days. Poultry, meat, milk and water have all been implicated in outbreaks and birds and dogs have been identified as sources. A species of campylobacter (Helicobacter pylori) has been linked to causing peptic ulcers.

Cancer   Cancer is a disease of uncontrolled cellular proliferation. Diet is thought to be involved in causing several types of cancer. The following are thought to be important for avoiding cancer:

- Avoid being overweight or obese.
- Avoid excess alcohol intake.

- Avoid eating pickled and smoked foods too frequently.
- Eat plenty of fresh fruit and yellow, red and dark green vegetables.
- Avoid eating foods high in fat.

People with cancer need to keep their food intake up because they often become underweight. For more detailed information *see* Section III (p120) and Section IV (p207). A study of breast cancer patients who attended the Bristol Cancer Help Centre, which advocates a vegetarian diet and meditation as therapy, showed that the patients were three times as likely to have a relapse compared with patients given conventional therapy. But the exact reason for this is not known and may or may not reflect on the treatment.

Canning   Canned, or tinned, food has been sealed and sterilized with heat. Although the process of sterilisation cooks the food it is not heated for long and many nutrients are well preserved. This is particularly so with fruit and vegetables which are processed within hours of being harvested.

Home canning and bottling, which is quite popular in North America, should only be undertaken if you really know what you are doing. The airless conditions within the tin favour the growth of clostridium bolutinum which causes the fatal illness botulism.

Caramel   When sugar is heated to about 150°C it undergoes chemical changes to form a brown coloured material called caramel. Caramel is a complex mixture of more than one hundred compounds. The colour of caramel is caused by a suspension of small particles. Caramel is widely used by the food industry as a food colorant. Four types are produced industrially by the reaction of a sugar, usually glucose, with a catalyst.

Type	Catalyst	Food use
Caramel I	sodium hydroxide	Colouring spirits, eg rum
Caramel II	sodium sulphite	Colouring vermouths
Caramel III	ammonia	Beer, gravy browning
Caramel IV	ammonium bisulphite	Cola drinks

Cola drinks and dark beers make the biggest contribution to intake and they contain about 4g/litre. The various types of caramel are broadly similar in chemical composition. The safety of Caramel III was called into question when rats were fed massive amounts because it lowered their white blood cell counts. This reduction in blood counts does not occur in human volunteers given large amounts of caramel. Caramel is recognized as a safe food additive (E150) in Europe, Australia and North America.

Carbohydrates   Carbohydrates are the main source of energy in almost all human diets. They are made by green plants from carbon dioxide and water under the influence of sunlight. Some of these carbohydrates make the supporting structure of the plant – the fibre – which is composed partly of cellulose. Others provide energy for growth and some may be stored as sugars and starches. Human beings are only able to digest starches and sugars and, unlike herbivores such as the cow, horse and rabbit, cannot digest cellulose.

Carbohydrates can be divided into starches (polysaccharides) and sugars (monosaccharides and disaccharides). As a rule, fruits are a source of sugar and seeds and roots a source of starches. There are two major types of sugar: the *monosaccharides* such as glucose, fructose and galactose and the *disaccharides* such as sucrose (glucose + fructose), lactose (galactose + glucose) and maltose (glucose + glucose).

Sugars are sweet to taste and the degree of sweetness varies with the type of sugar. Sweetness decreases in the following order:

- fructose (fruit sugar found in honey)
- sucrose (table sugar)
- glucose (dextrose)
- maltose (malt sugar)
- lactose (milk sugar).

Starches and sugars provide 3.75 kcal per gram. In naturally occurring foods sugar exists in combination with other nutrients and makes these foods sweet and palatable. Table sugar (sucrose) is derived from sugar beet or sugar cane and is extensively purified. Contrary to the widely held belief, brown sugar, molasses and honey differ very little from white table sugar in nutritional terms except that they provide small amounts of B-complex vitamins and iron (in the case of molasses).

The term 'complex carbohydrates' is often used to distinguish simple sugars from polysaccharides (starch). Starches consist of chains of glucose linked together. On digestion disaccharides and starches are broken down into their constituent monosaccharides and then absorbed – eg, on digestion starch yields glucose. Not all starch is fully digested and some passes into the large bowel where it can ferment causing flatulence.

Carbohydrates are not essential but they are desirable components in the human diet. They are thought to be a 'healthier' source of calories than fat or alcohol, although high intakes of sugar are undesirable since they lead to tooth decay. Consequently it is argued that it would be a good idea to limit our sugar and favour instead the starch found in bread, pasta, potatoes and rice – foods which also provide dietary fibre.

It is the sugar consumed between meals in the form of sweets and soft drinks that seems to be most harmful to teeth, and it is this that should be avoided. However, there is no need to be excessively abstemious in the use of jam or sugar in cooking – eg, in stewing fruit. Nor need you worry about the small amounts of sugar used as preservatives in foods like baked beans.

Carrots Carrots have little nutritional value except for their high carotene content. A 2oz (50g) serving provides about 6mg of beta-carotene.

The carotene from carrots is best absorbed in the presence of fat. The carotene is also better absorbed from tinned carrots than fresh carrots although, of course, tinned carrots are inferior in flavour. The excessive consumption of carrots or carrot juice can make your skin turn yellow but is not harmful.

Casein (caseinate) This is the curd protein in milk. It results from the action of rennin on milk. This reaction takes place in the stomach as part of normal digestion. It also occurs in making junket when rennet is added to warm milk. The milk sets and can be separated into solids, curd, and a liquid, whey. The casein is contained in the curd. Casein is widely used as a food ingredient in processed foods such as coffee whiteners. Casein has a high nutritional value as a protein.

Cellulite   Cellulite is the term used to describe the dimply fat that accumulates around the backs of women's legs. It has been said that it was invented by the French cosmetics industry. One professor, when asked for his opinion on cellulite, remarked that it was the French word for fat. There is no evidence that the fat that accumulates in middle-aged women is special. Creams that claim to dissolve cellulite just don't work. Nor should you be taken in by claims that you can 'spot reduce' fat.

Cereals   Cereal crops are by far the most important sources of plant food for man, both directly as cereals and indirectly as fodder for livestock (thereby providing meats and dairy produce). In terms of food production the major cereals are wheat, rice, maize, barley, millet, oats and rye. Barley is the major cereal crop in Britain and is mainly used for animal feeds, malting and brewing.

All cereals are rich sources of starch and a good source of protein. Cereals do not contain vitamins A and C but they are a good source of the B vitamins and vitamin E. These vitamins are concentrated in the outer coat of the seed. Milling and refining leads to losses of the B-complex vitamins and vitamin E. Refining does, however, remove mould contaminants (*see* Mycotoxins) which is perhaps why refined cereals became popular.

Overdependence on polished white rice leads to thiamin deficiency (beri-beri). Populations that eat large amounts of maize are at risk from niacin vitamin B_3 deficiency (pellagra). This is common in South Africa and used to occur among poor farmers in the southern USA at the turn of the century. It occurs because maize is low in tryptophan, which is converted into niacin in the body. Also, the niacin in maize is in a form that cannot be absorbed. But if maize is soaked in an alkaline solution during processing then the niacin can be absorbed. This is the process used when making tortillas.

Cereals contain a substance called phytic acid that interferes

351

with the absorption of calcium, iron and zinc. Unrefined cereals contain more phytic acid than refined cereals. Leavening a cereal with yeast, as in bread-making, helps break down the phytic acid and so makes the minerals more available.

Unrefined cereals are a rich source of the dietary fibre which helps prevent constipation. Some of the starches in cereals, such as rice and wheat, are resistant to digestion and have a similar effect to dietary fibre on large bowel function.

It is estimated that 1 in 2000 people are intolerant to gluten which is found in wheat and rye. Coeliac disease results from gluten intolerance. Allergies to maize are also common. Nevertheless, most experts recommend that in general we should increase our consumption of cereals giving preference to unrefined ones.

Cheese   At its simplest, cheese is milk in which the protein has coagulated forming a 'curd' as a result of acid or rennet being added (rennet is a substance extracted from the stomachs of suckling calves). It relies for its flavour on the effects of the rennet, the bacteria at work in it and the moulds which grow on it. The type of milk used also has a strong influence on the way cheese tastes, whether cow's milk (the majority of cheeses), goats' (Chevre) or sheep's (Roquefort, for instance) or even buffalos' (Mozarella). Pasteurized milk which is favoured by today's cheesemakers arguably produces a blander, less ripe flavour. Cheeses are usually graded by their consistency, from 'hard' to 'soft'. Here are some examples:

Very hard	Parmesan (ripened by bacteria)
Hard	Cheddar, Emmental, Cheshire (ripened by bacteria)
Semi-hard	Stilton, Roquefort (ripened by mould)
Soft, rinded	Brie, Camembert (ripened by bacteria)
Soft, unrinded	Cottage Cheese, Cream Cheese, Fromage Frais, Ricotta (unripened)

Cheese is a good source of protein, calcium, vitamin A and B-vitamins. Most cheeses are high in fat (mainly saturated) and salt (*see* table on p267, Section V).

Soft-rinded cheeses keep less well than hard cheeses and

can contain high levels of listeria. The government has warned pregnant women (as well as the young, the sick and the elderly) not to eat soft, rinded cheese because of the small risk of listeriosis. It matters not whether the milk is pasteurized – the worst ever outbreak of listeria poisoning came from a Swiss Vacherin cheese made from pasteurized milk produced in unhygienic conditions.

Ripened cheese contains tyramine and this can cause migraine in sensitive individuals.

Chilled foods   Chilling is the precise technology which suspends raw or cooked food just above freezing point. It is used for transporting a vast array of fresh foods as well as for storing dairy products and fresh meat in the shop. Ready-cooked dishes, known as 'cook-chill', have been found to contain potentially harmful bacteria in a number of surveys (including E-coli and listeria). Such dishes should be kept chilled before eating and heated very thoroughly. This is particularly important at the moment since many shops have been shown to have defective chiller cabinets which keep the foods at too high a temperature.

Chips   Chips have been frequently labelled as 'junk food'. In fact, properly cooked they are not only delicious but highly nutritious. People's objections to chips are that they are high in fat and often high in saturated fat. Cooking chips in vegetable oil instead of animal fats can decrease the saturated fat content. Thinly cut chips have a much higher uptake of fat than thick-cut chips. Frozen chips also absorb fat more readily. For eating at home, oven chips are particularly low in fat and, what fat there is, is particularly high in polyunsaturates. You can reduce the fat content of home-made chips down to the level of oven chips by blotting them on kitchen paper. Oven chips contain about 5 per cent fat, ordinary chips about 10 per cent fat and thin-cut chips about 15 per cent fat.

Cholesterol   Cholesterol is an important component of all tissues of the body. It is not required in the diet and can be manufactured in the body. High levels of cholesterol in the blood are associated with an increased risk of dying from heart disease. It is possible to lower blood cholesterol levels by reducing the intake of saturated fats (milk and meat fats) in the diet. With a few people reducing the amount of cholesterol actually consumed in the diet also lowers the level of blood cholesterol – the highest amounts of cholesterol are found in egg yolk and organ meats such as liver and brain. But generally it is saturated fat and not cholesterol in the diet that is critical. Cholesterol is found in all food of animal origin but is virtually absent in foods of plant origin.

Cholesterol is transported around the body attached to proteins called lipoproteins. These can be divided into different classes according to their density. Low-density lipoproteins (LDL) carry most of the cholesterol in blood. People with high levels of LDL in their blood are at high risk of heart disease. High levels of LDL and cholesterol are usually caused by a defect in a receptor that removes LDL from the blood. A diet high in saturated fat is believed to decrease the activity of this receptor. High-density lipoproteins (HDL) transport cholesterol from tissues to the liver – normally they only carry about a quarter of the cholesterol in the blood. People with high levels of HDL are at low risk from heart disease. Moderate alcohol consumption increases the level of HDL in non-obese people. Obesity decreases the level of HDL (*see* Section III, p104).

Chromium   Trivalent chromium is required for maintaining normal glucose metabolism. Low intakes of chromium have been linked to impaired glucose tolerance and non-insulin dependent diabetes (*see* p218). Liver, cheese, wheatgerm and peas are good sources of chromium.

Citrus fruit   Citrus fruits – eg, oranges, lemons and limes – are excellent sources of vitamin C. Children often find satsumas, tangerines and clementines easier to eat than oranges because they peel more readily. The peel of oranges is often treated with fungicides and wax but this matters little providing you don't eat large amounts of peel. Seville oranges for making marmalade should be unwaxed.

Cod-liver oil   Cod-liver oil is produced from the fish livers of the cod family (cod, pollock, saithe, whiting, haddock) by rendering the cod-livers in water. The oil is deodorized and vitamin E and anti-oxidants are added to prevent it from going rancid. Cod-liver oil is an excellent source of vitamins A and D and has long been recognized to be of value in the prevention and treatment of xeropthalmia and rickets. It is also a good source of the omega-3 polyunsaturated fatty acids. Claims have been made that cod-liver oil relieves some of the symptoms of rheumatoid arthritis. Trials with other fish oils suggest that supplements give mild relief of symptoms compared with a placebo treatment. Cod-liver oil also has beneficial effects on blood fat levels and blood flow (*see* Omega-3 Fatty Acids, p389).

Ten ml of cod-liver oil provides about 1200mcg vitamin A, 20mcg of vitamin D and about 2g of omega-3 fatty acids. Cod-liver oil BP is fortified and contains twice as much vitamin A and D. Cod-liver oil also contains glyceryl ethers which have been claimed to be of value in the treatment of cancer.

Coffee   The coffee tree is indigenous to Ethiopia but its cultivation and use as a beverage stem largely from Arabia. There are two types of coffee bean: Arabica (which tends to be grown in upland areas) and Robusta (which tends to be grown in low land tropical areas). The world's heaviest coffee consumers are the Scandinavians who consume 12kg/head/year. The British consume amount 3.5kg/head/year and the Americans about 5kg/head/year. Arabica coffee contains about half as much caffeine as Robusta. Arabica coffees are generally regarded as having a superior flavour. Arabicas are used for beverages brewed from ground coffee beans whereas Robustas are used mostly in instant coffees. Instant coffee is usually derived from a combination of Arabica and Robusta beans depending on which is cheapest at the time.

The roasting of coffee leads to the formation of the vitamin nicotinic acid. A cup of coffee provides around 1mg of nicotinic acid. Otherwise coffee is of no nutritional value except for any milk and sugar consumed with it.

Coffee is well known for its effects on the gut, inducing the urge to purge. This effect is stronger with decaffeinated coffee than ordinary coffee. There are at least 300 other organic substances in coffee that may be responsible for the effect.

Heavy coffee drinkers have an increased risk of heart

disease. Large consumption of certain types of coffee can increase the blood cholesterol level and this is unrelated to its caffeine content. Boiled (ie, percolated) coffee has this effect. Fresh filtered coffee does not raise blood cholesterol however. The effects on cholesterol of coffee prepared in a cafetière are unknown and contradictory findings have been reported with instant coffees.

Studies suggesting that coffee consumption increases risk of pancreatic cancer or other types of cancer have largely been discounted. Interestingly, recent studies suggest that coffee may decrease the risk of cancer of the large bowel.

Advice about coffee drinking

- Avoid coffee last thing at night if you have difficulty sleeping, or drink decaffeinated coffee.
- Avoid heavy coffee consumption (more than six cups/ day).
- Drink fresh filtered coffee in preference to boiled or percolated coffee.

Crisps and snackfoods   Crisps have somewhat unfairly been labelled as worthless junk by some health campaigners. Crisps are made from sliced potatoes fried in vegetable oils and coated in salt. Because of their large surface area they absorb a lot of fat (about one-third of their weight). The saturated fat content depends on the oil used. Crisps cooked in palm oil are high in saturated fats whereas those cooked in unhydrogenated vegetable oils will be low in saturated fat. Crisps are high in calories and are a useful source of vitamin C and potassium for children. Corn snacks and wheatsnacks are nutritionally inferior to potato crisps as they contain less vitamin C and also tend to be sold in larger packets. A small packet of crisps weighs about 1oz (28g) whereas a typical packet of corn chips is sold in 4oz (100g) packets. Although they appear salty, a packet of crisps contains no more salt than a slice of bread. As the salt is crystalline it gives an intense taste. Unlike sweets, crisps do not rot teeth. They should be avoided if you are trying to lose weight. 'Extruded' snacks (*see* Section III, p99–100) are of little nutritional value.

Detoxification diets   Besides the nutrients in food there is a vast array of other substances which if allowed to accumulate in the body would be toxic. Fortunately, we are adequately equipped with mechanisms that enable us to break down and excrete these toxins so they don't accumulate in the body (*see* p126). At the turn of the last century Metchnikoff suggested that many diseases resulted from the accumulation of toxins in the body. This led to the vogue for purging the bowels with an enema and detoxification diets. Practioners of unorthodox medicine and popular health writers often advocate detoxification diets which consist in the main of fruit, raw vegetables, water and yoghurt, but are devoid of meat, fish, alcohol and stimulants; the diets are typically prescribed for a week or ten days. These low-calorie diets lead to weight loss which is fine providing you are overweight. Some people experience severe headaches on withdrawing caffeine-containing drinks from their diet. Others claim a mild sense of elation after a few days on the diet. This is probably caused by a lack of calories rather than the elimination of toxins from the body. When food intake is low the brain switches from using glucose to ketone bodies as fuel and this triggers mood changes. There is little evidence that these diets do any good. They are based on a misconception that fruit and raw vegetables are low in toxins and that meat and fish lead to the accumulation of toxins in the body. In fact raw vegetables such as cabbage and onions are high in naturally occurring toxins whereas meat and fish are virtually devoid of toxins. Also the body can breakdown and eliminate toxins more efficiently on a high-protein diet provided by meat or fish.

Diabetes mellitus   Diabetes is the most common metabolic disorder in the population. It results in excess urine production and the presence of sugar in urine. The most common early symptom of diabetes is the need to get up several times in the night to pass water. It is not caused by a diet high in sugar. It can be controlled to some extent by diet (*see* Section IV, p218 for more detail).

Diet   Diet refers to the food eaten by a person, or a regular pattern of eating. More specifically it may mean a strict pattern of eating that must be followed for religious or medical reasons.

Escherichia Coli – E. Coli   There are many strains of this bacteria and some inhabit the large bowel without any harmful effects. This bacteria is often the cause of 'travellers' diarrhoea. It is usually caused by faecal contamination of food either via flies or food handlers. It is more common in warm climates such as the Mediterranean or Middle East where the warmth enables bacteria to multiply rapidly. The way to avoid contamination in the home is to ensure you always wash your hands after visiting the lavatory and before preparing food.

Eggs   Eggs are the ultimate in natural convenience foods. They are a good source of protein, and the yolk of egg is high in vitamins and cholesterol. The egg white consists mainly of albumen but also contains a substance called avidin. This prevents the absorption of biotin from the diet. However, it is destroyed on cooking. Biotin deficiency (a B vitamin) has been reported in people eating large amounts of raw eggs. Eggs, especially duck eggs, are susceptible to infection by salmonella. Cooking the egg kills the salmonella. Outbreaks of salmonella have been linked to the consumption of uncooked eggs such as mousse and home-made mayonnaise. Current government advice is that we should all avoid eating raw eggs and that pregnant women, the very young, the sick and the elderly, should not eat soft-boiled eggs. The risk is small and, providing you are healthy, you can probably get away with eating home-made mayonnaise, mousse or egg-flip but make sure they are freshly prepared.

Emulsifiers   These food additives enable oils to be mixed with water into an emulsion. They are found naturally in foods such as egg yolk and soya. They are needed to make foods like mayonnaise, margarine and fat spreads. The emulsifying substance is usually lecithin which is found in all cells inside the body.

Energy   Food is fuel and provides energy. The need for food energy must be met before all others. This is simple providing enough food is consumed. Food provides energy for muscular work and to maintain the body. Living requires energy and most of the food we eat is burnt up in the body to provide energy. Males require more energy than females. Needs for energy depend on age, sex and physical activity (*see* table on p360). The four sources of energy in our diet are protein, carbohydrates, alcohol and fat. Calories (more correctly kilocalories) or kilojoules are units used to measure the energy value of a food (*see* Section V, p247). Thus the number of kcal and kj per gram of the four nutrient is:

One gram of:	kcal	kJ
Carbohydrate	3.75	16
Protein	4	17
Alcohol	7	29
Fat	9	37

Fat provides more than twice as much energy per gram as carbohydrate, and alcohol almost twice as much. So it is easy to consume too much energy on a high-fat diet or with heavy drinking. Fruit and vegetables tend to be very bulky and are generally low in energy. Grains, meat, fish and dairy products, on the other hand, are high in energy.

Energy intake in excess of requirements is stored as fat. Inadequate energy intakes retard growth in children and causes weight loss in adults (*see also* Obesity). Many people have energy intakes below the recommended amounts yet obesity is common. Most experts agree that recommended daily amounts of energy are on the generous side and that future recommended amounts for energy are likely to be lower.

Recommended daily amounts of food energy

Age range		MJ	kcal
Boys			
1		5.0	1200
2		5.75	1400
3–4		6.5	1560
5–6		7.25	1740
7–8		8.25	1980
9–11		9.5	2280
12–14		11.0	2640
15–17		12.0	2880
Girls			
1		4.5	1100
2		5.5	1300
3–4		6.25	1500
5–6		7.0	1680
7–8		8.0	1900
9–11		8.5	2050
12–14		9.0	2150
15–17		9.0	2150
Men			
18–34	Sedentary	10.5	2510
	Moderately active	12.0	2900
	Very active	14.0	3350
35–64	Sedentary	10.0	2400
	Moderately active	11.5	2750
	Very active	14.0	3350
65–74		10.0	2400
75+		9.0	2150
Women			
18–54	Most occupations	9.0	2150
	Very active	10.5	2500
55–74		8.0	1900
75+		7.0	1680
Pregnancy		10.0	2400
Lactation		11.5	2750

Source: Department of Health. 1 MJ ≐ 1000 kilojoules

Enzymes These are biological catalysts. They kick off very specific chemical reactions. Most enzymes are made from proteins and their activity is destroyed on heating. Enzymes digest food components as well as regulate metabolism in the body. Enzymes are used commercially to make flavours. They are present naturally in food and can lead to vitamin losses and food spoilage. Blanching vegetables inactivates enzymes and is often recommended before home freezing.

Erucic acid This fatty acid is found in oilseeds, particularly in mustard oil and rapeseed oil. When an oil high in erucic acid is fed to monkeys, pigs, ducks or rats it leads to accumulation of fat droplets in the heart muscle (myocardial lipidosis). The animals, however, soon adapt and the fat droplets disappear after a few weeks. Varieties of rapeseed oil have been bred that contain no erucic acid and these are the ones used to produce rapeseed oil on sale in super-markets. An EC directive prohibits the sale of oils with more than 5 per cent erucic acid. Fatty acids (cetoleic and gadoleic acids) with similar properties to rapeseed are found in herring and mackerel oil as well as in partially hydrogenated fish oil. But there is no evidence that they cause any harm in the usual amounts consumed in human diets.

Essential fatty acids Certain polyunsaturated fatty acids cannot be made in the body and must be provided in the diet. They are commonly referred to as the essential fatty acids. They were originally called vitamin F. There are two families of essential fatty acids: the omega-6 family, derived from linoleic acid, which are found in vegetable oils such as sunflower oil; and the omega-3 family, derived from linolenic acid, which are found in some vegetable oils such as soya-bean and rapeseed oil and in oily fish.

Deficiency of essential fatty acids does not occur in people freely selecting their own diets but has occurred in babies fed skimmed milk and in patients with fat malabsorption. It is uncertain what the optimal intake is. More than the bare minimum is believed to offer some protection from heart disease but very high intakes may be harmful.

The UK has no recommendation on essential fatty acids but the Nordic countries (Denmark, Norway, Sweden, Iceland

and Finland) suggest that the optimum intake is between 9g and 26g of linoleic acid daily and 1–2g of the omega-3 fatty acid from both vegetable and marine sources.

Evening primrose oil   Evening primrose oil has been used as a folk medicine by the Inuits of North America for centuries. It is a polyunsaturated vegetable oil that consists mainly of linoleic acid (about 72 per cent) and gamma-linolenic acid (about 8 per cent). It has been claimed that its medicinal properties are due to the gamma-linolenic acid it contains. It has been advocated for the treatment of premenstrual tension, high blood pressure, eczema and arthritis. The only convincing evidence is the treatment of eczema where it offers mild relief of the itching and cyclic mastalgia (breast pain associated with periods). It is believed that gamma-linolenic acid is converted in the body to prostaglandin E1 which has anti-inflammatory effects. A large number of clinical trials are underway testing the claims made for it (*see also* Essential Fatty Acids, Fats, Premenstrual Tension). It should not be taken by people suffering from epilepsy.

Fat   Fat in the diet may be divided up into visible fats like cooking oils, butter, margarine and meat fat and invisible fats which are constituents of foods – eg, nuts, biscuits, sausages, milk and cheese. They contribute roughly equally to our total fat intake.

Fat consists of constituents called fatty acids. There are two main types: saturated and unsaturated fatty acids. Saturated fatty acids tend to be solid at room temperature.

There are two types of unsaturated fatty acids: monounsaturated and polyunsaturated. Fats rich in unsaturated fatty acids tend to be liquid at room temperature. We can make saturated and monounsaturated fatty acids in our body from carbohydrate or protein so they are not strictly required in the diet. But we cannot make certain polyunsaturated fatty acids (*see* Essential fatty acids) in the body and they must be provided by diet.

The industrial hardening of fat uses a process called hydrogenation (*see* Hydrogenation, Partially hydrogenated fats). This converts the unsaturated fats into saturated fats or into trans-unsaturated fats. They have higher melting points and behave like saturated fatty acids.

Need for fat in the diet

- A minimum of 4g a day of essential fatty acids needed.
- About 30g of fat a day is needed to ensure the absorption of the fat-soluble vitamins.
- Fat makes food more palatable. Fat acts as a carrier for the compounds that give food its characteristic flavours and aromas.
- Fat is a dense source of food energy. This is an advantage when energy needs are high in early life. But it is very easy to consume too many calories with a high-fat diet.

Adverse effects of high fat intake

- High intakes of saturated fat are linked to increased risk of heart disease.
- Diets high in fat are also high in energy and so are conducive to obesity.
- High intakes of fat are also linked with increased risk of cancer of the breast, bowel and pancreas, but the evidence is more controversial (*see* Section III, p119)

This table shows which foods are rich sources of the three main types of fatty acid and what the individual acids are:

Saturated

Lauric acid	Coconut oil
Myristic acid	Animal fats, coconut oil
Palmitic acid	Animal fats, palm oil
Stearic acid	Beef fat, butter, cocobutter, hydrogenated fats

Monounsaturated

Palmitoleic acid	Fish oil
Oleic acid	Olive oil, abundant in most fats
Elaidic acid	Butter, beef and lamb fat, hydrogenated fats
Gadoleic acid	Fish oil
Cetoleic acid	Fish oil
Erucic acid	High erucic rapeseed, mustard oil

Polyunsaturated fatty acids

Linoleic acid (essential)	Sunflower oil, corn oil safflower oil
Linolenic acid (essential)	Linseed oil, rapeseed oil
Gamma linolenic acid	Evening primrose oil, borage oil, blackcurrant seed oil
Arachidonic acid	Liver, brain and offal
Eicosapentaenoic acid (EPA)	Fish oil
Docosahexaenoic acid (DHA)	Fish oil, brain and offal

Favism   Favism is a disorder related to the consumption of broad beans in sensitive people, usually of Mediterranean extraction. These people have an enzyme deficiency (glucose-6-phosphate dehydrogenase) that makes their red blood cells susceptible to toxins called vicine and divicine found in broad beans. It results in anaemia. People without the enzyme deficiency can safely eat broad beans.

Fibre   Dietary fibre consists of the structural material from plants that cannot be digested. Fibre is not a nutrient but provides bulk to the diet and because of its water-retaining properties helps food pass through the gut faster. That is, it has a laxative effect. A high-fibre intake may offer protection against several diseases of the large bowel and certainly prevents constipation. The term 'non-starch polysaccharides' is sometimes used to describe dietary fibre. The richest sources of dietary fibre are bran, peas and beans and whole-meal cereals. Diets based on these foods tend to be very filling but are not very high in calories. So it is easier to follow a calorie-controlled diet if it contains a high proportion of fibre-rich foods.

Fibre is sometimes divided into two categories: soluble and insoluble. The soluble fibre (such as that found in pulses beans, peas and lentils) seems to be useful in helping to control some types of diabetes by slowing down the absorption of sugar into the blood. Insoluble fibre (eg, wheat bran) merely has a laxative effect.

Fish   Fish is a very fragile food resource and can easily be polluted. Fortunately, fish (excluding shellfish) from around

Britain is not generally polluted. Fish is an excellent source of nutrients, particularly protein. A small intake of fish can make a major contribution to the total intake of vitamins D and B_{12} as well as several trace elements – eg, selenium, fluoride and iodide. Fish oil also provides the omega-3 polyunsaturated fatty acids which are believed to help provide protection from heart disease. These oils are present in smoked fish but may be removed by processing from tinned fish, eg, tuna. They are present in tinned pilchards, sardines and mackerel however. Tinned whole fish are also a good source of calcium (derived from the dissolved bones).

Fish broadly can be divided into two categories: oily and lean.

- **Oily fish** include anchovy, bass, black bream, eel, herring, mackerel, pilchard, sprats, sardines, salmon, tuna, trout.
- **Lean fish** include cod, saithe (coley), haddock, hake, halibut, plaice, sole as well as cartillagenous fish such as dogfish, huss, monkfish, shark and skate.

Oily fish contain between 5 per cent and 30 per cent fat depending on when they are caught. They tend to be lowest in fat in summer and highest in winter. Oily fish spoil more rapidly than white fish. Spoilt oily fish can cause stomach upsets and a skin rash – this is called scombotoxicity or scomboid poisoning. It is thought to result from the growth of bacteria on oily fish such as mackerel. The need to eat mackerel fresh has been recognized for years. The term 'Holy mackerel' comes from the days when markets in Cornwall were specially allowed to open on Sunday to sell mackerel.

Eating fish

- The healthiest way to eat fish is steamed, baked or grilled.
- Eating raw fish carries a risk of getting worms (one of the hazards of Japanese food). Cold smoked fish does not carry this risk.
- Be careful small children do not choke on the bones – check their fish before serving it.

Fish oil   Fish oil is a variable commodity and its composition depends upon the type of fish used, the geographical location where the fish are caught, and the time of year. The composition of fish oil also reflects what the fish have been feeding on. Fish oils from cold water tend to be high in polyunsaturated fatty acids of the omega-3 series (*see* Omega-3 Fatty Acids) whereas tropical fish tend to be high in those from the omega-6 series. There are two types of fish oil:

- Fish liver oils – cod-liver, halibut and shark-liver oils. These tend to be high in vitamins A and D as well as in omega-3 fatty acids. Halibut and shark liver oils contain such high levels of vitamin A that poisoning can easily occur if they are consumed in excess.
- Fish body oils – normally derived from anchovy, cepelin, herring, menhaden and sardine. These are low in vitamin A and D but like the fish liver oils contain substantial quantities of omega-3 fatty acids. Cepelin, herring and mackerel oil contain quite high amounts of gadoleic and cetoleic acid (about 20 per cent). These fatty acids have toxic effects similar to erucic acid if consumed in large enough quantities (*see* Erucic Acid).

Fish oils can be contaminated if the fish are caught in polluted water. High levels of polychlorinated biphenyls (PCB) have been found in fish caught in the Baltic Sea. The levels of PCBs are low in Atlantic and Pacific fish oils. Most commercially available fish oils are monitored for these pollutants and the levels found in fish oils available in the UK are no cause for concern.

Fish body oils are a by-product of fish meal manufacture. Fish meal is used widely in animal feeds. Fish oil is one of the cheapest edible oils but it is unsuitable for direct use in food because it oxidizes rapidly. Consequently, most of the fish oil used in the UK, Canada and Europe is partially hydrogenated before use in food. It is widely used as an ingredient in margarine, compound cooking fats and bakery fats. The hydrogenation process destroys the omega-3 fatty acids. The safety of hydrogenated fish oil is well established. Hydrogenated fish oil was not previously used in the USA for historical reasons but the US Food and Drug Administration has recently approved partially hydrogenated fish oil for food use after reviewing specially commissioned toxicology studies.

Flatulence   One of the side effects of diets high in fibre is flatulence. This induced one leading physician to say 'Vegetarianism is harmless enough but apt to fill a man with self-righteousness and wind.' Flatulence is caused by bacteria living in the large bowel. The amount of gas produced is proportional to the amount of carbohydrates reaching the bacteria. On a diet high in fibre, more carbohydrates are available to the bacteria. Beans in particular are noted for their untoward effects. Beans contain two sugars (stacchyose and raffinose) that cannot be digested and so are available to the gut bacteria for gas formation. Jerusalem artichokes are also renowned for their effects. The artichokes contain a polysaccharide called inulin which cannot be digested. Onions and green peppers contain not only fermentable carbohydrates but also sulphur-containing compounds. The latter are responsible for the offensive smell of the emission!

Fluoride   Fluoride is the term for the ionized form of element fluorine. It is present in food and water. The richest dietary sources of fluoride are tea and sea fish. Drinking water is an important source of fluoride. Where levels are 1mg/litre it helps prevent dental caries, but high levels (usually in excess of 3mg/litre) can lead to mottling of the tooth enamel. Very high intakes cause fluorosis which affects bone health and kidney function. The safe range of intake is between 1.5 and 4.0 mg/day. Authorities recommend supplements of 0.25mg/day for children between two weeks and two years of age if the level of fluoride in water is low. 'Fluoridation' of water supplies which are low in fluoride to a level of 1mg/litre drastically reduces the risk of dental caries and has no harmful effects on health (*see also* Water).

Food poisoning   Confirmed cases of food poisoning have increased dramatically in the past decade. There are probably several million cases a year in all. Salmonella and campylobacter are the two most common food poisoning bacteria.

High-risk foods are: undercooked poultry, eggs, meat and

meat products, shellfish, and dairy products – eg, raw milk and soft rinded cheeses. Salmonella is particularly associated with poultry and eggs and listeria with soft cheeses. If contaminated foods are left for more than an hour and a half at a warm temperature then the bacteria, if present, can multiply rapidly. Food poisoning is thus far more common in warm weather. Salmonella is destroyed by heat and poultry should be cooked thoroughly. The government advises us not to eat raw eggs and not to serve soft eggs to the sick, the elderly, the very young and pregnant women. Pregnant women should avoid soft rinded cheese such as Brie, Camembert and Chevre (they are prone to high levels of the listeria bacterium).

How to avoid food poisoning:

- Observe personal hygiene. Wash your hands before handling food and cover up cuts and sores with a plaster.
- Keep cooked and raw food separate to avoid cross-contamination.
- Thaw frozen food thoroughly before cooking.
- Eat food as soon as it is cooked. If you keep it warm, then it should be kept piping hot.
- Keep cooked foods cold (less than 5°C).
- Avoid shellfish (especially cockles and mussels) from dubious sources.
- Keep pets off food preparation surfaces and wipe them down regularly with a disinfectant such as Detox.

Food supplements   'Food supplements' is the name given to a variety of pills and potions sold by health-food shops and supermarkets. They include vitamin and mineral supplements as well as more exotic extracts derived from food. Most people have no need for supplements – they get the nutrients they need from food. However, it is becoming recognized that food can also be used in the treatment and possible prevention of disease. For example, fish oil supplements bring mild relief to some rheumatoid arthritis sufferers and may help prevent heart attacks. Beta-carotene is believed to help protect against cancer. Food supplements are offered as an alternative to eating foods providing these nutrients.

Many of the claims made for food supplements are direct or implied health claims. The law controlling food supplements is more lax than that controlling medicines. It is not necessary to show that the product is efficacious or safe. Nor are there any compositional standards. Two supplements, tryptophan and germanium, were withdrawn by the Health Food Trade Federation in Britain following deaths related to their use in Japan and the USA. A study of people who used health-food shops found that they were only half as likely to die prematurely than the general population. However, the most probable explanation is that they are predominantly non-smokers, middle-class and health conscious.

Frozen food   Frozen food preserves the nutrients in fresh food very well, particularly if vegetables are frozen soon after being harvested. When they are fried, frozen foods take up more fat than fresh foods – this is particularly true of frozen chips and frozen fish.

Freezing can only stop bacterial growth, it cannot kill bacteria. So it is important to observe all the food safety rules relating to frozen food. Get frozen foods home and into the freezer as soon as possible. Ensure your freezer is working properly ie at minus 18°C or below. Thaw frozen food properly before cooking. For further information *see* Section V, p292.

Frying

- Shallow frying   Shallow frying is in many cases no worse than grilling. This is because it enables meat and meat products to shed as much fat as grilling does – think of the pan after frying sausages. And some foods like steak do not take up much fat from the pan so long as they are not finely chopped. Mince and beefburgers, therefore, do absorb quantities of fat (as well as often being high in residual fat). Shallow frying in polyunsaturated oil (eg, sunflower) or monounsaturated oil (eg, olive oil) is healthier than with hard fats such as lard, butter, beef dripping and solid vegetable fat. Although certain foods don't taste as good cooked this way.

- **Deep frying**   Deep frying is a much maligned method of cooking, although there are things to be said in its favour. A deep-fried chip, cut chunkily not thinly, will retain more vitamin C than a boiled potato. It is preferable to deep fry in liquid oils. Groundnut oil is one of the best because of its high smoke point. It is probably inadvisable to reuse polyunsaturated oils because they deteriorate on prolonged heating. You can minimize the uptake of fat by frying at a high temperature of about 180°C. If the temperature is low the frying does not seal the food and it soaks up fat. Excess fat can also be removed by blotting the food with kitchen paper.
- **Stir Frying**   This technique is popular with Chinese and South Asian cooking. 'Stir frying' is something of a misnomer. It relies more on steaming than frying. The oil is added to spread the flavour of garlic and ginger and to stop the food sticking to the wok. Only a small amount of oil should be used in the wok and the food is tossed frequently in its own steam. This prevents a large uptake of oil. Groundnut oil is preferred for stir frying by many cooks, but other liquid oils are quite satisfactory. Stir-fried vegetables should always be *al dente*. The technique with stir fry is to put the foods in first that require longer cooking (such as chicken) and to cut the vegetables into similar sizes so they cook at the same speed. Always start with a very hot wok.

Galactose and galactosaemia   Galactose is a sugar that is released on digestion of milk sugar (lactose). It can also be made in the body from glucose. About 1 in 40,000 babies are born with a condition that prevents them from metabolizing galactose properly. When they are fed milk, which is naturally high in lactose, it leads to a high level of galactose in their blood. If untreated this causes jaundice and brain damage. The disorder condition is called congenital galactosaemia. It is treated by feeding the baby a specially formulated lactose-free milk.

Garlic   Because of its pungency, garlic is generally regarded as a flavouring agent rather than a vegetable in its own right. Crushing the garlic liberates enzymes that release the pungent compounds. A series of related sulphur-containing compounds such as allyl disulphide and allyl trisulphide are responsible for the pungent odour of garlic and its medicinal properties.

Although garlic makes food taste nice, it makes your breath smell. The flavour of a food consists of a chord of different flavour notes. When they are played together they give rise to a pleasant sensation yet when played in isolation they may be discordant. The compound that actually makes your breath pong is allyl disulphide. It is known that even if you inject allyl disulphide into the blood stream it causes the breath to stink. You can also make your breath stink by rubbing a clove of garlic on the sole of your foot! But be careful because garlic can cause skin problems (contact dermatitis) for cooks.

Besides keeping vampires at bay, garlic has been claimed to have a number of medicinal properties. Allyl disulphide has been found to prevent the development of cancers in rats injected with chemicals that cause cancer. However, there is no evidence to suggest that people who eat a lot of garlic (eg, the French) are less prone to cancer. Allyl disulphide does have similarities with drugs used to treat heart disease. And garlic itself can increase the rate at which blood clots are broken down. But you have to eat extreme amounts – about 50g a day (that's about ten cloves). Garlic may also help lower blood cholesterol levels. In Germany, pills containing dried garlic powder are licensed as a medicine for cholesterol lowering.

Garlic has been claimed to relieve some of the symptoms of the common cold. Garlic 'pearls' have a medicinal licence for this purpose.

Germanium   Germanium is a non-essential element that is present in trace amounts in everyone's diet. A few years ago it was strongly promoted in health-food shops with the claim that it boosts the immune system. It could be regarded as an attempt to cash in on the market of sufferers of ME and AIDS. The toxicity of germanium has long been known inside the microelectronics industry where germanium is used to make transistors. Following reports of kidney damage and deaths resulting from the consumption of germanium in Japan, the Department of Health issued a warning in 1989 not to buy germanium supplements. The supplements were voluntarily withdrawn from health-food stores.

Gluten This is a protein found in wheat, oats, rye and barley. The amount of gluten varies from cereal to cereal and even in different types of cereal. Gluten is needed to develop the elasticity of dough in bread-making. As North American wheats are high in gluten they are favoured for bread-making, while British wheat, which is low in gluten, is better for biscuits.

Coeliac disease affects about 1 in 2000 people and is caused by an allergy to gluten. Patients with this disease must avoid wheat, oats, barley and rye. It is also advisable not to introduce gluten-containing cereals into the diets of children under the age of one if there is a family history of coeliac disease.

Goitre Goitre is a swelling of the thyroid gland which is situated at the base of the neck. It is caused by a dietary deficiency of iodine. Goitre is common in many isolated areas in Third World countries and is linked to the increased incidence of deaf mutism, cretinism and thyroid cancer.

Green-lipped mussel A food supplement known as 'Sea-tone' is extracted from the green-lipped mussel in New Zealand. It is sold as a treatment for arthritis. There is evidence that the extract does contain a weak, anti-inflammatory agent. But the *Pharmaceutical Journal* reported in May 1990: '[It] does not produce any subjective or objective improvement in patients with rheumatoid arthritis when given over an adequate period of time. It is an expensive preparation sold over the counter to patients desperate for improvement. No evidence has been found for it to be marketed as a useful drug.'

Guar gum Guar gum is derived from the cluster bean (Cyamopsis tetraglobula) and is used as a food thickener in foods like yoghurt. It contains types of fibre called glucomannans and galactomannans which when dissolved in water swell up to form a viscous mass like wallpaper glue or frog spawn.

Guar has been used by the pharmaceutical industry to slow

down the absorption of several drugs. It can also slow down the absorption of sugars from the gut. This is used to treat patients with non-insulin dependent diabetes since, if sugars are absorbed slowly, then less insulin is released. However, for the guar to be effective it needs to be part of a meal rather than taken as a supplement. It can be incorporated into bread and biscuits.

Guar gum has been sold as a slimming aid. The idea is that it makes you feel full. It has never been shown to be an effective weight-loss agent in the form it is sold by health-food suppliers. Tablets of guar gum can swell up and cause blockages in the throat or intestines. Another side effect is excruciating wind. *Guar gum is fine as a food thickener and as a medicine for the treatment of diabetes but is of no value for slimming.*

Hangovers   Hangovers are either caused by dehydration following excess alcohol intake or by substances other than alcohol in the drink. In most cases the hangover is caused by drinking too much alcohol. Sometimes it can result after consuming just two to three glasses of red wine or port. This is because these two drinks naturally contain vasoactive amines that can trigger a headache or migraine in sensitive people. If you persistently get a headache after drinking red wine, try changing to white wine. Here is a list of some alcoholic drinks listed in their order of likelihood of giving a migraine.

- Port, brandy, whisky, dark rum, sherry, strong cider, red wine, strong dark ale, barley wine, strong lager, strong ale, white spirits (vodka, gin, white rum), white wine, light ale, lager.

Hangover cures are the stuff of legend (and quackery). The truth is less exotic: a large quantity of water after heavy drinking is the most effective measure. One of the symptoms of a hangover is a 'cold sweat' caused by low blood sugar levels. This can be relieved by eating food, or by drinking a glass of orange juice if you feel too fragile to face food.

Heart disease   Heart disease is the main cause of death in the UK, USA and most European countries. A heart attack is not a bad way to go if you are old but it also kills many in their forties and fifties – especially men. Heart disease tends to run in families but you can't change your parents. The following steps can help prevent heart attacks:

- Maintain ideal body weight
- Avoid a diet high in saturated fat
- Don't smoke
- Take regular exercise

For people who have already had one heart attack, eating two good size portions of oily fish a week can help prevent a second heart attack. (*See* Section III, p110, and Section IV, p202).

Hydrogenation of fats   Oils can be converted into solid fats by making a reaction between hydrogen and a metal catalyst (usually nickel). This converts the unsaturated fats into saturated fats and also leads to the formation of trans fatty acids. Trans fatty acids are handled by the body similarly to saturated fatty acids. Although trans fatty acids may seem unnatural, they do occur naturally in the fat of ruminant animals (cows, sheep, goats). In fact, the level of trans fatty acids in butter is similar to the level in margarines 'high in polyunsaturates' (about 5–7 per cent). The highest levels of trans fatty acids are found in compound cooking fat such as Trex, Cookeen, White Cap (up to about 40 per cent) and in ordinary margarines (about 15 per cent). The safety of hydrogenated fat is well established (*see* also Margarine).

Hypertension   This is the term used to describe high blood pressure (*see* Section III, p108 and Section IV, p217). Blood pressure increases with age and about 15 to 20 per cent of adults develop hypertension. It is usually without symptoms but increases the risk of suffering a stroke or heart attack. It is more common in black races than white. Excess alcohol and being overweight may lead to hypertension but the cause is unknown in the majority of cases. Many people with hypertension benefit from cutting down on salt. This is best achieved by not adding salt at table or during the preparation of food.

Hypoglycaemia   This term is used to describe a low level of glucose in blood. The normal level of glucose in blood is maintained by the interaction of the hormones insulin and glucagon. If the level of blood sugar falls below this level it causes a 'cold sweat' and irritability. If it falls to very low levels, it leads to coma and death. For some people, mild hypoglycaemia can occur as a rebound effect after a meal high in carbohydrates. It can also occur after bouts of drinking. Relief from mild hypoglycaemia can usually be obtained by consuming a small amount of starchy food or sugar.

Iodine   In 1983 it was estimated that 400 million people in developing countries and 112 million in developed countries were iodine deficient. The intake of iodine is largely determined by the level in the soil. However, in Britain a high proportion of the iodine is supplied by milk. It has been suggested that some arises as a result of contamination with iodine disinfectants applied to the cows' teats! Others argue that it comes from the salt licks given to cattle.

Only a very small amount of iodine is required each day, about 75 micrograms (a microgram is a millionth of a gram). Where the intake of iodine is deficient it results in a condition called goitre. Iodine is needed to make the thyroid hormone which is made in the thyroid gland situated at the base of the neck. When iodine is in short supply the thyroid gland becomes enlarged: this enlarged gland is called a goitre. Goitre is more common in women than men because women produce more thyroid hormone during menstruation and child-bearing. It is called endemic goitre if it affects at least 5 per cent of a population. Goitre also increases the risk of thyroid cancer. Cretinism, which is a form of mental handicap, is common in areas where pregnant women have goitre and can be prevented by an adequate intake of iodine.

Soils low in iodine are found in many mountainous regions, and also in areas where the water supplies come from limestone. In the last century it was common in Derbyshire and was called 'Derbyshire neck'. Goitre is *no longer a major problem* in developed countries – the average British diet easily contains enough iodine. The prevalence of goitre has decreased because in areas where iodine is low in the soil, foods are fortified and people no longer rely on food grown locally. Sea fish is an excellent source of iodine so goitre is never seen in fishing communities. In Germany, salt is still iodized and in Switzerland iodide is added to chocolate – all to prevent goitre!

Iron   Iron is needed for blood formation. Our bodies only absorb about 10 per cent of the iron we eat from plant sources but a much higher proportion can be absorbed from meat. Vitamin C helps iron absorption by converting the iron into the ferrous state. Lack of iron in the diet causes anaemia (*see* Anaemia). Those most at risk of anaemia are toddlers, women of child-bearing age and vegetarians on rice-based diets. Iron deficiency anaemia is commonly caused by excess blood loss in women and may need to be corrected by supplements. Liver, meat and black pudding are particularly good sources of iron. Fish and poultry are fair sources. Wholewheat and dark green vegetables are quite high in iron but it is poorly absorbed. The UK recommended daily intake of iron is 10mg for men and women beyond child-bearing age, and 15mg for women of child-bearing age.

Excess iron intakes (greater than 75mg/day) are harmful and care should be taken to keep iron supplements out of the reach of young children.

Irradiation   This method of food preservation is now permitted in the United Kingdom and several other countries. It involves exposing the food to gamma rays or X-rays. Gamma rays are a higher energy type of X-rays and can penetrate through most packaging materials and food. The process does not make the food radioactive and when used in low doses does not lead to detectable chemical changes in the food. Hence it is not easy to detect if a food has been irradiated.

In low doses it can be used to inhibit sprouting in potatoes, to kill insects in grains and spices and to accelerate the ageing of freshly milled flour to make it suitable for breadmaking. In slightly higher doses it has been used to reduce the bacterial load of food, but doses greater than those legally permitted are needed to sterilize food. Irradiation will probably initially be used in place of insecticides to clean up spices.

Losses of vitamins B_1 and E occur during irradiation of some but not all foods, but other vitamins including riboflavin, niacin and vitamin C are more stable. The nutritional losses caused by food irradiation at the doses permitted are comparable to those caused by other methods of food preservation (*see* Section III, p145 for arguments for and against it). By law all food that has been irradiated must be labelled declaring the fact.

Labelling   Food labels are covered in a vast array of information that increases every year. The key elements to concentrate on are:

- The weight – use it to compare value for money with other products.
- Use-by dates – observe so as to minimize the risk of food poisoning.
- Ingredients list – the ingredients at the top are there in greatest quantity.
- Nutritional information – this allows you to see what exactly what the calorific value and the fat content are.

(*See* Section V, p245, for more detail.)

Lamb   Lamb is defined as meat from sheep under the age of one year. Lamb, like beef, is a good source of protein, iron, B vitamins and vitamin B_{12}. It is one of the few farm animals that is raised using traditional methods. Lamb, however, tends to be very fatty. Lean lamb is about 8.9 per cent fat, but lamb chops are about 35 per cent fat. There is no need to avoid lamb but it is healthier to discard the excess fat. Much of this is visible and can be trimmed off with a knife. The fat content of roast lamb can be greatly reduced by roasting it on a spit or on a tray above an oven tin.

Leg of lamb tends to be much leaner than other lamb joints. A 5oz portion of lean roast lamb will provide about 230 kcal and 10g of fat of which half will be saturated. That is about the same amount as in two and a half chocolate biscuits or an individual portion of butter.

Listeria monocytogenes   This bacterium is widespread in soil, water and the guts of animals. When it enters our bodies most of us are unaffected – as many as 1 in 5 of us carry it in our stomachs. But people with lowered immunity can contract listeriosis. Listeriosis is a food-borne disease rather than food poisoning as such. Those particularly at risk are pregnant women, babies, the elderly and the sick. The incubation period can last up to several weeks and the symptoms are initially very like those of flu. It can give rise to septicaemia, meningitis and abortion. The foods most likely to harbour high levels of listeria are soft, rinded cheeses and pâtés. Listeria is unusual in that it can multiply at lower temperatures than other bacteria.

Low-alcohol drinks   A 'low-alcohol' drink cannot exceed 1.2 per cent alcohol by volume. This means that low-alcohol beer is only three to four times weaker than ordinary beer and low-alcohol wine is about ten times weaker than wine.

'Alcohol-free' drinks must not exceed 0.05 per cent alcohol by volume thus you can drink as many alcohol-free drinks as you like without becoming inebriated. But it is possible for low-alcohol beer to make you drunk if you drink an unusually large volume.

There are a variety of low-alcohol beers and lagers which now offer quite reasonable quality. As far as low-alcohol wines are concerned they really are no substitute for the real thing.

Low-alcohol drinks won't give you a hangover but they might cause migraine in sensitive individuals.

Low-fat spreads   Low-fat spreads have been developed for a more fat-conscious generation of consumers. They have enabled the food manufacturer to sell half as much fat at the same price as margarine.

- Low-fat spreads typically contain 40 per cent fat
- Very low fat spreads contain about 20 per cent fat

There are no compositional standards for these products but most have vitamins A and D added to them in the same way that margarine does. Dairy spreads often do not have added vitamins because they are made with butter which is a good source of vitamin A. Low-fat spreads are unsuitable for cooking because of their high water content. They also need to be kept refrigerated to keep them emulsified. Most are low in saturated fat. As a rough guide low-fat spreads should contain less than 15g saturated fat/100g and very low fat spreads less than 10g saturated fat/100g (*see* Section V, p274, for more detail).

Macrobiotic   This is the application of Zen Buddhist philosophy to eating. Some foods are designated Yin and others Yang. The aim is to balance the Yin with the Yang. Unfortunately there are no clear guidelines to what is Yin and what is Yang. There are seven levels of macrobiotic diets – the most extreme consists of brown rice only and has led to several deaths. The less extreme macrobiotic diets are mainly vegetarian although they may contain fish and can be nutritionally adequate. In the main they consist of large amounts of unrefined cereals and smaller amounts of fruit and vegetables. Foods from the deadly nightshade family (including potatoes, tomatoes, aubergines, green peppers) are forbidden and fluid intakes are restricted. Adults following macrobiotic diets have lower blood pressure and blood cholesterol levels and tend to be underweight. The growth of children reared on macrobiotic diets is retarded and they are more at risk from rickets, anaemia and vitamin B_{12} deficiency.

Margarine   Margarine was invented by the French chemist Megemourine in 1869 as a cheap butter substitute. Margarine did not become popular until this century when catalytic hydrogenation was developed by the Dutch. This technique enabled the hardening of liquid vegetable oils by reacting them with hydrogen in the presence of nickel.

Margarine caused vitamin A deficiency when it first began to replace butter in Denmark. Margarine is now fortified with vitamin A to the same level as summer butter, and with vitamin D. It is sometimes coloured yellow with beta-carotene but more commonly annato or turmeric are used.

Margarine has the same fat content as butter. The early margarines were heavily hydrogenated and were low in polyunsaturated fats. In the mid-1960s soft margarines high in polyunsaturates were introduced and these now dominate the market. What goes into margarine depends on the world price for fats and oils. The cheapest oils are beef tallow, lard, fish oil, soya bean, rapeseed and palm oil.

Margarines high in polyunsaturated fatty acids are generally regarded as the healthiest type and contain plenty of vitamin E. For further information see Low-Fat Spreads and Section V, p274.

Metabolism   This is the body process which converts nutritive material into living matter or breaks it down to supply energy. The term 'metabolic pathway' is used to describe the well-defined chemical reactions, regulated by substances called enzymes, that lead to the build-up and breakdown of tissues and the conversion of food substances into energy. The term metabolic rate is used to describe the speed at which the body uses up nutrients to provide energy.

Microwaves   Microwaves cook food by agitating the water molecules in the outer 10 per cent, creating heat which is then conducted towards the centre of the food. This process is very similar to steaming and microwaves are excellent for cooking vegetables and fish.

However microwaves are imprecise machines for the following reasons:

- Different foods cook differently depending on consistency and shape.
- Microwaves are not evenly distributed within ovens and food can have 'hot spots' and 'cold spots'. This can lead not only to food burning on one side and being undercooked on the other, but also to inadequate defrosting.
- Some 'clockwork' timers are unreliable.

To ensure safe cooking follow the instructions on microwave dishes very carefully – particularly cooking and standing times (standing time allows proper conduction of the heat from the outer 10 per cent). Turn the food every now and again if you do not have a turntable. Use round dishes. Do not use metal containers or ceramics with metal glazes.

Migraine   Migraine is a common condition characterized by recurring intense headaches. In women it is often associated with menstruation. Female migraine sufferers usually find their symptoms disappear during pregnancy and after the menopause. Certain foods provoke migraine in susceptible people – eg, milk, cheese, fish, chocolate, oranges, alcohol, fatty fried foods, vegetables (especially onions), tea and coffee. It has been suggested that tyramine may be responsible for attacks in some people. Foods high in tyramine are pickled fish, cheese and Marmite. Red wine but not alcohol has been shown to provoke a migraine in some people. Lack of food can also cause a migraine attack!

Treatment consists of trying to avoid the precipitating factor. If an attack threatens the victim should immediately lie down. At this stage a few hours' rest may prevent the development of a full attack. Loud noise or bright light intensifies the headache or sickness.

Milk and cream   Britain and most countries in Northern Europe have diets which rely on dairy products for energy (calories), protein and a whole range of vitamins and minerals. Milk is an excellent source of all nutrients except iron.

Average milk consumption is four pints/head/week. While milk plays this central role, it and other dairy products are also the biggest contributors of saturated fat to our diet (milk alone provides 25 per cent of our saturated fat). Sales of skimmed and semi-skimmed milk have rocketed from 3 per cent in 1983 to 34 per cent of all milk sold in 1989 – a reaction to the link between saturated fat and heart disease. The consumption of skimmed milks is still lower in Britain than in North America and most other European countries. Only 11 per cent of the milk is drunk on its own in the UK, most is added to tea or coffee or added to food such as breakfast cereals. As a nation we still consume too much saturated fat.

Semi-skimmed milk contains half as much fat and vitamin A as full-cream milk, and skimmed milk is virtually free of vitamin A and fat. Otherwise skimmed and semi-skimmed milks contain similar amounts of nutrients to whole milk. For a table of milk and cream and their fat content *see* Section V, p266. Milk is a valuable source of riboflavin but this vitamin is destroyed rapidly if the milk is left in sunlight.

Children under the age of five have high requirements of energy and milk fat is a valuable source of calories and vitamin A. They should be given whole milk. For advice on baby milks, *see* Section IV, p165.

- **Pasteurized** milk has been heated to kill off certain food poisoning bacteria but is not completely sterilized.
- **UHT** milk is heated to a higher temperature to give it a longer shelf life.
- **Evaporated** milk is completely sterilized, higher in fat and lower in vitamins.
- **Condensed** milk is also sterilized and very high in sugar.
- **Homogenized** milk has had the fat more evenly distributed throughout it so there is no 'top of the milk' cream.
- **Green top** milk has not been pasteurized at all and carries a higher risk of bacterial poisoning.
- **Goat's and sheep's** milk are enjoying a revival. Greek and Greek-style yoghurts made from one or the other have become very popular. Goat's milk contains a substance that binds with vitamin B_{12} and prevents it being absorbed. Vitamin B_{12} deficiency has been known to occur in infants fed on goat's milk.
- **Cream** is high in saturated fat and it is not advisable to consume large amounts of it regularly. There is no reason why you should cease to enjoy cream with strawberries if you only indulge occasionally.

Minerals   About 1 per cent of our diet consists of essential mineral elements which are primarily needed for water balance, skeletal development and blood formation. A number of minerals are needed in small amounts and are widely distributed in many foods. Some mineral elements which are essential for health, for example iron and zinc, are poisonous in larger quantities. So excessively high intakes of minerals should be avoided. Special care must be taken to ensure that two minerals, calcium and iron, are present in the diet in adequate amounts and that sodium and chloride (salt) are not present in excess. Some non-essential minerals in the diet can be toxic if consumed in excess such as cadmium, germanium, lead, mercury (*see* Section III, p134).

Mineral hydrocarbons   These are a by-product of the

petroleum industry. They were until recently sprayed on dried fruit to stop it sticking together. The practice has now ceased since the government advised manufacturers that mineral hydrocarbons might accumulate in the lymphatic system in the body. Mineral hydrocarbons are still permitted in chewing gum and cheese rind in tiny quantities. We are advised not to swallow chewing gum or eat cheese rind of the sort found on hard cheese like Edam.

Monosodium glutamate (MSG)   This is used as a flavour enhancer in many processed foods. In oriental cooking it is used as liberally as salt. Glutamate occurs naturally in many foods such as soya beans and we also make it in our bodies. It has a chicken flavour. It has been blamed for causing 'Chinese Restaurant Syndrome'. The sufferer typically shows acute symptoms of food intolerance such as swelling of the lips, irritation of the eyes and vomiting. It has not been proved that MSG is the cause of Chinese Restaurant Syndrome. Allergies to foods such as shellfish which is widely used in Chinese cookery can produce similar symptoms.

Monounsaturates   This term is used to describe fats high in monounsaturated fatty acids (*see* Fats). Olive, peanut, hazelnut and rapeseed oils are high in monounsaturates. Oils high in monounsaturates are thought to be healthy substitutes for fats high in saturated fats such as butter, lard and solid vegetable fat. Oily fish, duck and goose fat are also high in monounsaturates. The incidence of heart disease is low in Mediterranean countries where most of the fat comes from monounsaturates (*see* Section III, page 110).

Mycoprotein   This is the name given to the protein produced by fungi. Quorn is the trade name of a commercially produced mycoprotein from Fusarium graminosum. It was approved for food use in the United Kingdom in 1984 and is awaiting approval in the United States. It is used as a meat substitute and is suitable for vegetarians but not vegans because the harvested Quorn is mixed with egg white. It is an extremely versatile material and can be used to make substitute 'meat' cubes for curries, casseroles and pies. It has a better texture than textured vegetable protein (*see* p407).

Mycoprotein is low in fat and relatively high in fibre. It is a good source of protein, thiamin and zinc but relatively low in B vitamins, iron and calcium.

Nutritional composition of Quorn

	per 100 grams
Energy kcal	86
Protein grams	12.1
Fat grams	3.4
Saturated fat grams	0.5
Carbohydrates grams	1.7
Fibre grams	6.8
Calcium mg	21
Iron mg	0.3
Zinc mg	9
Vitamin A	0
Vitamin B_1 (thiamin) mg	trace
Vitamin B_2 mg	0.12
Vitamin B_3 mg	0.5
Vitamin B_{12} mcg	0.05
Folate mcg	3.5
Vitamin C	0
Vitamin D	0

Mycotoxins   These are poisons produced by moulds that grow on foods. In medieval times, the consumption of rye bread contaminated with the mould ergot led to large outbreaks of ergotism which results in hallucinations and death (St Vitus' dance). The active constituents are called the ergot alkaloids and include lysergic acid which is related to the hallucinogenic drug LSD. One of the nastier effects of ergotism was the loss of limbs through gangrene.

In Russia during the Second World War, about 10 per cent of the population developed a disease called alimentary toxic aleukia. It caused diarrhoea, damaged the ability to fight disease and resulted in many deaths. It occurred because people were making bread from mould-infested grain.

These two examples illustrate that if an everyday food is contaminated, many people will be affected. Fortunately, measures are now taken to prevent the growth of mould on cereals and so these disorders are rare in developed countries (*see also* Aflatoxins, p129).

Nutrient A nutrient is any substance which provides the body with energy and the raw materials for growth and repair. The nutrients we need are protein, fat, carbohydrate, minerals, vitamins and water. Proteins and fats are needed to make the structural materials of cells and hormones. Both fat and carbohydrate are used to supply energy. Minerals are used to form the skeleton and body fluids. Vitamins are needed to direct nutrients down the correct metabolic pathway. Foods contain a mixture of nutrients. Some foods contain higher amounts of particular nutrients than others but when foods are combined they mutually supplement each other.

Nutrition This is the process by which living matter acquires substances called nutrients for growth, repair and energy. The science of nutrition is concerned with the need for food to support and sustain life. In its widest sense it includes food production and processing, factors that determine food choice, the digestion, absorption and metabolism of food and its effect on health. Dietetics is the application of nutrition in the therapy and management of disease.

Nuts All nuts with the exception of chestnuts are high in fat. A 50g packet of peanuts provides about 285 kcal and about 25g of fat. The fat in nuts is of the unsaturated type except in coconut where it is highly saturated. Coconut fat causes atherosclerosis when fed to animals.

- Except for chestnuts, nuts are a good source of protein.
- Almonds, brazils, hazelnuts and peanuts are rich sources of vitamin E.
- Nuts are prone to mould contamination. Never eat nuts if the shell is mouldy. The mould contains aflotoxins (*see* p129) and is harmful.
- Be careful not to choke on nuts. Peanuts are one of the commonest causes of choking. Never give children nuts to take to school and don't let them throw nuts in their mouths.

385

Oats   Oats grow well in cold climates and are a good source of protein and carbohydrate. They contain more fat, which is polyunsaturated, than other cereals. They are high in phytic acid which interferes with the absorption of calcium, zinc and iron. Oat gum has been shown to lower blood cholesterol levels when consumed in large amounts. Many oat products such as oatcakes, oatbiscuits and flapjacks are high in saturated fat. So don't be fooled into thinking that eating them will help lower your blood cholesterol. People with coeliac disease have to avoid oats because they contain gluten.

Obesity   Obesity is defined as the excess accumulation of body fat. In men it accumulates on the torso (apple-shaped) and in women around the bust, buttocks and thighs (pear shaped).

Measurement

Body density can be estimated by weighing a person in air and in water using Archimedes' principle. As fat has a lower density than muscle it is possible to estimate body fat by this method. But this is not really practical for the domestic bathroom. Measurement of skinfold thickness above the hip on the waist and between the shoulder blades can also be used. If you can pinch more than an inch on your waist you are probably a bit porky.

Body weight is a good index of obesity especially if it is related to height. Fat people tend to be short for their weight. The body mass index or 'Quetelet Index' is often used to classify obesity. It is calculated by dividing the weight in kilograms by the height in metres squared.

Body mass index

Normal	Less than 25
Overweight (plump)	25 to 28
Obese	Greater than 28

Some people with very muscular body builds are wrongly classified as overweight (*see also* Section III, p104).

Example of calculating Body Mass Index (BMI) for a man weighing 75kg who is 1.75 metres tall:

$$BMI = \frac{75}{1.75 \times 1.75} = 24.5$$

Health risks of obesity

The risk to health of being plump is not great, but the risk of many diseases such as diabetes increases greatly above a body mass index of 28. The female pattern of obesity is not as harmful with regard to heart disease as the male pattern. Obesity increases the risk of gall-stones, osteoarthritis, high blood pressure, cancer of the uterus, gall-bladder and breast. There are a number of ways of losing weight of which 'Dietary Management' is the least extreme:

Surgical treatment

- Jaw wiring to stop people eating, but many cheat by liquidizing food and sucking it through a straw.
- Surgical reduction of the size of the stomach – called banded gastroplasty. Carries risk of serious side effects.
- Liposuction – vacuums out the fat stores.

Drug treatment

- Appetite suppressants – some may be addictive and have side effects such as increasing blood pressure.
- Diurectic drugs – make you lose water not fat.
- Bulking agents – such as pectin, xanthan gum, guar gum. Never shown to be effective in the long term. Carry risk of intestinal blockage and cause flatulence.

Dietary management

- Low-calorie diet.
- Low-calorie diet with behavioural education.
- Very low-calorie diets.
- Meal replacements.

Many people find it easier if they slim with other people and join a slimming club. Slimming clubs and Weight Watchers can be recommended. However, if you are genuinely obese you should also seek medical advice.

Popular diets

Many of these are just variations of low-calorie diets – eg, the F-Plan Diet and the Hip and Thigh Diet. Many others are just gimmicks to make a quick buck. There is no magic about losing weight.

Quack remedies

Never send off for mail order products promising you weight loss without dieting. In every case we have investigated they have been no more than a con.

Offal   This is the general term used to describe the parts of the carcass that are not muscle. It includes the brain, heart, intestines, kidneys, liver, lungs, spleen and thymus. Certain offal from cows has been banned from entering the human food chain in the UK following the BSE scare. Most organ meats are low in fat with the exception of brain. They tend to be quite rich in cholesterol but that is not necessarily a drawback (*see* p353).

Brain

Brain is quite high in fat (about 10 per cent) and very high in cholesterol (about 2 per cent). It is popular in the Middle East. In view of the fact that certain spongiform encephalopathies can be transmitted by the consumption of brain it is best to avoid eating it.

Liver

The liver acts as sort of metabolic dustbin for the body where all the harmful substances are stored alongside nutrients. Liver is a very rich source of vitamin A and good source of iron. One 4oz portion would probably meet your needs for up to a month. It is probably advisable not to go overboard and eat it more frequently than once a week. The government has advised pregnant women or those trying to become pregnant to avoid eating liver because very high intakes of vitamin A in early pregnancy can cause birth defects.

Omega-3 fatty acids   These fatty acids include alpha-linolenic acid and its derivatives. They are a class of essential fatty acids. Vegetable oils such as linseed, perilla, soy bean and rapeseed oil are good sources of alpha-linolenic acid. Fish oils contain two of the derivatives in high amounts. These are eicosapentaenoic acid (EPA) and docosahexaenoic acid (DHA).

Small amounts of omega-3 fatty acids are required in the diet and these requirements are easily met by a normal diet.

The consumption of EPA and DHA but not alpha-linolenic acid decreases inflammation and prolongs bleeding time. Supplements of EPA and DHA in the order of 2–5g a day are used as medicines to lower raised plasma triglyceride levels (blood fats). EPA and DHA supplements do not lower plasma cholesterol levels at the doses commonly used despite claims to the contrary. Benefits of EPA and DHA supplements have been noted in the treatment of psoriasis, atopic dermatitis, rheumatoid arthritis and in preventing second heart attacks. Populations who regularly eat similar amounts of EPA and DHA as oily fish also have a low rate of heart disease. EPA and DHA supplements may make asthma worse in patients who are sensitive to aspirin.

At the time of writing MaxEPA, which is available on prescription only, and cod-liver oil are the only supplementary source of EPA and DHA that have a medicines' licence. No standards with regard to specifications, efficacy and safety exist for other EPA and DHA supplements.

Onions   The onion family (Allium species) includes onions, leeks, shallots and chives. Onions and garlic have been eaten since 3000 BC, and leeks were eaten by the Israelites before the time of their exodus from Egypt. Onions are primarily used to flavour food rather than for their nutritional value. An average onion weighs about 90g and provides about 20 kcals, 5g of sugar, 10mg of vitamin C and 16mcg of folate. It is thus of little nutritional value.

The pungent compound in onions is propyl disulphide, and in garlic it is allyl disulphide. Onions increase the rate at which blood clots are broken down if consumed in quite large amounts. Onions contain indigestible sugars and can cause flatulence. They can also precipitate migraines in sensitive individuals.

Organic food   Organic food and drink is produced without the aid of chemical fertilisers, pesticides, fungicides or herbicides. On average the produce is 50 per cent more expensive, largely because the farms are more labour intensive with lower yields.

There is good reason for buying organic produce if you believe that intensive farming threatens the environment. However, there is no reliable evidence that organic foods taste better or are better for your health. There are strict standards for farmers and food producers who wish to call their produce 'organic' (*see* Section V, p225). However these are not always adhered to and you have to be on your guard.

Osteoporosis   Osteoporosis means increased porousness of the bones due to lack of calcium salts. It is a condition that leads to brittle bones and is responsible for increased hip and leg fractures in the elderly. Osteoporosis is a consequence of ageing.

- It is more common in women than men, especially after the menopause.
- It is accelerated by a lack of physical activity.
- A good intake of calcium in early adult life may help protect against osteoporosis in old age.

Calcium *supplements* do not seem to be of benefit in preventing or treating osteoporosis beyond middle-age if you already have an adequate intake of calcium.

Regular physical activity and hormone replacement therapy (in women) help prevent osteoporosis.

Partially hydrogenated fats   Liquid oils can be converted into solid spreadable fats by partial hydrogenation (*see* Hydrogenation, p374). Partially hydrogenated vegetable oils are more stable than raw oils and are favoured for making biscuits. They contain fewer saturated fatty acids than fully hydrogenated fats. Partially hydrogenated fish oil is also widely used in margarines and bakery fats in Canada, the UK, Holland, Norway and West Germany. The proportion of partially hydrogenated fish oils used in fats is restricted to a maximum of 20 per cent in Canada because of concerns about a monounsaturated fatty acid similar to erucic acid (*see* Erucic Acid).

Pasta   Pasta comes in all shapes and sizes – eg, spaghetti, macaroni, tagliatelli, etc. It is made from ground durum wheat and water with or without eggs. Home-made pasta contains far more egg (often two to three eggs per pound of flour). The type of dried pasta available in shops nowadays was only developed towards the end of the last century. It should be poached rather than boiled to preserve nutrients and texture. Pasta is a good source of complex carbohydrates and protein. Most nutritional guidelines suggest we should eat more food like pasta. Wholemeal pasta is very high in dietary fibre. Marathon runners often binge on pasta two to three days before running to boost their glycogen stores – it gives them more stamina. On the other hand, if you are dieting, you need to limit the amount of pasta you eat (*see* p208).

Peanut butter   Peanut butter can be made with or without added fat, but all peanut butters are high in fat and should be used sparingly like butter or margarine.

Smooth peanut butter contains about 54 per cent fat. Hydrogenated fat is added to some brands and so is salt and sugar.

'Natural' peanut butter usually just contains peanuts and salt. Some brands contain palm oil which is high in saturated fatty acids. The 'natural' peanut butters are more likely to be contaminated with aflatoxins. Aflatoxin levels are routinely monitored in the peanut butters produced by the major manufacturers.

Pesticides, herbicides & fungicides   Providing pesticides, herbicides and fungicides are used according to good agricultural practice, they pose little hazard to health. The levels of these chemicals in foods are routinely monitored by governments and the major food companies. A recent government survey found that foods sold in health-food shops were much more likely to be contaminated than those from major food suppliers.

Advantages

- They increase the availability of foods and take much of the risk out of farming.
- They control insect-borne diseases and mould contamination of crops.

Disadvantages

- They may lead to the contamination of food with potentially harmful chemicals.
- They may endanger harmless insects and other wildlife higher up the food chain.

Pizza   Pizza consists of a bread base with a topping. The nutritional value depends upon what is on it. A traditional pizza is high in complex carbohydrates but many deep-pan pizzas are little better than fried bread. But pizza slices can often harbour food-poisoning bacteria, particularly in hot weather. Pizza is best consumed freshly cooked. Pizza freezes well and individual pizzas are a good fast food for children.

Polyphosphates   These are a food additive used to retain water in foods. They are commonly used in hams and in frozen food. Many frozen foods lose moisture when frozen and need water added. In the past, unscrupulous food manufacturers used polyphosphates to sell water instead of food but this practice has now been clamped down on. Polyphosphates break down on digestion to phosphates which are metabolized quite normally by the body.

Polyunsaturates   This term is used to describe fats that contain high proportions of polyunsaturated fatty acids (*see* Fats) – eg, safflower, sunflower, soybean and corn oils. These oils also tend to be high in vitamin E which protects the polyunsaturates from going rancid. Margarines 'high in poly-unsaturates' are usually made from these oils and must contain at least half of their fatty acids as polyunsaturates. You will sometimes see on the label 'all cis-linoleic acid'. Fish oils contain a different type of polyunsaturate (*see* Omega-3 fatty acids, p389).

Pork   Many people think of pork as fatty meat. Yet lean pork is lower in fat than chicken. Pork, like lamb and beef, is a good source of protein, iron, B vitamins and vitamin B_{12}. It is generally much cheaper than lamb or beef. The fat in pork is more unsaturated than that in lamb or beef but this depends on what the pig has been fed.

- It is healthier to choose lean cuts and trim off the excesss fat.
- Always cook pork thoroughly because it can transmit worms if raw.
- It is best to grill pork, because it often has patches of fat between the muscle tissues. This will reduce the fat content.
- Remember pork crackling is very fatty.

Potassium   Potassium is an essential mineral element that is needed for the fluid inside cells. Fruit, vegetables, meat and fish are good sources, but cereals are low in potassium. Potassium deficiency does not normally occur, but can arise following prolonged vomiting or diarrhoea. It can also occur in patients treated with diuretic drugs for the treatment of high blood pressure. Deficiency symptoms include weakness, anorexia, nausea, listlessness, drowsiness and irrational behaviour. Severe potassium deficiency can lead to heart failure. We need approximately 1.5–2g a day. Higher intakes of potassium are believed to help lower blood pressure. It has been suggested that adults consume 3.5g potassium a day by eating more fruit and vegetables.

Excessive intakes of potassium supplements or salt substitutes high in potassium are harmful and can result in heart failure.

Potatoes   Potatoes originate from South America. They are a good source of vitamin C mainly because of the relatively large amounts consumed. Storage leads to losses of vitamin C and new potatoes contain the most. Frying or baking are the best methods for preserving the vitamin. Boiling leads to losses in the cooking water and mashed potato contains the least. Crisps are a good source of vitamin C and a small packet provides two-thirds of the recommended daily amount for children.

The potato is a high-carbohydrate food and also provides useful amounts of protein and fibre. If you are trying to lose weight you should avoid fried potatoes and only eat potatoes in moderation.

Although it is fashionable to cook potatoes in their skins it does not enhance their nutritional value. Potato skin can contain both natural moulds and artificial contaminants (pesticides and fungicides).

Green and sprouted potatoes contain alkaloids called chaconine and solanine which are acutely poisonous when eaten in great excess. Small amounts of solanine can cause migraine and drowsiness (*see also* Chips and Crisps). The green and sprouting parts of potatoes should be removed before cooking.

Poultry and game   The term poultry includes chicken, duck, goose and turkey. Game includes rabbit, deer, pigeon, pheasant, partridge and venison. Venison is very similar to lean beef and rabbit is similar to chicken in composition. Poultry is a good source of protein, B-complex vitamins and vitamin B_{12}. But it is not such a good source of iron as red meat.

- Birds tend to store their fat underneath the skin. There is no need to remove the skin before cooking. So if you want to avoid the fat don't eat the skin. Goose and duck are much fattier (between 20 per cent and 30 per cent by weight) compared to chicken which is about 5 per cent fat.
- The white meat contains less fat than the dark meat but it also contains less iron.
- Game may contain lead shot which can damage your teeth – chew it carefully.
- Always cook poultry thoroughly because it is often contaminated with salmonella which can cause food poisoning. Be particularly careful when barbecuing chicken (*see* Section V, p309).

Pre-menstrual Tension　　Many women suffer from pre-menstrual tension (PMT) throughout their reproductive years but it mainly affects women over thirty years of age. More than half of women have some symptoms, and about half of these suffer badly enough to seek help. PMT is characterized by breast tenderness, feeling bloated, headaches and migraines, mood changes – eg, feeling tense, worried and irritable for no obvious reason. It is caused by changes in the levels of ovarian hormones during the menstrual cycle. Various changes in diet have been claimed to help alleviate the symptoms.

- A diet low in fat has been found to relieve breast tenderness in women.
- Vitamin B_6 supplements (pyridoxine) may relieve some of the symptoms but it has yet to be demonstrated in a properly controlled trial. Excessive intakes of pyridoxine taken by women in the United States have led to damage to the nervous system but the amounts taken were very high.
- Evening primrose oil has been claimed to relieve some of the symptoms of PMT. It is suggested that the gamma-linolenic acid contained in the oil increases the production of prostaglandin E1 which has anti-inflammatory effects. Despite the widespread claims for the benefits of evening primrose oil controlled trials have so far yielded inconclusive results.
- Many women find it helpful to avoid coffee and alcohol during the phase of their menstrual cycle in which they suffer symptoms.

Preservatives　　These are substances added to food to prevent food poisoning and the spoilage of food. Traditional preservatives include salt, sugar, vinegar, saltpetre, alcohol and spices. Benzoic acid and benzoates are widely used as preservatives in the food industry. Benzoates occur widely in natural foods – eg, cloudberries contain 2 per cent by weight benzoic acid. Some people show adverse reactions to benzoic acid but it is very rare. Sulphites and sulphur dioxides are also widely used to kill the yeasts that cause the sugars to ferment in food and alcoholic beverages. Sulphur dioxide is released when wines are opened. This is one reason you should open red wines about fifteen minutes before drinking them. Sulphur dioxide is very pungent and can trigger asthma. Organic acids such as acetic acid and proprionic acid are used to prevent mould growth in cereal products. They also occur naturally in many foods.

Protein   Protein is needed in the diet to provide structural material for the growth and repair of tissues. Requirements are highest in infancy and childhood. The need for protein changes little throughout adult life because the body can adapt to use protein more efficiently when it needs more.

The requirement for protein is linked to that for energy and about 5 per cent of our energy intake must be provided by protein. The need for protein may be greater during illness or when recovering from injury. Most staple foods, such as bread, rice and potatoes, provide about one-tenth of their energy as protein. Meat, fish, nuts, peas and beans, eggs and cheese are foods rich in protein. Breast milk contains 8.5 per cent of its energy as protein.

Proteins are large molecules and are made up of smaller units called amino acids. When proteins are eaten they are broken down in the stomach and small intestine into their constituent amino acids which are in turn absorbed. The body then synthesizes its own new proteins from these amino acids. Certain amino acids are also used to make hormones and similar chemical messengers. For example, phenylalanine is used to make adrenalin. There are twenty different amino acids commonly found in plant and animal proteins but the human body has a limited capacity to convert one amino acid into another. Certain amino acids must be provided in the diet because they either cannot be made from other amino acids or cannot be made in sufficient quantity. These are called the essential amino acids: isoleucine, leucine, threonine, valine, lysine, methionine, phenylalanine and tryptophan and, for infants, histidine.

Proteins can only be made by the body when all the necessary amino acids are present. If one of the necessary amino acids for the protein is absent then no protein synthesis can occur. In food of animal origin including milk and eggs, the amino acids are found in similar proportions to the those in the proteins in the human body. For this reason protein derived from food of animal origin is efficiently utilized by the body. Cereals and beans when eaten separately have low protein quality but when they are consumed together, the protein quality is as good as food of animal origin – eg, baked beans on toast.

As far as adults are concerned protein quality is not worth worrying about. However, children under the age of five need good quality protein. Children reared on vegetarian or vegan diets need to have a mixture of plant proteins (cereals and pulses) to give them high quality protein.

See over for table of recommended daily amounts for protein.

Recommended daily amounts of protein

Age range years	Occupational category	Protein g
Boys		
1		30
2		35
3–4		39
5–6		43
7–8		49
9–11		57
12–14		66
15–17		72
Girls		
1		27
2		32
3–4		37
5–6		42
7–8		47
9–11		51
12–14		53
15–17		53
Men		
18–34	Sedentary	63
	Moderately active	72
	Very active	84
35–64	Sedentary	60
	Moderately active	69
	Very active	84
65–74	Assuming a	60
75+	sedentary life	54
Women		
18–54	Most occupations	54
	Very active	62
55–74	Assuming a	47
75+	sedentary life	42
Pregnancy		60
Lactation		69

Source: Department of Health

Pulses – beans, peas and lentils   These are the seeds of leguminous plants. They are an excellent source of protein but need to be cooked well to destroy the many naturally occurring toxicants found in them (*see* Section III, p127). Mature pulses do not contain vitamin C but bean sprouts and green beans do. Green beans also contain beta-carotene which is absent from mature beans. Pulses are good source of soluble fibre and thus contain indigestible carbohydrates that give rise to wind (*see* Flatulence). Most pulses are low in fat with the exception of the soy bean. The soy bean is nutritionally superior to other pulses.

Raising agents   These are used to introduce air or gas into baked foods. They make bread and cakes rise. The most usual raising agent is carbon dioxide either produced by the action of yeast or by the reaction of bicarbonate with acid. Self-raising flour contains baking powder which is a mixture of sodium bicarbonate and tartaric acid.

Recommended daily amounts (RDA)   RDAs are estimates of the daily amounts of nutrients required. They are made for groups of people rather than for individuals. RDAs vary with age, sex, activity, pregnancy and lactation. The contents of vitamins and minerals in foods are often expressed as a percentage of the RDA. The RDA figure used in Britain is only a guideline by which to gauge the amount of nutrient present in the food. A portion of the food should provide at least 15 per cent of the RDA if it is to make a significant contribution to total intake. The EC has proposed a new table of RDAs for nutrients, shown below. If adopted only claims for these nutrients and vitamins could be made on food labels:

	Proposed EC RDAs for food-labelling
Vitamin A mcg	800
Vitamin D mcg	5
Vitamin E mg	10
Vitamin C mg	60
Thiamin mg	1.4
Riboflavin mg	1.6
Niacin mg	18
Vitamin B_6 mg	2
Folacin (folate) mcg	200
Vitamin B_{12} mcg	1
Biotin mg	0.15
Pantothenic acid mg	6
Calcium mg	800
Phosphorus mg	800
Iron mg	14
Magnesium mg	300
Zinc mg	15
Iodine mcg	150

Rice There are countless varieties of rice with long, medium and short grains. Most rice is consumed as white polished rice. The polishing of rice removes the rice bran and many of the B vitamins, particularly thiamin. If rice is parboiled before milling the losses of B vitamins are reduced. Parboiled rice is therefore nutritionally superior. Rice is a good source of protein and food energy. Rice contains less iron than wheat and where rice is the staple food iron deficiency is common. Brown rice or rice bran is high in phytate which interferes with the absorption of iron, zinc and calcium. Cooked rice should not be left lying around in warm conditions because food poisoning bacteria can grow on it (*see* Section V, p288).

Royal jelly Royal Jelly is a good source of food for bees. It makes an ordinary bee turn into a queen bee. The health benefits claimed for it – such as vigour, fertility and curing cancer – are not supported by any scientific evidence. Royal Jelly is exceptionally high in pantothenic acid but none of us are deficient in that anyway. There is no evidence that taking

Royal Jelly has any benefits at all. Some people are allergic to it. It is very expensive to buy as a food supplement.

Salmonella   There are around 2,000 strains of salmonella but salmonella enterididis phage type 4 now accounts for half of the confirmed cases of salmonellosis in Britain. Phage types 4 and 8 are commonly associated with poultry and eggs. Salmonella bacteria infect the gut wall causing diarrhoea, nausea, vomiting, headaches, fever and aching limbs. The incubation period is anything from six hours to two days.

Salt (sodium chloride)   Salt has been used for many years as a food preservative. For example, salting meat and fish and pickling vegetables. Small amounts of salt are needed in a diet (1–2g a day). The amounts naturally present in food are usually adequate. In very hot climates or where heavy manual work is undertaken the need for salt may be increased because of losses in sweat. Salt can also be lost from the body during severe attacks of diarrhoea and vomiting.

Dehydration is usually treated giving a solution of 1 teaspoon of salt and 8 teaspoons of sugar in a litre of water.

High salt intakes are linked with high blood pressure and stomach cancer. The World Health Organization recommends we should not consume more than 5g a day. Most salt in a diet is added at the table or during the preparation of food. Pickled and processed foods (especially bread) also tend to be high in salt. (*See* Section III, p108–9, and Section IV, p217 for advice on blood pressure.)

- Sea salt is produced by evaporating sea water. As it comes from sea water it also contains other minerals besides salt, including iodine.
- Table salt is usually derived from rock salt and mixed with magnesium carbonate so that it flows easily.
- Iodized salt is table salt to which iodide has been added.

Saturates   This term is used to describe fats rich in saturated fatty acids. As a rule they are solid at room temperature – eg, butter, lard, suet, coconut oil and palm oil. High intakes of saturated fat increase blood cholesterol levels and are linked with heart disease. Butter, full cream milk and fatty meats are the main source of saturates in our diet. You can cut your intake of saturated fat dramatically as follows:

- Change to semi-skimmed or skimmed milk from full-cream milk.
- Change from butter or ordinary margarine to a low-fat spread or a margarine high in polyunsaturates.
- Choose lean cuts of meat and trim off the excess fat in place of fatty meat and meat products.
- Use liquid vegetable oils instead of hard fats for cooking.

Selenium   Many parts of Northern Europe have soils which are low in selenium. It has been recognized as a problem by animal nutritionists for many years and in areas where selenium is low in the soil, animals are given salt licks or gastric implants containing selenium. Extreme selenium deficiency is called Keshan disease and causes localised damage to the heart muscle. Keshan disease has only been found in isolated parts of China where the soil is very low in selenium. North American wheat which is used in bread-making contains more selenium than British wheat.

Shellfish   Shellfish, which include molluscs and crusta-ceans, are notorious for causing food poisoning. A small minority of us also suffer allergies to shellfish. They most often result in urticaria (nettle rash).
Molluscs include cockles, clams, abalone, mussels, oysters, scallops, whelks and winkles. They are high in protein and low in fat. They are also high in vitamin B_{12} and several trace minerals. Oysters are very rich in zinc – one oyster contains about 4.5mg. There is no scientific basis for the claimed aphrodisiac properties of oysters. Molluscs are very prone to contamination by protozoa, bacteria and viruses (*see* Section III, p131). Food hygiene experts currently advise against consuming molluscs from British waters because many are polluted by sewage. Commercially farmed molluscs are safer to eat and are routinely tested for contaminates.
Crustaceans include crabs, crawfish, crayfish, krill, lobster, prawns and shrimps. They are high in protein, low in fat and

not particularly high in cholesterol (as has sometimes been claimed). There is no need to avoid crustaceans on a cholesterol lowering diet. They are also a good source of vitamin B_{12} and several trace elements. As they are filter feeders they also accumulate micro-organisms but because we don't eat their filters they are not as risky a food. One can safely eat crustaceans from the British waters.

Smoking, salting and pickling   These are three of the oldest methods of preserving food which they achieve by inhibiting bacterial growth. With more modern techniques such as canning, freezing and chilling, the need for these three processes has disappeared. But smoked fish, bacon and ham and pickled vegetables are now eaten for their distinctive flavours.

Heavy and regular consumption of any of these foods carries with it some health risks. They all contain carcinogens and salted food has been linked to the high prevalence of strokes in Japan (*see* Section III, p130).

Sodium   Sodium is a mineral element that is needed by the body as an electrolyte, rather like a car battery requires acid. Sodium is found in almost every food and so deficiency does not occur naturally. However, most of the sodium we eat is in the form of salt (sodium chloride) added to our food either at the table or during preparation and cooking. It has been observed that high blood pressure is rarely seen in communities that have low intakes of salt. Whereas in communities that have high intakes of salt high blood pressure is common – eg, in the North of Japan. High blood pressure is dangerous because it can lead to the rupture of a blood vessel in the brain and a stroke which causes either death or paralysis. As there are no positive advantages to be derived from eating larger amounts of salt than necessary it has been recommended by the World Health Organization that salt intakes should not exceed 5g daily. That is equivalent to 2g of sodium daily. Salt intake is most easily reduced by not adding salt to food during its cooking and preparation, and by avoiding processed or pickled foods with a high salt content. Although the taste of food may initially appear bland without salt you can soon adapt.

Soya   Soya beans originate from China and are widely used in Oriental cooking. In the United States soya beans are grown for oil production and the defatted soya bean meal is used for animal feed.

The soya bean provides good quality protein and, unlike other beans, is quite high in fat. Soya beans must be cooked well to destroy toxins (soyin) that occur naturally in a bean. For this reason most soya flours are sold heat-treated. Soya flour can be used in place of eggs in baking. Soya milk can be used as a substitute for cow's milk but needs to be fortified with vitamins and minerals. Allergies to soya, however, are relatively common.

Soya beans can be fermented to produce soya sauce (tamari) and bean paste (miso). They are very high in salt and contrary to claims often made are not a useful source of Vitamin B_{12}.

Soya beans are used to make meat substitutes such as textured vegetable protein. Traditional soya products such as bean curd (*see* p337) and tempeh (*see* p407) are widely used in Oriental cooking.

Staple food   A food which forms the mainstay of the diet is called a staple food. The nutritive quality of the staple food largely determines the quality of the diet. Generally, fruit and vegetables provide vitamins A and C and minerals but only small amounts of energy, protein, fat and energy. In part this is because they contain large amounts of water and so are very bulky. On the other hand, grains such as cereals, nuts, peas and beans, provide energy, protein, fats and, so long as they are not refined, adequate amounts of B-complex vitamins. Consequently, the major staple foods are either cereals (wheat rice, barley, maize, millet) or root crops (cassava, potatoes, yams). In Britain wheat is the staple food: it is used to make bread, cakes, biscuits, pastry and to thicken sauces.

Starch   This is a form of complex carbohydrate consisting of units of glucose joined together in a string. It is the main energy store of most plants particularly cereals and root crops. Starch is present in granules in plants and is poorly digested unless cooked. When starch is heated in water the granules burst and the starch becomes digestible. During digestion starch is broken down into glucose which is then absorbed and used to supply energy (*see* Carbohydrates).

Cereal grains, pasta, potatoes, yams, tapioca and sago are important sources of starch.

Steaming   With the exception of microwaving, this is incomparably the best way to cook green vegetables. They retain more of their colour and flavour as well as nutrients. You can buy saucepans in two parts which are dedicated steamers. But a cheaper option is an adjustable steamer which fits inside an ordinary saucepan. And, *in extremis*, a colander inside a saucepan with a lid over it will do the job adequately. Steaming is also a good way to cook fish and poultry.

Sugar   This is a crystalline, sweet-tasting substance obtained from a variety of plants. Table sugar is sucrose which is now mainly derived from sugar beet but in the past was derived more from sugar cane. There are other sugars besides sucrose which are found in fruit and milk (*see* Carbohydrates).

Sugar is rapidly digested and it is efficiently used to supply energy. Refined sugar provides no other nutrients. A high intake of sugar causes tooth decay. It is the frequency of sugar consumption that is most important, particularly that eaten in between meals. Besides causing tooth decay there is no good evidence that sugar is harmful in the diet, and it does make food taste nice!

Sulphites and sulphur dioxide   Sulphites and sulphur dioxide have been used in brewing and food preservation for many years. Sulphites when mixed with acid release sulphur dioxide. Sulphur dioxide kills yeasts and is also a bleaching agent. It oxidizes rapidly to sulphuric acid which in turn reacts with metal ions to form harmless sulphates. Sulphur dioxide is a pungent gas which if inhaled can trigger an asthmatic attack in those prone to the condition. Red wines are heavily sulphited and should be opened a while before they are consumed to allow the sulphur dioxide to escape.

Taste, flavour and mouthfeel   The pure sensation of taste is evoked by the contact of food with taste buds on the tongue and palate. We can detect four primary tastes (sweet, sour, salt and bitter). The tip of the tongue is most sensitive to salt and sweet, the back to bitter and the edges to sour and salt. In addition to taste is the flavour which is derived from the sense of smell. We are able to detect a very wide range of smells but compared with other animals our sense of smell is relatively underdeveloped. Many of the compounds which give food its flavour are soluble in fat and this is why adding fat to food makes it more palatable.

Mouthfeel is the term used to describe the texture of food in the mouth. Fat has a creamy texture. Aerated chocolate has been designed to give a specific mouthfeel. The tongue responds to different particle sizes: small particles feel watery, those of moderate size feel creamy and large ones dusty.

Tea   Tea is made from the leaf of the plant *Camellia Sinensis* which grows in hot and very wet mountainous areas such as Sri Lanka and Assam. The leaves are allowed to dry up on the plant and ferment. When tea leaves are infused in hot water, the caffeine and tannin are extracted. The caffeine is released faster than the tannin so that a freshly brewed cup of tea gives as much stimulus as one that has been brewed for a long time. If you put milk in the cup first the tannins fall to the bottom. But if you put the tea in first and then add the milk you will stain the cup. Tea has little nutritional value though it does provide fluoride (a cup of tea provides about 0.25mg of fluoride). The tannins in tea may interfere with our absorption of iron. Tea is a major source of the aluminium in our diet.

A number of bizarre claims have been made for the medicinal properties of tea. It has been claimed that certain types of China teas (Yunnan Toucha) lowers blood cholesterol levels. We tested it and it had no effect whatsoever.

Certain China teas have been sold as wonder slimming remedies. We have also tested these and can confirm that they won't make you lose weight, just money.

Herbal teas do not contain caffeine but may contain other pharmocologically active substances. Harmful effects have been noted with the consumption of certain herbal teas, particularly comfrey tea, and they are best avoided during pregnancy.

Teeth Dental caries is the term used to describe tooth decay. It is caused by the growth of bacteria on the teeth. The bacteria ferment carbohydrate and produce acid which dissolves the enamel of the teeth. This is most likely to occur where plaque (colonies of bacteria) is found – usually on the crowns or between teeth. Plaque grows best with sugar but also with starchy foods like bread. The risk of caries is greatly increased by the frequent consumption of sugary foods. Consequently the frequent consumption of sugary snacks should be avoided. Toddlers should never be given sugar solutions to suck inside a comforter. Sugar consumed as part of a meal has little effect on teeth. Brushing teeth regularly prevents the build-up of plaque. Teeth that have fluoride in them are more resistant to decay so fluoridation of water supplies helps prevent dental caries. Tooth loss is usually caused by gum disease which is also caused by bacteria. This can be prevented by good oral hygiene: brushing teeth regularly and removing residual food particles from between teeth with dental floss.

Tempeh Tempeh is a fermented press cake usually made from soya beans. It is a popular food in South East Asia, particularly in Java. The white fungus *Rhizopus oryzae* grows on the press cake. This increases the digestibility of the beans and reduces the capacity of the soy beans to cause wind. Tempeh is usually eaten fried as an accompaniment to rice and is of good nutritional value being a good source of protein and B-complex vitamins. Tempeh can be obtained in some Asian supermarkets in London. The same fungus is used to make Tempeh Bongrek from coconut. It is eaten by millions of people every day without any harm. But occasionally groups of people do die or become very ill after consuming even small amounts of it. If it is not made properly a bacterium called *Pseudomonas Cocovenenans* produces a toxic substance called bongkrekic acid. This leads to low blood sugar levels (*see* Hypoglycaemia) and is usually fatal. You shouldn't try to make tempeh unless you know what you are doing.

Textured vegetable protein (TVP) TVP is made from extruded soya. It is used as a meat substitute or extender. It is usually fortified with iron, zinc and vitamin B_{12}. It is a good source of protein but many TVP products contain high amounts of added salt.

Tryptophan   Tryptophan is an essential amino acid and is present as a constituent of many proteins. Tryptophan can be converted to nicotinic acid in the body: approximately 60mg of tryptophan will yield 1mg of nicotinic acid. Nicotinic acid is a form of vitamin B_3 (niacin). Thus tryptophan helps meet the requirements for niacin. So when assessing someone's intake of niacin you have to take into account the intake of tryptophan as well. The protein zein which is found in maize is very low in tryptophan and this is one reason why diets containing large amounts of maize result in niacin deficiency (pellagra).

Large amounts of tryptophan are taken as a supplement and can have drug-like effects. Tryptophan supplements have been claimed to induce sleep and other reports suggest they cause lewd dreams! Tryptophan was widely sold in health-food shops as a dietary supplement until late 1989 when they were suddenly withdrawn. It was discovered in the USA that a number of people who had been taking tryptophan supplements had developed a disorder called eosinophilic myalgia syndrome, which causes muscle weakness and death. More than 1,500 cases have now been identified in the USA quite apart from other cases in Britain and Japan. The tryptophan has been traced back to one Japanese manufacturer in whose factory it was contaminated.

Vega-testing   This is claimed to be a method of diagnosing food allergies. Its proponents cannot explain how it works, but say it draws on elements of acupuncture. Its opponents in conventional medicine say that it does not work and can be dangerous with diagnoses leading to restricted diets for no good reason.

Vegetable oils   With the exception of olive oil, most of the liquid vegetable oils currently used do not have a long history of use. All oils provide 9 kcal/g so if you consume large amounts you will be taking in a lot of calories. With the exception of coconut oil, they are all good sources of vitamin E. Olive oil, rapeseed, hazelnut and groundnut oils are high in monounsaturates and low in saturates. Sunflower, safflower, grapeseed and soya-bean are high in polyunsaturates and low in saturates. Palm oil and coconut oil are high in saturates. Some deep-frying oils are partially hydrogenated to make them more stable to heat. But most liquid vegetable oils are not hydrogenated.

Choose the oils which are low in saturates. Don't reuse oil for deep frying.

Vegetarians and vegans   There are currently in excess of one million vegetarians in the United Kingdom, and the number, particularly of young vegetarians, is increasing. Vegetarianism covers a broad spectrum of diets but all vegetarians exclude meat and fish:

- A lacto-vegetarian diet includes milk and its products.
- An ovo-vegetarian diet includes eggs.
- An ovo-lacto-vegetarian diet includes both eggs and milk products.
- A vegan or strict vegetarian diet contains no food of animal origin whatsoever.
- A fruitarian diet, which is the most extreme or ultimate form, consists only of raw fruit, nuts and berries. Fruitarian diets are unlikely to be nutritionally adequate and are not be be advocated.

The first stage in becoming a vegetarian is usually to give up eating red meat and this is followed by exclusion of poultry and fish. Some vegetarians give up cow's milk and products derived from it because they believe that the process of milk production is cruel (calves are taken away from their mothers and are either artificially reared or killed for veal so that the milk the cow produces can be used for human consumption). Others argue that cow's milk was intended for calves not man and that the consumption of cow's milk by man is unnatural. Some vegetarians object to eating eggs for similar reasons.

A vegan rejects the consumption of all food of animal origin, including milk and its products, eggs and honey, as well as food that has been processed using animal products. Vegans will not use animal products for other purposes either – eg, fur coats, leather shoes, or cosmetics that contain animal products or that have been tested on laboratory animals. Fruitarians believe that man can be sustained by a diet of fruit, nuts and berries and so they exclude grains and processed foods from their diet. Some believe that it is wrong to uproot living plants. Most fruitarians previously have been vegans and most vegans in turn have been vegetarians.

Nutritional adequacy

Both vegetarian and vegan diets can be nutritionally adequate providing care is taken. The main hazards to avoid are:

- a bulky diet (especially for children);
- vitamin D deficiency (see entry);
- vitamin B_{12} deficiency (see entry).

Health

Many studies have compared the health of vegans and vegetarians with the rest of the population but it is not easy to interpret them. Vegetarians often show a different attitude towards health compared with meat-eaters – for example, many are middle-class and tend not to smoke or drink. The period of time over which an individual has been a vegetarian is relevant, as are the reasons why one chose to become a vegetarian. In any study those who became vegetarians for health reasons will obviously bias the results, especially if the diet was adopted with the aim of curing a certain illness. However vegans and vegetarians are less likely to be obese and this confers benefits to health. On the other hand they are more at risk from deficiencies of vitamins B_{12}, D and iron. Some but not all vegetarian groups are less prone to heart disease. The general conclusion is that the health of vegetarians appears to differ little from that of meat-eaters. They may have slightly different patterns of disease but there is little evidence that they live any longer.

Vitamins   Vitamins are organic substances that are needed in small amounts in the diet to promote health. As the vitamins were discovered each was labelled with a letter of the alphabet. But once a vitamin had been isolated and its chemical structure discovered it was given a name – eg, vitamin A is called retinol. The alphabetical naming system still has some uses because some of the vitamins consist of a group of chemically related compounds with vitamin activity. For example, vitamin B_{12} exists in several forms – cyanocobalamin, sulphitocobalimin or hydroxycobalamin. It is also useful to refer to the B-complex vitamins as a group because they tend to occur together in the same types of foods. Some vitamins – the B vitamins and vitamin C – are soluble in water and others are soluble in fat – vitamins A, D, E and K.

With the exception of vitamin B_{12}, the water-soluble vitamins tend to be widely distributed in foods but never occur in particularly high levels. We can only store them for a limited time and so a regular intake is required. Signs and symptoms of a dietary deficiency of water-soluble vitamin deficiencies occur within about fifty days on a vitamin-free diet, but with vitamin B_{12} it may take up to four years.

Fat-soluble vitamins (A, D, E, K) need fat in the diet for their absorption. They are found in a narrower range of foods and are often found in very high levels. For example, liver and carrots both contain large amounts of vitamin A. An excess intake of fat-soluble vitamins cannot be excreted and is stored so a regular intake is not required. It is possible to get all the vitamin A required from one meal of liver a month.

Vitamins are required in the body because they cannot be made from other dietary components. There are large differences in vitamin requirements between species. For example, the only mammals that require vitamin C are man, monkeys and the guinea pig. Other mammals can make vitamin C from the sugar glucose in their bodies. It seems that some time in our evolution we lost the ability to make vitamin C. Vitamin C is abundant in fresh fruit and vegetables but not in grains and this is consistent with the notion that our ancestors evolved on a diet containing plenty of fruit and vegetables.

Vitamin supplements

Because small amounts of vitamins are necessary in the diet it does not follow that larger amounts will be better. There should be no need to take vitamin supplements if the diet is properly selected. By and large there are no significant vitamin deficiencies in Britain. It has been argued that if a diet is lacking one nutrient then it is likely to be lacking in several. For this reason many people take vitamin supplements as an insurance policy. While there is no harm in doing this there may well be no benefit. If you want to supplement your diet with vitamins and minerals we suggest you buy a multivitamin and mineral supplement containing the nutrients in amounts close to the recommended daily amounts.

Care, however, should be taken to avoid over-consuming vitamin supplements. An excess of water-soluble vitamins is not a major problem because it can be excreted in the urine. But high intakes can cause drug-like effects. For example, nicotinic acid in large amounts (greater than 80mg) will lead to flushing, nausea and even vomiting which can last for about two hours. Excessive intakes of fat-soluble vitamins are more of a problem because they cannot be readily excreted in the urine and so accumulate in the body. Deaths have been reported in people taking huge amounts of vitamin A. And the excessive consumption of carrot juice containing the provitamin A makes the skin turn yellow.

Vitamin deficiency diseases

Various disorders such as nightblindness, beri-beri, pellagra, rickets and anaemia have been recognised for centuries but the cause of these disorders – faulty nutrition – was only elucidated this century. This has led to the concept of vitamin deficiency diseases. Although there are thirteen vitamins recognized for man, the number of vitamin deficiency diseases that occur naturally is limited. These are deficiencies of vitamins A, C, D, B_{12}, thiamin, riboflavin, niacin and folate. Disorders resulting from deficiencies of the seven other vitamins only occur under peculiar conditions such as intravenous feeding. And 'vitamin' deficiency diseases are, in any case, rare in the developed world.

Vitamin A   Retinol is the chemical name for vitamin A. This fat-soluble vitamin is found in relatively few foods and all are of animal origin. The richest sources are liver, oily fish, eggs and butter. It is absent from skimmed milk. It is added to margarine by law so that it has a level of vitamin A equivalent to summer butter. Retinol can be made in the body from beta-carotene, which is present in many green, orange and yellow vegetables (*see also* Beta-carotene). Vitamin A is needed for vision, healthy skin cells and a normal immune system. Deficiency results in xerophthalmia (*see* p98) and this typically affects children under the age of five in developing countries where fat and vitamin A intakes are low.

It is not necessary to have a daily intake of vitamin A as it can be stored in the body. A single portion of liver can provide all the vitamin A required for a month. Vitamin A from the liver and other foods of animal origin comes in the form of retinol. Beta-carotene from plants is converted into retinol by our bodies. High intakes of retinol should be avoided in early pregnancy as it can cause birth defects, but beta-carotene can be consumed freely.

Vitamin B₁ (Thiamin)   Beri-beri is the term given to thiamin deficiency. It used to be common in South Asia among people who consumed large amounts of polished white rice. It is characterized by damage to the peripheral nervous system. Losing the sensation of touch is one of the symptoms and there is a characteristic wrist droop. It can also lead to paralysis of movement of the eyeballs (ophthalmoplegia). There is also a form called wet beri-beri where there is accumulation of water in the body (oedema) which can lead to heart failure and sudden death. Beri-beri is not seen in developed countries. But a form of thiamin deficiency occurs in down-and-out alcoholics that is characterised by loss of the sensation of touch and mental disturbances (confabulation – making up stories).

Vitamin B₁₂   Vitamin B₁₂ is often in short supply in vegan and vegetarian diets. The vitamin is made exclusively by micro-organisms. Cereals, fruits, nuts, pulses, vegetables and other plant foods are free from the vitamin unless contaminated by micro-organisms that produce it. Animals cannot make the vitamin and ultimately depend upon deriving it from these micro-organisms. Vitamin B₁₂ is stored in the liver and kidney and so it is found in high concentrations in these foods. It is also found in all animal flesh and dairy foods. The requirement for the vitamin is very small, about one microgram daily. The UK has no recommended daily amount for vitamin B_{12}, but in the US it is 2mcg. Average intakes among meat-eaters are in excess of this.

Vitamin B_{12} deficiency may take years to manifest itself as it takes four to five years to deplete body stores of the vitamin. The symptoms of vitamin B_{12} deficiency depend upon the intake of another vitamin called folic acid. Vegans and vegetarians tend to have high intakes of folic acid because they eat plenty of greens, nuts and unrefined cereals. So they rarely develop anaemia as a symptom of vitamin B_{12} deficiency. They usually present with neurological symptoms instead (the first symptom being a tingling sensation in the extremities followed by a loss of sense of touch). These early symptoms are reversible if vitamin B_{12} is given. If untreated the deficiency will progress to cause degeneration of the spinal cord, paralysis and may result in death. Vitamin B_{12} deficiency can also occur in breast-fed infants if the maternal intake is not adequate. Vegan mothers who do not take additional vitamin B_{12} have low concentrations of the vitamin in their breast milk.

Vegetarians who eat eggs and milk regularly are likely to have sufficient intakes of vitamin B_{12} but vegans may have very low intakes. Vegans are recommended to eat foods supplemented with the vitamin or to take supplements. The commercially produced vitamin is used to supplement a number of vegan foods particularly yeast extracts (Marmite, Tastex, Barmene) and some soya milks (Granogen and Plamil). Many breakfast cereals such as cornflakes are also supplemented with the vitamin. In Britain all meat substitutes are supplemented with vitamin B_{12}. A fairly regular intake (at least three times a week) is desirable as it is not possible to absorb more than about 3mcg of any dose given by mouth. Lacto-vegetarians who consume only small amounts of milk products (less than half a pint of milk or 2oz of cheese daily) should also consider supplementing their diet with the vitamin. The need for vegans to ensure that they have an adequate supply of vitamin B_{12} in their diet cannot be overemphasized.

Vitamin C   Ascorbic acid is the chemical name for vitamin C. It is found in fresh fruit and vegetables but is virtually absent from grains, meat and fats (except whale blubber). It is needed in the diet to prevent the disease scurvy. It takes about fifty days for a diet devoid of vitamin C to result in scurvy. It is characterized by poor wound healing, bleeding gums, haemorrhages under the skin and mental disturbances. As little as 10mg of vitamin C will prevent and cure scurvy but 20mg is needed for normal wound healing. The UK RDA for vitamin C is 30mg/day for adults. The US recommended daily amount is 60mg/day for non-smokers and 100mg/day for smokers. The higher recommendation for smokers was made because they have lower levels of vitamin C in their blood. The average adult intake of vitamin C in the UK exceeds 60mg.

Claims that high doses of vitamin C (1–2g per day) prevent the common cold have not been substantiated in controlled trials. However, they do help relieve some of the symptoms such as bronchitis. Ascorbic acid tablets are acidic and can erode dental enamel if sucked for prolonged periods.

Vitamin C is also used as a food additive in bread-making and as an anti-oxidant in fruit juices.

Vitamin D, rickets and osteomalacia   Vitamin D deficiency is probably the most prevalent vitamin deficiency seen in Northern latitudes. It causes rickets (bow legs) in children and osteomalacia (painful bones) in adults. Rickets is caused by low exposure to sunlight in the winter months coupled with a low intake of calcium. Rickets is far less common than in the past. Children affected with rickets have abnormally bowed legs because the process that leads to the deposition of minerals in the bone which gives it rigidity is impaired. Rickets and osteomalacia in the United Kingdom are now mainly confined to the Asian Indian population. Vitamin D can be made in the body by the action of sunlight on the skin but in the absence of sufficient sunlight it is necessary to consume vitamin D in the diet. The Indians make less vitamin D on exposure to sunlight than the white population. One reason for the decline in rickets in the UK could be the introduction of 'smokeless zones' in the 1950s which allowed more sunlight to penetrate in the cities. Another reason may well be the popularity of sunbathing. There are few dietary sources of vitamin D except for oily fish, liver and fish oils. Perhaps this is a suggestion that people who live in Northerly latitudes need fish in their diet. Some foods are fortified with vitamin D – eg, margarine and breakfast cereals.

Vitamin E   Vegetable oils (particularly sunflower seed oil), nuts, wholemeal cereals and leafy vegetables are good sources of vitamin E. Vitamin E protects essential fatty acids from damage by 'free radicals' in the body. The need for vitamin E is linked to the intake of polyunsaturated fatty acids – roughly 0.4mg is needed for each gram of polyunsaturated fat in the diet.

Deficiency does not occur in people on self-selected diets but does occur in premature infants and individuals with severe fat malabsorption. Deficiency results in an increased rate of breakdown of red blood cells, damage to muscle tissue and inflammation of fatty tissue.

There is no UK RDA for vitamin E. The USA RDA is 10mg. Average daily intakes of vitamin E in the UK are 7–9mg. This amount is probably adequate as it provides more than 0.4mg/gram of polyunsaturated fat. Vegetarians tend to have higher intakes.

It has been suggested that vitamin E may offer protection from heart disease and delay the ageing process. Vitamin E supplements often contain 10 to 100 times the RDA. Fortunately it is relatively non-toxic. Vitamin E is used as an antioxidant by the food industry to prevent rancidity of fat.

Water   Water is an essential nutrient but if you look in the library for books about water they are normally about sewage treatment. Water is the most abundant constituent of the human body accounting for as much as four-fifths of body weight. Fat people have less body water as a percentage of body weight than those who are lean. Body water continually needs to be replaced.

Our need for water depends upon how hot and dry it is. We normally lose about 1.5 litres a day from breathing alone but more in hot and dry weather. Water is also lost in sweat, urine and faeces. Some drugs called diuretics promote water loss in urine (coffee and alcohol have a diuretic effect).

Most adults typically drink about two litres of fluid a day. Another litre is provided by water in food. Adults need approximately 1ml of water per kcal of energy under normal circumstances but this rises to about 1.5ml per kcal when the individual is sweating a lot. Infants and children need about 1.5ml/kcal of energy expenditure. In hot weather, special attention needs to be given to the water needs of infants and the elderly whose thirst sensation may be blunted. Dehydration can also result following a bout of diarrhoea or because of intense physical exertion especially at high altitude. It becomes life-threatening when more than 10 per cent body weight is lost. Individuals can be rapidly rehydrated by giving a solution of one teaspoon of salt and eight teaspoons of sugar dissolved in a litre of water.

Toxicity of water can result from drinking water at a rate beyond the capacity of the kidneys to excrete it. The manifestations usually include a gradual mental dulling, confusion, coma, convulsion and even death. It is rarely observed in adults.

Tap water

Tap water is safe to drink in developed countries, is subject to monitoring for safety and has to meet certain standards. Water quality in terms of taste varies depending upon where you live and will contain varying amounts of minerals dissolved in it.

Some areas have high amounts of fluoride which can cause mottling of teeth in children, other areas have low levels of fluoride that increase risk of tooth decay. Ideally the level of fluoride should be 1 mg/litre to prevent tooth decay without causing mottling of teeth.

Nitrate levels are quite high in parts of the country where large amounts of nitrate are used as fertilizers. For example, in East Anglia. The EEC has set a maximum limit of 50mg nitrate/litre for drinking water. From time to time the levels exceed this limit in public water in parts of East Anglia. However, the levels of nitrate are below the levels known to cause harmful effects.

If you live in a chalk or limestone area then the water will be hard and will contain calcium salts – this makes it mildly alkaline. If you live in a granite area the water will be soft and slightly acidic. Most people prefer the taste of soft water but hard water may be healthier. Areas with hard water tend to have lower rates of cardiovascular disease than soft water areas. Soft water tends to dissolve lead from the plumbing. As a general rule only take water for drinking from the mains supply and run the water for a few seconds first. If you are worried about the quality of your water contact your local water authority and they will test it for you for free.

From time to time much play is made of the fact that British tap water does not meet EEC standards in all respects (the same is true of other European waters, by the way). The standards are set very high for all our benefit, but not meeting them in every respect *does not* mean that tap water is harmful.

Bottled water

Bottled water is equally variable in composition but is often not as closely monitored as tap water. A recent study published in 1989 found that out of thirty-seven brands of bottled water, twenty-four had levels of minerals exceeding the permitted maximum levels for drinking water in the USA. Perrier water was found to be high in mercury, Badoit was high in lithium and nitrate and Vichy St Yorre Royal was high in aluminium, boron, cadmium and lead. There is no need to drink bottled water for health reasons but by all means do so if you prefer the taste. Be prepared to pay a hefty premium over tap water. We would, however, strongly advise you to drink bottled water when travelling in developing countries.

Water softeners and filters

A variety of devices are available to soften and filter water. Some are ion exchange resins which replace the calcium and magnesium in water with sodium. These should be avoided by people with high blood pressure and should not be used to make up infant feeds. The more modern ion exchange resins replace the calcium and magnesium with hydrogen ions so making the water more acidic. Simple ion exchange filters do not remove nitrate from water. Some have charcoal filters to remove organic pollutants. The only really effective water purification system is reverse osmosis coupled with distillation but this is expensive and tends only to be used in hospitals and research laboratories to prepare pure water.

In Britain and America water filter salesmen now call more often than double-glazing reps. There are dozens of models most of which can remove 'off' flavours from tap water but very few of which can remove bacteria. (Since tap water contains very little bacteria this does not matter.) However if it is the flavour of chlorine that you object to then let the tap water stand for five minutes and the chlorine will evaporate. In our opinion most water filters are not worth it, unless you have a real objection to the taste of your tap water.

Xerophthalmia   This is the term used for vitamin A deficiency disease. It does not occur in Britain but is common in developing countries among children aged between two and five years. It results in:

- nightblindness – an inability to see under low light intensity;
- drying up of the tissues of the eye – this leads to infection of the eye and blindness;
- decreased resistance to infections like measles.

The requirement for vitamin A can be met by retinol which is found in liver, dairy fats and fish liver oils or by beta-carotene contained in green, orange and yellow vegetables such as spinach and carrots.

Yeast   There are several types of food yeast. Baker's yeast and brewer's yeast are strains of Saccharomyces cerevisae. This micro-organism breaks down starch into sugar and ferments the sugar to form alcohol. In doing so it also produces carbon dioxide. Yeast fermentation of bread, besides acting as a raising agent, also breaks down phytic acid – a substance found in cereals that otherwise interferes with our absorption of several minerals. Yeast itself is a rich source of B-complex vitamins. Thus yeast fermentation of flour improves the nutritional quality of the bread (*see* Bread). Yeasts are present on the skin of many fruits and are responsible for the spontaneous fermentation of grape and apple juice. Yeast extracts such as Marmite and Vegemite are made by allowing a concentrated suspension of yeast to dissolve itself. Salt is then added to preserve it. They are a good source of B-complex vitamins.

Yoghurt   Yoghurt is made by the fermentation of milk with Lactobacillus acidophilus. The lactic acid produced by the bacteria from the lactose in the milk causes the milk curds to coagulate. The fermentation process destroys the vitamin B_{12} in the milk. The level of fat in yoghurt depends on the milk used. Most commercial yoghurts are made from skimmed milk and so are low in fat. The creamy yoghurts only contain about 5–7 per cent fat, slightly more than ordinary milk but considerably less than cream. Fruit yoghurts, which are popular with children, typically contain about 15 per cent sugar. Guar gum is often added to yoghurt to make it feel thicker.

Zinc   Zinc is a trace element which we require in our diet. It is needed for normal reproductive function and healthy immunity systems and skin. Meat and seafoods (especially oysters) are good sources of zinc. It is also found in cereals but the presence of phytic acid may limit the amounts that are available to the body. Zinc deficiency occurs in isolated parts of the world where the soil is low in zinc and the diet contains a high proportion of unleavened bread. The leavening of bread with yeast breaks down phytic acid and facilitates the absorption of zinc. Dietary zinc deficiency causes impaired growth and delayed sexual maturation. The UK has no recommended daily amount for zinc. The USA RDA is 15mg for men and 12mg for women. Normal diets yield all the zinc we need. High intakes of zinc are toxic.

SOURCE NOTES

The authors would like to acknowledge the following journalists for the articles quoted in Section 1:

p15.   Oats and heart attacks: Chris Mihill, *Today*.
p15.   Polyunsaturates: Neville Hodgkinson, *The Sunday Times*.
p16.   Cancer ketchup: Julian Rollins, *Today*.
p17.   Cancer yoghurt: Emma Allen and Brian Wells, *Daily Star*.
p18.   Micro milk: Graham Brough, *Today*.
p18.   100,000 dead: Dr Vernon Coleman, *Sun*.
p19.   Coffee and babies: Chris Mihill, *Today*.
p19.   Woozy pilots: Ellis Plaice, *Today*.

Albert, A. *Xenobiosis*, Chapman Hall, London, 1987

Ashwell, M. (ed.), 'How safe is our food?', *British Nutrition Foundation Bulletin*, vol. 14, 1989

British Medical Association *The BMA Guide to Living with Risk*, Penguin, London, 1990

Dobbing, J. (ed.), *A Balanced Diet?*, Springer Verlag, London, 1988

Gregory, J., Foster, K., Tyler, H., Wiseman, M. *The Dietary and Nutritional Survey of British Adults*, HMSO, London, 1990

Hathcock, J. N. (ed.), *Nutritional Toxicology*, vol. 3, Academic Press, New York, 1989

Hobbs, B. C., Roberts, D. *Food Poisoning and Food Hygiene*, Edward Arnold, London, 1987

National Research Council, *Diet and Health*, National Academy Press, Washington, 1989

National Research Council, *Recommended Daily Allowances*, National Academy Press, Washington, 1989

Paul, A. A., Southgate, D. A. T. *McCance and Widdowson's Composition of Foods, and supplements*, HMSO, London, 1978, 1988, 1989

Taylor, S. L., Scanlon, R. A. (eds.), *Food Toxicology – A Perspective on the Relative Risk*, Marcel Dekker, New York, 1989

Yudkin, J. *The Penguin Encyclopaedia of Nutrition*, Penguin, London, 1986

INDEX

Note: Page references in bold indicate main entries in the directory at the end of the book.

spreads 275–6
textured vegetable protein (TVP) **407–8**
Thailand 131
That's Life (TV programme) 106–7
thiamin (vitamin B₁) **413**
thrombosis 116
Time Temperature Indicator 245
tinned foods *see* canned foods
tobacco-chewing 124
Tofu 337
tomato ketchup 16
tooth decay *see* teeth
toxicity and toxins 126, 153
    aflatoxins 28, 30, 129–30, 294–5
    compounds from cooking 142
    mycotoxins 129–30, 384–5
    naturally occurring 28, 30, 31, 32–3, 92
Trading Standards Officers 227, 278, 279
trans fatty acids 374
tryptophan 103, 351, **408**
Tunstall-Pedoe, Prof. Hugh 116
turkey feed 129
tyramine 381

UHT 233
UKROFS 229–30
Unigate 20–1
US Food and Drug Administration 327–8, 346, 367
US Food and Nutrition Board 96–7
US General Aviation Safety Leaflet 19
US Scientific Advisory Panel 32
use-by date 245–6
utensils, cooking 312–13

variety 74, 99
vegans *see* vegetarians and vegans
vega-testing **408**
vegetable oils 119, 311–12, 318, **408–9**
    erucic acid 361
    fats in, *table* 277
    toxic, Spanish 141
vegetables
    bacteria 288
    buying 224–5
    cancer protection 123–4
    for children 188
    composition, *table* 271
    cooking 307
    in dieting 211
    green 51–3, 77, 86, 296
    organic 227–8
    pulse 55, 87
    storage 295–6
vegetarians and vegans **409–10**
    babies 174
    breast-feeding 163, 164, 167, 341
    children 181, 188
    dieting 213–14
    health 410
    pregnancy 164
    principles 93
    questionnaire 56–7
    teenagers 193–4
    vitamin deficiency 56–7, 414
    young adults 196–7
    heart disease 116–17
venison 394
ventricular fibrillation 118–19
Vital milk 20
vitamin drops for babies 173

vitamins **410–16**
    A (retinol) 97, 102, 176–7, **412–13**
        deficiency 419
    B₁ (thiamin) 413
    B₆ supplements (pyridoxine) 395
    B₁₂ 56–7, 394, 410, **413–14**
        deficiency 414
        supplements 394, 414
    C (ascorbic acid) 97, 283, 411, 414–15
        in peas 234–6
        in potatoes 236–8, 295, 311, 393–4
        RDA 97
    D 178, 179, 415
    E 115, 333–4, **416**
    additives 143, 230
    in breast-feeding 163, 167, 341
    deficiencies 98–9, 102, 176–7, **412**, 414, 419
        alcohol 151
    excessive intake 103
    and intelligence 21–3
    labelling 252
    losses in cooking 310, 311
    losses in processing 234–8
    RDA 97, 251, 415
    supplements 395, 411–12
Voelcker, Dr Angustus 226
vulnerable groups 154–5

Waites, Prof. Will 26, 34–5
Warner, Dr John 27
washing up 298
waste 198–9
water 416–19
    added to foods 278–9, 392
    in babies' feeds 139, 165, 169
    bottled 23, 133, 283, 418
    fluoridation 155, 417
    nitrate 138–9
    sea 132, 401
    tap 23, 31, **417–18**
        lead 134, 169
water content of food 144
water softeners and filters **418–19**
weaning babies 171, 172–3, 174
weddings 316
weight
    chart 64
        infants 168
    questionnaire 57–63
    see also obesity; slimming
Weights and Measures Law 246
Wells, H.G. 144
wheat 404
Which? 288, 322
Widdowson, Dr Elsie 185
Wilcox, Dr 19
Wimpy 318
wine
    adulteration 140–1, 326
    alcohol 328, 329
    bottles 294
    organic 227
    preservatives 395–6, 405
women
    adolescent 191–2
    alcohol 148
    anaemia 98, 99
    breast cancer 124–5
    cholesterol level 112
    fertility 19

431